1987

Studies in Eighteenth-Century Culture VOLUME 16

EDITED BY *O M Brack, Jr.*
Arizona State University

PUBLISHED *for the*
AMERICAN SOCIETY FOR EIGHTEENTH-CENTURY STUDIES
by THE UNIVERSITY OF WISCONSIN PRESS

Published 1986

The University of Wisconsin Press
114 North Murray Street
Madison, Wisconsin 53715

The University of Wisconsin Press, Ltd.
1 Gower Street
London WC1E 6HA, England

First printing

Printed in the United States of America

LC 75-648277

ISBN 0-299-10940-2
ISSN 0360-2370

Editorial policy

The editors of *Studies in Eighteenth-Century Culture* select papers of the highest quality and broadest intellectual interest in eighteenth-century studies. Papers presented at regional and national meetings of the American Society for Eighteenth-Century Studies between 1 July and 30 June must be submitted by 1 August each year to be considered for publication. Generally papers written for oral presentation require revisions and the addition of scholarly apparatus. Contributions will be judged according to the highest standards of scholarship. Papers should be written in English, but quotations in foreign languages are permissible. Papers should not exceed 20 pages, as space is limited.

For documentation and presentation, papers should follow the *Chicago Manual of Style*, 13th edition. Double-space everything, including block quotations and footnotes. Footnotes should be numbered consecutively and typed on separate sheets following the text. Submit *three* (3) copies of the paper. Photocopies of illustrations should also be submitted in triplicate. The copies of the manuscript should be accompanied by a self-addressed envelope and enough loose stamps to cover the cost of returning one copy. Send manuscripts to the current editor.

Editorial Board for Volume Sixteen

125, 848

Contents

Preface

The maroon buckram binding and the typography are familiar but in a sense this volume represents a beginning. Although not immediately apparent since I have overstayed my three-year term as editor, this volume is a departure from previous ones. For the first time there is an associate editor and an editorial board, instituted with the hope that *Studies in Eighteenth-Century Culture* will have editorial continuity and that a more representative selection of quality essays from all disciplines will be solicited. An editorial policy has also been agreed upon and is published for the first time. New editorial procedures will not answer those critics who disguise their inability to review such a diverse collection of essays by harping on the lack of thematic unity. Much of the vitality of our society is in its diversity and I hope that the following essays demonstrate this diversity at its best.

"There are few things not purely evil, of which we can say, without some emotion of uneasiness, *this is the last.*" Although all has not been "delight in sublunary pleasures," one of the real pleasures of editing has been talking and corresponding with members I might not otherwise have met. Among these are the many editorial readers who have taken time from a busy fall semester to insure the quality of the volumes. For their support and assistance I am most grateful. I am happy to share any of the credit with them and take full responsibility for any failings since final editorial decisions were my own. I only hope that no one will say, he found it marble and left it brick.

O M Brack, Jr.

June 19, 1986

Studies in Eighteenth-Century Culture

VOLUME 16

Mise-en-Page, Biblical Criticism, and Inference during the Restoration

RICHARD W.F. KROLL

I

In recent years, the most pervasive critiques of method have demanded that cultural historians contemplate more strenuously than before the particular and concrete (or "material") conditions of the societies they seek to describe. This applies equally within and without the purview of Marxist economic analysis; but in so doing, the demand has merely exacerbated our methodological uncertainties about how technological and intellectual changes affect each other, if at all. A bold attempt to confront the difficulty occurs in Elizabeth Eisenstein's *The Printing Press as an Agent of Change*, which challenges us to reexamine the relationships between, on the one hand, the emergence of a full-scale print culture in Europe, and, on the other, our categorizations of the Renaissance, the Reformation, and the rise of early modern science.[1] Ultimately, however, despite the almost overwhelming detail combined with a certain descriptive indeterminacy, Eisenstein opts to view conceptual change as a (if not the) decisive product of technological innovation. To make this recognition, she implies, is to clarify what has hitherto been unnecessarily confused: in a characteristic pronouncement, she expresses impatience with the familiar problem of how scientific "advance" occurs, writing that "unless some new strategy is devised to handle this question, the old arguments will break out once again. . . . One advantage of bring-

3

ing printing into the discussion is that it enables us to tackle the open question directly without prolonging the same controversy *ad infinitum.*"[2]

I submit that no agreement over method has yet been made. For example, a recent issue of *Eighteenth-Century Studies* was dedicated to "The Printed Word in the Eighteenth Century."[3] Of the five featured articles, two were more or less traditionally bibliographical in focus (Feather, Amory); and two explored some of the political contexts and implications of publishing in France (Darnton, Gelbart). Only one attempted the more risky methodological territory lying between the demonstrable material or technological conditions of authorship and its more philosophical and conceptual implications, Martha Woodmansee's "The Genius and the Copyright: Economic and Legal Conditions of the Emergence of the 'Author.'"[4] Finding "an interesting interplay between legal, economic, and social questions on the one hand and philosophical and esthetic ones on the other," Woodmansee attempts to negotiate between them, in order to show how "fundamental" modern ideas like that of authorship could have arisen.[5]

Questions of causality aside, I want to argue here for a similarly fundamental conceptual shift which accompanied (or was accompanied by) a series of changes detectable in the field of printing, particularly in the typographic representation of Biblical texts, and occurring roughly at the time of the Restoration. An examination of the late seventeenth century yields an astonishing coherence among several apparently widely separated phenomena involving the physical production of books, the conditions of their publication, developments in Biblical and textual criticism, notions of historical evidence, attitudes towards literary representation, ideas about the cognitive processes of reading, and a distinctive understanding of the function of myth and narrative.

II

Before proceeding, I will take it as axiomatic that the two decades before the Restoration engendered the characteristic features and habits of what we might call "neoclassical" culture.[6] That general position unites the work of Michel Foucault, Robert Frank, Ian Hacking, Michael Hunter, Douglas Lane Patey, and M. M. Slaughter.[7] The new empiricism entailed a methodological approach which made it decidedly un-Baconian in character.[8] The work of Gassendi and Boyle was both typical and decisive: a scepticism about the reliability of signs, and about our capacities to perceive objects accurately could be contained by developing criteria of inference by which we might construct testable hypotheses.[9] As Locke makes very clear in the final chapter of his *Essay concerning Human Understanding*, the new methodology entailed a revision of "[*semeiotikē*], or *the Doctrine of Signs.*"[10] Boyle's famous distinction between the primary and secondary qualities of bodies (which Locke absorbed) makes very clear that any form of essentialism is no longer possible: signs resist anything more than inspection from without; they appear to us arbitrarily and sporadically; we must develop for ourselves an inferential mechanism using the immediate appearances of things; and any model of physical or moral coherence is the ultimate product of our private mental processes. In short, objects themselves, the raw material for our experience, have achieved a new ontological density.[11] M. M. Slaughter comments on some of the "potential problems in Boyle's corpuscular theory":

> One is that it is the goal of science to know the natures of things but since those natures consist in configurations of imperceptible particles those natures in principle may not be knowable. The second is that if our notions of genus and species are nominalistic by virtue of our inability to know the real natures of things, then it follows that a taxonomic method must yield results that are nominalistic and artificial rather than real.[12]

The world now represents a profound hermeneutical task both because our perceptions are unreliable and because signs appear to us as discrete entities with no organic connections among them: relations are made by our own inferences and analogies.

If ideas or signs impress themselves upon us as discrete, yet sequential events, it would seem natural to compare the mind to a space or room, or to a text. But I would argue that for Locke the analogy is more than a mere figure of speech. In his famous account of the cumulative nature of mental experience, Locke argues that the mind is a blank piece of paper on which experience imprints individual sensations by means of the corpuscular machinery of perception. That Locke uses the vernacular "white Paper," not the Latin *tabula rasa*,[13] and that for him the corpuscularian hypothesis was a physical, literal, mechanical explanation for the origin of mental ideas, should qualify our tendency to take Locke figuratively.[14] The mind also becomes a *camera obscura*, a space in which ideas serve as the individual counters of mental experience, of judgment, the exercise of reason, and of knowledge. Locke's *Essay* thus marks at once a conceptual revision of individual identity, of mental privacy that made eighteenth-century conceptions of reading possible, of mental space (the precondition of privacy), of textual space, and of historical space. Crucially, it exploits a shift in the understanding of textual space—the typographical and significative aspects of the printed page—that had already occurred before 1671, the year in which Locke completed Draft A of the *Essay*. [15] It also signals an epistemological relationship between that shift and new views of interpretative method and of knowledge itself. Neoclassical conceptions of cultural space seem to go well beyond an elaboration of Horace's *ut pictura poesis*, or the equally powerful and pervasive trope of architecture: [16] they seem to inhabit a dimension so concrete, so physical, and so mundane as to have been largely overlooked.

An example of the indifference to educing the conceptual principles implied by typography—the nature of the printed page—occurs in relation to Locke's largely unknown *A New Method of a Common-Place-Book*, originally published in Jean Le Clerc's *Bibliothèque Universelle*, but translated for posthumous publication in 1706. [17] It is not, one admits, a gripping work of philosophy or literature; but it clearly interested Toinard enough that he pressed Locke to make it public; [18] Locke writes in deference that "my obligations to you, and the friendship between us, compel me now to follow your advice." [19] Unlikely as it seems, the title too suggests some novelty. But intellectual historians have found it uninteresting precisely because they have commonly repressed any valid connection between ideas and their figurative or typographical embodiment. Yet the very tabular character of the commonplace book, with its emphasis on precise notation and its proper ordering, immediately recalls the atomistic nature of particular sensible signs in Locke's conceptualist economy, as well as the activity of analogy and inference essential to "reading" those signs. Locke emphasizes that the typography of the printed version represents the spatial arrangement of the original: "it is fit to acquaint the reader," he insists, "that this tract is disposed in the same manner that the common-place book ought to be disposed." [20] That disposition is for Locke a critical one; for the relationship between the "heads," which appear outside the margin, and the text that they signal, which appears within the margin, forms the crux of the semiological system. The physical distribution of the head in relation to its text perfectly enacts the inferential procedures of natural science: the head stands as a synecdoche, or as Sextus Empiricus' indicative sign, for the yet unmeasured whole. Thus, Locke is concerned "that only the head appears in the margin, and that it be continued on without ever doubling the line in the margin, by which means the heads will be obvious at first sight";[21] moreover, that "each head ought to be some important and essential word to the matter in hand, and in that word regard is to be had to the first letter, and the vowel that follows it; for upon these two letters depends all the use of the index."[22]

Locke's use of "essential" here indicates not an essentialism, but the deployment of a sign selected at random (the first letter and succeeding vowel) which stands to lead us into the whole it only partly signifies: it beckons from outside the margin to the body of discourse it signals, but which is inscribed *within* the page. Hence, in his commonplace book, we could say, Locke seeks to marry and domesticate typography and epistemology within the sphere of the new "Method" heralded by the pamphlet's title.

III

I would argue, then, that by the late seventeenth century, the Renaissance idea and consciousness of the text as conceptual space had undergone a metamorphosis. This was marked by at least two parallel revolutions: one, a change in the uses of textual scholarship and historical evidences; and the other, a change in the way Biblical texts were represented and printed.

I speak as readily of a "metamorphosis" as a "revolution" because, as histories of classical scholarship repeatedly remind us, both Erasmus and Joseph Scaliger have earned a permanent place in the history of textual criticism.[23] Further, Erasmus had, by the Restoration, achieved a symbolic resonance for the union of political comprehensiveness and moderate scepticism to which the Latitudinarian strain aspired. If Scaliger bequeathed a great corpus of classical scholarship and his work on chronology to the seventeenth century, Erasmus bequeathed a series of attitudes to the Greek New Testament text that had clear implications for classical and Biblical studies. Nevertheless, and crucially, neither left any method as such which a later age could adopt; and neither left any explicit statement of the methodological principles which could be said to have informed their practices.

Thus it would be a mistake to adopt Mark Pattison's eloquent endorsement of Scaliger as "the founder of historical criticism."[24] In claiming that he "first showed the way to that sound notion of textual criticism in which the genuine tradition is made the basis, and altera-

The *INDEX*.

The

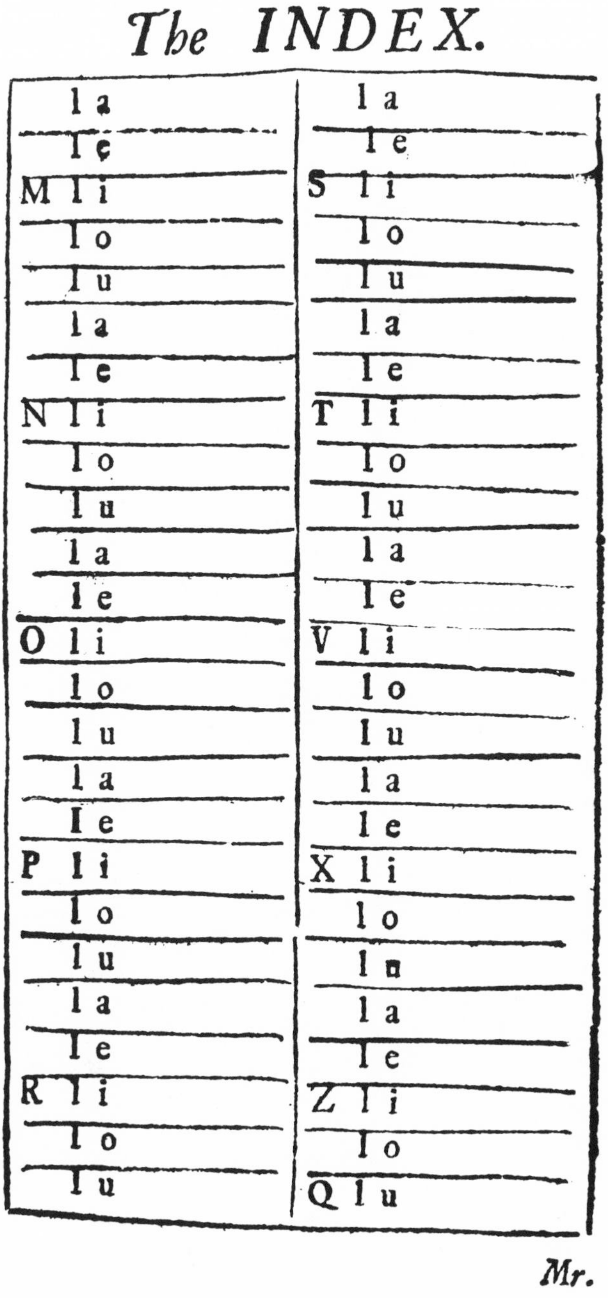

The INDEX.

	l a			l a	
	l e			l e	
M	l i		S	l i	
	l o			l o	
	l u			l u	
	l a			l a	
	l e			l e	
N	l i		T	l i	
	l o			l o	
	l u			l u	
	l a			l a	
	l e			l e	
O	l i		V	l i	
	l o			l o	
	l u			l u	
	l a			l a	
	l e			l e	
P	l i		X	l i	
	l o			l o	
	l u			l o	
	l a			l a	
	l e			l e	
R	l i		Z	l i	
	l o			l o	
	l u		Q	l u	

Mr.

Figure 1: John Locke, *A New Method of a Common-Place Book*. Courtesy The William Andrews Clark Memorial Library.

tion is only permitted on condition of establishing itself by rigorous proof," he imputes to Scaliger a systematics that Pattison could only have inherited from a post-Restoration (and post-Romantic) understanding of criticism.[25] Anthony Grafton's modern revaluation of Scaliger, though uncompleted, argues persuasively against the myth of Scaliger's sudden and preternatural originality: demonstrating in detail how Scaliger cannot be said to have applied a consistent method to his several editions of classical authors, he shows how the local, rhetorical anxieties and personal affiliations of the late sixteenth century constrained the pursuit of scholarship,[26] and how the common absence of any explicit statements about method (evincing perhaps a lack of any exact methodological consciousness) frustrates the historian's attempt to recuperate Scaliger.[27] Even Scaliger's edition of Manilius, though it lies "outside all normal traditions of sixteenth-century philology," writes Grafton, clearly "rested in part on unacknowledged borrowings of facts from Carrion and ideas from Pico."[28] "Scaliger's fate," Grafton concludes, "reveals something about the character of philology itself: that it formed part of a traditional curriculum and embodied a traditional set of mental and linguistic categories."[29]

It seems, in fact, slightly easier to situate Erasmus, for, following the pioneering work of Poliziano, Valla, Colet, and Reuchlin, Erasmus' New Testament of 1516 represents "that first flowering of the New Testament exegesis, based on criticism and philology, through which the Renaissance . . . was to prepare the way to modern exegesis."[30] And since, perhaps, we are here dealing with a single enterprise, it is possible to educe Erasmus' broad principles of criticism. Werner Schwarz argues that Reuchlin and Erasmus reinstituted the "philological" method of Biblical translation—in the early church represented by Origen and Jerome—and expounds Erasmus' procedures: first, Erasmus "compares several Greek manuscripts, indeed as many as he can lay his hands on to discover variants in their readings"; second, he "attempts to verify the reading of the Vulgate by means of old Latin manuscripts, as, for example, those lent to him by Colet in 1505"; third, he "uses the Fathers of the Church as independent witnesses for the early text of the Vulgate," taking "corruption of the manuscripts into account"; and lastly, "Erasmus attempts to explain the reason why the addition to the Greek text was made."[31]

But again, Erasmus' capacity to bequeath a systematic tool of criticism to the Restoration was limited. The edition of the New Testament was by no means an unqualified success, given that many contemporaries felt that Erasmus' scepticism about the Vulgate subverted Catholic exegetical traditionalism.[32] They were, of course, right: Erasmus' New Testament was an avowed part of his desire to recall the

Church to its pristine origins and to permit the individual to make probable judgments for himself. [33] Yet ironically, Erasmus' particular adaptation of moderate scepticism—culled from the tradition of academic scepticism best summarized in Cicero's *Academica* [34]—made him at once a textual critic and an ardent supporter of Catholic Church unity. More important, however, Erasmus too had no fully articulated method: although he appended a series of prefaces to his continually revised editions of the New Testament (the *Methodus, Apologia, Paraclesis, Ratio verae theologiae*), it appears that here, by "method," he understands principles of exegesis, less a strict hermeneutical model than a practical means of understanding and applying Scripture. [35]

Even the notion—which is peculiarly relevant here—that Erasmus and Scaliger might represent a new set of relationships between textual criticism or the world of scholarship, and a print culture, only applies generally. P. S. Allen and Anthony Grafton have made quite clear their belief that the idea of textual criticism can only become a reality in the context of a printing revolution; [36] but while Erasmus enjoyed close relations with Froben in Basle, and while "the arrangement of the Biblical texts" in the New Testament edition "shows the intention of the author," [37] Scaliger, in his edition of Catullus "did not carry over into his published notes the precision and meticulousness of his original collation," [38] which suggests that the relationship between scholarly precision and typographical detail was still very unstable at the end of the sixteenth century. [39]

In sum, as Neal Gilbert demonstrated twenty-five years ago, Renaissance notions of method display none of the concern with systematics which distinguish the new methodology of the late seventeenth century. Renaissance "discussion did not even touch upon the method of gaining valid and useful knowledge," he writes, "but concerned only the method of transmitting an 'already-established art,' or of pursuing a successful course of study." [40] As Basil Hall puts it, the sixteenth century rested content "with what seemed to be a reasonably authenticated text, and to inquire no further into textual criticism for its own sake." [41] Broadly speaking, the distinction lies between what we could call the synthetic and analytic approaches to knowledge, or between what Foucault refers to as a tradition of "commentary" and an attitude of "criticism." [42] As it looked back, the later age would even see itself engaged on an altogether different kind of project:

La différence qu'il y a entre eux et nous, est qu'on se picquoit bien plus d'érudition dans le siècle passé, que dans celuy-ci. . . . C'estoit le génie de ce tems-la, ou rien n'a esté plus en vogue, que la grande capacité, et une profonde littérature: on étudioit a fond les

Langues: on s'appliquoit a réformer le texte des ancien Auteurs par des interpretations recherchées, a pointiller sur une équivoque, a fonder une conjecture pour bien établir une correction: enfin on s'attachoit au sens littéral d'un Auteur, parcequ'on n'avoit pas le force de s'élever jusqu'à l'esprit, pour le bien connoitre; comme on fait a présent, qu'on est plus raisonnable, et moins sçavant: et qu'on fait bien plus d'estat du bons sens tout simple, que d'une capacité de travers. [43]

Thus, it was only in the late seventeenth century that a vigorous and searching scepticism about the nature of evidences could make possible the science of paleography, which, according to L. D. Reynolds and N. G. Wilson, denotes a watershed in the history of textual scholarship. Until then, "little or no interest [had been] taken in the date and origin of the manuscripts being used for editions of classical and Christian texts." [44] Stanley Morison sees the editors Herbert Rosweyde (1569–1629) and his successor Johann Bolland (1596–1665) as developing the "scientific investigation of hagiographic tradition." [45] The Maurists' production of the *Acta Sanctorum* (6 vols., 1668–80) was the setting for the next step. The Jesuit, Daniel von Papebroeck, or Papebroch (1628–1714), "Bolland's pupil and companion in his travels in search of manuscripts," [46] wrote part of the introduction to volume 2 of the April *Acta* (1675). [47] Here, he proved "that a charter supposedly issued by a Merovingian King Dagobert in 646 and guaranteeing certain privileges to the Benedictines was a forgery"; [48] and here we find "the first attempt to formulate rules of criticism": [49] his dissertation can be considered "the first sketch of a scientific classification of scripts and of the establishment of the criteria of comparison." [50] Papebroch cast in the process some aspersions upon the Abbey of St. Denis' diplomas, which prompted a "great work" by Dom Jean Mabillon (1632–1707), the *De Re Diplomatica*, printed in 1681, only three years after Richard Simon's *Histoire Critique du Vieux Testament*. Mabillon, a man of both immense learning and profound humility, realized that "as he worked" on *De Re Diplomatica*, "he saw the necessity and possibility of constructing a new discipline, if not a new science." [51] This became the science of paleography. [52] Knowles describes Mabillon's method thus:

Mabillon frankly admitted that the authenticity of a charter could not be proved by any metaphysical or *a priori* argument; a decision could be reached only after the expert had examined a series of different indications—the material used, the seal, the signature, the grammar and orthography, the modes of address, the plausibility of the dating, the intrinsic consistency of the whole document. In consequence, the certainty attainable in a favourable case could be no more than a moral certainty, but this was very different from doubt or complete scepticism.[53]

Paleography establishes once and for all the impossibility of recuperating the past as a seamless text, and signals a new historical consciousness which recognizes both the necessity and discreteness of particular materials or evidences, which includes indiscriminately a study of the "sacred" and "secular" past, and which only derives coherence from the mind of a critic, or the narrative of an historian.[54]

IV

If the late seventeenth century made a virtue out of necessity by invoking the time-worn preference for examples over precepts, it did so in terms which recognized that all forms of historical (and thence moral) knowledge have their origins in concrete particulars; and these required the reader or perceiver to infer their significance for himself (a process John Wallace has called "application").[55] Moreover, the method of inference and analogy assumed that all learning should proceed by an ostensive or demonstrative reference to particular objects, a procedure which would in turn develop in the mind of the child those desired habits of discernment, so frequently characterized as "Judgment." The visual possibilities of printing served all aspects of this epistemological model: the very typography of Johann Amos Comenius' well-known *Orbis Sensualium Pictus* (1658), the international best-seller of the century,[56] taught the meanings of words by reference to the things represented in the pictures, and conveyed the comparative meanings of foreign languages not only by the same process, but by the simple analogical device of placing words into parallel vertical columns. Nor is it accidental that the book depicts the very means of its own dissemination—writing, paper-making, printing, bookselling and bookbinding—nor again, that it depicts the clock in those spatial terms which made it such an attractive and persistent post-Cartesian metaphor for the process of inferring the hidden or occult workings of nature by observing indicative signs.[57] Indeed, the whole book moves constantly from the consideration of external, visible, and measurable signs to those invisible and unmeasurable matters that they could be thought to signify: thus lesson XXXVIII begins with "The outward parts of a man," moving to lesson XL, which deals with "The Flesh and the Bowels," to lesson XLI ("The Chanels & Bones") to lesson XLII ("The outward and inward Senses").

A second example of the confluence of printing and the new epistemology occurs in the history of John Ogilby's *Fables of Aesop Paraphras'd in Verse* (1651). The title page of the first edition declares that:

> Examples are best Precepts; And a Tale
> Adorn'd with Sculpture better may prevaile
> To make men lesser Beasts, than all the store
> Of tedious Volumes, vext the World before.

Perhaps the major publisher of the early Restoration, Ogilby seemed to endow this Renaissance cliché with new perceptual force: he turned each successive edition over to three of the finest illustrators in England before 1700, namely Francis Cleyn (1651 edition), Wenceslaus Hollar (1665 edition, printed by Thomas Roycroft),[58] and Francis Barlow (1666 edition, called the *Aesopics*).[59] Annabel Patterson finds in Ogilby's deployment of the fable a new political tact (and tack);[60] but I would add that the energy given to paraphrasis, which made the fable both more concrete and vivid, and to illustration repeatedly reinterpreted and reworked, powerfully suggests that the demand for particularity and inference applied to narrative found reinforcement in the new visual and typographical vocabulary.

Third, although we see little change between 1550 and 1660 in the ideological potential of the title page, graphic tokens of the new epistemological climate appear in this feature of the book. The title page can carry considerable weight in the argument because, as Stanley Morison puts it, "The history of printing is in large measure the history of the title-page."[61] Moreover, Margery Corbett and Ronald Lightbown claim, in their analysis of title pages printed after the late sixteenth-century in England, that the author (or in some cases the editor) was invariably responsible for the design of the title page prefacing his work.[62] They also emphasize that "the title-page is not a general statement of a moral or philosophical aphorism," because, rather than existing in isolation, it is "always closely related to the contents of the book for which it was made," regardless of subject.[63] To resort to the emblematic tradition as a means of explaining the machinery of the title page between 1550 and 1660, as Corbett and Lightbown do,[64] is finally to obscure the gulf that separates the title page of Hobbes's *Leviathan* (1651) from that of Michael Drayton's *Poly-olbion* (1612–22), or of Francis Bacon's *Instauratio Magna* (1620). Briefly put, the earlier title pages exhibit at most a casual scepticism about the possibilities of

LXXVII.

Uhrwerke.　　　Horologia.

Das Uhrwerk /	Horologium, n.2.	
theilet die Stunden ab.	dimetitur horas.	Hora , f. 1. die Stund.
Die Sonnuhr/ 1	Solarium , 1 n.2.	
weiset	oftendit	Oftendere , a. 3. weisen.
mit dem Schatten des	umbrâ gnómonis, 2	Umbra, f 1. der Schatte.
[Zeigers/ 2		Gnomon, m 3. der Zeiger.
wieviel es geschlagen ;	quota sit hora ;	
entweder an der Wand /	sive in pariete, [ticâ.]	Paries , m. 3 die Wand
oder im Compaß. 3	sive in pyxide magne-	Pyxis, f. 3. magnetica, t i.
		der Compaß.

Die

Figure 2: Johann Amos Comenius, *Orbis Sensualium Pictus.* Courtesy The Firestone Library, Princeton University.

inference, that is, of gathering the concrete particulars of knowledge into a coherent conceptual universe: the baroque fecundities of Drayton's title page deliberately confuse any sensible order among its many parts, in effect resisting all steady inference or anatomy of its putative metaphorical coherence; by the simple act of placing the architectural device within the reader's frame of vision, Bacon's admittedly less frenetic title page similarly entices us into an apprehension of a world in which intellectual voyages will ultimately yield—by sheer accretion—the totality of knowledge Bacon so desires. [65]

Although Hobbes's title page also serves a symbolic purpose, it does so by showing the reader the particular, atomic, precise relations of parts to the whole—most impressively in the body of the Leviathan himself. It thus presents itself as a complex figure of empirical figuration; and it achieves its effect by at least two concurrent strategies. First, the geography and perspective of the title page forces us to notice the disjunctions among its figures: the Leviathan appears grotesquely out of proportion to the harmonious and relatively realistic landscape, his sword and staff standing equally disproportionate both in relation to himself and to the landscape over which he looms. The other figures are simply divided off from each other by borders. Further, a peculiarly disturbing representational mechanism constantly conspires against any ease by which, having recognized the simply perspectival difference between the Leviathan and the landscape, we might seek to reconstitute them at some level of cognition *either* by treating them as figuratively (or representationally) analogous, *or* by a reverse process, as simply different. For the sword and staff (of the three chief elements of the scene) are at once the most immediately non-representational, and yet at the same time mediate most explicitly between the Leviathan and the landscape, especially in the case of the staff thrust out imperiously across the top right diagonal quarter of the page. We are in effect forced to contemplate at one and the same time how we might conceive differences among degrees of metaphorical—or at least figural—expression; and (because the relatively realistic landscape could imply the postulate of some real or actual world prior to representation) how we might imagine the derivation of figurative expression (language, universals) from such an actual world. The latter question, as the artificiality of the title page quite apart from its devices reminds us, cannot of course lead to something "outside" or "prior to" representation. Visually, we have been brought to the crux of Hobbes's linguistic philosophy.

The title page also pursues the empirical conundrum in an altogether simpler fashion, by ensuring that the meaning of its emblems

POLY-OLBION

GREAT · BRI · TAINE

By
Michael Drayton
Esq:

London printed for M. Lownes. I. Browne
I. Helme. I. Busbie.

Figure 3: Michael Drayton *Poly-Olbion*, Title Page. Courtesy The Firestone Library, Princeton University.

Figure 4: Francis Bacon, *Instauratio Magna*, Title Page. Courtesy The William Andrews Clark Memorial Library.

Figure 5: Thomas Hobbes, *Leviathan*, Title Page. Courtesy The Firestone Library, Princeton University.

(the Leviathan and the various figures in the lower half) is created empirically: that is, they enact the causal relations implicit in metonymy and synecdoche. We see the relations between parts and whole when we inspect the Leviathan closely: the body politic is constituted at its most basic by the totality of its citizens. Even this is an anti-essentialist view, just as is Hobbes's theory of political contract. There is nothing definable about society in the abstract, without our agreeing to make a society, which is a purely artificial construct. The elements of this whole—the people—are its precondition and irreducible minimum. Similarly, just as the canon is a physical part of military materiel, it comes to represent synecdochically that abstract indefinable, the military arm of the state. Thus Hobbes's title page precisely realizes the sceptical, atomistic and conceptualist foundations of its author's philosophy. [66]

V

The second great shift to which I referred earlier had occurred by 1657. In that year, Brian Walton completed the greatest Polyglot Bible ever printed, in six volumes and nine languages juxtaposed on the page for the reader's reference and examination. [67] It is a supreme instance of the merging of political conditions, the economics of publishing, the availability of technology, and conceptual change. At the most general level, the religious wars of seventeenth-century Europe had given England the edge in linguistic scholarship, and "England fulfilled the work begun at Alcala and Basle, Paris and Louvain, in the noblest of the Polyglot Bibles." [68] It was a many-faceted revolution: the second British book to be published by subscription, [69] its editorial achievement proved crucial for setting new standards in university publishing at Oxford; [70] and the work is considered "a landmark in the history of letter-founding in England, since never before had a work of importance been printed in [Britain] in any of the learned characters except Latin and Greek." [71] (This typographic achievement set a precedent for a smaller but still impressive and extraordinary publication issued in 1700, *The Lords Prayer In Above a Hundred Languages, Versions, and Characters*, which included such unusual types as Anglo-Saxon, Coptic, Ethiopic, Amharic, Arabic, Persian, Tartar, Gothic, Runic, Slavonic, Malabaric, and Chinese). The claim that Richard Simon's *Histoire Critique du Vieux Testament* (1678) initiates modern Biblical criticism, [72] tends to minimize a revaluation of Biblical texts that had occurred twenty-one years earlier, as the energy Simon devotes to Walton surely indicates. Basil Hall argues that "effective awareness of the significance of textual criticism for the ancient versions of the biblical text may be said to begin only with the *Biblia Polyglotta*."[73] This critical method served at once scholarly, epistemological, and political purposes, forming an early Arminian and Latitudinarian assault on Catholic and Puritan claims to absolute certainty.[74] The first great sixteenth-century Polyglot, the Complutensian Polyglot of Alcala (1514–17), had justified its arrangement of texts on the page in allegorical terms: the editors wrote, "We have placed the Latin translation of blessed Jerome as though between the Synagogue and the Eastern Church, placing them like the two thieves one on each side, and Jesus, that is the Roman Latin Church, between them."[75] But the historical integrity of Walton's Polyglot entailed a self-conscious espousal of inferential and probabilistic methods of reading: "Now care is taken that every private man may have [the original texts], and use them as his own," its preface declares.[76] The ideological implications of this position did not escape the Puritan John Owen, who, holding to the sanctity of Scriptural typography—the very Hebrew vowel-points even—reacted with outrage to this dispersion of the Biblical texts across not only one but two pages of the Polyglot. For its typography made quite clear that no single text or language comprised the authoritative Word of God, and that to choose the Hebrew Massoret over the Septuagint, for example, denied all the best principles of textual and historical criticism. Walton defended himself in *The Considerator Considered* (1659), arguing that Owen's "*fears* and *jealousies*" had led him to claim that a comparative study of texts would open the floodgates to "Papists, Atheists [and] Antiscripturalists."[77] From Walton's perspective, Owen "must needs cry out, [*dos pa zō*], as not seeing any means of being delivered from utter uncertainty in and about all sacred truth. . . . Hence are all these tragicall exclamations, fearfull outcries of correcting the Originalls by the help of Translations . . . of Printing the Originalls, and defaming them, gathering up translations of all sorts, and setting them up in competition with them."[78]

The potential consequences of textual fragmentation, allied with the general sceptical tenor of the age, could indeed have been catastrophic for Christian truth. But Walton, Edward Pococke, and Henry Hammond, his co-editors, belonged to a different and positive tradition of scholarship, stretching back at least to Isaac Casaubon and Hugo Grotius, whose *De Veritate Christianae* became a publishing phenomenon in its own right, beginning in England with the 1650 edition. Grotius confronted the potential collapse of the Biblical texts

AUCTOR.
Kirch. Chin.
Illuſtr. 162.

BRACHMANICA.

ग्रा लि ३ नो मि ३ क्ली प म्र ऱ्र ३ मिलि म्र
म क्लीप. मि प म्र ३ नो मि ३ ह व म
ग्रा द्रे म ने ३ ३ म ३ म ह व म्र
धी म्र न् मो ल्ला मो म म्र ग्री क्ष ३ ऱ्र ३ मि म्र प ३ ऱ्र ३ ने ३
ग्रा नि म्र मे म्र म कु ने लि ट म ३ ३ म मो ल्ला म्र म द्री प
प ३ द्री मि ते न लि म्र द्रे लि म न् म्र मो क्ष ३ प ३ म्र म्र
द्री मि लि म्र म्र द्रे ले मो लि ३ म म्र लि म्र
प ३ ने मो म्र ऱ्र द्रे क्ष म ऱ्र लि ३ ने म्र नी म्र लि म्र
मे द्रे ने लि ले न नो म्र म्र मा ल्ला

ग्रा मि ३.

—————————————————————

Superior Typus *non verſio* eſt Orationis Dominicæ,
ſed ipſiſſima *verſio vulgata*, Brachmanicis notis expreſſa.
Itaque legendi ratio nulla alia hîc locum obtinet Verſio verò Orationis Dominicæ in Linguam Brachmanicam
autori nondum, ut videtur, innotuit.

SINICA.

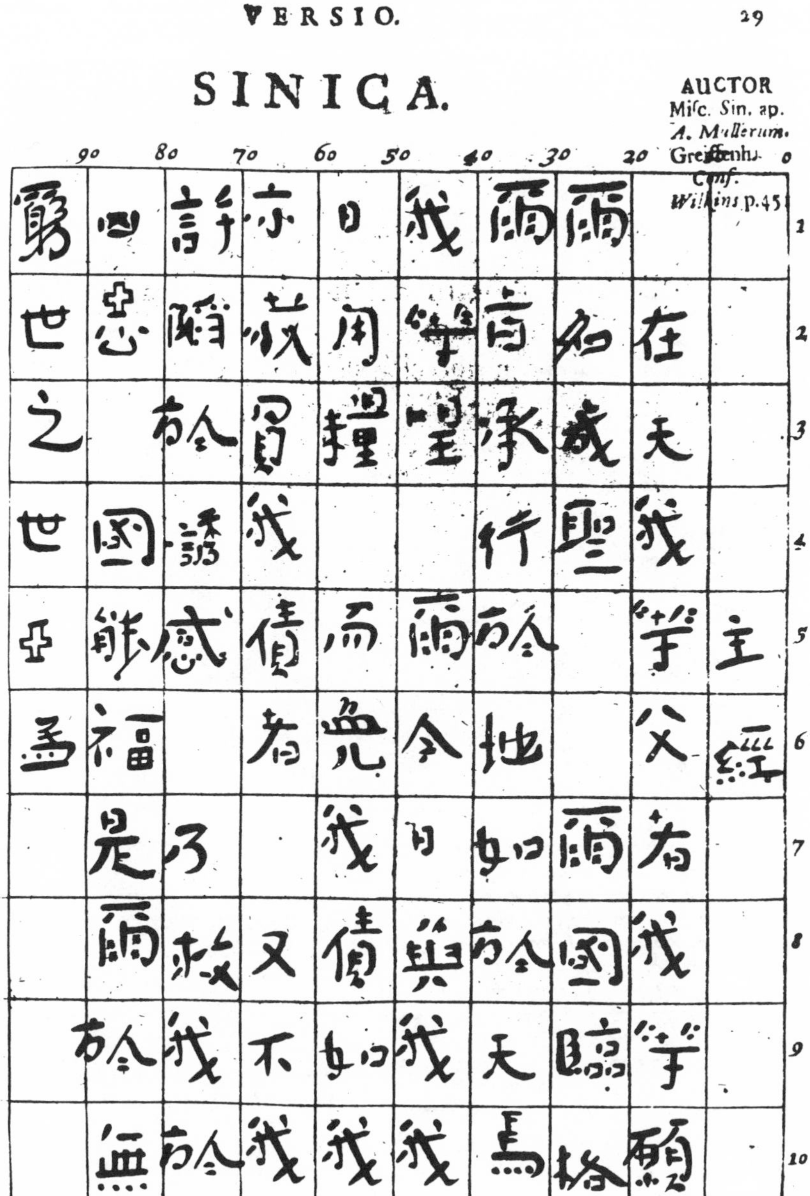
VERSIO.
29
SINICA.
AUCTOR
Misc. Sin. ap.
A. Müllerum.
Greiffenh.
Conf.
Wilkins p.45

Figure 6: *The Lord's Prayer in Above An Hundred Languages.* Courtesy The William Andrews Clark Memorial Library.

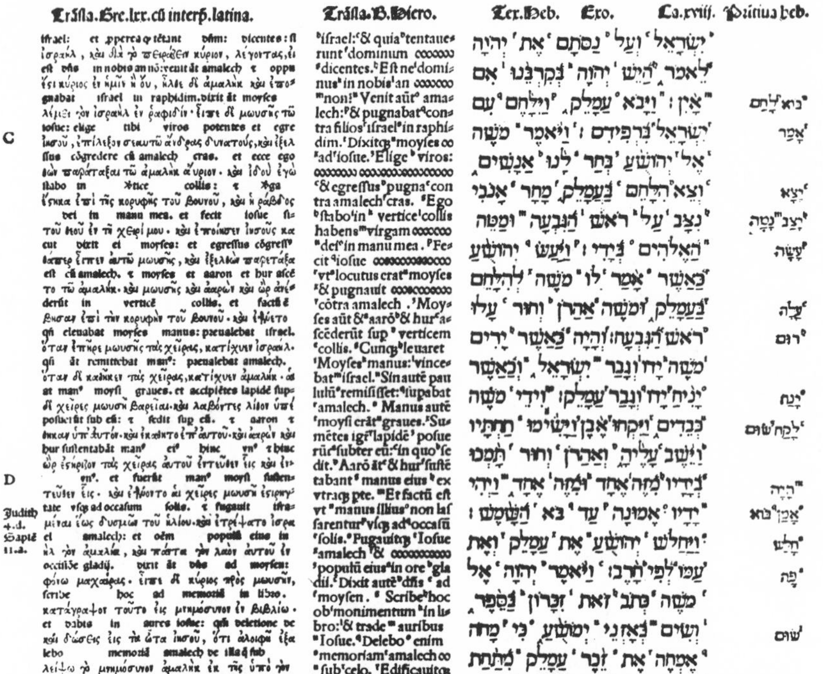

Trāsla.Gre.lxx.cū interp.latina. Trāsla.B.Hiero. Ter.Heb. Exo. Ca.xviij. Priitiua heb.

Transla.Chal. Interp.chal. Priitiua chal.

r ii

Figure 7: The Complutensian Polyglot. Courtesy The Firestone Library, Princeton University.

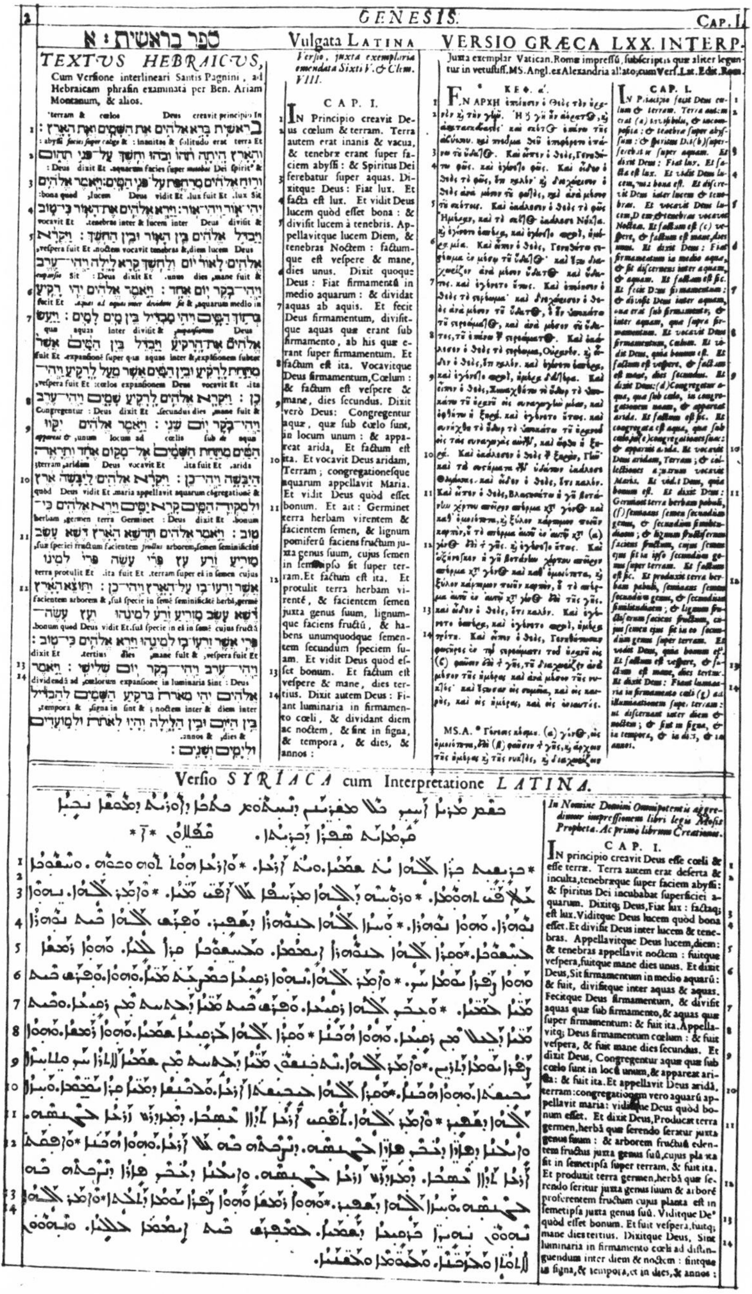
GENESIS. CAP. I.

TEXTUS HEBRAICUS, Cum Versione interlineari Santis Pagnini, ad Hebraicam phrasin examinata per Ben. Ariam Montanum, & alios.

Vulgata LATINA
Versio, juxta exemplaria emendata Sixti V. & Clem. VIII.

CAP. I.

1 IN Principio creavit De-
2 us cœlum & terram. Terra
autem erat inanis & vacua,
& tenebræ erant super fa-
ciem abyssi: & Spiritus Dei
3 ferebatur super aquas. Di-
xitque Deus: Fiat lux. Et
4 facta est lux. Et vidit Deus
lucem quòd esset bona: &
5 divisit lucem à tenebris. Ap-
pellavitque lucem Diem, &
tenebras Noctem: factum-
que est vespere & mane,
6 dies unus. Dixit quoque
Deus: Fiat firmamentū in
medio aquarum: & dividat
7 aquas ab aquis. Et fecit
Deus firmamentum, divisit-
que aquas quæ erant sub
firmamento, ab his quæ e-
rant super firmamentum. Et
8 factum est ita. Vocavitque
Deus firmamentum, Cœlum:
& factum est vespere &
9 mane, dies secundus. Dixit
verò Deus: Congregentur
aquæ, quæ sub cœlo sunt,
in locum unum: & appa-
reat arida, Et factum est
10 ita. Et vocavit Deus aridam,
Terram; congregationesque
aquarum appellavit Maria.
Et vidit Deus quòd esset
11 bonum. Et ait: Germinet
terra herbam virentem &
facientem semen, & lignum
pomiferū faciens fructum juxta genus suum, cujus semen
in semetipso sit super ter-
12 ram. Et factum est ita. Et
protulit terra herbam vi-
rentē, & facientem semen
juxta genus suum, lignum-
que faciens fructū, & ha-
bens unumquodque semen-
tem secundùm speciem su-
am. Et vidit Deus quod es-
13 set bonum. Et factum est
vespere & mane, dies ter-
14 tius. Dixit autem Deus: Fi-
ant luminaria in firmamento cœli, & dividant diem
ac noctem, & sint in signa,
& tempora, & dies, &
annos:

VERSIO GRÆCA LXX. INTERP.
Juxta exemplar Vatican. Romæ impressū, subscriptis quæ aliter leguntur in vetustiss. MS. Angl. ex Alexandria allato; cum Vers. Lat. Edit. Rom.

Versio SYRIACA cum Interpretatione LATINA.

Figure 8: Bishop Walton's Polyglot. Courtesy The William Andrews Clark Memorial Library.

head on, but argued that Scriptural history itself could become not the infallible but the sufficient epistemological grounds of Christian orthodoxy.[79] The actions and narratives adumbrated—however indistinctly—in the Biblical texts became, retroactively, the very grounds for their validity, since to allow the probability of Christ's life, miracles, death, and resurrection is at once to create several distinctions: first, between the events *qua* events and the records we inherit from the past; and second, between essential and inessential (and thus potentially divisive) articles of faith. We can subsequently validate the authority of the texts that inscribe these events.[80]

The actions to which the accumulated manuscripts and fragments repeatedly refer become the epistemological focus of argument: just as simple sensible signs become the building-blocks of the new empirical fabric of knowledge, so individual actions become the irreducible atoms of full-scale narrative. Narrative, in turn, and not the fragments that record it, becomes the means of stabilizing the Biblical texts, although such security must be achieved conceptually, in the mind of the critic or reader by an inferential activity. This explains the rather sudden emergence of the Biblical "harmony," I would argue, beginning with John Lightfoot's *The Harmony of the Foure Evangelists* (1644).[81] For the harmony objectified the action of the reader upon the dispersed narratives of Scripture, especially the Gospels, and dramatized both a scepticism about the original coherence of evidence and the capacity of the interpreter to make sense of it and convert it into narrative terms.[82] A nineteenth-century inheritor of this tradition captures the purposes and method of the harmony as follows: "It is simply an arrangement by which the corresponding parts of different documents may be brought together before the eye and compared—a method not peculiar to Biblical study, but familiar to all students of literary and historical documents."[83] And this conception is realized most fully and explicitly in Jean Le Clerc's *The Harmony of the Evangelists* (1701).[84]

The page is divided into four columns, one for each Gospel, while a bottom section is devoted to a paraphrase of the whole.[85] The relations between the discrete accounts of the various Gospels and the act of interpretation which would mold them into a coherent narrative are thereby enacted on the page. Le Clerc comments that "any man that has eyes may be convinc'd merely from dipping into this Book," that the "entire History" of Christ "has not been related by every particular Evangelist"; the reader may thus "see one [writer] proceeding in a Relation, when all the rest are silent."[86] Le Clerc does not attempt to ignore the evangelists' "broken Narrative" because it in no way embar-

MATTHEW.	MARK.	LUKE.	JOHN.
C H A P. XIV.	C H A P. VI.	C H A P. IX.	C H A P. VI.

21 And they that had eaten were about five thoufand men, befides women and children.	44 And they that did eat of the loaves, were about five thoufand men.	14 For they were about five thoufand men.	10 So the men fat down, in number about five thoufand.
☜	☜	☜	☜
			☞ 14 Then thofe men when they had feen the miracle that Jefus did, faid, This is of a truth that prophet that fhould come into the world.
			☜
22 And ftraightway Jefus conftrained his difciples to get into a fhip, and to go before him unto the other fide, while he fent the multitudes away. 23 And when he had fent the multitudes away,	45 And ftraightway he conftrained his difciples to get into the fhip, and to go to the other fide before unto Bethfaida, while he fent away the people. 46 And when he had fent them away,	☜	
☞	☞		☞ 15 When Jefus therefore perceived that they would come and take him by force, to make him a king,
he went up into a mountain apart to pray :	he departed into a mountain to pray.		he departed again into a mountain himfelf alone.

Women and Children, whom *Jefus* thus entertain'd, and who perceiving this wonderful Miracle, concluded he was that extraordinary Prophet whom God had promis'd to fend unto 'em, namely, the *Meffiah*.

Jefus immediately order'd his Difciples (who obey'd him with fome reluctancy at parting with him) to go on board, and fail over before him to the other fide of the Lake over againft *Bethfaida*, where he then was, while he himfelf ftaid to difmifs the Multitude. After which, underftanding that feveral of thofe whom he had thus miraculoufly treated were refolv'd to take him by force, and proclaim him King over them, he withdrew into a Mountain alone to fruftrate their defign, and that he might be uninterrupted in his Devotion. The Apoftles in the mean time, who

G g

Figure 9: Jean Le Clerc, *The Harmony of the Evangelists.* Courtesy The William Andrews Clark Memorial Library.

27

rasses him to conceive of narrative as a web woven from particular (and apparently isolated) events. (He has, after all, a clear precedent for this view in Locke's *Essay*, in the meditations on "Duration"). What chronological arrangement does for the Gospels is to show that these events are interdependent, not incoherent or contradictory.[87] For Le Clerc, "'tis plain [the Evangelists] have given us the same story in substance, tho' differing in some Circumstances; which Variety arises from different Memories of the Historians, and their different purposes of writing in a short or more copious Stile."[88]

The typographical arrangement of the *Harmony*, I emphasize, demonstrates Le Clerc's probabilist method: the view that meaningful history arises from "the connexion and dependence of one Story upon another," while recommending the value of chronology and sequence, reminds us how literary narrative (like words and the experience they describe) should always refer to particular events, if we are not to lose ourselves in the mists of language; and the fusion of these events into a coherent whole, by echoing the nature of mental experience, stimulates or revives in the mind "a clear and distinct Notion of them."[89] A belief in this effect assumes that, despite the vagaries of textual and historical evidence, and the obscurities of language, we can gain an insight into the originative acts which beckon to us from beyond discourse and which yet—Le Clerc knows full well—depend on that very discourse for their continued life in the minds of future generations.

NOTES

1 Elizabeth L. Eisenstein, *The Printing Press as an Agent of Change: Cultural Transformations in Early Modern Europe* (Cambridge: Cambridge Univ. Press, 1979; reprint, 1982).

2 Ibid., 688.

3 *Eighteenth-Century Studies* 17, no. 4 (1984).

4 Woodmansee is clearly conscious of the difficulties she raises. She writes: ". . . here we find an interesting interplay between legal, economic, and social questions on the one hand and philosophical and esthetic ones on the other. The problem of how these two levels of discourse—the legal-economic and the esthetic—interact is one that historians of criticism have barely explored. This is unfortunate because it is precisely in the interplay of the two levels that concepts and principles as fundamental as that of authorship achieved their modern form" (*Eighteenth-Century Studies*, 17 [1984]:440).

5 Ibid.

6 I use the word "neoclassical" advisedly, to indicate a prevailing set of epistemological assumptions over a given historical period, rather than a single nexus of esthetic requirements.

7 Michel Foucault, *The Order of Things: An Archeology of the Human Sciences* (New York: Vintage Books, 1973); Robert Frank, *Harvey and the Oxford Physiologists: A Study of Scientific Ideas* (Berkeley: Univ. of California Press, 1980); Ian Hacking, *The Emergence of Probability: A Philosophical Study of Early Ideas about Probability, Induction and Statistical Inference* (Cambridge: Cambridge Univ. Press, 1975); Michael Hunter, *Science and Society in Restoration England* (Cambridge: Cambridge Univ. Press, 1981); Douglas Lane Patey, *Probability and Literary Form: Philosophic Theory and Literary Practice in the Augustan Age* (Cambridge: Cambridge Univ. Press, 1984); M. M. Slaughter, *Universal Languages and Scientific Taxonomy in the Seventeenth Century* (Cambridge: Cambridge Univ. Press, 1982).

8 See Frank's description of the methodological revolution in the 1640s and 1650s (*Harvey*, ch. 4). Hunter takes very decided issue with the notion of a primarily "Baconian" science in the Restoration. For a recent restatement of the still common view that Bacon had prime methodological significance for the period, see Neal Wood, *The Politics of Locke's Philosophy: A Social Study of "An Essay concerning Human Understanding"* (Berkeley: Univ. of California Press, 1983), ch. 4.

9 See for example, Slaughter, *Universal Languages*, 189–90.

10 John Locke, *An Essay concerning Human Understanding*, ed. Peter H. Nidditch (Oxford: Clarendon Press, 1975; reprint, 1979), 4.21.4.

11 I owe this suggestion to discussion with Professor Eric Rothstein.

12 Slaughter, *Universal Languages*, 197.

13 Locke, *Essay*, 1.3.22: "for white Paper receives any Characters."

14 For Locke's corpuscularian explanations for perception, see *Essay*, 2.1.6; 2.8.4. Locke writes: "the impulse of such insensible particles of matter of such peculiar figures, and bulks, and in different degrees and modifications of their Motions, causes the *Ideas* of the blue Colour, and sweet Scent of that Flower to be produced in our Minds" (*Essay*, 2.8.13).

15 In *An Essay for Understanding of St. Paul's Epistles*, Locke explains the causes behind the "obscurity" of the Pauline Scriptures, among which he numbers "the text itself." The first of the "external" textual problems is

> The dividing of [the Epistles] into chapters, and verses, as we have done; whereby they are so chopped and minced, and, as they are now printed, stand so broken and divided, that not only the common people take the verses usually for distinct aphorisms; but even men of more advanced knowledge, in reading them, lose very much of the strength and force of coherence, and the light that depends on it. Our minds are so weak and narrow, that they have need of all the helps and assistances that can be procured, to lay before them undisturbedly the thread and coherence of any discourse; by which alone they are truly improved, and led into the genuine sense of the author. When the eye is constantly disturbed in loose sentences, that by their standing and separation appear as so many distinct fragments; the mind will have much ado to take in and carry on in its memory, an uniform discourse of

dependent reasonings; especially from the cradle been used to wrong impressions concerning them, and constantly accustomed to hear them quoted as distinct sentences, without any limitation or explication of their precise meaning, from the place they stand in, and the relation they bear to what goes before, or follows.

Locke's subject is the necessity of logical and argumentative coherence, and resistance to the axiomatic power of language which he enshrines in the *Essay*, but his language nevertheless renders the argument spatial and tactile, just as he regards the mind in spatial terms and thus displays an extraordinary sensitivity to the printed page. (John Locke, *An Essay for the Understanding of St. Paul's Epistles*, in *The Works of John Locke*, 11th. ed. [London: W. Otridge et al., 1812], 8:vi–vii).

16 For the frequency of the architectural trope, I am indebted to discussions with Dr. Simon Varey.

17 John Locke, *A New Method of Making Common-Place-Books* (London, 1706). Included in this issue are Le Clerc's meditations on the use of commonplaces, as well as a discourse by John Wallis on teaching the deaf and dumb (dedicated to Robert Boyle).

18 Spelled variously: the *National Union Catalogue* refers to him as Nicolas Thoyonard (1629–1706). The *Method* refers to him as Toignard, while E. S. de Beer, in his edition of Locke's correspondence, refers to him as Toinard. Toinard was also the author of a *Harmony*, which Le Clerc wanted Locke to have published. It was published a year after Toinard's death.

19 Locke, *A New Method*, in *Works* 3:308.

20 Ibid., 3:308–9.

21 Ibid., 3:311.

22 Ibid., 3:330.

23 On the history of classical scholarship, see: Rudolph Pfeiffer, *History of Classical Scholarship from 1300 to 1850* (Oxford: Clarendon Press, 1976); L. D. Reynolds and N. G. Wilson, *Scribes and Scholars: A Guide to the Transmission of Greek and Latin Literature*, 2d ed. (Oxford: Clarendon Press, 1974; reprint, 1978); John Edwin Sandys, *A History of Classical Scholarship*, 3 vols. (Cambridge: Cambridge Univ. Press, 1908); Ulrich von Wilamowitz-Moellendorff, *History of Classical Scholarship*, trans. Alan Harris, ed. and intro. Hugh Lloyd-Jones (London: Duckworth, 1982).

24 Mark Pattison, "Joseph Scaliger," in *Essays* (Oxford: Clarendon Press, 1889), 1:133.

25 Ibid., 1:161.

26 Anthony Grafton, *Joseph Scaliger: A Study in the History of Classical Scholarship*, vol. 1, *Textual Criticism and Exegesis* (Oxford: Clarendon Press, 1983), 227.

27 Grafton writes about the sixteenth-century concept of method thus: "the classical scholars and chronologists of the sixteenth century had one great problem when it came to argument about first principles: they could not, for the most part, talk about method in general terms. There was no tradition of general debate about method in either study; there was no literary

genre in which it could be cast and no vocabulary in which it could be framed." While Scaliger could appeal rather loosely to Sextus Empiricus, "he never managed to define in a systematic and detailed way the methods and presuppositions of a good critic" (*Scaliger*, 6–7).

The Restoration revision of method presupposed the revaluation of the Epicurean canon, as presented by Diogenes Laertius in ancient times, and as revamped by Pierre Gassendi in *De Vita et Moribus Epicuri* (1647) and *Philosophiae Epicuri Syntagma* (1658), as well as by such English thinkers as Walter Charleton in his *Physiologia Epicuro-Gassendo-Charletoniana* (1654). Sextus Empiricus alone never offers adequate machinery or criteria of inference. Part of the interest in Erasmus in the Restoration was owing to his Christianized revaluation of Epicurus in the *Colloquies*, one of his most widely printed works. (See Marie Delcourt and Marcelle Derwa, "Trois Aspects Humanistes de l'Épicurisme Chrétien," in *Colloquium Erasmianum* [Mons: Centre Universitaire de l'État, 1968], 119–33).

28 Grafton, *Scaliger*, 228.

29 Ibid., 229.

30 Fr. Louis Bouyer, "Erasmus in Relation to the Medieval Biblical Tradition," in *The Cambridge History of the Bible*, vol. 2, *The West from the Fathers to the Reformation*, ed. G. W. H. Lampe (Cambridge: Cambridge Univ. Press, 1969; reprint, 1980), 493.

31 Werner Schwarz, *Principles and Problems of Biblical Translation: Some Reformation Controversies and their Background* (Cambridge: Cambridge Univ. Press, 1955), 144–46. For other assessments of Erasmus' New Testament, see: Roland H. Bainton, *Erasmus of Christendom* (New York: Scribner's, 1969), 131ff.; Marjorie O'Rourke Boyle, *Erasmus on Language and Method in Theology* (Toronto: Univ. of Toronto Press, 1977); Johan Huizinga, *Erasmus and the Age of Reformation* (New York: Harper, 1957), 111.

32 On the series of attacks on Erasmus, see P. S. Allen, *Erasmus: Lectures and Wayfaring Sketches* (Oxford: Clarendon Press, 1934), 66–74; and Schwarz, *Principles and Problems*, 62ff. Albert Rabil writes that Erasmus thought that "even after we have done all that is humanly possible to clarify the texts, much remains unclarified" (*Erasmus and the New Testament: The Mind of a Christian Humanist* [San Antonio, Texas: Trinity Univ. Press, 1972], 125).

33 Rabil, *Erasmus and the New Testament*, 126.

34 Marjorie O'Rourke Boyle, *Rhetoric and Reform: Erasmus' Civil Dispute with Luther* (Cambridge, Mass.: Harvard Univ. Press, 1983), 18–19.

35 See Rabil, *Erasmus and the New Testament*, ch. 3.

36 Allen, *Erasmus*, 31–32; and Grafton writes, "the invention of printing made possible a new level of precision in textual scholarship" (*Scaliger*, 14).

37 Schwarz, *Principles and Problems*, 143. See also Allen, *Erasmus*, 109–37 for Erasmus' relations with his printers.

38 Grafton, *Scaliger*, 166. Grafton also records Scaliger's frustration with Estienne's unauthorized changes of his texts (ibid., 127).

39 The standard work on authorial and editorial control of the printed page still appears to be Percy Simpson, *Proof Reading in the Sixteenth, Seventeenth,*

and Eighteenth Centuries (London: Oxford Univ. Press, 1935). The situation does not seem to have improved remarkably even after Ben Jonson's famous supervision of William Stansby's folio edition of the *Workes* in 1616. By contrast, the example of Clarendon's *History of the Rebellion* (1702) provides evidence of strict authorial and editorial control of the proofs. (In this case, the effective author/editor being the Earl of Rochester). The problem is complex owing to the nature of the evidence. (See Simpson, *Proof Reading*, 90–94).

40 Neal W. Gilbert, *Renaissance Concepts of Method* (New York: Columbia Univ. Press, 1960), 231.

41 Basil Hall, "Biblical Scholarship: Editions and Commentaries," in *The Cambridge History of the Bible*, vol. 3, *The West from the Reformation to the Present Day*, ed. S. L. Greenslade (Cambridge: Cambridge Univ. Press, 1963; reprint, 1968), 63.

42 I take "analytical" to emphasize the *a priori* disjunctiveness of evidences and "synthetic" to assume a basic coherence among them. Foucault writes: "faced with existing and already written language, criticism sets out to define its *relation* with what it represents; hence the importance assumed, since the seventeenth century, by critical methods in the exegesis of texts; it was no longer a question, in fact, of repeating what had already been said in them . . . " (*The Order of Things*, 80–81). In some ways, I suspect that "criticism" only became a possibility as new evidences came to light. For example, the Alexandrine Codex was only discovered in 1627, and the first palimpsest recognized in 1692. (See F. F. Bruce, *The English Bible: A History of Translations* [New York: Oxford Univ. Press, 1961], 128; and Reynolds and Wilson, *Scribes and Scholars*, 175).

43 Père Rapin, Preface to "Comparaison de Thucydide et de Tite Live," in *Oeuvres* (Amsterdam, 1709), 1:175–76, quoted in Gilbert, *Renaissance Concepts*, 226.

44 Reynolds and Wilson, *Scribes and Scholars*, 170–71.

45 Stanley Morison, *Politics and Script: Aspects of Authority and Freedom in the Development of Graeco-Roman Script from the Sixth Century B.C. to the Twentieth Century A.D.*, ed. and completed by Nicolas Barker (Oxford: Clarendon Press, 1972), 315.

46 Ibid.

47 Dom M. D. Knowles, "Jean Mabillon," *Journal of Ecclesiastical History* 10 (1959): 160.

48 Reynolds and Wilson, *Scribes and Scholars*, 171.

49 Knowles, "Mabillon," 160.

50 Morison, *Politics and Script*, 315.

51 Knowles, "Mabillon," 160.

52 Morison, *Politics and Script*, 315. Percy Simpson sees the great classical scholar Richard Bentley as "the pioneer of a new textual method" (*Proof Reading*, 147), which I read as a tacit recognition of this revolution.

53 Knowles, "Mabillon," 160.

54 The notion that "modern" historical thought began as a post-Romantic phenomenon receives its most classic expression in Friederich Meinecke's

Historism: The Rise of a New Historical Outlook, trans. J. E. Anderson (London: Routledge and Kegan Paul, 1972). Ernst Cassirer takes this attitude to task, writing that it was the Enlightenment that established the essential methods that made post-Romantic history possible: the eighteenth century "tries to grasp the meaning of history by endeavoring to gain a clear and distinct concept of it, to ascertain the relation between the general and the particular, between idea and reality, and between laws and facts, and to draw the exact boundaries between these terms" (*The Philosophy of the Enlightenment,* trans. Fritz C. A. Koelln and James P. Pettegrove [Princeton, N.J.: Princeton Univ. Press, 1951], 197). In other words, the eighteenth century developed a hypothetical and empirical method for judging historical evidences, which is the thrust of Arnaldo Momigliano's "Ancient History and the Antiquarian," in *Contributo alla Storia Degli Studi Classici* (Rome: Edizioni di Storia e Letteratura, 1955), 67–106. He writes, "the Age of the Antiquities meant not only a revolution in taste: it meant a revolution in historical method. . . . The Age of Antiquities set standards and posed problems of historical method which we can hardly call obsolete today. . . . [The modern] distinction between original authorities and non-contemporary historians became the common patrimony of historical research only in the late seventeenth century" (p. 68). This is precisely the final argument of Joseph M. Levine's painstaking study, *Dr. Woodward's Shield: History, Science, and Satire in Augustan England* (Berkeley: Univ. of California Press, 1977): "historically the discipline of history, with all its ancillary techniques, did in fact take its rise in close relation to natural science . . . " (p. 292). It is also worth noting that Ezechiel Spanheim's *Dissertatio de Praestantia et Usu Antiquorum* (1664) is generally regarded as initiating modern numismatics.

55 John M. Wallace, "Dryden and History: A Problem in Allegorical Reading," *ELH* 36 (1969): 265–90; and "'Examples are Best Precepts': Readers and Meanings in Seventeenth-Century Poetry," *Critical Inquiry* 1 (1974): 273–90.

56 In the seventeenth and eighteenth centuries, it was published in Europe at least twenty-six times. The first English edition appeared in 1659. The Author's Preface to the first English edition speaks of the power of the senses—especially sight—in impressing ideas upon the mind, and paraphrases the famous adage about that mental machinery: "Now there is nothing in the understanding which was not before in the sense. And therefore to exercise the senses well about the right perceiving the differences of things, will be to lay the grounds of all wisdom, and all wise discourse, and all discreet actions in one's course of life" (Johann Amos Comenius, *Orbis Sensualium Pictus* [London, 1659], sig. A3^v).

57 Both Boyle and Locke refer to the Strasbourg clock in this connection. See Locke, *Essay,* 3.6.9; and Robert Boyle, *Some Considerations Touching the Usefulness of Natural Experimental Philosophy* (1663), in M. A. Stewart ed., *Selected Philosophical Papers of Robert Boyle* (Manchester, England: Manchester Univ. Press, 1979), 160, 170, 174.

58 Roycroft was also the printer of the *Biblia Polyglotta*.

59 See Edward Hodnett, *Francis Barlow: First Master of English Book Illustration* (Berkeley: Univ. of California Press, 1978), 79, 143, 167ff.; and Katherine S. Van Eerde, *John Ogilby and the Taste of His Times* (Folkestone, England: Dawson, 1976).

60 Annabel Patterson, "From Aesop to Michael K: The Life and Times of the Political Fable" (paper presented at Princeton University, April 1985).

61 Stanley Morison, *First Principles of Typography* (New York: Macmillan, 1936), 16. S. H. Steinberg develops this idea in *Five Hundred Years of Printing*, 2d ed. (Harmondsworth, England: Penguin, 1961), 145ff.

62 Margery Corbett and Ronald Lightbown, *The Comely Frontispiece: The Emblematic Title-Page in England, 1550–1660* (London: Routledge and Kegan Paul, 1979), 35.

63 Ibid.

64 Ibid., 14–34.

65 Although we could designate Bacon an "empiricist" in his emphasis on experiment, he does believe in the possibility of an essentialist taxonomy. M. M. Slaughter writes,

> Bacon's new empirical method would remedy the deficiencies of the Aristotelian method by requiring observation and experimentation before the classification of phenomena and the framing of definitions. As in the case of Aristotelian science, however, classification and, even more so, definition are the ends of his scientific activity.
>
> While Bacon is identified with the new science and the scientific revolution, there is evidence that his acceptance of classification and definition as this end and means of science can be traced to an implicit acceptance of Aristotelian essentialism (*Universal Languages*, 94).

Just as his methodology proposes no real use of hypothesis, requiring the creation of models, so the world proposed by his title pages is ultimately coherent, as if adumbrating his peculiar form of realism.

66 A much more curious item in the printing history of the Restoration occurs in the form of Joseph Moxon's *Practical Perspective* (London, 1670) and exemplifies a similar relationship between Restoration visualism and inferential modes of representation. Moxon was a Fellow of the Royal Society, a maker of mathematical instruments, Hydrographer to Charles II, and master printer. He enters histories of printing because he was responsible for "the earliest full specimen of types issued by an English type foundry," and, even more so, because he printed and published *Mechanick Exercises* (1677–83), which included the first practical treatise in English on the art of printing, and "one of the first books which could be purchased in installments." (See Colin Clair, *A Chronology of Printing* [London: Cassell, 1969], 88; idem, *A History of Printing in Britain* [London: Cassell, 1965], 141; also Steinberg, *Five Hundred Years*, 220.)

In *Practical Perspective*, Moxon intended a guide "Usefull for all *Painters, Engravers, Architects*, &c. and all others that are any waies inclined to Speculatory Ingenuity." What makes the book unusual is its combination of interest in the perspectival challenges for those attempting to overcome optical and perceptual difficulties created by the distortions of optical devices, with its attempt to print illustrations of figures distorted by convex and concave mirrors or lenses. If we take the distorted perspective as representing what the viewer sees, Moxon assumes an inferential mode of measurement by which, in seeing either a whole or part of the representation, we could in some way produce a model (or hypothesis) of the originally coherent figure. Any segment of the distortion stands in a strangely metonymic relationship to its putative "cause." As far as I can establish, most Renaissance handbooks on perspective did not concern themselves with this particular issue. (See Willi A. Bärtschi, *Linear Perspective: Its History, Directions for Construction, and Aspects in the Environment and in the Fine Arts,* trans. Fred Bradley [New York: Van Nostrand Reinhold, 1981]; Samuel Y. Edgerton, Jr., *The Renaissance Rediscovery of Linear Perspective* [New York: Harper and Row, 1975]; William M. Ivins, Jr., *On the Rationalization of Sight: With an Examination of Three Renaissance Texts in Perspective* [New York: Metropolitan Museum of Art, 1938]). It seems no small coincidence that Moxon's book would appear at a time when perspective was finally being understood in a mathematical light, especially in the work of Girard Déargues (1593–1662) and Brock Taylor (1685–1731). (See Bärtschi, *Linear Perspective,* 15–16). [See figure 10]

67 The languages were Hebrew, Greek, Latin, Aramaic, Syriac, Arabic, Ethiopic, Samaritan, and Persian. See Basil Hall, *The Great Polyglot Bibles* (San Francisco: Book Club of California, 1966), [20].

68 Hall, "Biblical Scholarship," 92.

69 Clair, *History of Printing,* 140.

70 Harry Carter writes: "The congeries of learned editors of the *Biblia Sacra Polyglotta* or London Polyglot Bible must be considered as ancestors of the English university presses of later times. Their Bible . . . set a standard in textual criticism which would in future be demanded of learned publishing, a standard which only institutional presses could hope to maintain. It was the co-operative achievement of scholars among the Anglican clergy, conceived at a time when many of them had been deprived of their benefices and had taken refuge in Royalist Oxford" (*A History of the Oxford University Press,* vol. 1 [Oxford: Clarendon Press, 1975], 41–42).

71 Clair, *History of Printing,* 140–41. This predates by a very few years Fell's reorganization of the Oxford University Press, which included obtaining a set of types, now known as the Fell Types. (See Nicolas Barker, *The Oxford University Press and the Spread of Learning: An Illustrated History, 1478–1978* [Oxford: Clarendon Press, 1978], 14–18.)

72 Richard Popkin, "Bible Criticism and Social Science," in *Boston Studies in the Philosophy of Science* 14, ed. Robert S. Cohen and Mark W. Wartofsky (Dordrecht, Holland: D. Reidel, 1974), 339–60.

73 Hall, "Biblical Scholarship," 64.

74 The use of typography as an adjunct to an epistemologically moderate

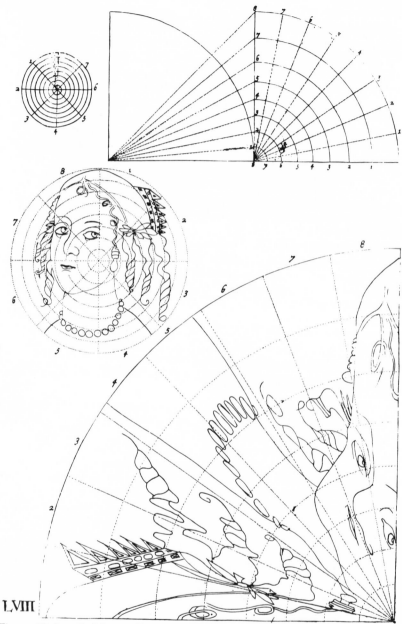

LVIII

Figure 10: Joseph Moxon, *Practical Perspective*. Courtesy Department of Rare Books and Special Collections, Rush Rhees Library, University of Rochester.

model of reading is also to be found in Erasmus, a figure of considerable reverence to the English hermeneutical tradition which I describe here. (See Schwarz, *Principles and Problems*, 143; 156–57.)

75 Hall, "Biblical Scholarship," 51. A similar principle informs the commented Latin Bible of 1498. Werner Schwarz comments: "Even the set-up of the pages reveals the traditional principle. In the middle of each page there is the text of the Bible in rather large letters. Between these lines the interlinear gloss is printed in small letters. The Bible verses are surrounded by the following commentaries:

1. The ordinary gloss.
2. The *Postillae* of Nicholas of Lyra . . .
3. Moral and additional explanations.

The purpose of this arrangement is proudly announced in the preface: the reader need not turn a page in order to study the commentaries, which are printed in closest proximity to the Bible text. The reader is thus supposed to understand the text in accordance with the tradition which encloses, like a large frame, the official Latin version of the Bible" (*Principles and Problems*, 48).

Although Erasmus revised his edition of the New Testament following the readings of the Complutensian Polyglot, one of the editors of the Polyglot, Zúñiga, found the implications of what Erasmus had done so disturbing that he proved a vigorous critic, arguing that "if Erasmus, relying on his knowledge of secular literature, had not been vainglorious, he would not have made a new translation, but would have written notes only, where, during the century-long tradition, the text had become corrupt" (ibid., 164).

76 Hall, *Great Polyglot Bibles*, [2]. Hall also mentions that the London Polyglot is so accurate a version that it has been reproduced for modern Bible scholars.

77 Brian Walton, *The Considerator Considered: Or, A Brief View of Certain Considerations upon the Biblia Polyglotta* (London, 1659), 88.

78 Ibid., 85. Owen is attacking the Polyglot from what Schwarz calls the "inspirational" view.

Richard Bentley, the greatest classical scholar since Scaliger, and the discoverer of the Homeric digamma, proposed an edition of the New Testament that in its rigor anticipated the editions of the nineteenth century. He never published it, but his letter to Archbishop Wake (in 1716) and his proposals for the scheme (1720) show his awareness of the relationship between the philosophy of textual criticism and the way those texts might appear typographically. He argues that the low standards of present editions of the New Testament are owing to printing: "The New Testament has been under a hard fate since the invention of printing," he writes, "After the Complutenses and Erasmus, who had but very ordinary MSS, it has become the property of book-sellers. Rob. Stephens' edition, set out and regulated by himself alone, is now become the standard." He assures the archbishop that he need not fear a collapse of the text, for "I find that by taking 2000 errors out of the Pope's Vulgate, and as many out of the Protestant Pope Stephens', I can set out an edition of each in columns, without using any book under 900 years old, that shall so exactly agree word for word, and, what at first amazed me, order for order, that no two tallies, nor two indentures can agree better." In his *Proposal*, he aims to confirm his readings: "[The author] makes use of old versions, Syriac, Coptic, Gothic and AEthiopic, and of all the Fathers, Greeks and Latins, within the first five centuries; and he gives in his notes all the various readings (now known) within the said five centuries. So that the reader has under one view what the first ages of the Church knew of the text; and what has crept into any copies since, is of no value or authority."

Without acknowledging Walton, Bentley is following very closely the textual and typographical model first established by the *Biblia Polyglotta*. To make a sample collation (of the Apocalypse), Bentley's assistant, John Walker, received help from the Maurists, of whom the most distinguished successor to Mabillon was Montfaucon. (See James Henry Monk, *The Life of Richard Bentley, D.D.*, 2d ed. [London: J. G. and F. Rivington, 1833], 1: 398–401; 2:119–33.)

79 The attack on "infallible" grounds of Christian truth in favor of the "sufficient" (or probable) persuasiveness of Scripture in the "plain" places occurs, for example, in Viscount Falkland's *Discourse of Infallibility* (London, 1651), 197–98:

> . . . the Scripture cannot prove every thing in *foro contentioso* I beleeve, but all necessary Truth, I beleeve it can: for only those, which it can, are such: I denie not, but that a contentious person may denie a thing to be proved, when his own conscience contradicts his words, but so he may Arguments drawn from any other ground as well as Scripture, so that if for that cause you refuse to admit of proofes from thence, you might as well for the same, refuse to admit of any other kinde of Arguments: and certainlie, if the Scriptures (I meane the plaine places of it) cannot be sufficient ground of such and such a point, surelie it cannot be a sufficient ground to build a ground upon, as the Churches Infallibilitie.

80 Thus Grotius can admit of numerous inaccuracies and prevarications in the Biblical texts themselves without damaging their substantive claim that "there was such a Person as *Jesus* of *Nazareth*, who lived heretofore in *Judea*, when *Tiberius* was Emperor of *Rome*"; "that the same *Jesus* was nailed to a Cross by Pontius Pilate, Governor of Judea"; that he wrought miracles that depended on more than human power; and that, historically, he rose again, which proves the truth of his doctrine (Hugo Grotius, *The Truth of the Christian Religion* [London, 1680], 48; 50ff.; 55–62).

81 John Lightfoot, *The Harmony of the Foure Evangelists* (London, 1644). See also, John Lightfoot, *The Harmony of the . . . Old Testament* (London, 1647); John Lightfoot, *The Harmony, Chronicle and Order of the New Testament* (London, 1655); Samuel Craddock, *The Harmony of the Four Evangelists* (London,

1668). Lightfoot was the textual editor for the Samaritan text in the Polyglot (see Simpson, *Proof Reading*, 144).

82 Lightfoot claims that the harmony reduces the Scriptural texts "into their proper order," and takes them "up in their proper places, in which the naturall Method and genuine *Series* of the Chronology requireth them to be taken in" (*The Harmony of the . . . Old Testament*, 1). This is not unrelated to the older, Erasmian tradition of paraphrase, which is an exercise in mediating between the literal text and its natural or probable meanings. Thus Henry Hammond, also an editor of the Polyglot, published a *Paraphrase and Annotations upon all the Books of the New Testament* (London, 1653), in which he requires the reader to exercise a comparative philological method to grasp the probable sense of the Scriptures.

83 William Arnold Stevens and Ernest de Witt Burton, *A Harmony of the Gospels for Historical Study: An Analytical Synopsis of the Four Gospels*, 12th ed. (New York: Scribner's, 1904), iii.

84 Jean Le Clerc, *The Harmony of the Evangelists. Being the Whole Text of the Four Gospels Dispos'd According to the Order of Time in which the Things Related in Them were Done* (London, 1701). Le Clerc, a long-time correspondent of Locke, editor of the *Blbiothèque Universelle* in which an *abregé* of the Essay had first appeared, as well as the original of *A New Method of a Common-Place-Book*, also published one of the first systematic expositions of critical method in the *Ars Critica* (1697). Momigliano calls this work "the most important" of the textbooks "chiefly concerned with textual criticism" ("Ancient History," 81).

85 Owen had attacked Walton for including a paraphrase in the Polyglot, accusing him of claiming for it the same status of Scripture proper (see Walton, *Considerator Considered*, 112–18).

86 Le Clerc, *Harmony*, 584.

87 Ibid., 596.

88 Ibid.

89 Ibid., sig. A4. The degree to which narrative details are widely felt to have a new ontological density combined with an affective power can be seen in John Edwards, *An Inquiry into Four Remarkable Texts of the New Testament Which Contain Some Difficulty in Them: With a Probable Resolution of Them* (Cambridge, 1692), and *A Discourse concerning the Authority, Stile, and Perfection of the Books of the Old and New Testament* (London, 1694). Edwards later violently attacked Locke's *The Reasonableness of Christianity* as a Socinian tract, prompting Locke's *Vindications*. Oddly, however, they both work towards an effectively similar epistemological stance towards Scripture, though from very different angles. Edwards categorically denies that Scripture as such is textually corrupt, a point which places him in the same "inspirational" camp as Owen; but he radically undercuts that premise by emphasizing that our perceptions of Scripture are fallible, and that therefore any interpretation is bound merely to be "probable" (to use his word), governed often by our individual inclinations, passions and wills. He invokes Grotius at this point: "the excellent *Grotius* acquaints us that he pick'd out

the Best and most Convictive Arguments (as he thought) to prove the *Truth of Religion*, and particularly the *Christian*; and yet some of them, as *Signatures, Fire Ordeal*, &c. are neglected by other Learned Men; for Evidences work more or less, according to the Diversity of Mens Genius's and Dispositions . . . " (*A Discourse*, xi). The Holy Spirit encourages "the Diversity of Interpretations" (ibid., xi). Edwards' unoriginal defence of Christ's parables illuminates the connection between the particular concrete persuasiveness of "Evidences" and that of narrative in general. Not only do parables partly hide the truth from the herd, nor only stimulate a kind of forensic diligence on the part of the reader/hearer, but they also incarnate and particularize the lofty truths of God: "it is very entertaining and pleasant to hear the most Heavenly Matters express'd and set forth by those which are earthly and worldly; because hereby at once both our Minds and our Corporeal Senses are gratified. We are let into Celestial and Spiritual Mysteries by those Objects which are sensual and bodily: we attain to an Insight of those things which are supernatural and extraordinary, by a Representation of those which are merely natural and common" (ibid., 23). Recalling Luther's famous dictum that *"Esop's* [sic] *Fables is the best Book next to the Bible,"* he reminds us that many parables "are Representations of usual and common Occurrences, and such as the Generality of our Saviour's Hearers were daily conversant with; and for that very Reason were made use of by him, as being most moving and affecting" (ibid., 27).

Women, Class, and the Growth of Magazine Readership in the Provinces, 1746–1780

JAN FERGUS

Historians of the eighteenth century have recently begun to direct attention to provincial towns and provincial culture. A work like Penelope Corfield's *The Impact of English Towns, 1700–1800*[1] makes clear that despite the centrality of London in every sense, provincial towns became increasingly important in the economic, social, and cultural life of eighteenth-century England. With over 10 percent of the population in 1801, London had been, of course, the center of the book trade, and probably of readership as well, during the previous century. Yet the reading habits of the remaining portion of the population during that time can provide more reliable indications of the popularity of fiction or the dissemination of information, as well as changes in taste, than can a study of reading in the metropolis. Fortunately, some business records of the Clay family of booksellers, who operated in four midland market towns, are deposited in the Northamptonshire Record Office. These records offer an opportunity to investigate the development of the provincial reading public in England during the last half of the eighteenth century.

The Clays' main bookshop was located in Daventry between 1742 and 1781. At various times during that period, John Clay and, after him, his son Thomas Clay operated shops in Rugby and Lutterworth. Another son, Samuel Clay, also ran a short-lived bookshop in Warwick, August 1770–July 1772, and took over the Rugby shop after his brother Thomas died in 1781.[2] These towns were merely the centers of the Clays' activities, however; sales were made to customers who resided as far as ten or fifteen miles away from the nearest shops. As a result, the Clay customers include subscribers for magazines drawn from a fairly large area in the midlands—an ellipse about forty miles long and as much as thirty miles broad, covering parts of the three counties of Northamptonshire, Leicestershire, and Warwickshire.

The records of the Clay shops are incomplete, particularly for the three decades before 1770 (see table 1 for a list of surviving Daventry day books). During this period, the Warwick shop was not yet in operation. Because two rival bookshops were already well established when the Warwick shop opened in 1770, the records of this shop can give only an incomplete view of customers' interest in subscribing to magazines: many customers are likely to have subscribed through the other two shops. Accordingly, the Warwick records have been used sparingly in this study.[3] By contrast, in Daventry, Rugby, and Lutterworth, no rival booksellers seem to have existed between 1746–1780. Unfortunately, for the three decades before 1770, no records at all survive for Lutterworth, and those for Rugby include only the eighteen-month period just before 1770. These omissions are less serious for a study of readership of the magazines than they are for a study of any other part of the audience, however, because monthly lists of *all* magazine subscribers, including those served by the Rugby and Lutterworth shops, were kept in the better-preserved Daventry records. As a result, we have at least a glimpse into the growth of magazine readership within this provincial area between the mid-forties and the mid-sixties, along with a rather concentrated view of developments in the seventies, a decade especially important for magazines.

As table 1 clearly illustrates, the decades before the seventies saw a large growth in provincial magazine readership, a growth which seems to be traceable in part to the emergence of new magazines during this period (see table 2.1). The *Critical Review*, for example, issued in 1756, shows a pattern of steady growth in readership, followed by retention of those readers. Its history reverses that of most specialized magazines issued during the fifties and sixties (and later as well), which tended to reach their largest audiences among the Clays' customers relatively soon after first being issued, and then to decline in circulation, sometimes genteelly over a long period (as does the *Gentleman's*), sometimes rather precipitously (as in the case of the *Court and City*).

Nonetheless, even though almost all the specialized magazines introduced in the fifties and sixties were defunct by the early seventies—including such titles as the *Christian's*, the *Newgate*, *Martin's*, the *British*, the *Wonderful*, and so on—they apparently did succeed in enlarging the audience for magazines. During the period 1764–66, some 180 customers subscribed to magazines, about four times the number in the earliest years recorded, 1746–48, and about three-fourths of the total achieved later in 1770–71 and 1774. In other words, by the mid-sixties, this particular provincial audience had nearly reached its limit—with one major exception. The magazines had not succeeded in attracting many women as subscribers, despite the appearance of several designed especially for them. For example, although nine women took magazines between December 1764 and March 1766, only one ordered a copy of the *Court Miscellany, or Lady's New Magazine*. She requested the October 1765 issue, but she does not appear among the lists of subscribers at any point before the records end in March 1766. The *Court Miscellany* was first issued in July 1765, and had six male subscribers by December of that year; it ceased publication in 1771. By contrast, in the seventies the new *Lady's Magazine* immediately attracted and sustained a substantial readership, and both the numbers and the proportion of its female subscribers grew over the next decade (see table 2.2). Thus, while women constituted 4 or 5 percent of total magazine subscribers during the previous three decades, in 1770–71 the percentage doubled (to nearly 10 percent) and reached a high of about 16.7 percent by the end of the decade.

Overall, some 110 women were magazine subscribers over the periods covered by all the Clay records for Daventry, Rugby, Lutterworth, and Warwick (see table 3). On the surface, this figure compares favorably with the approximately sixty women altogether who bought or borrowed fiction from the Clays during this time. Those women constituted, however, about a fourth of the total number of customers who bought or read book-length fiction; the 110 women who subscribed to magazines comprise a much smaller proportion of the entire audience for magazines—at least a thousand customers and probably more. A comparison between these two audiences is worth making because it partially substantiates the claims of scholars like Robert D. Mayo that readers read much of their fiction in the magazines rather than in book form.[4] When I began this study of women subscribers, I hoped to find that here the usual clichés about the new reading public—female, middle-class, and addicted to fiction—would at last find some support, even though I had found little evidence for a sizeable audience of this kind among Samuel Clay's buyers and borrowers of books.[5] And in fact, women subscribers to the magazines do substantiate these clichés to some extent. Magazines, after all, were a bargain compared to book-length works of fiction, offering for sixpence a variety of short and long tales, essays, and so on. Accordingly, during and after 1770, which may be a watershed year for middle-class female readership, as it certainly is for novels[6] and for magazine fiction,[7] over 40 percent of the fifty-four women whom I have been able to identify as subscribers to magazines were tradesmen's or farmers' wives or daughters (a total of twenty-three women). They almost equal the twenty-five wives and daughters of professional men who subscribed in this decade.

So far, I have been implying that subscribers and readers were identical, and that women who subscribed to or read magazines could easily be distinguished from men. Obviously, no such easy identification or separation is possible. Many readers could share one subscription, and some certainly did. At one point, three men shared a subscription to the *Critical Review*, and in at least four instances, women living in the same or adjoining parishes transferred from one to another a subscription to the *Lady's Magazine*. Such instances certainly do not exhaust the possibilities for shared readership. All members of a household receiving a magazine could have read it, not to mention friends and relatives.

The task of separating readers from subscribers and men from women is further complicated by the existence of what I will call "concealed" women subscribers—women whose subscriptions were recorded under someone else's name, typically a husband's or father's. A number of subscriptions, for example, go along for years under a man's name, and then suddenly his wife's name appears. In one case, Dr. Knowler, a clergyman, took the *London Magazine* for at least twenty-eight years until his death in 1774, at which time his wife assumed the subscription for another three and a half years. This case is easy to interpret; presumably, both husband and wife were reading the *London Magazine*. What are we to make, however, of the case of William Deacon, a surgeon, who subscribed to the first issue of the *Lady's Magazine* (dated August 1770)? He was replaced as the subscriber by his wife Catherine for four months beginning in the following December. When the records resume after a three-month gap, however, Mr. Deacon was again the recorded subscriber and remained so for the life of the subscription, another six years. Both were still living when the subscription was cancelled. Thus, only because the records are fairly complete for this decade do we have any indication that Mrs. Deacon ever was a subscriber—for a total of four months out of more than seven years. Altogether, about twenty-five other cases of concealed women subscribers emerge in 1770 and afterward; in other words, nearly a fourth of all women subscribers (27 of 110) were concealed. Most of them were married women like Mrs. Deacon, but six were single women whose brothers or fathers were originally and primarily listed as subscribers. If more Clay records survived, no doubt further instances of concealed subscription would emerge.

The causes and consequences of the phenomenon of concealed subscription have important implications for studies of women readers. For example, over half of all the women who subscribed to magazines were single (a total of 57),[8] and a significant segment were widowed, leaving a rather small group of married women as subscribers. Certainly the fact that married women did not exist legally, so that in business transactions their husbands would be likely to obtain credit and to receive bills, must have contributed in some degree to the phenomenon of concealed subscription—though without accounting for it entirely. If this condition or the small disposable income available to many women sufficed to explain concealed subscription, then women who bought and borrowed books would be about as rare as those who subscribed to magazines, and most of them would be single—but such is not the case. Between September 1746 and March 1748, for example, while women constituted only 4 percent of John Clay's subscribers to magazines, they composed about 7.5 percent of his book buyers (24 of approximately 320) and 14 percent of the book borrowers (6 of 42), according to a preliminary count. In addition, only about one-fourth of the women who bought books at this period were single (as opposed to more than half the total numbers of women who subscribed to magazines). Some further explanation for the small proportion of married women who subscribed to magazines must exist, and more important, the possibility that many married men were subscribing for their wives must be considered. In other words, a thorough study of women who subscribed would entail an equally thorough study of the men who did, a massive undertaking. For the present, however, we must assume that married women's interest in magazines may be underrepresented in the figures recorded in tables 1–3.

Those women who can be identified as subscribers to magazines divide themselves clearly into two quite different audiences: the large one of the 1770s and the smaller, earlier audience. The early audience is traditional in its composition and tastes. In categorizing women subscribers through parish records and other archival materials, I have followed the eighteenth-century practice of determining a woman's class primarily by that of her husband and secondarily, if she was unmarried, by that of her father. Thus, the "professional class" noted in table 3 consists of the wives and daughters of members of the professions—clergymen, doctors, lawyers, and officers. I can identify no women in the next two classes—wives and daughters of farmers and tradesmen—who were subscribers to magazines before 1770. Instead, eight of the total of fifteen subscribers before 1770 are members of the gentry or professional classes. While I cannot identify the remaining seven with any certainty, various clues indicate that at least six of them also belonged to these classes. In other words, during the three brief periods covered by the Clay records before 1770, women subscribers generally belonged to the two classes which traditionally produced readers, the professional class and the gentry, and the tastes of these women were primarily conservative. They preferred the oldest magazines, the *Gentleman's* (six subscribers) and the *London* (two subscribers).

Women's comparative lack of interest in novelty almost completely vanished in the seventies, when women subscribers multiplied (see tables 1 and 2.2). The *Lady's Magazine* was by far the most successful in attracting women readers: sixty-two women altogether subscribed, or about 56 percent of the total number of women who subscribed over the four decades covered by the Clay records. In addition, table 2.2 shows that at first the magazine drew even more men as subscribers than women. The runner-up in popularity among women, the *Town and Country Magazine,* obtained about one-fourth as many women subscribers as the *Lady's:* seventeen altogether (about 15 percent of the total; see table 3).

Some interesting differences exist in the classes of women who subscribed to these two magazines. The *Lady's Magazine,* for example, was especially attractive to tradesmen's and farmers' wives: 72 percent of the women whom I can identify as belonging to these groups subscribed (or eighteen of twenty-five women), whereas by contrast a little more than half the women whom I can identify in each of the other classes did so (twenty-four of thirty-nine). Indeed, the *Lady's Magazine* can almost be said to have created middle-class women subscribers among the Clays' customers. The *Town and Country,* on the other hand, which offered "chronicles and scandals in high life"[9] as well as various kinds of fiction and other staples of the popular miscellanies, largely attracted members of the gentry and professional classes among its women readers: no identifiable tradesmen's wives and just two farmers' wives subscribed. Like the *Lady's,* however, the *Town and Country* initially attracted provincial men as subscribers even more successfully than it did women: in the areas served by the Daventry, Rugby, and Lutterworth shops, thirty-four men and six women were readers within two years of issue. Moreover, the magazine managed to sustain a substantial readership for some time. This history, like that of the *Lady's Magazine,* was remarkable. Again, while it was not unusual for new magazines to attract a large number of new readers at first, ordinarily the audience evaporated quickly. The *Court and City Magazine,* issued between the *Town and Country* and the *Lady's,* offers a good example. Having obtained fifteen subscribers within a year of issue, only one of whom was a woman, it dropped to four by the end of the following year. Its readership elsewhere must have been comparable, for it ceased publication at that point.

A climax for subscriptions to magazines was reached in 1774–75, as table 1 indicates. Twenty-nine magazines were taken, including highly specialized ones like the *Lawyer's,* the *Macaroni,* the *Builder's,* the *Musical,* and the *Medical.* However, the approximately 240 readers recorded in this year seem to represent a saturation point. Indeed, in the seventies, the number of readers—male and female—does not vary as much as or in proportion to the number of magazines. While about 190 subscribers took sixteen different magazines during the last six months of 1771, only about 210 took the thirty-one magazines available in the first eleven months of 1777. That is, although the number of magazines taken by the Clays' customers nearly doubled in six years, the subscribing audience increased by only a little more than 10 percent during the same period. Apparently, after the success of the *Lady's Magazine* and the *Town and Country* in enlarging the provincial audience, in part by attracting new women readers, increasing numbers of magazines had to draw on virtually the same pool of provincial readers. Furthermore, these new readers tended to be rather fickle. Table 3 indicates that very few women subscribers to the *Lady's Magazine,* particularly farmers' and tradesmen's wives and daughters, held their subscriptions for more than two years. Overall, only twelve of the sixty-two subscribers did so. Alternatively, they may have made arrangements to share one another's subscriptions. For all these reasons, the Clays' provincial magazine audience seems to have reached a kind of plateau in this decade.

Although the women who subscribed to the *Lady's Magazine* generally did so for short periods, then, they nonetheless subscribed in increasing proportions. The total number of subscribers in any month dwindled over the decade from a high of thirty-four to a low of eighteen, but the proportion of women who subscribed rose from about 50 percent to over 70 percent over the same period. The magazine's extreme popularity with women makes it a worthwhile case study. Although its success with tradesmen's and farmers' wives and daughters was remarkable, in fact the *Lady's* appealed to all classes of women.

Unlike the *Town and Country*, it was domestic and decorous in tone. And according to Jean Hunter's analysis of the contents, during the 1770s about one-fourth of the magazine was devoted to morals and manners and another fourth to tales. Travel, poetry, theatre, foreign news, essays in French, and a variety of other material made up the balance.[10] Furthermore, like other popular miscellanies, it drew heavily on its subscribers for unpaid submissions.

This policy of printing readers' works both exploited and flattered readers—a winning combination. Decorum seems to have been the most important criterion used in selecting which readers' contributions to publish: almost the only criticisms ever directed at readers' submissions to the magazine concerned the presence of sentiments inappropriate or unflattering to ladies. Indeed, the editor explicitly stated, "though we acknowledge the reception of many a piece, we are too delicate to say, 'they are unworthy of publication,'"[11] a delicacy not observed by the editor of the *Town and Country*, who did not scruple to call "W's *Poem on Writing . . . indeed a very trifling Essay on the Subject,*" or to comment that "J. L. *of* Watford *assures us his Epitaph, is an Original; we sincerely believe it, and that it never will be copied.*"[12] Strikingly, the editor of the *Lady's* adopts a female persona, unlike the editor of the *Town and Country*. The soothing and flattering tone of the *Lady's* must have encouraged amateur writers, for the editor constantly apologizes for having no space to include all the "favours" received.

According to Jean Hunter's analysis of four years in the 1770s, about 40 percent of those submitters and contributors who can be identified by sex were male.[13] This figure suggests that we must not be too ready to assume that male subscribers to the *Lady's Magazine* were gratifying their wives or daughters only. Indeed, I have been able to identify exactly five contributors to the *Lady's* during the 1770s who were also customers of the Clays, and none were women. If any of the Clays' women customers submitted their own work, they probably did so under assumed names. (Most of the works attributed to women in the magazine use such names as Matilda, Eloisa, Clarinda, and so forth.) The male contributors were a tapster, a schoolmaster, two schoolboys, and the very minor poet Benjamin West. The tapster's case is the most interesting. He was the only one among them to subscribe to the *Lady's*. Moreover, only he and Benjamin West actually saw their works in print; the others' contributions were simply acknowledged.

William Gough, tapster at the Globe, an inn at Dodford (a few miles from Daventry), apparently shared his subscription to the *Lady's Magazine* with a Mr. Hewitt, probably the innholder. Hewitt subscribed to the *Lady's Magazine* in his own name sometime before July 1771, and maintained the subscription at least through January 1772. At this time Gough was about thirty-two years old and had been married for over four years to Mary Freeman, a literate woman, who was twenty-two and pregnant with what seems to have been their only child. By the time the Clay records resume in 1773, Gough had replaced Hewitt as the subscriber, remaining so until the end of 1777, when the records are interrupted. Gough died in March 1779; subsequently Hewitt took up the subscription again. [14]

Hewitt's original subscription was to Wheble's *Lady's Magazine*. Although I have generally conflated them in the tables and in my analysis, there were two *Lady's Magazines* between April 1771 and December 1772. One was printed by Wheble, the original publisher, the other by Robinson and Roberts; the latter had been sold the rights to the magazine by its originator. Robinson and Roberts sued Wheble to stop publication, and won, but Wheble continued to publish nonetheless, printing an indignant account of and attack on the decision in his July 1771 issue. [15] Students of literary property in the eighteenth century will not be surprised at Wheble's indignation or at his willingness to equate publication with ownership. He eventually stopped printing the magazine in 1772; Robinson and Roberts triumphed in the end. During the time that both were available, however, Wheble's magazine was the more popular of the two among the Clays' customers: a total of thirty-six subscribers chose Wheble's magazine while sixteen took Robinson and Roberts'; some of these subscribers vacillated between the two.

To return to William Gough, the tapster-poet: by September 1771, his first work was published in Wheble's magazine, an enigma and an answer to another reader's enigma. In the next fifteen months, Gough published at least five more enigmas, four answers, a poetic rebus on the town of Southam, his birthplace, and another poetic rebus in praise of Wheble's magazine. In this last work, each successive letter of the title, "Whebles Ladies Magazine," is the subject of a one- or two-line rebus. The first line, for example—"A Grain well known all England round"—refers to wheat and supplies the first letter, *W*. Gough concludes with four lines that must have applied to other male readers of the magazine:

> Join these initials, and with ease,
> You'll find what doth my fancy please.
> Altho', ye wits, I must declare,
> 'Tis chiefly to amuse the fair. [16]

Despite this rather sheepish praise of Wheble's magazine, Gough was prepared to subscribe and submit to Robinson and Roberts' magazine by 1773, after Wheble had stopped publishing: Gough's poetical enigmas appear there in that year. His work for Wheble is more interesting, however, for his friends submitted answers to his enigmas, and exchanges developed that reinforced a sense of community among the audience, in which distinctions between writers and readers tended to disappear.

The case of William Gough suggests that students of the reading public must not expect to distinguish clearly or easily between male and female audiences. The case of the *Lady's Magazine* as a whole, however, allows us to observe a successful formula for appealing to a new audience within a particular genre. What the *Lady's* seems to have done is to model itself on the even more successful *Town and Country*. The *Lady's* adopted the *Town and Country's* emphasis on short, entertaining pieces, many of them fictional, but rejected its focus on scandal as well as its sophisticated or acerbic tone in favor of a domestic, decorous one, deifying propriety. Equally important, the *Lady's* specialized; it addressed itself to women, a segment of the population which had to content itself otherwise with magazines aimed at men or at a generalized male and female audience. Admittedly, however, those earlier magazines addressed to women did not survive long. If we are to account for the *Lady's* success, we must look at the ways in which it exploited its readers—in part by flattering them with the assumption that they all could write, in part by encouraging them to see themselves as a writing and reading community.

A number of earlier magazines addressed to women invited readers' participation—some of them even before the *Tatler* and *Spectator*, as Mayo has pointed out[17]—but they did so less persuasively. Oliver Goldsmith's "Mrs. Stanhope," for example, in the *Lady's Magazine, or Polite Companion for the Fair Sex* (1759–63), called for readers' submissions in a qualified, unencouraging, even ambiguous way:

> If any of the sex, whose situation in life is not entangled in the cares
> of it, and whose minds have had leisure and opportunity to seek for
> knowledge, shall think proper to contribute their assistance to so
> well-meant an undertaking, the favor will be duly acknowledged.
> And this is all proposed by an invitation to a correspondence.[18]

This statement, while it firmly restricts the class of possible contributors, does not clearly indicate whether the contributions will be published or not. Indeed, Mrs. Stanhope explicitly states that her intention is "not to make all her fair readers turn writers."[19] By contrast, the *Lady's* of 1770 began with a somewhat less ambiguous invitation in its advertisements. The first one that appeared in the *Northampton Mercury* on 20 August 1770, claimed that "Any Favours from Correspondents will be thankfully received" and noted that "letters to the Editor are requested and received" by the printer Wheble.

Apparently, the advertisements sufficed. Although the first issue makes no reference to a policy of encouraging readers' submissions, in the second a paragraph addressed to correspondents appears. [20] By the third issue, the paragraph is headed "To our Correspondents," and it becomes a regular feature, generally increasing in size—in Wheble's magazine, to half a page by May 1771, and a full page within a year of publication. In this portion of the magazine, the *Lady's* engaged in dialogue with potential and actual contributors—soliciting and acknowledging contributions (most of which were never printed), calling for partially printed works to be completed, promising to publish other works. The magazine directly and almost intimately addressed its readers and writers, claiming the existence of a homogenous, eager, delicate, and discerning audience, many of whom were clamoring for continuations of one another's literary productions. Indeed, some readers apparently offered to continue works abandoned by their authors. In such an atmosphere, distinctions between writers and readers evaporate. The reader, in this formulation, is a writer. By promulgating this formula, the *Lady's* allowed its readership to modify and shape it to some extent. In 1770, creating an audience—one that included a substantial portion of middle-class women readers—apparently required allowing that audience to take some part in creating the magazine.

NOTES

1 Penelope Corfield, *The Impact of English Towns, 1700–1800* (Oxford: Oxford Univ. Press, 1982).

2 Jan Fergus, "Eighteenth-Century Readers in Provincial England: The Customers of Samuel Clay's Circulating Library and Bookshop in Warwick, 1770–72," *Papers of the Bibliographical Society of America* 78 (1984): 159–61.

3 The nine women who subscribed through the Warwick shop are included in the totals listed in table 3, as are those in another eccentric group—the five women listed as magazine subscribers in NRO ML478, Samuel Clay's Rugby day book for 1781–84.

4 Robert D. Mayo, *The English Novel in the Magazines, 1740–1815* (Evanston, Ill.: Northwestern Univ. Press, 1962), 1–2.

5 Fergus, "Eighteenth-Century Readers," 171–72.

6 J. M. S. Tompkins, *The Popular Novel in England, 1770–1800* (1932; reprint, London: Methuen & Co., 1969), 13; Tompkins points out, however, that the number of novels published yearly declined in the mid-seventies.

7 Mayo, *English Novel*, 2.

8 Two of these women were subscribers both as single and then later as married women; I have counted each as one subscriber and have included them among the fifty-seven single women here. Three other single women seem to be combined with their mothers in the subscription lists; I have considered them as three subscribers, not six, since the subscriptions in each case seem to be continuous.

9 Mayo, *English Novel*, 185.

10 Jean Hunter, "The *Lady's Magazine* and the Study of Englishwomen in the Eighteenth Century," in *Newsletters to Newspapers: Eighteenth-Century Journalism*, ed. Donovan H. Bond and W. Reynolds McLeod (Morgantown: School of Journalism, West Virginia University, 1977), 112.

11 *Lady's Magazine, or Entertaining Companion for the Fair Sex* 12 (1781): 114.

12 *Town and Country Magazine, or Universal Repository of Knowledge, Instruction, and Entertainment* 3 (1771): 226.

13 Hunter, "The *Lady's Magazine*," 109.

14 See Warwick County Record Office parish records on microfilm: Southam, Reel 1; Northamptonshire Record Office, parish registers for Dodford (106p/1–4) and Weedon (344p/3).

15 John Wheble's *Lady's Magazine* 2 (1771): 41–52.

16 John Wheble's *Lady's Magazine* 3 (1772): 432.

17 Mayo, *English Novel*, 18.

18 *Lady's Magazine, or Polite Companion for the Fair Sex* 1 (1759): 165.

19 Ibid.

20 *Lady's Magazine* 1 (1770): 84.

Table 1. Subscribers and Magazines, 1746–1780, Daventry (includes Rugby and Lutterworth)[a]

Dates, Daventry Day Books[b]	Magazines Subscribed To	Total Subscribers[c]	Women Subscribers	Women Subscribers as % of Total Subscribers
Sep 1746– Mar 1748 (NRO D64)	3	50	2	4
Jul 1758– Sep 1759 (NRO D2931)	11	120	5	4.2
Dec 1764– Mar 1766 (NRO ML692)	20	180	9	5.6
Jan 1770– Mar 1771 (NRO D2930)	15	240[d]	23	9.6
July 1771– Feb 1772 (NRO D7719)	16	190	23	12.1
Mar 1773– Jan 1774 (NRO ML699)	18	190	23	12.1
Jan 1774– Feb 1775 (NRO ML89)	29	240	32	13.3
Jan 1777– Dec 1777 (NRO ML88)	31	210	35	16.7
Mar 1779– Sep 1780 (NRO ML10)	19	210	35	16.7

[a] In the one surviving Warwick record, thirty subscribers, nine of them women, took seven magazines between August 1770 and March 1772. These records are eccentric for various reasons, however, and are therefore not included here.

[b] The day books, along with other Clay business records, are deposited in the Northamptonshire Record Office; catalog numbers given in parentheses.

[c] Total subscribers rounded off to nearest ten. Until computer analysis of the records is available, these figures cannot be exact, though they are substantially accurate.

[d] Subscribers (5) listed in Rugby day book for 1768–1770 (NRO D2925) but not in the Daventry day book beginning in January 1770 (NRO D2930) are included in this figure.

Table 2.1. Circulation History: Magazines with More Than Ten
Subscribers per Month, 1746–1765[a]

Magazine	Subscribers per Magazine in Selected Months (Women Subscribers within Totals in Parentheses)					
	Dec 46	Jan 48	Dec 58	Jan 59[b]	Dec 64	Dec 65
Gentleman's (1731+)	24 (1)	24 (1)	22 (1)	26 (2)	21	19 (2)
London (1732–85)	7	5	24 (1)	25 (1)	32 (2)	31 (2)
Universal (1747–1815)		7	9	11	15 (1)	14 (1)
Martin's (?–1765)			13	15	7	
Monthly Review (1749+)			10	11	8	10
Critical Review (1756+)			4	4	7	6 (1)[c]
Royal (1759–71)				[d]	17	14

[a]Other magazines, whose circulation figures never reached more than ten per
month, taken by women during this period: 1758–59, Ladies' New Magazine; Grand
Magazine of Magazines (one woman each); 1764–65, Gospel (first version); Christian's;
Beauties of Magazines; Candid Review; Wonderful Magazine; Universal Museum (one each).
Some women took more than one copy of these magazines.

[b]The fairly substantial changes in subscriptions during the month between December 1758 and January 1759 are reasonably typical. As a rule, many subscriptions
were cancelled after the December issue, and many began with the January issue.

[c]The woman here indicated as a subscriber—Miss Spateman, a clergyman's daughter—
ordered one copy of the Critical Review but was never listed as a regular subscriber.

[d]The Royal Magazine had ten subscribers for its first issue (July 1759).

Table 2.2. Circulation History: Magazines with More Than Ten
Subscribers per Month, 1770–80[a]

Magazines	Dec 70[b]	Dec 71[b]	Dec 73	Dec 74	Jan 77	Nov 77	Dec 79	Aug 80
	Subscribers per Magazine in Selected Months (Women Subscribers within Totals in Parentheses)							
Gentleman's (1731+)	24 (1)	24 (1)	15 (1)	17 (1)	18(1)	17 (1)	10 (1)	12 (1)
London (1732–85)	30	26	23	22 (2)	20 (2)	18 (4)	16 (1)	20 (1)
Universal (1747–1815)	11	12	6	7	7	7 (1)	11 (1)	10
Monthly Review (1749+)	8	11	11	10	7	7	13	13
Critical Review (1765+)	10	10	9	7	10	9	9	11
Court and City (1770–71)	14 (1)	3 (1)						
Town and Country (1769–96)	39 (6)	48 (6)	43 (5)	42 (5)	37 (4)	34 (5)	32 (5)	28 (5)
Lady's (1770+)	22 (11)	33 (11)[c]	27 (9)	34 (13)	28 (14)	26 (14)	23 (15)	18 (13)
Everyman's (1771–73)		23 (1)	3					
Oxford (1768–76)	14	7	3					
Westminster (1772–85)			16 (1)	12 (2)	10 (1)	10 (1)	9 (2)	11 (1)
Sentimental (1773–77)			13 (2)	6 (2)	3 (2)			
Musical (?)[d]				11	3	5		
Theatrical (?)[d]					5 (1)	11 (4)	11 (2)	9 (1)
Gospel (1774–84)					12 (1)	12 (1)	11 (1)	8 (1)

[a] One other magazine was taken by women during this period, but its circulation never reached ten per month: *Alamode Magazine*, 1777, four women.

[b] The figures for December 1770 and December 1771 do not include magazines sent by John Clay to his son Samuel at Warwick. These magazines were circulated to Warwick customers, and the names of subscribers appear in Samuel Clay's Warwick day book D2929. John Clay's day books D2930 and D7719 simply list Samuel as the subscriber and indicate numbers of each magazine sent to him.

[c] During December 1771, two versions of the *Lady's Magazine* were published, the first one by Wheble, and a later rival by Robinson and Roberts. During this month, John Clay had thirty-three subscribers to the two magazines and Samuel Clay had six. Of the total of thirty-nine subscribers in December 1771, thirty took Wheble's and nine took Robinson and Roberts' magazine; twelve of the subscribers to Wheble's were women, as were four of the subscribers to Robinson and Roberts' *Lady's Magazine*.

[d] Mayo does not list the *Musical* or the *Theatrical* magazines; all other dates are taken from his work.

Table 3. Women Subscribers: Daventry, Rugby, Lutterworth, and Warwick, 1746–84

Class	No. of Total Women Subscribers	No. of Total Women Subscrib-ing 2+ Years[a]	*Lady's*[b]	*Gentleman's*[b]	*London*[b]	*Town & Country*[b]
Gentry	12	5	5 (1)	2 (1)	1 (1)	3 (3)
Professional	27	12	16 (6)	2 (1)	3 (1)	5 (3)
Farmers' wives, daughters	8	0	6	0	0	2
Tradesmen's wives, daughters	15	3	12 (2)	0	0	0
Unidentified	48	9	23 (3)	4	2 (2)	7 (2)
Totals	110	29	62 (12)	8 (2)	6 (4)	17 (8)

[a] The figures for total number of women who subscribed to a particular magazine for two years or more include women who took magazines other than the four most popular ones (*Lady's, Gentleman's, London,* and *Town and Country*). In two cases, women took more than one of these magazines for two or more years each: Mrs. Ashley, a member of the gentry, subscribed to the *London* and the *Town and Country,* and Miss Warren of Bugbrook, sister of a clergyman, subscribed to the *Town and Country* and the *Gentleman's.*

[b] Numbers in parentheses indicate total number of subscribers in that class whose subscriptions lasted two years or more.

Berkeley, Shaftesbury, and the Meaning of Politeness

LAWRENCE E. KLEIN

As an object of inquiry, George Berkeley has been a property almost entirely of philosophers.[1] The result of this attention has been that, while Berkeley's relations to certain aspects of the discourse of his era have been widely studied, his relations to other aspects of this discourse have been relatively neglected. One implication of this philosophical focus has been that examination has concentrated largely on the early works in which Berkeley worked out the theory of vision and the ideas comprising his so-called immaterialism, while the later works have been neglected.[2]

One of Berkeley's later works which has received little attention from those interested in his philosophy is *Alciphron*, a dialogue (or really a set of dialogues among the same participants), first published in 1732.[3] The central concern of *Alciphron* is religion and belief. The dialogue is, in the concluding words of a rather long subtitle, "An Apology for the Christian Religion, against those who are called Free-Thinkers."[4] Indeed, this dialogue is one between two free-thinkers and two serious Christians.[5] One possible and obvious approach to *Alciphron* is to consider it in the context of the continuing early eighteenth-century discussions about the nature of and relations among such topics as natural and revealed religion, reason and faith, matter and spirit, the Trinity, miracles, and so forth.[6]

Alciphron, however, is not a single-minded text:[7] not only is it a dialogue between freethought and religion, but also it is a dialogue about "politeness." To show this, I will first define that key term in early eighteenth-century English discourse, then show how Berkeley inserted it into the dialogues offering a critique of the notion, and, finally, indicate how Berkeley appropriated a redefined notion of politeness for his own use.

In so doing, I hope to broaden our understanding of the relationship between George Berkeley and another eminent Augustan, Anthony Ashley Cooper, the third earl of Shaftesbury. Berkeley's attitude toward Shaftesbury is usually seen as a mixture of genuine philosophical complaint about Shaftesbury's moral thought and of rather scandalously *ad hominem* commentary on Shaftesbury's person.[8] However, it will become clear here that Berkeley was taking on more than just Shaftesbury's moral thought and that there was a discursive justification for the entire range of Berkeley's criticisms of Shaftesbury. This justification was the fact that the sort of "politeness" to which Berkeley was objecting in *Alciphron* found its most elaborate, interesting, and influential expression in the writings that comprise Shaftesbury's *Characteristicks* (first published in 1711).

The word "politeness" was at the center of a discursive phenomenon of considerable importance and complexity in late seventeenth- and early eighteenth-century England.[9] At that time, "politeness," with a distinctive set of related words, came to occupy a central place in English discourse. The vocabulary of "politeness" helped organize, characterize, and evaluate a diverse and extensive set of human interests and activities. Because "politeness" found a home in texts of great diversity, it meant many things. However, for present purposes, the word "politeness" can be understood to designate a cultural ideal of urbane sociability, appropriate for a secular elite. In the early eighteenth century, the word "polite" ranged most typically over the personnel, the venues, and the characteristic activities, interests, styles, and cultural productions associated with that ideal of urbane sociability.

In the first place, "politeness" was the way gentlemen and ladies were to deport themselves in each other's company. The "company" which it presupposed consisted of social interactions that were neither intimately private nor formally public, but rather semi-public and informal. Accordingly, its characteristic milieux were drawing rooms and salons, coffee-houses and chocolate-houses, parks and squares. It was recognizably urban in provenance, and it often did not hesitate to sneer at rural life and cultural provinciality.

This urbane sociability was epitomized in polite conversation. On one hand, polite conversation was well informed. In substance, it dwelled on politics, history, the arts and belles-lettres, and, self-reflectively, the social world itself (in the form of either social gossip or reflection on social mores or even practical ethics). On the other hand, polite conversation had to be pleasurable. The criteria of "politeness" in expression were, to name the most obvious: ease, freedom, naturalness, pliancy, open-endedness, and humor. (Similarly, "politeness" disparaged all dryness, stiffness, affectation, dogmatism, and solemnity.) Thus, at its best, "politeness" aspired to a combination of learning with sociability. "Politeness," so conceived, could be applied to more than just conversation. The same set of criteria and aspirations were talked of frequently in this era as relevant to "polite writing," "polite learning," "polite philosophy," "polite arts," and so forth. These areas of discourse to which the language of "politeness" was applied became embedded with ideas of gentlemanliness and urbane sociability.

Its growing presence in English discourse at the very end of the seventeenth century forced important writers to take "politeness" into account; their use of "politeness" in turn reinforced its currency and significance. In other words, at the same time that "politeness" was becoming a verbal furnishing of the age, the generation of Swift, Addison, Steele, and Shaftesbury (the four were born within five years of one another) came of age and clearly was unable to ignore "politeness." What their situation called for was not simply taking a stand, pro or con, with respect to "politeness," but, rather, absorbing "politeness" into discourse, making sense of it, and evaluating it. It is possible to say that each of these writers valued "politeness" at the same time that he endeavored to strip away the cant associated with it.

In this collective attempt to take "politeness" seriously, Shaftesbury is of particular interest, for he made it the focus of his entire endeavor in moral and cultural criticism. In absolutely central remarks, Shaftesbury is found merging his philosophical endeavor with a desire for "politeness." For Shaftesbury, "To *philosophise*, in a just Signification, is but To carry *Good-Breeding* a step higher." [10] He thus declared that one of his principal aims in *Characteristicks* is "to recommend MORALS on the same foot, with what in a lower sense is call'd *Manners* and to advance PHILOSOPHY . . . on the very Foundation of what is call'd *agreeable* and *polite*." [11] In so assimilating a notion of philosophy to a notion of "politeness," Shaftesbury was creating an ideal of a philosopher-gentleman. His *Characteristicks* was meant to be an embodiment of "polite philosophy": there he bares the metaphysical presuppositions and explores the modes of insight that allow a continuity between "politeness" and philosophy; moreover, these philosophical investigations are embedded in and related to surrounding discourses concerned with the criticism of society and politics, arts and letters; and all of this is performed with such striking profuseness, discursiveness, and heterogeneity that Shaftesbury has seemed to many (Berkeley among them) to have carried the ideal of urbane sociability motivating his writing to rather oppressive lengths. [12] Nonetheless, Shaftesbury did bring to a peak the sort of pattern I am designating here as "politeness."

In *Alciphron*, Berkeley was contending with "politeness" of the sort just sketched. His freethinkers, who spoke a language continuous with the one I have been discussing, were meant to be representatives of "politeness." Conflating freethinking with "politeness" in this manner allowed Berkeley to pursue a critique of "politeness" at the same time that he attacked atheism. Of course, Berkeley was here no mere reporter on "politeness," but its parodist: by exaggerating, even if only mildly, he produced ludicrous effects.

To begin with, Berkeley's freethinkers are polite gentlemen. Both are urbane "men of fashion" (1.1.33). They are also specifically urban, visitors who have left behind the delights of the Town for a brief stay in the country, where the dialogues take place. [13] Alciphron (for whom the dialogues are named) is the elder of the freethinkers. He is characterized as both worldly and learned, though, at this point in his career, a bit moody, having indulged rather excessively in the "amusements of the Town." Lysicles, the younger freethinker, is depicted as an Alciphron-in-training; he combines a bit of letters and a bit of the world and now he has fallen into intimacy with "men of pleasure and free-thinkers" (1.1.32). The upholders of religion in the dialogue, who are named Euphranor and Crito, are also gentlemen, but, by contrast to the freethinkers, they live in the country and advocate sobriety, study, and reflection. As will be evident, through both their actual comments and their handling of the dialogue, Euphranor and Crito cast doubt on the claims of "politeness" as such claims are articulated by Alciphron and Lysicles.

The identification of freethinking with "politeness" is made not only through the characterization of the participants in the dialogue, but also through explicit statements. Lysicles, for example, hails the exalted social demography of modern philosophy. "Our philosophers," he says, "are the best bred men of the age, men who know the world, men of pleasure, men of fashion, and fine gentlemen" (1.11.47). This elite provenance of freethinking is reiterated at many points during the dialogues. References are frequent to the progress of freethinking among the "better sort" (1.3.36; 1.9.44), "people of fashion," "good company," "men of parts and breeding," "men of rank and fortune" (1.12.51), and "the politer sort of men" (2.24.106). Thus, Berkeley situates freethinking in the elite social domain of "politeness."

However, he also is situating freethinking in the geographical milieu of "politeness." At one point, the dialogues are interrupted by the appearance of fox hunters, "half-a-dozen sun-burnt squires, in frocks, and short wigs, and jockey-boots." What follows is a short piece of characterization, worthy of the *Tatler* or *Spectator*, in which the plain squire and the town gentleman are juxtaposed. The reader is informed that Lysicles, "being a nice man and a bel esprit, had an infinite contempt for the rough manners and conversation of fox-hunters, and could not reflect with patience that he had lost, as he called it, so many hours in their company." Lysicles finds it "strange that men should be diverted with such uncouth noise and hurry, or find pleasure in the society of dogs and horses!" Finally, Lysicles reflects: "How much more elegant are the diversions of the town!" (5.1.174–75) Lysicles is aggressively urban here, as is Alciphron when he specifies his chosen arena as the "drawing-room or assembly of polite people" (1.11.48).

The freethinkers also attest to their "politeness" in direct professions. Alciphron, in particular, radiates the "polite" assumptions of the age, demanding of the others: ". . . what is it that gives one man a better mien than another: more politeness in dress, speech, and motion? Nothing but frequenting good company. By the same means men get insensibly a delicate taste, a refined judgment, a certain politeness in thinking and expressing one's self" (1.11.50). This sounds as if it were cribbed from Shaftesbury, but it could have been cribbed as well from many other works. Alciphron aspires to politeness, refinement, and taste, toward which the means are company and conversation. It is "polite conversation," he points out, "which constantly keeps the mind awake and active, exercising the faculties, and calling forth all its strength and spirit, on a thousand different occasions and subjects . . ." (1.11.50). [14] This is the conventional wisdom of the "polite" world, articulated in scores of essays, letters, handbooks, and dialogues emanating in the early eighteenth century. [15]

The commitment to "politeness" was a commitment to style. According to Lysicles, those "bred in the modern way" make a "better figure," expressing "better things in a better manner." As Crito rephrases him, exaggerating the rhetoric of "politeness" only a bit, those who frequent places of "polite" resort are "in the way of hearing many instructive lectures, seasoned with wit and raillery, and uttered with spirit. Three or four sentences from a man of quality, spoke with a good air, make more impression and convey more knowledge than a dozen dissertations in a dry academical way" (1.11.48).

Implied in this valorization of "manner," "air," and "figure" is the disapprobation of those without taste, precisely those writers of "dissertations in a dry academical way." This attempt to seize learning and assimilate it to "politeness" involves wresting it from the insufficiently sociable domain of the academician or the even more hermetic realm of the solitary scholar. Lysicles refuses the title of philosopher to dons "in square caps and long gowns" and hails the end of "the reign of pedantry": "Our philosophers, said he, are of a very different kind from those awkward students who think to come at knowledge by poring on dead languages and old authors, or by sequestering themselves from the cares of the world to meditate in solitude and retirement" (1.11.47). For the freethinkers, philosophy has vacated the groves of Academe for the pleasures of the Town.

It should be evident that the discourse of the freethinkers was charged with "polite" language and sentiment. It need only be added that, while Berkeley's object was often the general vocabulary of "politeness," at other times he was taking specific aim at the third earl of Shaftesbury. The freethinker Alciphron is a Shaftesburian, or rather he is dripping with Shaftesburian pretensions. He is the articulator in the dialogue not only of Shaftesbury's characteristic moral ideas, but also of Shaftesbury's more general concern with "politeness."[16] Alciphron's allegiance to Shaftesbury is made clear at several points, but not with more humor than in the fifth dialogue. In the midst of proffering a critique of the unfortunate impact of clerics and academics on learning (itself derived from Shaftesbury), Alciphron refers to the third earl himself as a model of "good writing." In fact, Alciphron asserts: "I am never without something of that noble writer about me." And, with that, Alciphron whips out an essay by Shaftesbury, from which Crito declaims a long passage. The great textographical joke is that a rather prodigal swatch of Shaftesburian prose is set on the page as poetry (5.21–22.197–200).

Berkeley's objection to the ideal summed up in the term "politeness" is simply that the aspirations advertised as politeness are only intellectual pretensions. Whatever positive opinions the freethinkers hold and whatever noises they make about their commitment to reason and examination, the fact is, says Berkeley, that, when seriously engaged in intellectual combat, the freethinkers hide behind "politeness" or its components. In his own coterie, the freethinker talks a hard line, declaiming against prejudice and urging reason and examination. But when the freethinker is indeed pressed by reason, he laughs at logic and assumes "the lazy supine airs of a fine gentleman, a wit, a *railleur*, to avoid the dryness of a regular and exact inquiry" (4.13.158). [17]

Thus, gentlemanliness was neither the matrix nor the vehicle of insight, as it was asserted to be by advocates of "politeness." Rather, gentlemanliness in discourse was revealed as evasiveness, an evasiveness reenacted numerous times in the course of the dialogues. For instance, when Euphranor argues that God speaks to men constantly in his own way, Alciphron is not very impressed by the Berkeleian theory of God's visual language (which is being put in Euphranor's mouth at this point). Alciphron objects that "this dissertation grows tedious, and runs into points too dry and minute for a gentleman's attention. . . . There is a certain scholastic accuracy which ill suits the freedom and ease of a well-bred man" (4.12.156). In another instance, Lysicles, when he meets resistance to his assertion that the soul is material, smugly asserts: "My notions sit easy. I shall not engage in pedantic disputes about them." To this, Euphranor pointedly responds: "This, I suppose, is said much like a gentleman" (6.14.247). [18] For Berkeley, then, gentlemanliness could not serve as a model for intellectually serious pursuits. Rather, it was a poor apology for lack of industry and an inability to concentrate. [19] Indeed, the very criteria, which "polite" writers thought conducive to significant discourse (freedom and ease, the avoidance of dryness and tedium), Berkeley saw as a refusal of true intellectual engagement.

Among other things, then, the dialogue *Alciphron* is a satire on intellectual fatuity, in which "politeness" is shown to be the refuge of the intellectual laggard. However, a further dimension of Berkeley's critique involves the separate notion that "politeness" is a highly impolite mode of discourse. This claim can be seen at a point in the dialogues at which Alciphron is criticizing forensic pedantry whether manifested by contemporary religious controversialists or by medieval scholastics. In Alciphron's view, scholasticism was Gothic and unpolite. In response, Crito, while not defending the medieval scholastics, does assert that ". . . whatever futility there may be in their notions, or inelegancy in their language, in pure justice to truth one must own they neither banter nor rail nor declaim in their writings, and are so far from shewing fury or passion that perhaps an impartial judge will think the minute philosophers [that is, the freethinkers] are by no means to be compared with them, for keeping close to the point, or for temper and good manners" (5.19.194). In Crito's view, the scholastics may have entertained insubstantial ideas and utterly lacked taste in their writings, but at least they knew how to engage in reasoned debate and, moreover, they did it with "temper and good manners." Berkeley seems to be saying that the trouble with the "polite" style of discourse is not only its intellectual diffuseness, but also its underlying bad manners. "Politeness" is thus unmasked as a species of unpoliteness.

Berkeley makes this point in other ways as well. I pointed out earlier that the spread of "politeness" involved the embedding in discourse of the figure of the "polite" gentleman. Berkeley takes this figure and transforms it. In Berkeley's view, the model of "polite" discourse is not a truly polite conversational idiom, but rather a repellent social persiflage. Crito paints a striking picture of the conceited social wag, "tipping the wink upon one, thrusting out his tongue at another . . . often affecting the countenance of one who smothered a jest, a sometimes bursting out in a horse-laugh." Such a figure is a disgrace not just in any public arena, but even—and this is interesting—"in a private visit among well-bred men!" The figure that Berkeley has offered is really quite unsociable—rather impolite, one might say. Moreover, this very figure, says Berkeley, is the one "that certain great authors, who in this age would pass for models, and do pass for models, make in their polite and elaborate writings on the most weighty points" (6.32.284). There is no doubt that Shaftesbury is the target here. Elsewhere in the dialogue, Shaftesbury has been identified as one whose "tinsel" is made to pass for "good writing." His "affected strains" are made to pass for "wit," his "obscurities" for "depths," and his "pedantry" for "politeness" (3.15.136). [20] Thus, the figure inscribed in so-called polite discourse is not the polite gentleman at all, but rather a species of social boor, a social bully. "Politeness" is not just bogus in its cognitive claims; it does not even manage to be properly polite.

Thus, it appears that in *Alciphron* Berkeley was engaged in a reexamination of that notion of "politeness" which was a popular idiom in his era and which had been given a particularly influential formulation in Shaftesbury. Where Shaftesbury was arguing in his intricate way that "politeness" and philosophy were closely related in aim and in method, Berkeley was arguing that the language of "politeness" was a species of cant and that Shaftesbury was mired in bad faith. However, it is important to recognize that Berkeley was not jettisoning all notions of politeness so much as denying Shaftesbury's claim to be taken as a model of politeness.

In other words, a recognition of Berkeley's critique of "politeness" (as "politeness" was articulated by contemporaries) has to be balanced with an appreciation of Berkeley's attachment to a notion of politeness. He once described himself as "one who values no happiness beyond the friendship of men of wit, learning, and good nature,"[21] an epithet with a distinctly "polite" ring to it. The case for Berkeley's own politeness would touch on several points. First, as we have seen, his criticism of the language of "politeness" relies on a standard of manners in behavior and style, against which that language has been found wanting. Similarly, his criticism of Shaftesbury is that Shaftesbury's claim to be a model of taste for the age is belied by (what Berkeley saw as) the tastelessness of Shaftesbury's writing. Moreover, elsewhere in *Alciphron*, Berkeley argues that Christianity has been a source of politeness in European history: like nothing else, Christianity has "visibly softened, polished, and embellished our manners" (5.12.186). This of course indicates the use to which he could put, when needed, a concept of the refinement of manners. Finally, it is hard not to see the dialogue *Alciphron* itself as a piece of "polite" writing by the standards of the age. That is, a notion of politeness seems to have been a criterion for the production of the text. The dialogue *Alciphron* is unusual among treatises against freethinking. Not only is it a dialogue, but it is a dialogue among gentlemen with defined characters. Moreover, it is a dialogue rendered with a considerable amount of narrative zest and laced with wit and humor. If any religious treatise could find an audience in the "polite" world, this one could. Its literary quality may not be that of the great Augustan satires in prose and poetry; but anyone who has read any of the Boyle lectures, which are a solemn monument of Anglican polemic against atheism, will appreciate the considerable "politeness" of Berkeley's *Alciphron*.

A fitting motto for Berkeley is found in the mouth of one of his own freethinking dialogists. It addresses both sides of Berkeley's relationship to politeness, and it also addresses the concern of this paper to examine an unexplored aspect of the canonical philosopher. The freethinker Alciphron, in the midst of complaining of the tediousness of argumentation and the hostility of gentlemanly politeness to scholastic dryness, utters the relevant words with a sigh: "In so polite an age [as this], who would be a mere philosopher?" (4.12.156) The point is twofold: first, in a polite age, even Berkeley attempted, in his own way, to bring together the gentleman and the philosopher; second, whatever of a strictly philosophical nature is found interesting in Berkeley by modern-day philosophers, it is an act of historical justice to examine as well those parts of Berkeley which do not fit the modern idea of a philosopher. Such an examination not only restores Berkeley to his age, but also reveals that age in one of its characteristic patterns.

NOTES

1 This impression is easily gained from an examination of two bibliographies of Berkeley scholarship: T. E. Jessop, *A Bibliography of George Berkeley*, 2d ed., rev. (The Hague: Martinus Nijhoff, 1973) and Colin M. Turbayne, "A Bibliography of George Berkeley, 1963–1979," in Colin M. Turbayne, ed., *Berkeley: Critical and Interpretive Essays* (Minneapolis: Univ. of Minnesota Press, 1982), 313–29. Except for works of a biographical character, the significant exceptions are John Redwood's treatment of Berkeley in connection with deism (cited in note 6), a number of essays by Donald Davie on Berkeley as a writer, and, more recently, the Berkeley section of John Ricchetti's *Philosophical Writing: Locke, Berkeley, Hume* (Cambridge, Mass.: Harvard Univ. Press, 1983).

2 The writings that most intrigue philosophers are those written within the several years on either side of the original publication in 1710 of Berkeley's canonical philosophical work, *A Treatise concerning the Principles of Human Knowledge*. Aside from the *Principles*, the works by Berkeley most frequently examined are: the philosophical notebooks, from 1707–1708, in which Berkeley first worked out his philosophical positions (published posthumously as *Philosophical Commentaries*); *An Essay towards a New Theory of Vision* (1709); and the *Three Dialogues between Hylas and Philonous* (1713), which defended the *Principles*. Having written these, says Professor Pitcher in his study of Berkeley (p. 1; cited in note 3), Berkeley "had completed the great works that give him a secure place in the history of philosophy."

3 *Alciphron* is mentioned only perfunctorily in G. J. Warnock, *Berkeley* (1953; reprint, Notre Dame, Ind.: Univ. of Notre Dame Press, 1983); Jonathan Bennett, *Locke, Berkeley, Hume: Central Themes* (Oxford: Clarendon Press, 1971); Harry M. Bracken, *Berkeley* (New York: St. Martin's Press, 1974); George Pitcher, *Berkeley* (London: Routledge & Kegan Paul, 1977); and J. O. Urmson, *Berkeley* (Oxford: Oxford Univ. Press, 1982).

If *Alciphron* were to appear in philosophical treatments of Berkeley, it would appear in treatments of Berkeley's ethics. However such treatments have usually confined themselves to the analysis of Berkeley's tract, *Passive Obedience* (1712): this is true in Pitcher's work (Chapter 12), perhaps the most comprehensive recent philosophical account of Berkeley. *Alciphron* is, however, a rich source of Berkeley's ethical ideas, a fact recognized in Paul J. Olscamp, *The Moral Philosophy of George Berkeley* (The Hague: Martinus Nijhoff, 1970), 4–5.

4 George Berkeley, *Alciphron*, in *The Works of George Berkeley, Bishop of Cloyne*, ed. A. A. Luce and T. E. Jessop (1948; reprint, Nendeln, Liechtenstein: Kraus Reprint, 1979), 3:21. All subsequent references to *Alciphron* are in the body of the text and indicate the dialogue number, the section number, and the page number of Volume 3 of this edition.

5 It should be noted that the entirety is narrated to the reader indirectly by a fifth character, present but nonparticipant in the original dialogues.

6 Such an approach is taken by John Redwood in *Reason, Ridicule and Religion: The Age of Enlightenment in England 1660–1750* (London: Thames and Hudson, 1976), 60–68.

7 It is a "polyphonic" text in the sense developed by Mikhail Bakhtin with respect to the novel (or to what he calls "novelistic discourse"). See the recent edition by Michael Holquist of Bakhtin's essays, *The Dialogic Imagination* (Austin: Univ. of Texas Press, 1981), 11–12, 48–51, 61, 66–83, 260–63.

I should add here that the sense in which I use the word "language" or "vocabulary" or "rhetoric" (as in "the language of 'politeness'") owes much to the notion of a language developed by J. G. A. Pocock in, among other places, the essays in *Politics, Language and Time* (New York: Atheneum, 1973).

8 For an expression of this opinion (and references to others who share it), see Olscamp, *Moral Philosophy of Berkeley*, 165–66. Olscamp's treatment of the Shaftesbury-Berkeley relationship is interesting for taking into account many areas of agreement between Shaftesbury and Berkeley (p. 166). The conclusion of this paper adds another.

9 This summary of the language of "politeness" is a dense condensation of part of the author's doctoral dissertation, "The Rise of 'Politeness' in England, 1660–1715," The Johns Hopkins University, 1983. A considerably longer account than this appears in "The Third Earl of Shaftesbury and the Progress of Politeness," *Eighteenth-Century Studies* 18, no. 2 (Winter 1984–85), 186–214.

10 Anthony Ashley Cooper, third earl of Shaftesbury, *Characteristicks of Men, Manners, Opinions, Times,* 2d ed., corrected (London, 1714), 3.161 ("Miscellany," 3.i). The same passage appears in the more readily available John M. Robertson edition of 1900 (London: Grant Richards), 2.255.

11 Shaftesbury, 3.163 ("Miscellany," 3.ii; Robertson, 2.257).

12 For instance, see George Saintsbury's comment in *A History of Criticism and Literary Taste in Europe* (New York: Dodd, Mead, and Co., 1904), 3:157–58: "There are few writers of whom more different opinions have been held, in regard to their philosophical and literary value, than is the case with Shaftesbury. . . . It is difficult to put the dependence of that difference in an uncontentious and non-question-begging manner, because it concerns a fundamental antinomy of fashion in which this curious author strikes opposite temperaments. To some, every utterance of his seems to carry with it in an undertone something of this sort; 'I am not merely a Person of Quality, and a very fine gentleman, but also, look you, a philosopher of the greatest depth, though of the most elegant exterior, and writer of consummate originality and *agudeza*. . . . ' Now this kind of 'air' abundantly fascinates some readers, and intrigues others; while, to yet others again, it seems the affectation, most probably of a charlatan, certainly of an intellectual coxcomb, and they are offended accordingly. It is probably unjust (though there is weighty authority for it) to regard Shaftesbury as a charlatan; but he will hardly, except by the fascination aforesaid or by some illegitimate partisanship of religious or philosophical view, escape the charge of being a coxcomb. . . ."

13 The editors of *The Works of George Berkeley* suggest at several points, on the basis of the appositeness of the descriptions, that the fictive location of the dialogues is the area around Newport, Rhode Island, where Berkeley wrote them (3:31 n., 65 n., 174 n.). However, at the beginning of the seventh dialogue, it is said explicitly that the freethinkers have come from London for a brief stay in the country. This is not a trivial point, because the geographical contrast between Town and Country is meant to reinforce the contrast between the specious "politeness" of the freethinkers and the sober integrity of the country gentlemen.

14 Similarly, Alciphron says: "Proper ideas or material are only to be got by frequenting good company" (1.11.48).

15 Compare Alciphron's view to those presented in *The Management of the Tongue* (London, 1706), an anonymously assembled *bricolage* of "polite" opinion: "Whoever will live in Society must make himself Sociable; and the only way to learn to be Sociable, is to be often in Society. Conversation is the great Book of the World, which teaches the use of other Books: Learning is rustical without it, and deprived of all manner of Charms: Study improves the Talents of Nature, but they are wrought on by Conversation. . . ." (pp. 2–3).

16 Alciphron rehearses Shaftesbury's ideas of moral and aesthetic sense in 3.3–12. 116–32. (Reference is also made to the author Cratylus, in whose name Shaftesbury's views are again summarized [3.13.132ff.]. It is as Cratylus that Shaftesbury is lampooned as the neurasthenic blue blood projecting, in his works, various fantasies onto the actual world.) Alciphron also regards Shaftesbury as the "admired critic of our times," the mender of the "taste of the age" (5.32.200).

17 The notion that freethinkers alternate between declamatory and bantering discursive styles is also brought up in 1.4.37.

18 This intellectual shiftiness is instanced again in 2.7.75–76, and commented on in 6.29.276–77.

19 Berkeley also cuts down the cognitive pretensions of "polite" conversation, ridiculing the claim that everything can be learned from conversation. He has Lysicles trumpet, rather naively, the observation that "conversing with ingenious men . . . is a short way to knowledge, that saves a man the drudgery of reading and thinking" (4.18.165). Conversation can thus only elicit a specious knowing appropriate to drawing-room chatter, but nothing else.

20 Shaftesbury's discursive manner is also the subject of criticism or insinuation at 5.22.200, and 5.25.204.

21 Letter to Alexander Pope, 1 May 1714, in *The Works of George Berkeley*, ed. Luce and Jessop, 8:83.

"Horse-bogey Bites Little Boys";

or

Reid's Oeconomicks of the Family

CHARLES STEWART-ROBERTSON

The unborn child, it was said, is little more than an "oyster." Thereafter, of course, it might emerge into the graduated spheres of "Nature," "Society," and "Education" until, *foris familiate*, it would be prepared itself to practise the "Art" of parenting.[1] Along the way, it had seemingly run up the entire gamut of rights, from the testy issue of a delayed succession in the face of a real or only probable "being, in the womb"[2] to that of redress against unnaturally harsh or cruel punishment meted out by its own parents or guardians.[3] At the end, it stood to inherit rights and obligations commensurate with those under which it had only just survived, been nurtured, and found itself trained up to civic virtue. Such is the life of this child-oyster in a shell.

By a different, and for Thomas Reid favoured analogy, life for this or any other creature of nature is a veritable parade of "wombs" and "imperceptible beginnings," of "coats of Mail" and "strait Boddices," all of which confine, determine, but ultimately release their charges. Here the infant is a "caterpillar," and the "tender Charities" governing the relations among the succeeding parts or phases, as indeed among husbands and wives, children and brethren, are "as so many adamantine Chains."[4] The butterfly, the caterpillar, and the chrysalis are each, in turn, the nourishing abode for the other; each is likewise a "covering" or "narrow case" which, notably in respect of the second, threatens to become its successor's "grave"; each must "exhaust" itself to the "last agony" in order to "burst" those bonds which would deny life to the next. Caterpillar-man is truly a unity in diversity: "An embrio in the Womb, a child of two or three years old and a Man adorned with all the Accomplishments of knowlede° Wisdom and Virtue which men in their present state attain differ one from the other as the egg, the caterpillar and the butterfly. Yet all are one and the same animal in the different Stages of its progressive state."[5] Freed at last from the exigencies of struggle and imprisonment, metamorphosed from butterfly to man and back again, this creature is not "fitted to take its pastime in the Air."

It, or he, is now fitted, moreover, to speak for himself and through speech to bind himself into the larger, and higher, circle of civilization wherein is gathered, "out of its brutish existence in the wilderness," [6] what Cicero aptly called our "scattered humanity" (*dispersos homines*). In part, the implied rite of passage conveys the child out of the precarious latency of tacit consent, through the articulation of explicit contract, into the more reflective climes of reasoned discourse and communication among his fellows. In part also, it sets the passions on a path of education, from a state of unbridled to one of well-governed and refined expression; in doing so, it fosters the growth not only of moral action but, more critically, of civil order. The latter path was at root Baconian, a simple yet apparently neglected matter of *cultura* or *georgica animi*. Widely adopting Bacon's methods of husbandry, eighteenth-century Scottish prelectors were themselves transformed, from early metaphysicians and ontologists to late pneumatologists and "Georgicians."[7] In large measure, theirs was truly a transformation of and by "Speech"; for they found themselves increasingly fascinated, even as they were shaped, by the powers of language both general (or theoretical) and specific (or practical). Without speech, as Reid remarks in a long digression under the heading of "Contracts and Covenants,"[8] "human Life would be a most dismal state of being."

Naturalistic, jurisprudential, and linguistic concerns are thus manifestly interwoven into the fabric of Reid's lectures on Oeconomicks, or Private or Domestic Jurisprudence, at Glasgow after 1764. As initially conceived, these issues were all to have positioned themselves under the spreading canopy of the term "Pneumatology." Within a year, his bold scheme having failed of time as much as of vision, he would apportion his discussion of man under the conditions and culture of Nature to his private "12 o'clock" class.[9] Effectively, this reallocation of materials would thereafter separate by the space of some three months (late December to late March) phases in the child's evolution—from "oyster" to citizen, as it were—which Reid clearly believed to be integral. Indeed, had Reid not been quite so faithful to his mentors, Bacon and Turnbull, in giving testimony to the essential unity of "Mind and Body,"[10] this adventitious wrenching apart of a conceptual whole might well have jeopardised his own, if not subsequent *studia humanitatis* during the latter half of the century. As it was, Reid seems to have been able to rekindle his enthusiasm for the naturalistic aspects of the child's upbringing several months later, during his jurisprudential prelections on the Oeconomicks of the family.[11] Conversely, the parental obligations unfolded in the latter were never far from his mind as he traced man's rude beginnings within the "Society" of Nature. The communicative bondings of imitative gesture and conventional language, moreover, were visibly at work in both, stalking his analyses with innuendo as well as declamation. In short, the vision undone by practice was in practice restored.

What I have called the fabric of Reid's inquiry into man's domestic state, and in particular that facet of it which concerns the intertwinings of husbands and wives, parents and children, must therefore be judged, even against its chronology, to be more or less a continuous piece. It is important to bear in mind that continuity (or the hypothesis of continuity), even as one proceeds to abstract text from text, and to tug at the very threads of coherence.

Although not central to our task, it is perhaps fitting, and certainly traditional, to address briefly that marital state which Reid regarded as Nature's, and God's, provision for the conception of the child-oyster. Jurisprudential writers, from as early as Xenophon in his *Oeconomica*, and Justinian, had included wives, children, and slaves under the aegis of the *paterfamilias* and within the category of the *familia*.[12] Reid's more immediate sources, Grotius and Pufendorf, Gershom Carmichael (almost certainly) and Turnbull's Heineccius, not to mention Hutcheson and Reid's Aberdonian contemporaries, Fordyce, Gerard, and Beattie, had fallen into the simple rhythm of a tripartite (less frequently, fourfold) division and progression.[13] Thus, consideration of the obligations holding between parents and their children was regularly set between a particular author's views of marriage and his examination of the duties incumbent upon masters and servants (or slaves). To this pattern, Reid appears to have given his early and ready consent.[14]

Beginning then with the "Marriage Relation," Reid found himself at no loss for words. Indeed, he fairly warms to the subject of the "Passion of Love between the Sexes."[15] Yet immediately he cautions against confusion: those who conceive of this "natural Passion" in terms of the "sensual Appetite," he admonishes, "know nothing of its Nature nor even felt its influence."[16] As his earliest lectures at Glasgow indicate, it was a subject in which he was well versed. Moreover, the hand of Nature but also, as we shall see, of God was clearly evident in Reid's script.

In the still tentative and unpolished jottings of April 1765, with Grotius, Pufendorf, and less certainly Hutcheson close by his elbow,[17] Reid provides the first glimmerings of what the "Nature" of that "Passion" might be. It is the stuff of which not only Love but "Jealousy" is made; for this "passion gives an attachment & preference to one object which it is impossible to have to more than one," and "cannot be satisfied without a like reciprocal⁵ attachment and preference in the person beloved" (a "return," incidentally, which Reid insists cannot be "the effect of force or fear").[18] Therein, as Reid remarked in what appears to be an early fragment from the same period, lie the "mutual Comfort & happiness of both parties."[19] Such too, in addition to the "regular propagation of the human Race & the right Education of Children," are the "ends" of "this Institution" of Marriage.[20]

Some sense of the heights to which that "mutual Comfort & happiness" might go, and to which Reid was prepared to follow on this "very noble Subject," may be found in what is presumed to be a later, and certainly more finely kempt, stretch of lecture notes.[21] The key is again raised to accommodate the "Serious Nature" of this "Passion" of Love which, unlike the unbridled "sensual Appetite," is "compounded" of "Esteem Sympathy [and] Benevolence . . . all of them modified in a peculiar manner." The peculiarity, of course, is still to be found in the factor of "like Attachment and Preference in the person Beloved"[22] which, in this short fragment on Marriage, Reid had rather cemented with divine injunction. (The "helpmeets" are now "commanded" to "cleave" unto one another, marriage "being the institution of God himself."[23]) This "Attachment," however, now finds the wings to carry Reid aloft in a burst of poetic fervour:

> It finds or conceives in its Object some Superlative Worth Merit and Beauty, that engrosses the whole Mind, and the more it dwells upon this object the more it is moved to an Enthousiastick° Admiration. The very language of Love, like°ˢ that of the more rapturous flights of poetry, shews a high degree of Enthousiam, a kind of Inspiration. The mind is elevated above itself by being constantly filled

with the Idea of an Object which is, or at least is conceived to be, of Superlative dignity and Beauty. The Natural Effect of this Passion in both Sexes is to produce an Elevation of Mind [,] a quickness of Discernment, ˢa vigor of Resolutionˢ Generosity Courage and tenderness. [24]

Significantly, the "Elevation" which this proper, but still very "Natural" passion produces in the Mind very likely took root in Cicero's *De officiis;* specifically, in that passage from Book 1 (4.12) in which the much-revered Tully traces the effects of that same hand of "Nature," now gloved with "the strength of Reason" *(vi rationis),* on the "social Offices" and affairs of man.

In his own unfinished translation of *De officiis,* which ends shortly after the passage quoted below, Reid strives to maintain that lofty tone. In doing so, moreover, he exposes once again that naturalistic base from which not only his thinking, but also the higher reaches of society, beyond the family, seem to proceed. Here is Reid's translation:

> The same Nature by the force of reason conciliates man to man, both in conversation and in the intercourse of social Offices; and chiefly begets a superior affection to [theirᶜ] hisˢ children; it impels himᵒˢ to enter into societysᵒ and communitys,ᵒ hold assemblies and Solemn[itiesᶜ] meetings [,] & for these purposes to seek after those things which are requisite both for food and dress; not for [themselvesᶜ] himselfˢ only but for [theirᶜ] his wife children and others who are dear to him and whom he ought to protect: Which cares rouse the mind and prepare it for the management of greater affairs. [25]

The notions that a man's wife and children are naturally "dear to him" and that he "ought to protect" (or provide for) them are critical here, since they mark for Reid, as for other writers opposed to the reviled doctrines of Hobbes, the thin line which both separates and conjoins nature and morality. As Reid reiterates in the fourth of his prelections on the Culture of the Mind, the condition of man reared solely under the "culture of Nature" may "in thought" be distinguished from that in which he is subject to "human Society," while "the first can never be ˢin fact & realityˢ without some degree of the last." [26] Equally then, the "intention of Nature" (or as Reid would also have it, the "Intention of the Supreme being") [27] concerning that aspect of human life wherein men "may be considered barely as Men" [28] can be separated only by the lightest reins of abstraction from the "dictates" of "Reason" whereby the "Government of a Family," and thence the "full" extent of civil society, is ordered.[29] The "Oeconomy of Nature" and Oceo-nomical Jurisprudence" are but an abstract moment, and a page or two of lecture notes, apart.[30]

"We therefore send Hobbes a packing," wrote Turnbull in a note to Heineccius' *Methodical System of Universal Law.*[31] Fearful perhaps that the naturalistic account of Hobbes would generate the wrong impression, and foster a *patria potestas* untempered by the tenderest of parental affections as well as by God's gift of reason,[32] Scottish thinkers launched a counteroffensive on behalf of both parents and children. Characteristically, the offensive would begin amidst "Animals Male and Female," "Oviparous" and "Viviparous."[33]

Although the manners would differ, it was clear that the various species of "brute Animals" not only enjoy the "Appetite of procreating their kind," but also experience "such a Care of their Young as is necessary to their preservation & Education."[34] Care and "the indigence of the Children," or what Gerard categorized as the "Necessity of Children," and the "Naturale Affection of parents"[35]—these were the principal thrusts to be used against what Reid mistakenly interpreted as Hobbes's "imagined" view that authority rests "upon Generation," and Gerard's more accurate reading of *De cive* (9.1.2), that "dominion over the infant first belongs to him who first hath him in his power," namely the mother. (Gerard calls this "a kind of Occupation.")[36] In his lectures on the "Culture of Nature," Reid had earlier depicted that "indigence" as being more dramatic among human progeny. "The infant enters into Life," he declared, "in a state of greater weakness and imbecillity than the Young of any other Species; with more Wants, and less ability to supply them."[37] The point was so well put that it almost led him to obfuscate one of the essential platforms of the Scottish position.

Having seen fit to render the child-oyster so vulnerable, Nature must now surpass herself in equipping its Parents with "a strong parental Affection and tenderness." But here Reid adds a qualifying phrase—"especially to the Mother"—and promptly allows the thought to carry him away: "[the Mother] whose Age and Experience enables her to supply the necessities of her helpless offspring; and whose innate Affection disposes her to watch over it by night and by day; and to be more attentive to its wants and its dangers than her own."[38] "Age and Experience" will scarcely distinguish the young mother with her first child but, more important, Reid is perilously close to drawing a likeness between human Parents and that domestic "Quadruped," the cow, for whom "the Care of the Mother alone seems sufficient."[39] If the Mother's tenderness is "sufficient," then perhaps it is also exclusive, as Hobbes was trying to suggest in his argument for maternal dominion over the child, at least for the first of the three widely accepted periods of nurture and entitlement.[40] Yet such a concession flies in the face of both the naturalistic and jurisprudential cases which Reid, among others, was trying to build.

Parental authority belongs to "both parents," Grotius had emphasised and Pufendorf, noting that "each parent shares equally in [the] generation," joined in the refrain; so too did Heineccius, Turnbull, Hutcheson, Fordyce, Gerard, and, of course Reid himself,[41] It is "Common to both Parents," he early stipulates, adding eventually that "the necessities of Children and their wants . . . would be impossible for the mother alone to supply."[42] The "task" which this latter remark implies, and which in fact Reid makes explicit,[43] should not, of course, be confused with the question of responsibility; having the *power* or natural capability and having the *right to exercise* that power are quite different things. The sheer contiguity of naturalistic and jurisprudential concerns, however, was apt to mislead, and too often did.

Was it perhaps the great jurist himself who had inadvertently sown the seeds of confusion? The "right of parents over children," Pufendorf had insisted, was based on a "two-fold claim: First, because the very law of nature, by reason of its command that man be sociable, had laid upon parents the care of children, and, to provide against its neglect, has at the same time implanted in them the most tender affection for their offspring."[44] The "implant" and the "command," Nature's providence as well as its governance through Reason: the principles were wedded into a language as intimate as the conjugal relation itself.[45] Indeed, one might say that there had been founded a society of terms as natural and as binding as that primitive society of husband and wife—what Reid calls this "lasting Attachment and League of Love and Fidelity,"[46]—and the secondary one which would eventually exist between parents and children. Such societies have their natural ends as well as beginnings, but it would be the course over the long run which would ultimately count. "Man of all Animals," attested Reid in a marginal addendum, "has the longest infancy, & his Education is a long Work."[47]

That "long Work" which Nature had intended, and for which she had made provision of "the Natural Affection planted in [the] breasts" of both parents, bound children and parents alike in a common task; for the former, of submission, gratitude, imitation, and respect; for the latter, of a sound and healthy regimen, moderation in punishment and, in due time, the equitable distribution of goods and properties. As Heineccius, Turnbull, and later Reid, kept ever before them, the "duties of [this] society" were to be "deduced from its end"; "parental power" was to be "estimated" or measured against this end; and the "Nurture and admonition of the Lord" was to be enlisted towards the fulfillment of it. That "end" was rather two-fold for it involved, more immediately, the educating or training up of children and, more remotely, their entrance "as full members of Society."[48] At this point, that division which was never real, but only an abstraction, becomes for the first time a reality for both parent and child. While the natural affection of the one for the other continues for as long as the "Children are in life"—descending even "to the third & fourth Generation, & to all the Subsequent Generations a Man can see"[49]—the authority of the parents diminishes, then ceases altogether. Their authority, Gerard instructs his charges, "is not perpetuale . . . Neither is [it] Unlimited in its Extent[;] it is given for certain Ends, & it is just No farther than it answers them: it only reaches to the Means by which parents can be Useful to their Children."[50]

The tables begin to turn; indebtedness shifts proportionally with utility; the once "young unexperienced° & giddy" children become "Seniors grave & experienced."[51] This giddiness had, in a sense, made of the child a natural receiver of the wisdom of his elders; for he was possessed not by a god (as the term implies), but by a "Natural Principle" of "implicit Belief" in whatever the "Mother or Nurse" should tell him.[52] In time, he would himself become an "infuser" of "Sentiments and Notions" into the young mind.[53] It was all a matter of perspective. "In all these different States," Reid observes, "we may easily discover the Parents° duty by putting ourselves in the Situation of the Child, & that of the child by putting ourselves in the state of the Parent."[54] Apparently, Reid had absorbed more than he realised from Adam Smith's doctrine of Sympathy.

The alternation of perspectives had a more serious, and controversial, aspect to it, however, one which taxed and absorbed the minds of all who touched upon the Oeconomicks of the Family. The "giddy" child, not to mention his "oyster" predecessor, could only be *presumed* to have agreed to an arrangement under which he would be subject to his parents even to that point, just short of *foris familiate*, where he would respectfully seek the latter's "consent" to marry.[55] Gerard was prepared to reject the presumption altogether. The "foundations" of child indigence and parental affection were sufficient, he argued, to "support [the] State" of mutual obligation, "Without supposing as some have done Any Tacit Contract between Parents & their Children—It cannot be founded on this [he continued], because the Children refusing to submit Would Annule the Authority of Parents;

this Authority indeed arises without any Consent from [the mere] justice of the Case—."[56] Fordyce had to acknowledge that any "just Sense of the Connexion" could scarcely have been "formed" when Nature began to "dictate the first Lines of filial Duty."[57] Turnbull, after Heineccius, ties the presumption of "consent to this society" to "no other principle" than that whereby the parental "right and power to direct their children's actions" is "estimated" by the "proper education" of those children; in short, he makes it conditional upon the parental fulfillment of its natural duty.[58]

Hutcheson, like Gerard and to some extent Fordyce, had been content to lay the respective obligations of power of direction and obedience to that power on Nature's shoulders. Only when the child has "come to the full use of reason" does Hutcheson speak of "consent," and then it is on the Socratic presumption that because the child has "voluntarily" chosen to remain in the family, he has "consented to this subjection."[59] This latter view had earlier been adopted by Grotius who, in respect of the infant, remarked simply that "it is fair that he who is not able to rule himself be ruled by another."[60] This "fairness" is apparently the "Justice of the Case" of which Gerard spoke above. Yet all is not fair even in infancy: "When children have a separate Property,"[61] notes Reid (for example, through a "donation, legacy, or inheritance") "the parents °ᵃare not°ˢ the proprietors but [only] the Guardians."[62] The point had been taken from Grotius, and disseminated through Hutcheson.[63]

Although "all men grant" it—especially the author of *Leviathan*—Robert Filmer had confessed his amazement that "a child can express consent, or by other sufficient arguments declare it before it comes to the age of discretion."[64] Reid noticed the dissension.[65] What he appears not to have realised fully, perhaps because, like his mentor Turnbull, he slightly underestimated Pufendorf,[66] was the extent to which the German jurist had rightly fitted the instrument of language to the natural conditions of childhood and, in the process, drawn the appropriate conclusions concerning rights and obligations. In a telling remark from *De jure naturae et gentium*, Pufendorf sets the tone for, as well as seeding the aspirations of, the Scottish debate and its participants. "This consent," he writes as he builds towards his conclusion,

> being reasonably presumed, has the same force as if it had been expressed. . . . Just as he whose business is conducted by another in his absence, and without his knowledge, is understood to have contracted an obligation, as if from a tacit contract, to repay the other what was paid for his advantage. From this *it is patent, that the sover-*

eignty of a parent over a child is actually established when he accepts and rears it, and undertakes to mould it, as well as he can, into a useful member of human society.[67]

What Pufendorf had in fact taught Scottish thinkers was a new regard for the social significance of language; that is, for the use of speech, whether by "natural" or "conventional" signs, as a means not only of rational discourse and commitment but, more important, of civil order itself.[68]

On 21 and 22 March 1765, Reid turned to the question of those "Obligations" under which man is placed "in the Use of Speech."[69] The concerns were, of course, general ones: "Every man desires to be trusted in his declarations and therefore ought to deserve it"; "Want of regard to Truth [is] a Sign of the utmost depravity" and detrimental to "the good of Society"; and finally, the "Effect of Faith . . . procures Credit and Trust," the latter being "one of the chief engines of business." But there were other, perhaps more disturbing and certainly equally lasting, issues. A week earlier, Reid had complained vehemently against the "Right of Succession in Entails" (whereby the order of descent, in terms of heirs, is fixed and specified).[70] He expresses particular anxiety on behalf of "the younger Children ˢwhose right naturally is equal,ˢ"[71] but who must endure "straitningº . . . in their Education and provision after they have been brughtº up in Opulence."[72] More succinctly, they stand to be deluded in their expectations.[73] When he reaches the subject of "Speech," a few days later, Reid is still mindful of the innocent.

There were, of course, many positive things to be said about Speech, and about our "obligations in the use of it." Viewed most "extensively," Speech may be said to comprehend "every Sign whether natural or Artificial by which men can affirm or deny[,] accept or refuse, promise or contract, threaten or Supplicate, praise or blame, encourage or discourage, and in a word by which we can communicate to others our thoughts our Sentiments our purposes our passions and affections." Through speech, moreover, a "young man may learn more of things of real Importance to his happiness in one Month than he would have been able to discover by his own natural and unimproved powers in a long life."[74] Yet even the salient points could not quite conceal the dangers awaiting the young.

Imitators of the "Language of those about them," they most certainly are; believers too, by virtue of "particular Instincts" with which they are endowed. Citing Theocritus' *Idylls* (15.40), Pufendorf had sounded the alarm: "No; I'm not going to take you, baby. Horse-bogey bites little boys."[75] The possibilities for deception were endless. The child had been "presumed" to give his consent to parental authority; could it also be presumed that the parent had consented to tell it the truth? Conscious undoubtedly of the pitfall, Reid inscribed in the margin: "This point ought to be treated more fully."[76] His misgivings on this issue, more immediately on behalf of the child, but also in the interests of society as a whole, never quite abated.[77] The critical notion of "Contract" was, to him, inseparably linked with the very existence of a "Moral Faculty" in man, in "Minors" (albeit less assuredly) no less than in adults.[78]

The child-oyster—to whom Grotius ascribed "no rights," arguing that "a thing which does not exist" can have "no attributes," but whom Pufendorf defended, although it was not yet "a part of the world," as long as it had been conceived and was "still in the womb"[79]—might yet become "eminent for genius." George Campbell, in an address before the Philosophical Society in Aberdeen, conjectured that such eminence most likely fell to "children of parents in the middle stations of life," who had been "habituated to a life of temperance and sobriety, alike exempted from the ˢidleness andˢ debaucheries of affluence and from the penury and toils of indigence."[80] Later the same year (1765), Gerard wondered "whether children do not take more after the mother than the father, & if they do what are the causes of it."[81] The naturalistic search for "causes" would have intrigued Reid, who by then was settled in Glasgow. Nevertheless, he had not altogether been left out; for in April 1761, he had himself explored the roots of "Moral Character"[82] and, earlier still (perhaps in 1758), seems to have reflected on the question, "To what Causes are the Differences in Character among Men owing?"[83] In the latter, the rights of the child-oyster are evenly balanced against the obligations of the Mother. The "inquiry into . . . Causes" is here less determinable than that which will begin "after a Man is born," but it clearly does not stay itself for want of curiosity.

> How far Mens Character which they bring into the World with them is influenced by that of their immediate or more Remote Parents. by the Conduct and Regimen of Mothers in Conception & Gestation. by Climate & Air[,] is perhaps a Matter that we have not sufficient Data to Determine[.]

With a characteristic gesture, Reid rests his case precisely where it had begun.

NOTES

1 These terms are extracted from a segment of the unpublished MSS of Thomas Reid, housed as the Birkwood Collection in the Archives of the Aberdeen University Library. The transcriptions here and throughout this paper constitute part of the editorial work currently underway for the Reid Publication Series. Where necessary, the editor's notation system, which has appeared elsewhere in print, will be explained in the notes. The document in question, MS 2131/4/I/30, is part of Reid's "Lectures on the Culture of the Mind," specifically that which treats of the "Culture of Nature." This particular lecture is numbered "2 Lect" and, while undated, is clearly later than Reid's first attempt to effect a progression from the Culture of Nature to those of Society and Education; see MS 2131/4/I/31 (dated Dec. 1765 and Jan. 1766).

2 Sir James Dalrymple, Viscount of Stair, deals with that "weighty and subtile question"—namely, "Whether that person who falls to be nearest heir at the time of the defunct's decease, may not then be entered, though there be a nearer in possibility, or in hope?"—in his *Institutions of the Law of Scotland*, ed. by David M. Walker (1693; reprint, Univ. Presses of Edinburgh and Yale, 1981). bk. 3, title 5 ("Heirs, etc."), 50, pp. 715–16. On one part of the complex issue at least, he is quite resolute: "There is no question, but when a nearer heir is really or probably in being, in the womb, though unborn, that the service must be stopped till the birth. For in all things tending in favour of those unborn, they are accounted as born: and that not only for presuming that there is a living child, not a false conception, but presuming that it is a male child, not a female" (p. 715). The highly intricate case which he subsequently cites—from the years 1647 and 1648—involving a Marion Weir and a Major James Bannatine, does not, alas, admit of such an easy resolution! (pp. 716–18)

3 Although his is by no means the only defence of the right of the child to rid itself, if need be, of "that inhuman and unnatural Yoke," David Fordyce's plea on behalf of the child is perhaps one of the most spirited and certainly one of the most popular. See his "The Elements of Moral Philosphy," which was first published anonymously in the second volume of Robert Dodsley's *The Preceptor* (1748), and later separately, as well as posthumously, under the author's own name (1754); bk. 2, sec. 3, ch. 3, 313 (1748 ed.). As the dating alone might indicate, Fordyce's work owes at least a partial indebtedness to Hutcheson's English version of his own *Philosophiae moralis institutio compendiaria, ethices & jurisprudentiae naturalis elementa continens. Lib. III* (1742), entitled "A short introduction to moral philosophy, in three books," and published just a year before Dodsley's *Preceptor*, in 1747. That indebtedness is clearly acknowledged (*vide* pp. 278, 289, 312, and 316 of Fordyce's "Elements"), although again it is not exclusive. Hutcheson's strenuous objections to Hobbes's treatment of children as nothing but "a piece of goods

or chattels" (Hutcheson's words), in *De cive* (ch. 9), had clearly set loose a contagion of Scottish moral indignation. For a similar reaction, just a decade later, see Alexander Gerard's lectures on "Practical Oeconomics," as recorded by George Forbes in 1748 (Aberdeen University Library, M. 205.2, fol. 749).

4 MS 2131/4/I/30 ("2 Lect," fol. 2). Cf. Reid's use of the caterpillar analogy once again, but now under the heading of "Oeconomical Jurisprudence," in MS 2131/7/VII/15.

5 MS 2131/4/I/30 ("2 Lect," fol. 8). (The superscript *o* indicates that the word was so spelled in the original.)

6 *De oratore*, trans. E. W. Sutton and H. Rackham (Loeb Classical Library ed.), 1.8.33. Reid cites this passage, with obvious approval and apparently fervent manner, in the opening address of what he himself termed his "Lectures on the Culture of the Mind," MS 2131/4/I/1.

7 The source of their inspiration was Bacon's *Of the Advancement of Learning* (1605) and its Latin sequel, *De dignitate et augmentis scientiarum* (1623), esp. bk. 7, ch. 3. I have treated the issue of the "Pneumatics and Georgics of the Scottish Mind" in a paper of this title read at meetings of the South Central Society for Eighteenth-Century Studies, Baton Rouge, Louisiana, March 1985 (forthcoming in *Eighteenth Century Studies*).

8 *Vide* MS 2131/8/IV/7 and 4/III/4 (the two seemingly remote MSS being in fact one continuous and integrated text). We shall have occasion to return to the subject matter of this jurisprudential lecture at a later stage. Then, unless otherwise stated, I shall use the original, not integrated, folio numbers; where passages from each of the once-separate MSS are used, the fol. numbers will correspond with the order of the MS numbers.

9 The master plan made its abortive appearance under the marginal heading "Lect 1" beginning on fol. 1 and continuing into fol 2 of MS 2131/4/II/11. It called for a fourfold division of "Pneumatology" into the following areas: the "Physiology of the Mind"; the "Culture of the Mind"; the "Connexions of Mind & Body" (eventually identified as the basis for "Eloquence"); and the "Nature Attributes and Government of the Supreme Mind." It was a bold and ambitious conception ill suited, unfortunately, to the limited time frame of his "publick class." The four headings were never to appear again on that stage. Within a year (that is, at the beginning of the 1765–55 session), Reid had cancelled Parts Two and Three, and moved their theatre to the so-called special or private "12 o'clock" hour. Cf. MSS 2131/4/II/1 (fol. 3), 4/I/6, and 8/I/15.

10 Reid reaffirms this ruling presupposition concerning the "connexions" between "Mind and Body" in more than a few places; see, for example, MSS 2131/4/I/1, 4/I/13, 4/I/27, 4/I/29, and 4/I/31. Bacon had professed the doctrine of the "League of Mind and Body" in *De augmentis*, bks. 4 and 5, while Turnbull's reiteration of the "faith" appears in both his *Theses Academicae* of 1726 and his later *Principles of Moral Philosophy* (London, 1740), esp. vol. 1, ch. 2. Gerard too is profuse in his affirmations of fidelity to the principle.

11 In a marginal addendum to his discussion of the "care" which "both parents" should employ "in maintaining their ofspring°," Reid remarks: "To this shedule° ought to be prefixed some general Observations upon the Oeconomy of Nature in the propagation of Animals" (MS 2131/7/VIII/17 [fol. 1]). Those observations—which would, if our hypothesis is correct, be rather for most of his charges a reminder or review—are in fact contained in a MS headed "Oeconomical Jurisprudence" and consisting of three quarto pages of text, much of which is devoted to "the Oeconomy of Nature in brute Animals and the Means which the Divine Providence has contrived for preserving the Species in every Tribe while the individuals perish." MS 2131/7/VII/15. It is here, as noted above in note 4, that Reid has recourse once more to the analogy of the caterpillar. Cf. Hutcheson's phrasing in his *System* (1755), bk. 3, ch. 1, ii.

For his assistance not only in transcribing MSS 2131/7/VII/15 and 17, but also in noting their connection, I am very much indebted to my assiduous coeditor of Reid's Lectures on Jurisprudence and Politicks, Dr. Knud Haakonssen.

12 Justinian introduces this subject by distinguishing those who are subject to others (*quae alieno juri subjectae sunt*) from those who are *sui juris*, and then announcing that he will seek identification of the latter by ascertaining just who the former might be. Slaves, children, and legitimate wives are thence herded into the category of *alieni juris*. See *Institutes*, trans. T. C. Sandars (London, 1922; reprint, Westport, Conn.: Greenwood Press, 1970), bk. 1, titles 8–12. Reid encouraged his students to read "Xenophon in the fifth book of his Memorabilia commonly called his Oeconomicks" where, he added, Xenophon had provided "an Account of a long conversation of the Divine Socrates upon the Administration of a Family." MS 2131/7/VII/7 (fol. 2); cf. MS 2131/7/VII/20 (fol. 3). Xenophon sounded just the right note for the eighteenth-century Scottish prelector: "Now if God grants us children, we will then think out how we shall best train them" (*Oeconomicus*, trans. E. C. Marchant [Loeb Classical Library ed.], 7.12).

13 The fourth division, from Justinian's *Institutes*, bk. 1, title 13, involved the relation of the tutor to his pupil (*De tutelis*).

Grotius, whose presence is more than faintly visible in Reid's discussion, treats of all three relations in Book 2, Chapter 5 of *De jure belli ac pacis libri tres* (1625; reprint, 1642). Pufendorf's accounts in *Elementorum jurisprudentiae universalis libri duo* (1660; reprint, 1672), bk. 2, obs. 5, and *De officiis hominis et civis juxta legem naturalem libri duo* (1673; reprint, 1682), bk. 2, ch. 2–4 are succinct, but relatively sparse in comparison with his detailed and weighty approach in *De jure naturae et gentium libri octo* (1672; reprint, 1688), bk. 6, ch. 1–3. Turnbull's translation "with Notes and supplements" of Heineccius' *A Methodical System of Universal Law* (1741)—a formidable combination, incidentally, of rigorous logic and vigorous commentary—deals with the trilogy of duties in vol. 2, bk. 2, ch. 2–4. In his posthumously published *A System of Moral Philosophy, in Three Books* (London, 1755), vol. 2, bk. 3, ch. 1–3, Hutcheson perpetuates the tripartite structure, now under the general heading, "Of Civil Polity." (Cf. his earlier *Philosophiae moralis institutio compendiaria* [1745], bk. 3, ch. 1–3.) Beattie like Gerard kept that tradition alive in the North, even as Reid was maintaining it in the South. See J. Rennie's notes of Beattie's "A Compendious System of Pneumatology," Glasgow University Library, MS Hamilton 55, under "Oeconomicus," sec. 1–3; cf. Geo. Forbes' notes of Gerard's lectures on "Oeconomicks"—the "Relations & Duties of a family" (500^v–01^v)—in AUL MS M.205.2 (731^v seq.).

14 Cf. MS 2131/8/IV/7 (fols. 7 and 8) and 4/III/4, dated "Apr 2" through "Apr 4," as well as 7/VII/20 (fol. 1), dated "Apr 14 1768"; 7/VII/15 (fol. 1); and 7/VII/1a (fol. 1), n.d.

15 MSS 2131/8/IV/7 (fol. 7), 4/III/4, and 7/VII/18 (fol. 2).

16 MS 2131/7/VII/18 (fol. 2).

17 MS 2131/8/IV/7 (fol. 7) and 4/III/4. In an unusual gesture of documentation, Reid specifies that he is now examining "Book 2[:] Of the Right & duties arising from the Domestic Relation." Unfortunately, he omits the name of the author from whom he is deriving his materials. Grotius is the most likely candidate, for his treatment of the subject is contained in "Book Two" of *De jure belli ac pacis*. The title, however, does not as readily match. Either Pufendorf's *Elementorum jurisprudentiae universalis* or his *De officio hominis et civis*, but not *De jure naturae et gentium*, might fit the Book number, but again not the title. The same is true of Heineccius' *A Methodical System*. Hutcheson comes closest in respect to the title particularly in *A System of Moral Philosophy* (the words "rights" and "duties" and "domestic relations" appearing *within* Chapter 1)—but the book number is off by one (Book 3, not 2). The textual evidence of fol. 8 points to Grotius, but is scarcely conclusive.

18 MS 2131/8/IV/7 (fol. 7) and 4/III/4. (The superscript *s* indicates that the word in question has been inscribed above the regular line of text.) On the subject of Jealousy, see also Pufendorf, *De jure naturae et gentium libri octo*, trans. C. H. and W. A. Oldfather (1682; reprint, Oxford: Clarendon Press, 1934), bk. 6, ch. 1, 15.

19 MS 2131/6/V/34^v. On the *recto* side of this single leaf, Reid has made several lists of topics from "Space Duration and Number" to various "Powers." The notes on both sides are obviously rough drafts, although the two paragraphs *verso* in a small and fine hand would appear to be more finished, as though they had been made ready for insertion in another and fuller discussion. The document is undated.

20 These latter two "ends" of marriage are particularly noticeable in Heineccius' *Methodical System*, vol. 2, bk. 2, ch. 2, sec. 25–27, as translated by Turnbull. The approval of the translator is equally apparent in the ample, and often forceful notes; cf. sec. 27: "For certainly it would be better not to procreate, than to give a bad education to children . . . mankind receive great hurt from any one who is a disgrace to the kind on account of his bad education. How unhappy was it for mankind that there was a Nero?"

21 MS 2131/7/VII/18, which Dr. Haakonssen has shown to be continuous

with 7/VII/17. That Reid was in no wise ashamed to dwell at length on the subject of "the natural passion of Love between the Sexes" may be witnessed in a kind of prelector's aside from the same document (fol. 1): "It may appear a light and trivial Subject to those who have never been accustomed to think of it as Philosophers. But [it] is really a very noble Subject of Philosophical and moral Speculation." Does the slightly defensive tone suggest just a twinge of anxiety on Reid's part lest he should be mocked?

22 MS 2131/7/VII/18 (fol. 2).

23 MS 2131/6/V/34. Although it is not clear precisely who a certain "inspired writer" might have been, who has reinforced this idea in Reid's mind—for it would never have been too far away,—a highly likely candidate is Pufendorf, or perhaps, through him, Milton ("On [the Doctrine and Discipline of] Divorce"), whom the former had some cause to fault "perhaps because [he had been] irritated by his own [i.e. Milton's] domestic infelicity." The phrasing of "help meet," "institution," and "in the State of innocence" is more prevalent in Pufendorf than in most (although that need not suggest that it was uncommon). See *De jure naturae et gentium*, bk. 4, ch. 1, sec. 1, 2, 24.

24 MS 2131/7/VII/18 (fol. 2). (The superscripts ˢ———ˢ enclose an entire phrase written above the line; *os* indicates a word—here "like"—inscribed over another.)

25 MS 2131/2/II/8 (fol. 5). (The superscript *c* indicates that a word, or part of a word, has been cancelled or lined out.) The MS in question is unfortunately undated, although I suspect that it was early enough—and probably not undertaken in the first hectic years at Glasgow, but in a space of more leisure—to have caught some of the glow of William Duncan's widely read translation, along with the original Latin, of *Select Orations of Marcus Tullius Cicero* (London, 17—; the first English-only edition appeared in 1777). Duncan had been Professor of Natural and Experimental Philosophy at Marischal College, Aberdeen, between 1752/3 and 1760.

Walter Miller translates the last part of this passage as follows: ". . . [Nature] further dictates . . . the effort on man's part to provide a store of things that minister to his comforts and wants—and not for himself alone, but for his wife and children and the others whom he holds dear and for whom he ought to provide [*tuerique debeat*]; and this responsibility also stimulates his courage and makes it stronger for the active duties of life" (Loeb Classical Library ed.).

26 MS 2131/4/I/18, "4 Lect" (fol. 1), n.d. Cf. MS 2131/4/I/10: "I conceive therefore that the gradual Improvements of the human Mind are partly produced immediately by Nature *or rather by the Author of Nature*, partly by our Intercourse with our fellow Men in Society, & partly by Art used by those who have the training of us or by our selves when we arrive at years of Discretion" ("3 Lect" [fol. 1], n.d.).

27 Cf. MSS 2131/7/VII/17 (fol. 1) and 7/VII/20 (fol. 1); also the earlier 8/IV/7 (fol. 8) and 4/III/4, as well as 7/VII/15.

28 MS 2131/7/VII/15.

29 MSS 2131/7/VII/15 and 6/V/34.

30 Both terms appear on fol. 1 of 7/VII/15, which then goes on to treat the "Oeconomy of Nature" as 7/VII/17 does of "Oeconomical Jurisprudence."

31 Heineccius, *Methodical System*, vol 2, bk. 2, ch. 3, sec. 52, 45 n.

32 See Hutcheson, *System of Moral Philosophy*, bk. 3, ch.2, 190: "The parental affection naturally secures to [children] this emancipation [from Hobbesian subjection or 'slavery'], as the reason God has given them intitles them to it."

33 MS 2131/7/VII/15 (fol. 2).

34 Ibid. (fol. 1).

35 AUL, MS M.205.2 (746). Cf. Reid, MS 2131/8/IV/7 (fol. 8) and 4/III/4.

36 Reid denies that "Parental Authority" is founded "upon Generation. as Hobbs° grossly imagines." MS 2131/8/IV/7 (fol. 8). Cf. Gerard, M.205.2 (746); Pufendorf, *De jure naturae et gentium*, bk. 6, ch.2, 2–4 (the last section here perhaps misleading Reid: ". . . the act of generation gives rise to an *occasion* of acquiring some right over offspring"—the italics mine; the emphasis Pufendorf's); Turnbull's Heineccius, *Methodical System*, vol. 2, bk. 2, ch. 3, 52, 45 n., where Hobbes is rebuked for deriving "paternal power from occupancy"); and finally Grotius, who subtly argues: "By generation parents acquire a right over children—both parents, I mean, the father and the mother" (*De jure belli ac pacis*, bk. 2, ch. 5, 1).

37 MS 2131/4/I/30 (fol. 10).

38 Ibid.

39 MS 2131/7/VII/15 (fol. 2). In one other location, Reid tinkers with the natural differentiation of the sexes, to the point where, having provided the husband with "more hardness and Robustness of Constitution for toil & labour," nature must endow the wife with "tenderness & delicacy fitted to domestick Oeconomy and Order, and for the nursing and training of children in their tender Years" (MS 2131/6/V/34).

40 See, for example, Grotius, *De jure belli ac pacis*, bk. 2, ch. 5, 2, 1. The first period is that of "imperfect judgement," the second that of "mature judgement," and the third (and sometimes most contentious) "after the son has withdrawn from the family." The distinction has its origins in Aristotle's *Nicomachean Ethics* and *Politics* (esp. 1.13). Cf. Reid, MS 2131/7/VII/20 (fol. 4).

41 See Pufendorf, *De jure naturae et gentium*, bk. 6, ch. 2, 1. The question of "Sovereign" or "supreme authority" was, of course, a different matter, as Pufendorf was quick to argue. It is "contrary to rule," he notes, "that two should together hold the supreme authority over the same person" (bk. 6, ch. 2, 5). Usually the man, but under certain circumstances the woman, occupied that role. Heineccius adds the important qualification that, even allowing for the husband's "prerogative in the conjugal society," he cannot "command something manifestly base and hurtful to his children"; for neither the mother nor the children can be "obliged" to consent to anything "morally impossible" (*Methodical System*, vol. 2, bk. 2, ch. 3, 53).

Gerard, like Reid, couples the joint responsibility of the father and the mother for the child's well-being with the fact that "both have Naturale Affection—" AUL MS M.205.2 (747ᵛ). Hutcheson earlier added the somewhat novel twist that, not only does "parental power" belong "equally" to "both parents," but "the wife is wronged when she is deprived of her equal share, unless where she has voluntarily consented . . . to submit all domestick matters to his last determination" (*System of Moral Philosophy*, vol. 2, bk. 3, ch. 2, 2, 190). Cf. Heineccius, *Methodical System*, vol. 2, bk. 2, ch. 3, 53.

42 MS 2131/7/VII/17 (fol. 1).

43 Ibid.

44 Pufendorf, *De jure naturae*, bk. 6, ch. 2, 4.

45 The admixture occasionally reaches the finer elevations of logic: "We may therefore certainly conclude," reasons Reid at one stage, "on the one hand that if the maintenance and education of children had not been imposed by the Author of Nature upon fathers as well as mothers, that the father would naturally have been as indifferent about his own children as about the children of another. And on the Other hand from the parental Affection being common to both parents we may as certainly conclude that Nature intended that both Parents should exert this Natural Affection in the care of the common offspring°" (MS 2131/7/VII/17 [fol 1]). Two familiar "corollaries" were also in place: first, that the father should not be "frustrated" in his knowledge of just whom he was "to care for" as *his own* offspring; and second, that the mother should cooperate in this matter by remaining absolutely "chaste." Reid's concern was that the father, being uncertain, would be unable to "Exercise" his "Parental Affection" (fol. 2). Robert Filmer had taught him perhaps to be sceptical in this regard, for the author of *Patriarcha* had expressed the view that "no child naturally and infallibly knows who are his true parents," yet must obey "those that in common reputation are so," otherwise the commandment to obedience "were in vain." See his "Observations on Mr Hobbes's *Leviathan; or His Artificial Man—A Commonwealth*," in *Patriarcha and Other Political Works*, ed. Peter Laslett (Oxford: Basil Blackwell, 1949), 11.245.

46 MS 2131/7/VII/18 (fol. 1); cf. 7/VII/20 (fol. 3).

47 MS 2131/7/VII/17 (fol. 1); cf. 7/VII/20 (fol. 1).

48 Heineccius, *Methodical System*, vol. 2, bk. 2, ch. 3, 52–55; and Reid, MSS 2131/6/V/34 and 7/VII/20 (fol. 4).

49 MS 2131/7/VII/18 (fol. 4).

50 AUL MS M.205.2 (749). Reid likewise questions "how far their Authority reaches," in MS 2131/8/IV/7 (fol. 8) and 4/III/4.

51 MS 2131/7/VII/20 (fol. 4).

52 Compare this point as elaborated by Reid in his lectures on the Culture of Nature, MS 2131/4/I/30 (fol. 10), with a curious, and much earlier query, dated "Dec 1, 1758," MS 2131/6/III/5 (fol. 3): "Is it not from a Natural Principle that Children believe every thing that is told them?" Reid adds: "they swallow down with a greedy Belief whatever is told [them] til they are by Experience convinced that they do by this means expose themselves to deceit."

53 For a different approach to the infusion, see my earlier article, "The Well-

Principled Savage, or the Child of the Scottish Enlightenment," *Journal of the History of Ideas* 42 (1981): 503–25.

54 MS 2131/7/VII/20 (fol. 4).

55 See MS 2131/7/VII/20 (fol. 4). Hutcheson finds the child "cruel and ungrateful" who does not "first" try to obtain the consent of his parents to marry someone from outside the bounds of the familial society to which he has hitherto been subject. (*System of Moral Philosophy*, vol. 2, bk. 3, ch. 2, 4, 195.)

56 AUL MS M.205.2 (747).

57 Fordyce, "Elements," bk. 2, sec. 3, ch. 1, 307. Fordyce adds: "But when the Child is grown up, and has attained to such a degree of Understanding, as to comprehend the *Moral Tye* . . . he must be conscious that he owes to [his parents] these peculiar Duties." (Is that "must" a moral ought or a desperate hope?)

58 Heineccius, *Methodical System*, vol. 2, bk. 2, ch. 3, 50–52.

59 Hutcheson, *System of Moral Philosophy*, vol. 2, bk. 3, ch. 2, 188–89, and 3, 193.

60 Grotius, *De jure belli ac pacis*, bk. 2, ch. 5, 26 and 2.

61 MS 2131/8/IV/7 (fol. 8) and 4/III/4.

62 MS 2131/7/VII/20 (fol. 4).

63 Grotius, *De jure belli ac pacis*, bk. 2, ch. 5, 1, 2. The words in parentheses are indeed Hutcheson's; cf. his wording on this point in *A System of Moral Philosophy*, vol. 2, bk. 3, ch. 2, 2, 192–93.

64 Filmer, "Observations on Mr Hobbes's *Leviathan*," 11.245.

65 MS 2131/8/IV/7 (fol. 8) and 4/III/4: "Hobbe's Notion[;] Filmers," is the extent of the textual evidence here, but as usual it is just enough and, indeed, says plenty.

66 Turnbull, in the same comment upon Heineccius cited above (note 58), affirmed that "Pufendorf's way" does not "satisfy us"; the way, namely, of deriving parental authority "partly from the nature of social life, and partly from the presumed consent of children." Turnbull's dissatisfaction, however, is all the more curious in so far as Pufendorf appears to have laid down much the same sort of condition which Turnbull, following Heineccius, had attached to the "presumed consent"; namely that (in Pufendorf's words), "as the parent by his acknowledgement of a child declares that he will fulfil the obligation enjoined by nature . . . so . . . the infant, although unable . . . expressly to promise . . . contracts an obligation towards his parents by reason of their care for him. . . ." See *De jure naturae et gentium*, bk. 6, ch. 2, 4.

67 Pufendorf, *De jure naturae et gentium*, bk. 6, ch. 2, 4 (italics mine). Cf. bk. 3, ch. 6, 5, in which Pufendorf deals with the question, "how long children [may be thought to] continue in a weakness of reason which prevents their contracting an obligation[?] . . ." In a manner not unlike that of Reid, in the early notes on child credulity from 1758 (MS 2131/6/III/5), Pufendorf observes: ". . . since a tender age, even when able to understand the conduct

of business, is carried away by quick and usually ill-considered impulses and makes promises lightly, is credulous, eager to have a reputation for liberality, inclined to cultivate influential friendships, and ignorant of whom to trust, many states have safe-guarded it by law, that, in contracting obligations, younger persons must follow the authority of others who are more prudent, until it is felt that their hasty impulses have abated."

68 See Pufendorf, *De jure naturae et gentium*, bk. 4, ch. 1, "On Speech and the Obligations that Attend it." In Section 1, he writes: ". . . in order that this instrument, of the greatest usefulness for the life of man, may gain its end in binding together the family of men, and that man may not become less sociable through the use of speech than through silence or dumbness, the law of nature is understood to command that *no man shall decieve another by the use of signs which have been instituted to express his thoughts.*" Cf. Hutcheson's chapter on "The Obligations in the Use of Speech" in *A System of Moral Philosophy*, vol. 2, bk. 2, ch. 10. Many of the illustrations in Section 2, for example, are gleaned directly from Pufendorf. Hutcheson does, however, add the Scottish qualification that Nature must also have "implanted a moral feeling in our hearts to regulate this power [of communicating with each other]."

69 MS 2131/8/IV/7 and 4/III/4 (fol. 3, 4; fol. 1).

70 MS 2131/8/IV/5 (fol. 3, 4), dated "Mar 14 1765."

71 Cf. MS 2131/7/VII/1a (fol. 1).

72 Approaching the matter from a different angle, he reflects: "Entails seem to lesson too Much the Parental Authority which Nature had ordained for the benefite° of Children, and for the Punishment of those who are incorrigibly vicious."

73 Pufendorf cites Lucretius' "unthinking childhood may be deluded" (*De jure naturae et gentium*, bk. 4, ch. 1, 15).

74 MS 2131/8/IV/7 (fol. 3, 4) and 4/III/4.

75 Pufendorf, *De jure naturae et gentium*, bk. 4, ch. 1, 15. Such was J. M. Edmonds' rendering of the line in 1912, as used in the Oldfather translation of *De jure naturae* (*The Greek Bucolic Poets*, Loeb Classical Library ed.). A. Lang translates the mother's rebuke to her crying baby more prosaically as:

> No, child, I don't mean to take you.
> Boo! Bogies! There's a horse that
> bites! Cry as much as you please, but
> I cannot have you lamed.
> (Theocritus, Bion
> and Moschus
> [London, 1928])

K. J. Dover, in his edition of the *Idylls* (London: Macmillan, 1971), interprets Praxinoa's censure to mean, "I'm going out to see something nasty that would only frighten you." Μορμώ, the demon who bites, is therefore somewhat akin to the stern parental warning, "Hot!" Something of this tone is captured in Borriss Mills's more recent verse translation (West Lafayette, Ind.: Purdue University Studies, 1963/68):

> No, I won't take you, baby. Bad horsey!
> Bites! Go ahead and cry. I can't have
> you crippled for life.

That a horse may bite is, of course, no matter of deception; bogies are another thing.

76 MS 2131/8/IV/7 (fol. 4) and 4/III/4.

77 On 1 April 1768, for example, Reid raised before the Literary Society of Glasgow the query, "Whether the Supposition of a tacit Contract at the beginning of Societies is well founded[?]" Cf. the subject matter of MS 2131/2/II/10.

78 MS 2131/8/IV/7 (fol. 2) and 4/III/4. Cf. also 7/VII/2 and 4 (where Reid's challenge to Hume figures most prominently), and 2/II/10, which treats of "tacit (or quasi) contracts."

79 Grotius, *De jure belli ac pacis*, bk. 2, ch. 4, 10: ". . . the fact must be recognized that a person who is not yet born has no rights, just as a thing which does not exist has no attributes. If then the people, from whose will the right to rule arises, changes its will, it does not injustice to those yet unborn, since they have not yet acquired any right." Pufendorf counters: "Now by him who is not yet a part of the world we understand one who has not yet been conceived, not one who is still in the womb; for this latter is treated in many matters of law as a member of society" (*De jure naturae et gentium*, bk. 4, ch. 12, 10). Not surprisingly, the issue here was that of rights for the unborn in connection with the transference of property.

80 Campbell's query was entitled, "Whether the manner of living of parents affects the genius or intellectual abilities of the children?" It was delivered before the Society on 22 January 1765 (Question 72); Aberdeen Philosophical Society *Minutes*, AUL MS 539[1]. The final, albeit still incomplete, paragraphs of Campbell's address have been located among the papers of another member of the Society, Thomas Gordon; see AUL MS 3107/3/10.

81 Query 76, for 13 August 1765; *Minutes*, AUL MS 539[1].

82 Query 44 entitled, "Whether Moral Character consists in Affections wherein the will is not concerned; or in fixed habitual and constant purposes?" for 15 April 1761; *Minutes*, AUL MS 539[1]. Reid appears to have returned to the subject in an address before the Literary Society in Glasgow, on 9 May 1766. See Glasgow University Library, MS Murray 505.

83 MS 2131/6/IV/2 (fol. 2). Although the match is not exact, Reid's query is fairly close to that put down by Mr. Farquhar (Minister at Nigg) for 15 November 1758: "Upon what the Characters of Men chiefly Depend?" Query 15; *Minutes*, AUL MS 539[1].

In Florid Impotence He Spoke:
Edmund Burke and the Nawab of Arcot

REGINA JANES

In his excellent little book on Burke, C. B. Macpherson asks, "Why should [Burke's] speeches and writings, most of which were partisan pleadings on some issue of the day, still command attention?"[1] But the *Speech on the Nabob of Arcot's Debts* did not command Macpherson's attention; it is not mentioned in the text. Nor is that in the least surprising. Arguably Burke's greatest speech, it is a masterwork by a master craftsman. The speech exposes an intricate system of corruption and complicity in corruption that extends—in the grand manner—from the scourged backs of the lowliest Indian cultivator and English revenue officer to the pampered pockets at the highest levels of British politics. One of Burke's more peopled speeches, its characters, Dundas, Rumbold, Fox, Pitt, Benfield, Atkinson, Macartney, the Nawab of Arcot, the Raja of Tanjore, Haidar Ali, are deployed like musical instruments: themes appear and reappear as characters are doubled, paralleled, contrasted, isolated. Like Dido's hide, the argument gradually takes in more and more ground, proceeding from paradox to paradox, until the mass of iniquity is complete and the argument ends where it began: in an image of Henry Dundas, at the last a great sow suckling his reports from the Secret Committee. The speech has been plundered for its figures and its pictures: Haidar Ali as a storm looming over the Carnatic; Dundas as a blushing bride with six great chopping bastards at his or her androgynous heels; Pitt as a gleaner, picking up straws with painful precision and recovering with a broad-cast squandering of Indian revenues; the tapeworms, the sensitive plant, the giant phantom of debt, the chalice of fornications, the briar and the oak. The images are familiar; they are often quoted; and they are all that seems to remain of the speech.

There is good reason for that. Save for the comparably pecuniary *Speech on the Sixth Charge*, this is the least theoretical of Burke's Indian speeches. There is no invocation of natural law; there is no discussion of rights, chartered or otherwise; there is little description of the nature and obligations of empire. The speech fits awkwardly in the history of the East India Company and the British empire in India since it accuses the Board of Control, the great ministerial instrument of reform, of corruption. It is less detailed in its historical accounts than other of Burke's Indian speeches. Perhaps most important, it requires sustained attention to the details of a dead scandal, to the minutiae of distasteful and defunct pecuniary transactions. It is not surprising that the reward of Burke's efforts now should be not unlike their reward at the time: "Why bother? It's all settled anyway."

Burke delivered the speech only after he had tried and failed to alter from behind the scenes the determination of the Board of Control relative to the Nawab's debts. He spoke almost five hours, until one in the morning, and received no answer to the allegations in the speech apart from the humiliating vote of 164 to 69 against his side of the question. Undeterred, goaded, or newly inspired, he revised the speech over a longer period than almost any other. (Six months elapsed between delivery and publication, and there is evidence of revision and circulation of the speech.[2] Only the *Speech on American Taxation* saw a greater delay—nine months—but without comparable evidence of revision or circulation.) The speech is also fitted with more apparatus than any other: like the writings, it has an epigraph; like a few of the speeches it has a preface or "advertisement"; like the committee reports, it has an appendix as long again as the speech. But the *Speech on the Nabob of Arcot's Debts* alone has all three. Five months before he died, Burke was to remind French Laurence to build him a cenotaph in the history of the impeachment. But the *Speech on the Nabob of Arcot's Debts* is the monument he built for himself, and it was his last sustained look at the affairs of South India. What makes the speech peculiarly interesting and appropriate as a monument, apart from its formal structure, is that within the text, Burke elaborates all the reasons that the text cannot perform its ostensible function: to persuade (the Board of Control to reconsider its decision, the house to investigate that decision). Every argument Burke advances is a reason that his argument will be disregarded, as well as a reason that the argument must be made.

Formally, within the published text, British corruption in Britain encloses British corruption in India. Quite unlike anything else Burke wrote, this text progresses towards its defeat through a series of opening, enlarging, and closing circles. At the end of the speech, Burke inscribes himself as one who serves, though he only stands and waits. In the language of funerary monuments, his is one of those bodies dead in the Lord, awaiting the call of the trumpet, awaiting a greater man to come: "Let who will shrink back. I shall be found at my post. . . . Whoever therefore shall at any time bring before you any thing towards the relief of our distressed fellow-citizens in India, and towards a subversion of the present most corrupt and oppressive system for its government, in me shall find, a weak I am afraid, but a steady, earnest, and faithful assistant."[3] Burke at his "post" brings the speech round to a point before it began, to the epigraph from the Emperor Julian in the published text. The initial image is a closed circle in which Rumbold and Dundas alternate as accused and accuser in an endless round. But that closed circle evokes Dundas's Secret Committee reports with which the body of Burke's argument will end some sixty pages later, closing another circle. The allusion to British corruption in Madras, through Rumbold, once its governor, who had contrived to remit to China £58,000 in six months on an annual salary of £20,000,[4] will end in an accusation of British corruption in Britain, through Dundas and Pitt, who had won an election. Fox's India bill is periodically invoked, its provisions a bulwark against the corruptions that Pitt's bill has let in; its justice, humanity, and honor vindicated; its memory apostrophized in the one example of florid, failed rhetoric in the speech: "O illustrious disgrace! O victorious defeat! May your memorial be fresh and new to the latest generations! May the day of that generous conflict be stamped in characters never to be cancelled or worn out from the records of time!" (502). This is a bit much, and it does not end here. There are two laments over the fallen, the members defeated in 1784, one toward the beginning of the speech (488), one toward the end (551). Pitt's unpaid revenue officers in England reappear as unpaid armies in India. The metaphorical scourged backs of British petty offenders become, horribly, the literally scored, flayed back of the Indian cultivator "lashed from oppressor to oppressor, whilst a single drop of blood is left as the means of extorting a single grain of corn" (533). The single stone Burke casts into the pool against the decision of the Board of Control makes ripples that widen to reveal corruption and its effects in India and then spread until they reach the House of Commons itself, the shore from which the stone was flung.

But the pool soon recovered its smoothness; the shore remained un-moved. Perhaps Burke's most obviously self-defeating argument was his concluding flourish: the just accusation that Pitt and Dundas, out of gratitude to the Nawab's creditors for their assistance in the election of 1784, were settling his debts without official enquiry. The corrupt manipulation of the debts in India had found an interest with ad-ministration and tainted, in a small way, the house itself. Burke exag-gerates the number of members introduced into the house in 1780 by Paul Benfield, the principal manager of the debt, but William Pitt had committed the same exaggeration when he complained of Indian cor-ruption in an earlier parliament.[5] Burke does not exaggerate in his ac-count of Atkinson's management of the 1784 election and the consulta-tions between creditors and ministers over the provisions of Pitt's India Act. But he widens his charge to include the purchase of "even whole parliaments in the gross" (548). So old as to be venerable, this was the traditional, creaking complaint of an out-voted opposition. At one in the morning, it might have made anyone doze. The additional, inevitable implication that the benches opposite are upholstered with Indian chintz seems scarcely calculated to elicit the cushions' applause and votes.

If the broad, sweeping charge with which Burke ends must fail, the narrow ground from which he begins is equally hopeless. The ground was one that could not be rejected logically or legally; it could only be rejected politically and practically, and so it was. The speech on the debts attacks two decisions taken by the Board of Control established in Pitt's India Act of 1784: to settle without further enquiry the Nawab of Arcot's debts to three sets of European creditors and to award the districts of Arni and Hanumantagudi, claimed by the Raja of Tanjore, to the Nawab. Both decisions overturned recommendations by the Court of Directors, the governing body of the East India Company, and the first violated a provision of Pitt's India Act of 1784. The act had required the Court of Directors to settle those debts after an enquiry into their merits. In obedience to the statute, the directors had begun their investigation in London, had encountered great difficulty sub-stantiating the debts, and had ordered their government at Madras to continue the investigation. The Board of Control had then altered the directors' despatch to Madras so as to eliminate the order for further investigation and to substitute a plan of settlement without investiga-tion. The directors entered a protest, and Burke made a speech. But the decision to violate the letter of the statute by those who had made the statute had already been taken and Burke had already failed in his attempts to reverse that decision.

In the abstract, Burke's situation was hopeless enough, but the particular circumstances of the Board's decision compounded the difficulty. It was Henry Dundas on the Board of Control who had prevented the enquiry and who continued to prevent it in the house by opposing Fox's motion for papers.[6] But it was also Henry Dundas who, as chairman of the Secret Committee in 1781 and 1782, had first introduced into the House of Commons in 1782 resolutions that enjoined, among other things, the investigation of the debts. The last of Dundas's twenty-five resolutions "respecting the government of the Presidency of Fort St. George" had recommended that "just Distinctions . . . be made between the Claims of the different Creditors; and that, in all these Proceedings and Regulations, the Chief object of Attention should be directed to the Discovery and Punishment of Peculation by any of the Company's Servants, and, above all, to the more entire Prevention of it in future."[7] On the occasion of those earlier resolutions, Burke had written triumphantly to his kinsman William, then agent for the Raja of Tanjore: "I told you before, that the Lord Advocate continued in the same happy train of thinking, which your early Impressions formed him to. His Speeches, as well as his Resolutions relative to Tanjour, and the oppressions and usurpations of the Nabob, were such, as if your own honest heart had dictated them."[8] But now "a singular revolution" had occurred (485). Burke and Dundas had not been allies in 1782; they had remained on opposite sides of the house, but they had cooperated, and Burke had been anxious to seduce Dundas to the Rockingham connection. From the spot where Burke now stood, it was very clear that Dundas had betrayed both a common cause and a high cause, and it is not surprising that the metaphors of the speech make Dundas an androgyne. Nor, since Dundas had set the policy, could there be the faintest hope that the policy was founded in error, mistake, ignorance, anything that could be rectified or set right by speech.

The principal remaining feature of the speech and the parliamentary situation that militated against Burke is the same feature that defeats the modern reader: the impenetrable thicket of addition, multiplication, and rates of interest. Burke cuts through it, all the while telling the reader how dangerous, intricate, shifting, and mysterious it is, but his path tends to close up behind him. Even C. H. Philips termed the speech "obscure."[9] The listener tires and falters as he tries to keep up with the calculations. The demonstration of mastery makes the pupil revolt from the lesson and long for the bell. The reader can skim the hard bits, but doing so deprives the speech of its foundation in hard-earned fact and weakens both the force and the logic of Burke's conclusions. Arguments from such authorities should be handled with care, but it was Paul Benfield's agent in the House of Commons, Nathaniel William Wraxall, who testified on the basis of this speech that Burke understood the affairs of Madras better than any man in England. [10]

But these are small matters, though intractable enough and central to Burke, compared to what the speech almost inadvertently reveals about the impossibility of persuasion. In this exemplary act of resistance to power, Burke voices most of the reasons that an ethical or moral appeal running counter to established, entrenched interests must fail. The first problem to which he adverts is that invincible human indifference to anything far off and remote. At the beginning of the speech, he chides the house for "our total neglect" of so important a concern as India. The countermodel he holds up is a god-like perspective "of this frame the bearings, and the ties, / The strong connexions, nice dependencies, / Gradations just" [11]: the house should have had "steadily before our eyes a general, comprehensive, well-connected, and well-proportioned view of the whole of our dominions, and a just sense of their true bearings and relations" (488). To possess such a view requires a vantage point well above the globe itself, rather like that of Bathurst's angel in the *Speech on Conciliation*. But that is not an easy position to reach.

By the end of the speech, the neglect Burke reproves at the beginning has become more ominous. At the beginning, neglect is dangerous. To it Burke attributes the loss of the western empire. By the end, neglect acquires something of the character or nature of sin, a moral failure that speaks of a hardened heart. "I confess," says Burke, "I wish that some more feeling than I have yet observed for the sufferings of our fellow-creatures and fellow-subjects in that oppressed part of the world, had manifested itself in any one quarter of the kingdom, or in any one large description of men" (549). The rebuke implicates Burke's own party as well as all others, but the salvation Burke proposes is only the astonishment of posterity at the actions of this moment. (The pronouns of Burke's peroration are significant: there is a "call upon *us*," "*I*" will be at my post "*whoever*" leads forward a plan. The "us" is universal; the "I" certain; the "whoever" impossibly vague. Its vagueness suggests that no one Burke knows means to lead him, certainly not Fox who made the motion Burke supports in this speech. Burke knows how to praise his friends when they propose to go into action.) As Michael Ignatieff has pointed out, the weakest, the most inefficacious of appeals is the bare appeal to a common humanity. When Burke charges his audience with lack of fellow feeling, he acknowledges that a considerable part of his argument has been built upon a mirage: compassion for the natives of India who must pay this debt through bodily labor and deprivation. Burke puts it, of course, a little more vividly: "It is therefore not from treasuries and mines, but from the food of your unpaid armies [opportunity cost], from the blood withheld from the veins, and whipt out of the backs of the most miserable of men, that we are to pamper extortion, usury, and peculation, under the false names of debtors and creditors of state" (496). Burke's language attempts to generate the appropriate feelings, pity, revulsion, and rage, but the fact remains that our friends and neighbors are extortion, usury, and peculation, while the victims are remote, poor, and alien. When the image comes round again, as images do in this speech, we find that ministry indeed know who their friends are by a natural sympathy: "They were touched with pity for bribery, so long tormented with a fruitless itching of its palms; their bowels yearned for usury, that had long missed the harvest of its returning months; they felt for peculation, which had been for so many years raking in the dust of an empty treasury; they were melted into compassion for rapine and oppression, licking their dry, parched, unbloody jaws" (523). It is not, it would seem, that ministry lack the proper feelings, but that they direct them to improper, inappropriate objects, possessed of a parliamentary interest. If the problem at the opening of the speech is that the audience does not know enough, the problem at the end, when such deficiencies of information have presumably been supplied, can only be that the word has fallen on stony ground.

Burke does not depend solely upon compassion for his argument, of course. He also invokes interest, but unfortunately the only interest available to him for invocation is the public interest. He attacks the preference of the private debt over the public debt of the company and the consequent diversion of funds from such public uses as the company's administration, military, and investment, to private pockets. He suggests that pampering the Nawab and his creditors undermines the authority of the public government at Madras, and from time to time he casts doubt on the Nawab's loyalty to the British interest. But neither the Nawab's loyalty nor the creditors' machinations then posed a threat to the British hold on Madras, and the company could be relied upon to look to the public debt. While there was a public interest to be appealed to, there was no public pressure to make that appeal effective.

Burke makes a more capacious appeal to the public interest in his insistence on the responsibility of government for the welfare of the people. But that interest contravenes the interest of the company and reveals that magnanimity, justice, and benevolence are merely the grander, public relatives of compassion, a private virtue. To the depredations of Haidar Ali in war and the predations of creditors and ministry in peace, Burke contrasts the accomplishments of "real kings, who were the fathers of their people . . . [moved] by the ambition of an unsatiable benevolence, which, not contented with reigning in the dispensation of happiness during the contracted term of human life, had strained, with all the reachings and graspings of a vivacious mind, to extend the dominion of their bounty beyond the limits of nature, and to perpetuate themselves through generations of generations, the guardians, the protectors, the nourishers of mankind" (522). Such men built and maintained reservoirs and watercourses that provide Burke with his most concrete image of India: "mounds of earth and stones, with sluices of solid masonry," "properly scoured and duly levelled" watercourses (522). The Carnatic had recently been devastated by war, and Burke's argument in context goes to the need to restore the country before it is required to pay any debts, public or private. But he extends the argument to repudiate not only the private debt, but also the public debt to the company:

> But I, Sir . . . do positively deny that the Carnatic owes a shilling to the Company; whatever the Company may be indebted to that undone country. It owes nothing to the Company for this plain and simple reason—The territory charged with the debt is their own. . . . In peace they go the full length, and indeed more than a full length, of what the people can bear for current establishments; then they are absurd enough to consolidate all the calamities of war into debts; to metamorphose the devastations of the country into demands upon its future production. What is this but to avow a resolution utterly to destroy their own country, and to force the people to pay for their sufferings, to a government which proved unable to protect either the share of the husbandman or their own? (530)

However just, the argument is problematic. The burdens of empire were in large part sustained by the practice of conquering territory and making the conquered pay the expenses incurred while conquering them. In the Carnatic, where the company had not conquered the Nawab but had established him in power and treated him as an independent ally, the company received a share of the Nawab's territorial revenues and charged the Nawab with the expenses incurred in assisting him and themselves in wars with the French and invasions by Haidar Ali. Burke's objection reduces the company from a profit-making institution to a trusteeship and barely allows the legitimacy of the company's receipt of the territorial revenues to pay for its army, civil administration, and investment. Burke was an imperialist for the power, glory, and responsibility of it, not the profit. But eighteenth-century colonial administrators were praised, by Burke among others, for their success in increasing revenues. Very early on, the revenues were absorbed in keeping up military and civil establishments, but the Indian empire was to pay for itself, both in its maintenance and in its expansion. It was unlikely that either the company or the parliament would be pleased with the prospect of sustaining, restoring, and supporting the Carnatic.

Although Burke called the preference of the private debt over the public debt "no more than the preference of a fiction over a chimera" (531), he did not intend seriously to argue that the public debt should be given up. Instead, he suggested other methods for managing the public debt so as to prevent it from propagating the private debt. But he was clear that the debts of the Nawab to his European creditors should be disallowed because they were fictitious and because the country could not bear their weight. Burke certainly overestimated the purity of fraudulence in the debts. Although part of the debt was as collusive as Burke maintained, some part of it had been legitimately incurred, for legitimate purposes. He did not overestimate the inability of the Carnatic to pay, however. The Board of Control estimated that the debt would be repaid in eleven years. It was finally paid off in nineteen years, with a new debt contracted in the meanwhile, as Burke predicted. When that second debt came to be inquired after in 1805, the Carnatic was in name as well as in effect the company's own. Those claims were investigated, as Burke had once requested, and 95 percent of the total claims were disallowed, one in twenty only judged legitimate. [12] New circumstances led to a new disposition towards the creditors and the debt.

The futility of Burke's arguments in 1785 did not, however, hinge entirely on the disposition of his audience. Far more devastating is his analysis of the situation in India, an analysis that reveals the collapse of external constraints on British power and thus necessitates the useless appeal to internal restraint. The speech unveils a dismal portrayal of the progress of power that far outgoes any practical recommendations Burke would ever make and undermines Burke's own arguments on behalf of the imperial enterprise.

"Tribute," Burke tells us, "hangs on the sword," as he denies the right of the Nawab of Arcot to receive any tribute from the Raja of Tanjore (536). The statement implies the right to exact tribute from those one conquers. But we have already seen Burke's reservations about the sums the company levied on its Indian dependencies, even for public purposes. Ordinarily enthusiastic about the glories of British acquisitions, Burke mentions in the speech a successful levying of tribute that had helped restore the revenues received from the Carnatic. But the account is curiously cautious: the British commander is praised, but the description is flat. There is little rejoicing in the accomplishment and less in the language: an account tells us "that there has been a recovery of *what is called* arrear. . . . It was brought about by making a new war. After some sharp actions, by the resolution and skill of Colonel Fullarton, several of the petty princes of the most southerly of the unwasted provinces were compelled to pay very heavy rents and tributes, who for a long time before had not paid any acknowledgment. After this *reduction* . . . that province was divided into twelve farms" (527; emphases added). There is a "reduction," not a conquest; those conquered are "petty princes," not "great princes"; and war is brought, by the British, to "the unwasted provinces." Burke deliberately and ironically deflates the one source of tribute that he grants is legitimate: direct conquest.

But direct conquest was not the only method of expansion or acquisition. Much cheaper and as effective was the practice of exacting lands, cities, and cash from erstwhile "allies," small states that had enlisted as supporters of the British in regional conflicts; among them was Tanjore. Such states were encouraged to show their loyalty, good will, and deference by handing over territory, contracts, and the conduct of their foreign policy. Here there was tribute without conquest by means of the simple possession of power without its exercise, and here Burke's language was less cautious. Tanjore is "a small kingdom, not obtained by our arms; robbed, not protected by our power; [it has made us grants of territory and subsidy] for which no equivalent was ever given, or pretended to be given." The latest "outrageous and insulting robbery of that country" has been to "force from [the Raja] a territory of an extent which they have not yet thought proper to ascertain, for a military peace establishment, the particulars of which they have not yet been pleased to settle." In the event of any future wars in the region, his revenues are to be confiscated "until all the debt which the Company shall think fit to incur in such war shall be discharged; that is to say, for ever" (534–35). Well, yes, indeed, that is how it was done. In 1799, fourteen years later, the then Raja of Tanjore formally and finally resigned the administration of his country to the British. In 1801, though both were then dead, Wellesley discovered that this very Nawab of Arcot and his eldest son and successor had all along been "public enemies of the British Government in India,"[13] and

Arcot too disappeared as an independent entity. As Burke remarked proleptically enough, "[The Raja's] sole comfort is to find his old enemy, the Nabob of Arcot, placed in the very same condition" (535).

Burke is clear as to the circumstances that made both oblitera- and extortion possible: "The Nabob of Arcot, and Raja of Tanjore, have, in truth and substance, no more than a merely civil authority, held in the most entire dependence on the Company." What pre- served them for a few years was their utility as administrators and their providing a resource and income for the servants of the com- pany. "The Nabob, without military, without federal capacity, is ex- tinguished as a potentate; but then he is carefully kept alive as an independent and sovereign power, for the purpose of rapine and ex- tortion. . . ."(536). "Thus these miserable Indian princes are con- tinued in their seats, for no other purpose than to render them in the first instance objects of every species of extortion; and in the second, to force them to become, for the sake of a momentary shadow of re- duced authority, a sort of subordinate tyrants, the ruin and calamity, not the fathers and cherishers, of their people" (537). It is a highly col- ored and rhetorically charged picture, and it omits the fact that the company needed the assistance of native rulers in the collection of revenue. But it is none the less exact and prophetic. In time the extor- tion would cease to be an entrepreneurial affair, managed by individ- uals, and would be confined to institutional channels, with certain In- dian princes continued in their seats less for the sake of extortion than for the sake of the rhetorical effect of their subordinate tyranny: its revelation of the superiority of British rule to that of Kipling's native states, "the dark places of the earth." Examining the debts of the Nawab would check one form of extortion, but it would have no effect on the wider problem of spoliation that Burke also attacks and that is inseparable from empire itself and intrinsic to conquest. Moral senti- ment might reject such practices, but self-interest tends to carry more weight in human affairs.

When moral exhortation fails, it has long been customary to appeal to divine vengeance, that last, unreliable resource. Burke does so, not for the first or for the last time relative to the affairs of India, but in a form that marks the desperation of the appeal. Towards the end of the speech, he advances a damning but puzzling image.

> The commonwealth then is become totally perverted from its pur- poses; neither God nor man will long endure it; nor will it long en- dure itself. In that case, there is an unnatural infection, a pestilen- tial taint fermenting in the constitution of society, which fever and convulsions of some kind or other must throw off; or in which the

vital powers, worsted in an unequal struggle, are pushed back
upon themselves, and by a reversal of their whole functions, fester
to gangrene, to death; and instead of what was but just now the delight and boast of the creation, there will be cast out in the face of
the sun, a bloated, putrid, noisome carcass, full of stench and poison, an offence, a horror, a lesson to the world (549).

The image is a shocking one, but it is also puzzling: how does "the
constitution of society" find itself in such a fix?

The answer is thirty pages earlier, in the only Indian of the work
who possesses a character beyond that of victim. At the center of the
speech is not Dundas, not Benfield, not the Nawab, not the Raja, but
Haidar Ali, ruler of Mysore. Haidar Ali had twice driven the British to
the sea. In 1769, he concluded a treaty with a chastened presidency at
the gates of Madras. In 1780 he swept over the Carnatic with such
force that a Secret Committee in the House of Commons was created.
That committee eventually justified his actions and laid the blame for
the war on the provocations of the Madras presidency. Burke wields
Haidar Ali as an instrument of divine justice, a diabolical weapon of
vengeance. The "scene of woe" that burst on the Carnatic, "the like of
which no eye had seen, no heart conceived, and which no tongue can
adequately tell," a scene of "fire, sword, exile," and famine, had in
fact been seen before, but in Old Testament prophecy, even to the
"captivity, in an unknown and hostile land." When Haidar Ali "found
that he had to do with men who either would sign no convention or
whom no treaty, and no signature could bind, and who were the determined enemies of human intercourse itself," he does not "act," he
"decrees." And his decree falls upon "the country possessed by these
incorrigible and *predestinated* criminals . . . those against whom the
faith which holds the moral elements of the world together was no
protection" (518–19; emphasis added). A case of Satan driving out
Satan, Haidar Ali enacts the judgment Burke called for. On invasion
followed famine. A nation "perished by a hundred a day in the streets
of Madras; every day seventy at least laid their bodies in the streets,
or on the glacis of Tanjore, and expired of famine in the granary of
India" (519). But Burke withholds the "circumstances of this plague of
hunger. . . . I find myself unable to manage it with decorum; these
details are of a species of horror so nauseous and disgusting; they are
so degrading to the sufferers and to the hearers; they are so humiliating to human nature itself, that on better thoughts, I find it more ad-
viseable to throw a pall over this hideous object, and to leave it to your
general conceptions" (519–20). Here, for reasons of decorum, Burke
hides the intimacies of starvation. Later, he will not be so delicate, but

will describe a body consuming itself and its end: "the vital powers, worsted in an unequal struggle, are pushed back upon themselves, and by a reversal of their whole functions, fester to gangrene, to death; and instead of what was but just now the delight and boast of the creation [conventionally man], there will be cast out in the face of the sun, a bloated, putrid, noisome carcass, full of stench and poison, an offence, a horror, a lesson to the world" (549). Those are the bodies perishing by a hundred a day in the streets of Madras, by seventy a day in Tanjore, where the living lay out the dead for burning. But the sufferer is no longer man, the victims of Haidar Ali's invasion; the sufferer is the commonwealth when authority secures public robbery. The 'delight and boast of the creation' is the British constitution. The image withheld in India, Burke thrusts on Britain, in a wish for some evidence of divine justice when human persuasion fails, as fail it must.

Haidar Ali was dead. He had died in 1782; a peace had been concluded with his son Tipu Sultan in 1784. Though Burke knew it and all his auditors knew it, a reader would not know it from the speech itself. For the duration of the speech, Haidar Ali looms as a menace, lives as a threat. But however much Burke expresses vindictive rage and revels in the justice of disaster, the instrument of a disastrous justice was gone. One more external restraint had collapsed, and the vehemence of Burke's imagery erupts from the certainty that there was nothing to be done. Neither in England nor in India was there the will or a way to halt the racking of ryots or the despoiling of princes. Nor would investigating the debts of the Nawab of Arcot have prevented all the ills Burke complains of, though it would have prevented some.

The lesson to be drawn from Burke's failure is not one that he would have liked: that the powerless must be empowered for their own protection, that the powerful cannot be trusted to protect those who have no power over them. Humanitarian gestures without power are useful only as monuments. They are only words, only images. But words and images have their uses, as do monuments. They may remind us of the inevitability of failure, but they also remind us of the continuing presence of resistance and the continuing need for resistance, in very different worlds.

NOTES

1 C. B. Macpherson, *Burke* (New York, 1980), 13. At issue in the *Speech on the Nabob of Arcot's Debts*, 1785, was a decision by the Board of Control, estab-

lished by Pitt's India Act of 1784 and dominated by Henry Dundas. The Board had ordered the East India Company to establish a fund from the revenues of the Carnatic (the region west and south of Madras) to pay off the European creditors of Muhammad Ali, Nawab (or governor) of the Carnatic (or Arcot, from its capital city). For decades, the Nawab had been borrowing from Europeans to pay his troops and household, to finance schemes of territorial expansion, to repay the Company for past military assistance and meet its demands for present subsidy, and to provide presents, bribes, and interest on the loans already made. Many of the loans were legitimate, but a large part was suspected to be fictitious. Pitt's India Act (like Dundas's and Fox's unsuccessful bills of 1783) had enjoined the settlement of the debt after investigation by the Court of Directors, the ruling body of the East India Company. Having begun an investigation and encountered difficulties ascertaining the legitimacy of the debt, the Directors had ordered their government at Madras to continue the investigation. It was this order that the Board of Control had countermanded, directing that the debt be settled and the claims accepted without further investigation. In the election of 1784 that had decimated the supporters of the Fox-North coalition, considerable support had been thrown to Pitt by the creditors and their agents. In particular, Richard Atkinson, attorney for Paul Benfield, the principal creditor, had worked closely with government in managing the election. In 1783, while Fox's India bill was depending, Burke had been the recipient of much suasion by some creditors, who sought terms like those the Board of Control gave a year later. Burke inferred, plausibly enough, that the Board of Control had now repaid the creditors for their support in the election. In the fall of 1784, Burke met with members of government to attempt to reverse the decision. Having failed, he spoke against the decision in February 1785.

2 *Correspondence of Edmund Burke,* ed. Thomas W. Copeland et al. (Chicago, 1965), 5:211–12. In October, Burke indicated that his "Dundas speech" had appeared earlier than he had intended; he had meant to wait for the town to fill, but had forgotten to send instructions to the printer (230–31).

3 *Writings and Speeches of Edmund Burke,* ed. P. J. Marshall (Oxford, 1981), 5:552; further citations from this edition appear parenthetically in the text.

4 *Second Report from the Committee of Secrecy on the Causes of the War in the Carnatic . . . 27 June 1781,* in *Reports of Committees of the House of Commons* 7 (London, 1806), 282. Rumbold claimed that he was merely remitting a fortune he had acquired earlier (413).

5 7 May 1782, *Parliamentary History* 22 (London, 1806): 1419.

6 As P. J. Marshall has pointed out, Fox's motion and Dundas's refusal "were somewhat unreal gestures": the papers desired had already been published and were available to the public (*Writings and Speeches* 5:550 n. 1).

7 24 April 1782, *Parliamentary History* 22:1321.

8 [25] April [1782], *Correspondence* 4:447.

9 C. H. Philips, *The East India Company 1784–1834* (Manchester, 1940; reprint, 1961), 40.

10 *The Historical and the Posthumous Memoirs of Sir Nathaniel William Wraxall,* ed. Henry B. Wheatley (London, 1884), 4:82.

11 Alexander Pope, *Essay on Man,* 1.29–31.

12 James Mill, *History of British India,* 4th ed., ed. H. H. Wilson (London, 1840), 5:36.

13 Percival Spear, *Oxford History of Modern India,* 2d ed. (Delhi, 1978), 100–101.

Swift's Directions to Servants and the Reader as Eavesdropper

JANICE THADDEUS

Because Swift never completed the *Directions to Servants,* commentators have either remarked briefly on its occasional brilliance or ignored it altogether. Generations of students read the extended selection reprinted in W. A. Eddy's edition of the *Satires and Personal Writings* (1932),[1] but the *Directions* has dropped out of current anthologies. This is a special loss, since the *Directions* is a good introduction to Swiftian irony; it appeals to students, who can identify with the footman-persona's position as member of a crafty underclass. The one exception to this general scholarly neglect is Herbert Davis's detailed consideration of the various texts and manuscripts.[2] Much else, then, needs to be said. To begin with, if modern readers are to interpret the *Directions* intelligently, they must first consider three related substrata: the position of servants in the early eighteenth century, Swift's attitudes toward mutual subordination in general and servants in particular, and the literary background.

Servants in aristocratic or simply wealthy households at the beginning of the eighteenth century were cruelly caught in the peculiar set of inconsistencies which characterized society in England. Within the great family—that is, the extended family which included the full household of parents, children, and servants—patriarchal assumptions governed social and monetary relationships. But in all relationships outside the family the assumptions were egalitarian.[3] Within the family matrix masters instilled severe religious values and limited their servants' sexuality. Servants were expected to attend family prayers and in theory at least they were hindered from marrying. Quite simply, servants were supposed to commit all of their emotions and energies to their employers. Reverend Patrick Delany, Swift's successor as Dean of St. Patrick's, defined the situation in one of his *Sermons upon Social Duties and Their Opposite Vices* in 1750: "your time and strength are no longer your own, when you are hired; they are your master's, and to be employed in his service; and consequently you cannot employ them as you please, but as he directs: nor can you misemploy them, or with-hold them from him without manifest fraud and injustice."[4] This view was difficult enough to maintain at any time, and especially difficult in Great Britain, where, as Randolph Trumbach puts it, "outside of the dynamics of individual families, the shape of English society was determined by the fluidity and the egalitarian relations characteristic of kindred structures" (2). Trumbach emphasizes "the impossibility of demanding patriarchal deference from a contractual employee in a commercial and highly politicized society" (137). Increasingly, as patriarchal values began to shift inexorably toward egalitarian values, the position of servants became more and more problematical. Fissures had begun to appear long before Dr. Delany wrote his sermon in 1750.[5] By 1720 the family chaplain had virtually disappeared, and with him the custom of joining together for the disciplinary activity of family prayers. Servants who had been recruited from the minor gentry also gradually vanished, increasing the chasm between master and hired help. As early as 1724 Defoe addressed his *Great Law of Subordination Consider'd* to the question of the "Insolence and Unsufferable behaviour of SERVANTS in England."[6] The situation was unstable. And the inevitable result was discord.

Swift himself treated his servants on patriarchal assumptions, although his relationships with them were tinged with his own unconventionality, as many of his friends and colleagues remarked. Thomas Sheridan tells us that "he had often some whimsical contrivance to punish his servants for any neglect of his orders, so as to make them more attentive for the future,"[7] giving as an example the fact that when a new maidservant was hired, he always told her that his only requirement was that she shut the door both upon entering and leaving a room. When one of his servants asked permission to attend her sister's wedding, Swift was so generous—offering not only the time, but a horse and attendant—that the girl in a flurry forgot to close the door. Swift allowed her to ride half the distance, and then caused her to be called back in order to remind her of what she had forgotten. He then allowed her to proceed to the wedding. Delany tells a similar story, which we also find in Laetitia Pilkington. When Swift's large and pock-marked cook Sweetheart overdid a roast, he peremptorily told her to fix it. Of course she insisted that this was impossible, to which he replied that in the future she should commit only such faults as could be mended. Delany also notes approvingly that Swift carefully hired servants who did not stand too much on their dignity, warning them, for instance, that his groom and his footman took turns polishing his scullion's shoes.[8]

Swift clearly defines the theory behind these actions in his sermon "On Mutual Subjection." His argument is, in essence, that it was excessively inconvenient for people always to insist on their private rights: "Thus, Servants are directed to obey their Masters, Children their Parents, and Wives their Husbands; not from any Respect of Persons in God, but because otherwise there would be nothing but Confusion in private Families."[9] Swift pursues the argument through a political analogy: in the family, as in the state, disobedient acts undermine authority, and authority is essential. A nation serves its prince and vice versa, and "in the like manner, a Servant owes Obedience, and Diligence, and Faithfulness to his master, from whom at the same time he hath a just Demand for Protection, and maintenance, and gentle Treatment" (144). The theory is neat, but the facts were resistant. All readers of the *Journal to Stella* remember Patrick's capers. Swift always had difficulty finding good servants, especially in Ireland. When Saunders McGee died in 1722, Swift lamented his loss, saying he was the only good servant he had ever had. Swift buried him in St. Patrick's, and put up a plaque, though he was advised to omit from the plaque that McGee was a "friend" as well as a servant. To Knightley Chetwode he wrote, "I have lost one of my best friends as well as the best servant in the kingdom."[10] By contrast, his servant Tom was "drunk as a Dog," and had to be turned off; Will was drunk as well, but Swift kept him and often sent him on rather difficult missions.[11] On a larger scale, his steward Gillespy had let his affairs slip so badly in 1716 that Swift had to fire him.[12]

But if Swift was in general dissatisfied with his servants, and treated them like children, he also always maintained as a part of his paternalism an ultimate sense of their human needs, especially that of independence. This concern may in part derive from Swift's own experience. In his fragment of an autobiography, Swift accused his parents of an "indiscreet" marriage, claiming that he had "felt the consequences" of his own resultant poverty "during the greatest part of his life."[13] Since this indiscreet father had died before Swift was born, Swift was dependent on others as servants were, and like a servant he competed by his wits rather than through family influence. Later, he fell in love with the child of the marriage between Sir William Temple's housekeeper and his steward. Esther Johnson's parents were servants.[14] Because of his father's early death and Stella's background— two substantial reasons—Swift could easily identify with those who were in a dependent position, and understand their desire for autonomy. In harsher terms, Samuel Johnson makes a similar point: "He seems to have wasted life in discontent, by the rage of neglected pride and the languishment of unsatisfied desire."[15]

Swift also appears to have respected his servants' minds. Faulkner claimed convincingly in the preface to the 1762 edition of the *Works* that Swift indefatigably revised every poem until he was satisfied that his servants could understand it, "for I write to the Vulgar, more than to the Learned."[16] Swift carefully hedged his esteem—the servants were ignorant. He simply wished to address the individual whom Johnson later called the common reader, and some of those individuals were near to hand. On the other hand, most authors did not consider their servants' opinions worthy of notice, and Swift was exceptional in his desire to honor their free responses.

In keeping with Swift's sense of the need for independence, he managed his servants' funds with care. Delany observes that whenever Swift had them do work beyond the line of duty, he paid them the wages he would have given a hired laborer. When they had saved a year's wages, he paid them interest, "and took singular delight in seeing it accumulated to a sum, that might set them up in the world, in case he died; or they found it advisable to quit his service: which they seldom did."[17] He ultimately offered the position of verger of St. Patrick's Cathedral to the butler who had copied the fourth *Drapier's Letter*, as a reward for his loyalty, but the butler preferred to stay on in his accustomed place.

However, the way in which Swift offered this thirty-pound-per-year position to his servant is important as an indication of the way readers should approach the *Directions*. During the time when the butler might have collected the £300 offered for betraying the author of the fourth letter, he vanished for a night and a day, and when he returned Swift would not believe the story that he had simply been drunk, and insisted that even if he had been merely drunk, such thoughtless behavior was insufferable. He turned the poor man off for the duration of the proclamation. After the legal situation had cooled, according to Deane Swift, the butler returned to "his former station, until one morning the Doctor suddenly commanded him to strip off his livery and put on his own cloaths. The butler stared with surprise, wondering for what crime he had deserved to be turned out of his place, which his master observing, asked him if he had no cloaths of his own to put on? he told him he had. Then go your ways, said the Doctor, and as soon as you have thrown off your livery and dressed yourself, come back to me again." [18] When the butler returned again, Swift offered him the job as verger. Swift had deliberately manipulated his butler into distrust, anger, and fear—and then reversed these emotions. Readers find in the *Directions* similar manipulations of their attitudes toward the persona-footman.

The best template of the odd familiarity combined with contempt which infuses the *Directions* appears in Laetitia Pilkington's *Memoirs*. The following incident occurred during a dinner at Swift's house about four years after he published *Gulliver:*

> He placed himself at the Head of his Table, opposite to a great Pier-Glass, under which was a Marble Side-board, so that he could see in the Glass whatever the Servants did at it. . . . The Dean then turning his Eye on the Looking-glass, espied the Butler opening a Bottle of Ale, helping himself to the first Glass; he very kindly jumbled the rest together, that his Master and Guests might all fare alike. "Ha! Friend," says the Dean, "Sharp's the Word, I find you drank my Ale, for which I stop two Shillings of your Board-Wages [19] this Week, for I scorn to be out-done in any thing, even in cheating." [20]

Swift's butler steals, but then he democratically mixes up the sludge in the bottom of the bottle so that everybody else gets a share of the ale and its bitter dregs. Swift is watching, noting every action, and like the butler, he wants to excel at what he's doing, even though in this case it is to identify with the servant while he cheats his master, and to overcharge him for what he has taken. The similarity to the tone and content of the *Directions* is striking. Swift's footman-persona advises his butler: "If any one desires a Glass of Bottled-Ale; first shake the Bottle, to see whether any thing be in it, then taste it, to know what Liquor it is, that you may not be mistaken; and lastly, wipe the Mouth of the Bottle with the Palm of your Hand, to shew your Cleanliness (17)." The only action which Swift's actual butler omitted was wiping the bottle with his presumably filthy hand. It is the similarity of passages like these which has led readers from the eighteenth century to the twentieth to emphasize that Swift drew his examples from life. Two of these statements will suffice. Johnson said of the *Directions* and *Polite Conversation:* "It is apparent that he must have had the habit of noting whatever he observed; for such a number of particulars could never have been assembled by the power of recollection" (48). Irvin

Ehrenpreis concludes that "one has a disquieting sense that Swift is competing with the servants."[22] In Pilkington's account, Swift is certainly competing with his butler.

There is no doubt that Swift observed his servants closely, even obsessively, and this close observation is reflected in the *Directions.* Evidence of this meticulousness appears, for instance, in the seventeen suggested replacements for broken candlesticks, which include a "Lump of Butter against the Wainscott," a loaf of bread, and a "Powder-horn" (14). This mixture of dirt, stink, and danger registers what Claude Rawson has called "the radical unruliness of things."[23] Swift's hodgepodge lists suggest that life always verges on chaos. Even efficiency and neatness clash. In the instructions to the chambermaid, for instance, Swift's footman advises: "When you sweep your Lady's Room, never stay to pick up foul Smocks, Handkerchiefs, Pinners, Pin-cushions, Tea-spoons, Ribbons, Slippers, or whatever lieth in your Way; but sweep all into a Corner, and then you may take them up in a Lump, and save Time" (55). This pile of things dropped by negligent or lazy people—the mistress, the seamstress, the maid herself—represents the clutter which always threatens. Although the maid saves time by sweeping the whole tangle into a corner, she will lose time when she needs to sort it again later. This unruliness of things is aggravated by unruliness of mind:

> You are sometimes desirous to see a Funeral, a Quarrel, a Man going to be hanged, a Wedding, a Bawd carted, or the like: As they pass by in the Street, you lift up the Sash suddenly; there by Misfortune it sticks: This was no Fault of yours; young Women are curious by Nature; you have no Remedy, but to cut the Cord; and lay the Fault upon the Carpenter, unless no Body saw you, and then you are as innocent as any Servant in the House. (55–56)

The chambermaid's desires, as Swift's footman imagines them, shift as abruptly as newspaper headlines. Her mind is as cluttered as her mistress's floor, and as disobedient as the window sash.

The observation was close and full, but it was also extended. Swift said that he had begun working on the piece as early as 1704, long before he even moved to Ireland, that he had tinkered with it off and on during the remainder of his life, and that he had never finished it; it was published only after his death in 1745.[24] Leslie Stephen concludes simply that in the *Directions* "he has accumulated the results of his experience in one department."[25] The accumulated detail in the *Directions* certainly is realistic, but Swift's own life was not the only source. As I have already mentioned, the literary influences are equally important.

There were three kinds of books dealing with servants being published at this period: complaints, lofty exhortations, and practical advice. The *Directions* reflects all of these species, especially the last. Defoe's *Great Law of Subordination Consider'd*, mentioned above, is typical of the complaint literature. Defoe describes the difficulties inherent in the system of subordination and lists the behavior in servants which he most deplores—a litany of sauciness, swearing, drunkenness, and thievery. His book shows that Swift was not alone in noting servant misbehavior, and even that he was not alone in being close to obsessive about it. And yet Defoe, himself middle class, was extremely sensitive to the problems of the lower classes. What I am trying to stress here is that Swift, although certainly higher in the social scale than Defoe, could complain bitterly—just as bitterly as Defoe did—about the servant problem, and yet be extremely sensitive to servants' difficulties. Defoe's sensitivity produced *Moll Flanders*. Swift's sensitivity took a more ironic form; in the *Directions* he combined his sympathy with complaint.

During the course of Swift's many revisions to the *Directions*, he called it by two other working titles: the "Whole Duty of Servants" and "Advice to Servants."[26] Both of these titles indicate literary connections, the one to lofty exhortation, the other to practical advice. "The Whole Duty of Servants" obviously relates to *The Whole Duty of Man*. Swift had echoed this popular handbook on the title page of the Drapier's letter to the common people of Ireland, which was published in 1724, just before he may have begun transcribing the *Directions*. Allestree's book was "necessary for all families," and Swift's was "very proper to be kept in every family." Deane Swift noticed the similarity of phrase (186). In the case of the *Drapier's Letter*, the purpose was to give the work greater credibility, implying that it had been written by a reader of *The Whole Duty of Man*. In the *Directions* Swift's chosen persona, the footman, represents *The Whole Duty of Man* in reverse. The conduct book's ideal servant remains meek and diligent not only when his master's "eye is over him," but also when he is secure from punishment. Swift's footman drops the plates as soon as he is out of hearing. According to the *Whole Duty* a servant should never waste his master's goods or purloin: "Indeed, this sort of wastefulness is worse than common theft." Swift's footman wastes and purloins to the maximum of his ingeniousness. The perfect servant is also supposed to be meek and patient "under the reproofs of his master," an ideal which Swift's footman obeys in the letter, but hardly in the spirit. Finally, the *Whole Duty* insists that a servant must be constantly diligent, never indulging in "idleness and sloth, nor yet to company-keeping, gaming, or any other disorderly course, which may take him off from his master's business."[27] Swift's footman would have his fellow servants stop in an alehouse at every snug opportunity. Books in the genre of lofty exhortation could be extremely fulsome; Thomas Seaton's *The Conduct of Servants in Great Families*, for instance, implies that servants who are "vigilant, to seize the Opportunities of being Religious more than Others" may after death reach a world where their "Mansion shall be better than his."[28] In Ecclesiastes, source for the title of the *Whole Duty of Man*, fearing God constitutes that duty. God watches and judges everything. In the *Directions*, as in *Gulliver*, Swift simply omits God. In the *Directions* no one is watching. Masters don't watch servants; servants don't watch masters. God has vanished. This is a world where everyone is out for himself.

Swift's book chiefly reflects the third genre: practical advice. Most of the practical handbooks were written by professional writers, anonymously or not, and they were rather sedate. Edward Laurence's *The Duty of a Steward to His Lord* (1727), for instance, in measured language emphasized the seriousness of the job and the time it required.[29] But one popular manual resembles the *Directions* in so many ways that Swift must have deliberately parodied some of its elements, although he may not have been directly parodying this particular book.

This manual is the anonymous *Compleat Servant-Maid, or, the Young Maidens Tutor*, which had reached its sixth edition by 1700. Although limited to women, the *Compleat Servant-Maid* follows an outline similar to Swift's. It begins with "General Directions to Young Maidens" and then moves specifically to individual positions, giving a list of them at the front of the book: "Waiting-Woman, House-Keeper, Chamber-Maid, Cook-Maid, Under-Cook-Maid, Nursery-Maid, Dairy-Maid, Laundry-Maid, House-Maid," and "Scullery-Maid." The moral attitudes of this handbook are, to say the least, confused. In the general directions, for instance, this advice appears:

> If you would endeavour to gain the esteem and reputation of a good Servant, and so procure to yourself [not] only great Wages, but also great gifts and Vales, the love and respect of your Lady or Mistress, and the blessing of God Almighty upon all of your lawful endeavours, you must in the first place, be mindful of your duty to your Creator, according to the advice of Solomon, Eccles. 12.1. *Remember thy Creator in the days of thy Youth.*[30]

The implication here is that wages come first and that God gives them, the sort of connection which disturbed readers of *Pamela*. Anonymous continues in this vein: "Lastly, if you behave your self civilly and be neat, cleanly, and careful to please, you will be cherished & encouraged, not only with good words, but good Gifts." [31] If the subordinate classes please both God and man they will receive lots of extra money. From this attitude it is only a very brief step to the assumption that if you *appear* to be neat and cleanly and careful to please, you will also receive gifts.

Anonymous's language is also notable. It is distinctly lower class, what Carey McIntosh has called Mollspeak. [32] "Be careful," says the *Compleat Servant-Maid*, "that you waste not, or spoil your Ladies or Mistresses goods, neither sit you up junketing a nights, after your Master and Mistress be a-bed" (ca. 6). Daniel Defoe, Richard Allestree, Thomas Seaton, and in his own right Jonathan Swift would not use "junketing a nights," but Swift's footman speaks of "junketing"— three times. Anonymous also suggests that chambermaids avoid trifling, and does so in archaic and colloquial terms, with the addition of a proverb, also typical of Mollspeak: "Be not subject to change, but still remember that a rolling stone never getteth Moss, and as you gain but little money, so if you tumble up and down you will gain but little Credit" (63). [33] One feels that this writer simply is not very intelligent, and one does not feel that way about Swift's footman. The use of a proverb is a borrowable habit, and though Swift's footman rarely indulges in this practice, he does intone one particularly longwinded proverbial reference: "Be not proud in Prosperity: You have heard that Fortune turns on a Wheel; if you have a good Place, you are at the Top of the Wheel" (43). [34] But if proverbs are not Swift's footman's forte, slang is. "Learn all the new-fashion Words, and Oaths, and Songs, and Scraps of Plays that your Memory can hold," he advises (35). He suggests to the cook and butler: "You can junket together at Nights upon your own Prog"; tells the butler to "flirt" the mouth of a bottle into the cistern; refers to a miser as "a covetous Huncks"; and occasionally lapses from slang into mere awkwardness. [35] Especially at the beginning, the footman uses colloquialisms, and his references are vague, as if Swift wanted his chosen mouthpiece to betray his origins by committing faults of the sort which were rejected by those careful with their English. Swift seems to have added this first section last, and part of his purpose may have been to set the character by his language.

Anonymous also includes other details which Swift similarly adopts (although in heightened form). For one thing, unlike most writers, Anonymous is not above suggesting that "your Close-stools and Chamber-pots be daily emptied, and kept clean and sweet" (143), a scatological possibility which Swift characteristically pursues. The strictly devotional handbooks did not provide precise instructions for household tasks, but Anonymous expatiates at length on such domestic details. And Swift does the same.

Although the women in Anonymous's book like to junket and tumble up and down, they are on the whole uninventive in their misbehavior. The nurserymaid, for instance, is presumed ignorant enough to need the following earnest advice concerning the children in her charge:

> You must also be extraordinarily careful & vigilant, that they get not any falls, through your neglect, for by such falls, many (the cause at first being unperceivable) have grown irrecoverably lame or crooked. Therefore if any such thing should happen be sure you conceal it not, but acquaint your Lord or Lady, Master or Mistress thereof, with all convenient speed, that so [sic] means may be used for their Child's recovery before it be too late. (104–5)

Swift's advice to his nurserymaid is more likely to protect the feckless servant from punishment:

> If you happen to let the Child fall, and lame it, be sure never confess it; and, if it dies, all is safe. (64)

Swift has adopted the genre of practical advice, and while he imitates the style he simultaneously subverts the content.

He also adds a number of new elements. The most obvious of these, and the most important, is his persona, the ex-footman who speaks this Mollspeak, and who is writing this book in order to address his ex–partners in service. If we go back to Laetitia Pilkington, and recombine the elements slightly, we have the situation in the *Directions*. Swift and the servant have collapsed uneasily into one voice, and that voice is ostensibly talking to the servant-audience. The reader is now Pilkington, the observer or eavesdropper. Although the most fascinating quality of this book is the interplay between the ostensible reader and the eavesdropper, readers have always tended to overlook that interplay, emphasizing one audience or the other. When Dodsley first printed the *Directions* in London, he printed it straight, without a preface.[36] Dodsley himself was a former footman, writer of three poems addressed to his fellows in service. In 1720, Dodsley had defined the need for obedience and subordination in these severe terms:

> Purchas'd by annual Wages, Cloaths, and Meat
> Their is our Time, our Hands, our Head, our Feet.[37]

Dodsley suggests that those who cannot accept these terms should simply leave. For Dodsley, then, it must have seemed perfectly natural that the *Directions* was aimed chiefly at the servants themselves. Other readers have made this assumption. J. Jean Hecht in his book on servants (1956) says, "The diverting ironies of Jonathan Swift's *Directions for Servants* [sic] were intended to shame the class out of its misconduct" (87). Swift's Dublin publisher George Faulkner, on the other hand, was aiming toward an Irish public. As Swift had frequently complained, Irish servants could not read, so they were not a likely audience. Faulkner clearly stated in his preface that "the Author's Design was to expose the Villanies and Frauds of Servants to their Masters and Mistresses" (5). Swift himself had written to Faulkner in 1739 saying that the *Directions* was "very useful, as well as humorous,"[38] a characteristically ambiguous phrase. At any rate, when one turns to the work itself, recognizing the existence of this double audience helps us to read it.[39]

So far, I have drawn eclectically from Swift's treatise to illustrate its language and its attitudes. To analyze the double audience, I will concentrate in detail on one passage where Swift's footman directs his reader-footman about the complications involved in making coffee:

> If you are ordered to make Coffee for the Ladies after Dinner, and the Pot happens to boil over, while you are running up for a Spoon to stir it, or are thinking of something else, or struggling with the Chamber-maid for a Kiss, wipe the Sides of the Pot clean with a Dishclout, carry up your Coffee boldly, and when your Lady finds it too weak, and examines you whether it hath not run over, deny the Fact absolutely, swear you put in more Coffee than ordinary, that you never stirred an Inch from it, that you strove to make it better than usual, because your Mistress had Ladies with her, that the Servants in the Kitchen will justify what you say: Upon this, you will find that the other Ladies will pronounce your Coffee to be very good, and your Mistress will confess that her Mouth is out of Taste, and she will for the future suspect herself, and be more cautious in finding Fault. This I would have you do from a Principle of Conscience, for Coffee is very unwholesome; and out of Affection to your Lady, you ought to give it her as weak as possible: And upon this Argument, when you have a Mind to treat any of the Maids with a Dish of fresh Coffee, you may, and ought to subtract a third Part of the Powder, on account of your Lady's Health, and getting her Maids Good-will. (39–40)

We must consider this excerpt from four points of view: the ostensible reader, or reader-as-servant; the eavesdropper, or reader-as-master (or mistress); the author-as-footman; and the author-as-Swift. The reader-as-servant sees that making coffee is a delicate matter, if not a difficult job. It requires care and attention, even alacrity. The household does not appreciate this fact, and keeps its spoons in an inconvenient place, forcing a servant to hop here and there, exhausting himself in the process. But his job is so dull and the enforced passivity is such ("you are ordered") that (to switch to Swift's second person) you are always thinking of something else and inevitably making a mess of things. You are not allowed to get married, so you are rather sex-starved, and you need affection, so you grab the chambermaid at every lucky opportunity. In spite of these and similar problems, you must always put the best face possible on all of your actions to avoid being whipped or losing your job altogether. Therefore, you should never be merely passive; instead, you should always be as manipulative as possible. And your language, dense with verbs and parallel clauses, strengthens this manipulative tactic. You are running, thinking, struggling; you wipe, carry, deny, swear. You must barrel through, making excuses, inventing lies, using whatever methods you can muster to maintain your position with those who have power over you. Remember that in front of company your mistress will always be embarrassed to admit that you are an inadequate servant and will hesitate to chastise you, and that you can always appeal to the company as witnesses. Lie, then, and lie boldly.

In Swift's holograph manuscript for the directions to the butler, the cook, and the footman, he noted in the margin, "find a reason." [40] And throughout the manuscript the reasons are often added as an afterthought, though they provide much of the humor. Here, with the fulsome tone of the tracts and the disingenuousness of the books of advice, the footman-reader receives the message that he is to invoke a "Principle of Conscience," in this case a crocodile concern for his lady's health (but not her maid's health). The mock assumption is that he cares, has "affection" for his lady, since he is part of the family (mentioned frequently elsewhere, though not in this particular paragraph), but that he is in an extremely ticklish position, and to survive must always look to his advantage.

On the other hand, this piece would rouse his mistress to indignation and a passel of clichés: servants are always chasing one another's tails, they lie like dogs, they'll steal you blind. "God sends Meat, but the Devil sends Cooks." Above all, they are simply incompetent. The deuce take them. "You can't make a Silk Purse out of a Sow's Ear." [41] Her response would be a mixture of fear, indignation, and despair.

Elsewhere in the book, she might be forced to recognize that though servants may be knaves, she is a fool—or worse. [42] The footman advises that his fellow-footmen should "Never wear socks," while serving meals, because "as most Ladies like the Smell of young Mens Toes" (and Swift had *added* "of young Mens Toes"), "so it is a sovereign Remedy against the Vapours" (41). How to reply to this? In addition, the mistresses in this book are "so proud and lazy, that they will not be at the Pains of stepping into the Garden to pluck a Rose, but keep an odious Implement sometimes in the Bed-chamber itself" (60). Swift is emphasizing that disposing of other people's excrement is demeaning, but why not include the master as well as the mistress? Swift is vexing the reader, sowing discord more often than he calms it.

Swift-as-author provides no solution. If, as he wrote to Faulkner, this piece is to be "very useful," how is it so? Swift himself, as Laetitia Pilkington told us, watched his servants incessantly, identified with them, outdid them even in cheating, and embarrassed his guests. Pilkington adds, "Dinner at last was over to my great Joy; for now I had Hope of a more agreeable Entertainment than what the squabbling with the Servants had afforded us" (56). Swift's footman's mistress—and most people—would hesitate to put their guests in this position. It is not a helpful method of dealing with the problem.

In this particular passage Swift confounds the footman-as-author with his footman-audience. Elsewhere in the *Directions* the footman's true opinions of his job (and possibly Swift's more detached judgment) more forcefully appear. Any self-respecting human being is looking to escape servitude: "To grow old in the Office of a Footman, is the highest of all Indignities" (44); and, in a sadder tone, "poor Servants have so few Opportunities to be happy, that they ought not to lose any" (41). A servant has the right to snatch happiness: his lot is so often bleak. This is the message which Swift's footman ultimately delivers to his fellow servants, a message certainly different from Faulkner's claims about exposing villainies, and one which will surely not console the eavesdropper, who wants to know how to find a good cook, and how to live with her once she's been found.

To sum up more clearly the dual attitude which we as readers must derive from the *Directions*, I quote Laetitia Pilkington on Swift's method of entertaining guests:

> The Dean set about making the Coffee; but the Fire scorching his Hand, he called to me to reach him his Glove, and changing the Coffee-pot to his Left-hand, held out his Right one, ordered me to put the Glove on it, which accordingly I did; when taking up Part of his Gown to fan himself with, and acting in Character of a prudish Lady, he said, "Well, I do not know what to think; Women may be honest that do such Things, but for my Part, I never could bear to touch any Man's Flesh—except my Husband's, whom perhaps," says he, "she wished at the Devil."

"Mr. P——n," says he "you would not tell me your Wife's Faults; but I have found her out to be a d——ned, insolent, proud, unmannerly Slut." I looked confounded, not knowing what Offence I had committed.—Says Mr. P——n, "Ay, Sir, I must confess she is a little saucy to me sometimes, but—what has she done now?" "Done! why nothing, but sat there quietly, and never once offered to interrupt me in making the Coffee whereas had I had a Lady of modern good Breeding here, she would have struggled with me for the Coffee-pot till she had made me scald myself and her, and made me throw the Coffee in the Fire; or perhaps at her Head, rather than permit me to take so much trouble for her."

This raised my Spirits, and as I found the Dean always prefaced a Compliment with an Affront, I never afterwards was startled at the latter (as too many have been, not entering into his peculiarly ironical Strain) but was modestly contented with the former, which was more than I deserved, and which the Surprize rendered doubly pleasing. (58–60)

In this scene, Swift himself is making the coffee, and doing a fine job of it, and Pilkington is being good enough not to interfere. But Swift is making this coffee for his friends, not his betters, out of conviviality, not necessity. He accepted and supported the hierarchical society of the early 1700s, liked to have people know their place, but realized that *forcing* them to keep that place diminished their humanity. In *Gulliver,* he solved this problem by creating a genetically inferior class to perform the duties of servitude. The yahoos were slaves, but the sorrel nag was by his genetic makeup a servant. In England, fortunately or unfortunately, these distinctions were not so clear. At one point in the manuscript version of the *Directions* Swift clearly called his piece "Directions to Poor Servants."[43] Whether he meant poverty-stricken, unfortunate, or even badly trained, the implication is that Swift felt sorry for the objects of his satire. Caught between the throes of a great family about to die and an egalitarian family about to be born, Swift prefaced his affront by a compliment. The reader-as-eavesdropper must hear the compliment as well as the affront.

NOTES

1 *Satires and Personal Writings by Jonathan Swift,* ed. W. A. Eddy (London: Oxford Univ. Press, 1932), 229–50.

2 This essay prefaces the *Directions to Servants and Miscellaneous Pieces 1733–1742* in *The Prose Works of Jonathan Swift,* ed. Herbert Davis (Oxford: Basil Blackwell, 1973) 13:vii–xxiii. Whenever clear, page citations to this and

other works will appear in parentheses in the text. Carol Houlihan Flynn's work-in-progress "Physical Economy: the Body Employed by Swift and Defoe" contains a fascinating section on the *Directions,* arguing that "the calculated lunacy of Swift's *Directions* emphasizes the primacy of matter."

3 The clearest and most detailed discussion of these competing attitudes as they apply in family life can be found in Randolph Trumbach, *The Rise of the Egalitarian Family* (New York: Academic Press, 1978). Cissie Fairchilds in *Domestic Enemies: Servants and Their Masters in Old Regime France* (Baltimore: Johns Hopkins Univ. Press, 1984) and Sarah C. Maza in *Servants and Masters in Eighteenth-Century France: The Uses of Loyalty* (Princeton: Princeton Univ. Press, 1983) describe a similar ambiguity.

4 In J. Jean Hecht, *The Domestic Servant Class in Eighteenth-Century England* (London: Routledge, 1956), 72.

5 Ann Kussmaul (*Servants in Husbandry in Early Modern England* [Cambridge, England: Cambridge Univ. Press, 1981]) points out that as early as the end of the seventeenth century farmers redesigned their houses to provide totally separate quarters for servants—separate entrances, separate stairs, etc. Only the kitchen was common ground. By 1815 farm workers were mostly hired day laborers (177). Like domestics, the farm laborers were passing through a period of inconsistency. Kussmaul writes, "Service in husbandry is an institution fraught with ambiguity. Servants were hired workers and family members" (69).

6 Daniel Defoe, *The Great Law of Subordination Consider'd* (London, 1724), title page.

7 Thomas Sheridan, *The Life of the Rev. Dr. Jonathan Swift,* 2d ed. (London, 1787), 380.

8 Patrick Delany, *Observations upon Lord Orrery's Remarks on the Life and Writings of Dr. Jonathan Swift* (London, 1754), 187, 214.

9 Swift, *Irish Tracts 1720–1723 and Sermons,* vol. 12 of *Prose Works* (Oxford: Basil Blackwell, 1948), 145.

10 Irvin Ehrenpreis, *Swift, the Man, His Works, and the Age* (Cambridge, Mass.: Harvard Univ. Press, 1962–83), 3:323.

11 *The Correspondence of Jonathan Swift,* ed. Harold Williams (Oxford: Clarendon Press, 1963–65), 2:153.

12 Swift, *Correspondence* 2:229–31, passim.

13 Ehrenpreis, *Swift* 1:28.

14 John, Earl of Orrery, in his *Remarks on the Life and Writings of Dr. Jonathan Swift* (London, 1752), claims that Stella's low birth was the principle reason Swift was so reluctant to marry her (24); however, Orrery objects to the *Directions* on the grounds that Swift was bothering to satirize "the lower classes of mankind," who should be allowed to "pass on unnoticed" (284), so that it is possible that Orrery was appealing to his own prejudices. Orrery also noted vividly that Swift liked to lodge "at night in houses where he found written over the door *Lodgings for a penny.* He delighted in scenes of low life" (34).

15 Samuel Johnson, *Lives of the English Poets*, ed. George Birkbeck Hill (Oxford: Clarendon Press, 1905), 3:61.

16 *The Poems of Jonathan Swift*, 2d ed., ed. Harold Williams (Oxford: Clarendon Press, 1958), 1:xxiv n. 2.

17 Delany, 186.

18 Deane Swift, *An Essay upon the Life, Writings, and Character of Dr. Jonathan Swift* (London, 1755), 191.

19 "Board-Wages" were an allowance given for obtaining food outside the household in lieu of actual board. The custom was widespread and presumably prevented pilfering. In the *Directions* everyone is rushing to filch food, both to eat and to barter with.

20 *Memoirs of Mrs. Letitia Pilkington* (Dublin, 1748), 1:54–56.

21 Ehrenpreis, *Swift* 3:835.

22 Claude J. Rawson, *Gulliver and the Gentle Reader* (London: Routledge, 1973), 99.

23 Swift, *Prose Works* 13:xxii.

24 Leslie Stephen, *Swift* (London: Macmillan, 1882), 202.

25 L. J. H. Bradley, in a letter to the *Times Literary Supplement* (11 February 1926), 99, mentions a religious tract called *Advice to Servants* (London, 1738), whose title Swift might have been echoing when in 1738 Swift himself referred to his MS as "Advice to Servants" in a letter to Faulkner (*Correspondence* 5:121). Bradley was unable to locate a copy of this tract, and I have not found it either. The title "The Whole Duty of Servants" appears in a letter to Gay and the Duchess of Queensberry (28 August 1731), *Correspondence* 3:493.

26 Richard Allestree, *The Whole Duty of Man* (London, 1733), 222–24.

27 Thomas Seaton, *The Conduct of Servants in Great Families* (London, 1720), 122.

28 See Hecht, *Domestic Servant Class*, 39.

29 *The Compleat Servant-Maid, or, the Young Maidens Tutor*, 6th ed. with additions (London, 1700), A5. This book was first published in 1677. Preceding it by two years was *The Gentlewoman's Companion* (presumably by Hannah Woolley, although this attribution is now being questioned), which includes much the same advice, and at times in the same words. It seems that Anonymous plagiarized Woolley, adding extra and much more crass and uneducated observations.

30 Ibid., ca. 6; the copy I read was imperfect, and the pagination was unclear.

31 Carey McIntosh, *Common and Courtly Language: The Stylistics of Social Class in Eighteenth-Century British Literature* (Philadelphia: Univ. of Pennsylvania Press, 1986), passim.

32 In [Hannah Woolley], *The Gentlewoman's Companion*, 3rd ed. (London, 1682), this passage reads: "Be not subject to change, *For a rouling Stone gathers no Moss;* and as you will gain but little *Money,* so if you ramble up and down you will lose your *credit*" (291).

33 Davis notes that this passage appears in no MSS and conjectures that it may have been found among the "scattered Papers" Faulkner mentions in his preface (xix). Davis notes further that there is a "perplexing change of

tone" (xix) in the footman's section, which seems to alternate between minute details and paragraphs warning about the wicked ways of the world. Davis's observation supports my argument that the *Directions* had literary as well as factual sources.

34 Swift, *Prose Works*, 13:27, 25, 50, 27.

35 Faulkner wrote to the London printer, W. Bowyer, on 1 October 1745 that he would like some help: "As you are famous for writing prefaces, pray help me to one for Advice to Servants," but the London edition appeared without a preface, as noted, and most scholars conclude that Faulkner had to write his own. *Prose Works* 13:x, and n. 2.

36 In Hecht, *Domestic Servant Class*, 73.

37 Swift, *Correspondence* 5:172.

38 Swift did write (or at any rate Dean Swift and Faulkner respectively published) straightforward though fragmentary pieces called "Laws for the Dean's Servants" and "The Duty of Servants at Inns." The "Laws," dated 1733, threaten to dock servants for drunkenness, sneaking out without permission, and other misdemeanors. The servant at an inn has to check *everything;* he must even taste the ale and check to be sure that there are no cats under the bed. He must also be tour-master, aware if there is "any Thing worth seeing" (Swift, *Prose Works* 13:163–65). The references to servants in Swift's poems are surprisingly gentle, if not uniformly so. *The Humble Petition of Frances Harris* (1701), telling how she lost her life savings and how she wishes the parson to take up a collection for her, evokes her childishness, but kindly. Written in Mrs. Harris's voice, this poem, like the *Directions*, reflects some of a servant's linguistic habits (Swift, *Poems* 1:68–73). When "Desponding Phillis" in *The Progress of Love* (1719) foolishly marries her butler, the two of them deteriorate comically as well as rapidly, but they manage at least to make a living: "They keep at Stains the old blue Boar, / Are Cat and Dog, and Rogue and Whore," (1:222, 225). The most appealing sexual moment in all of Swift's works takes place in *A Description of the Morning*, where Betty, who had slept with her master, "softly stole to discompose her own" bed in order to mask that fact (1:124). Betty the servant is deft and attractive—no glass eye, no stinking ooze.

39 Rothschild MS 2275, The Wren Library, Cambridge, England; Swift, *Prose Works* 13:18, 211. There is a more extensive copy made by an amanuensis, with Swift's corrections, in the Forster Collection at the Victoria and Albert Museum. Davis's edition gives all the variant readings.

40 Swift, *A Compleat Collection of Genteel and Ingenious Conversation, etc.*, vol. 4 of *Prose Works*, 182, 190.

41 See Peter Steele: "all the canonical deception of *Directions to Servants* depends upon a readiness in the masters to be practised upon equivalent to the readiness of the servants to practise. The pretender in Swift is almost always a knave, but he is parasite to a host of fools." *Jonathan Swift: Preacher and Jester* (Oxford: Clarendon Press, 1978), 94.

42 Rothschild MS, title page; Swift, *Prose Works* 13:17, 211.

Richard Bentley and John Dunton:
Brothers under the Skin

ROBERT ADAMS DAY

Many readers have been struck by the extraordinary capaciousness of the satirical net that Swift casts in *A Tale of a Tub;* in the sections concerning the abuses of learning, for instance, where he is not afraid to name names, the victims of his satire range from the late laureate to Tom D'Urfey (though to be sure Dryden was dead by 1704, and a Catholic to boot). But clearly Swift is not concerned to spare either eagles or tomtits, or—to preserve the metaphor of a net and include Hobbes in our discourse—leviathans or minnows.

One ill-assorted pair of Swift's victims here—certainly a leviathan and a minnow—have probably never been considered together before; nor, one would think, is there any reason except sheer love of paradox to mention Richard Bentley, D.D., and John Dunton in the same breath. On the one hand the Master of Trinity, the Newtonian divine chosen to inaugurate the celebrated Boyle Lectures against atheism, considered by many to be the foremost classical scholar of his age, and on the other an eccentric (or mad) little self-educated bookseller, operating out of the Black Raven in the Poultry, equally notable for his shameless self-advertising and his participation in some rather shady dealings concerning the promotion of popular works of piety: what could these two have in common?

One answer will immediately occur to many readers: Swift had a violent personal grudge against both. It is common knowledge that he had made a fool of himself with his "Ode to the Athenian Society" before discovering that that august body consisted principally of John

Dunton; he and Sir William Temple had engaged in acrimonious and abortive negotiations with Dunton over a scheme to publish a history of England; and he had seen his admired patron ignominiously flattened by Bentley in the controversy over the authenticity of the epistles of Phalaris. But a heavily-documented recent study has persuasively argued that Swift was far more objective about Temple, far less a slavishly admiring partisan, than we had thought; and as for the Phalaris controversy, the consensus at the time and for many years later was in fact that Temple, the Honorable Charles Boyle, and the Christ Church wits had scored a resounding victory over the oafish pedant Bentley.[1] It is more to Swift's credit to assume that something more significant than personal animosity led him to bestow his satirical attentions on Bentley and Dunton. I want to argue here that Swift had perceived, in certain writings both of which we can be sure he knew, a fundamental and identical threat to good letters and polite learning as he understood them. I refer to Bentley's *Dissertation on Phalaris* (1697 and 1699) and Dunton's *A Voyage Round the World* (1691).

Very few modern scholars have read either of these. But they deserve more attention than they have received for many reasons, and notably for our purpose because, however disparate their subject matter, they both shrilly proclaim the arrival on the scene of a new kind of writer—Typographic Man, in full bloom—a new attitude toward audience, self, and subject matter, which I have chosen to call Eyethink, and a new style, which, borrowing a term from the Russian Formalist critics, I shall call *skaz*.

To detect and articulate these literary phenomena, which I am quite sure that Swift perceived only vaguely and intuitively, but with no less alarm for all that, we need to adopt a view of literary history which has only recently been brought to our attention, notably by Walter J. Ong: the view that the gradual replacement in the West of oral and preliterate culture by writing and then by typography has exerted a steady and powerful, but only very gradual, influence on the development of discourse—the history of utterance, so to say, from Homer to Wordsworth to Allen Ginsberg.[2] Space does not permit an elaborate exposition of this theory, but we must note at least that in a preliterate society discourse, in order to be preserved, must above all be *memorable*—qualifying this requirement with the observation, contrary to one's first impression, that "memorability" need not have anything whatever to do with weightiness of content—and therefore such discourse must be narrative, not analytical or expository, in arrangement, must be filled with formulas, must be repetitious, heavily patterned in thought and sound, and so on. These characteristics do not disappear with the advent of writing (which is at first thought of merely as a means of preserving discourse, *not* as a mode of composition); when writing permits them to be classified and codified they become rhetoric, formally taught and learned. But rhetoric, at least until Hugh Blair and Adam Smith, is never considered a mere ornament, but continues to be seen as a primary means and indeed a necessity of composition. However, with the increasing influence of typographic culture, classical education, based on extensive memorization and on rhetoric, begins to wither away, and so do the community-dictated values and traditional commonplaces (or *topoi*) of rhetorical discourse.

It is not much of an exaggeration to say that in pre-Commonwealth England, with the number of printers limited by the Stationers' Company and censorship an ever-present threat, virtually *any* discourse was necessarily thought of as an oration—what oft was thought but ne'er so well expressed.[3] The Commonwealth, with its torrent of pamphlet literature and newsletters of every conceivable complexion, and its myriad authors of every persuasion and every degree of education from bare literacy to the doctorate, changed all that. And though the Restoration naturally brought a renewal of government control of discourse, with the activities of Sir Roger L'Estrange and other licensers of the press, it was too late to turn the tide. One need only compare the size of Wing's short-title catalogue with that of Pollard and Redgrave's to see what had happened.

The oration in every respect is governed by auditory values and the presence, real or imagined, of a very responsive audience, to be pleased and swayed, sometimes to retort. But with printing easy and cheap (and virtually unrestrained as to content), several new conditions arise. The "audience" is no longer a collective felt presence, hearing; it consists of remote, vaguely conceived individuals, seeing: *patres conscripti* metamorphosed into *dear Reader*. They can re-read (a vitally important factor if the discourse is nonmemorable) but they cannot respond; and therefore a new kind of author-reader intimacy is generated. The author need not woo the collective audience with the devices of the classical *exordium*, nor yet carefully prepare his transitions; he can present his unmediated self instantly, just as it is, and "buttonhole" the individual reader with direct address. The reader can react only by throwing the book aside or by submitting, ruefully or not, to a potentially or actually offensive intimacy. The existence, increasingly felt if not understood, of this new sort of audience in turn creates a new author, who operates by Eyethink, not Earthink, and who writes *skaz*. That is, either innocent of a classical, rhetorical, Latinate training, as with Dunton, or choosing to forget it for the time being, as with Bentley, he practises what we in the twentieth century take so much for granted and value so highly, but which was genuinely new and shocking in 1700—authentically subjective self-expression, unmediated by the elaborate strategies of rhetoric.[4] He jots down whatever comes into his head, as fast as he can write (the tape recorder unhappily being as yet unknown) and hurries it off to be printed. The result is that the idiosyncratic individuality of the writer, with his whims (Dunton called them maggots) and blunders and characteristic tricks of speech, is directly conveyed to the reader, and we have something new in discourse. It is naive, unadorned, idiomatic speech, an idiolect in fact, transferred to paper, which is what the Russian Formalists meant by the term *skaz;*[5] it is not the voice of the orator, nor yet the artful persona of the classical rhetorician pretending to be naive or briefly impersonating his stupid opponent. It is the genuine, unmediated personality of the real person writing— what Michael Wigglesworth across the Atlantic at Harvard was calling "a bare and naked stile that hath never a ragg of eloquence to its back, made up wholly of common and road-way expressions like ordinary table-talk," and what Sir Philip Sidney in his *Defence* had called "words as they fall chanceably from the tongue."[6] But such discourse has yet another, and new, dimension.

Thinking for the eye, or Eyethink, is also "I-think" in the sense of egomania, or so Bentley's and Dunton's contemporaries thought; several critics remarked that Dr. Bentley's only subject in *Phalaris* was really himself,[7] and Dunton repeatedly boasted that his own personality was his sole and darling theme. From the point of view of orality theory, the wheel has come full circle: the only kind of discourse that could be preserved and transmitted through time in preliterate eras— memorable utterance—is being challenged and obliterated by thoroughly forgettable discourse—preserved purely by the means of cheap paper—the egotistical babble of just anyone turned author, who, as Dryden remarked, faggots his notions as they fall.[8]

What this regained paradise of undisciplined utterance might contain is best shown by example.

> . . . and then my Father (who had something too of the *Ramble* in his Brain, you may see by this, as well as his Son, whence you may take Notice, I'm no degenerate Branch, nor does Evander ramble from his virtuous progenitors, tho' in good earnest he almost does from his Sence, pray Reader put me right again, whereabouts was I

before I stept over the unconscionable Essex stile of this over-grown bursten-gutted Parenthesis—O—then my Father went a-rambling, to shew his Son the way. . . . [9]

Here's your justness of thought! . . . At this rate our friend Homer (as poor and blind as some have thought him) was the ablest *Jack of all trades* that ever was in nature. Hippias the Elean . . . was an *idiot evangelist* to him. . . . Take my word for it, poor Homer, in those circumstances and early times, had never such aspiring thoughts. He wrote a sequel of songs and rhapsodies, to be sung by himself for small earnings and good cheer, at festivals and other days of merriment; the *Ilias* he made for the men, and the *Odyssey* for the other sex. [10]

But, how to lug it in,—ay, there's all the craft,—what's a Man the better for having—*two Hogsheads at the Door;* For look ye now, and do but consider my case,—I could cry I'm so pull'd and tormented—to talk of Life; and all those pretty things that I intended,—how I *lookt abroad* when I first saw the Light, found the Bubby, and all that, (*but first the Brandy-bottle*). . . ." [11]

But what a dutiful child had mother *Clito* the herb-woman! For her sake alone her son Euripides could wish to be rich, to buy her oil to her salads. But what had the old gentleman the father done, that he wishes nothing for *his* sake? 'Tis a fine piece of conduct that our Sophist has shewn. He had read something of our poet's mother, for she was famous in old comedy for her lettuce and cabbage. . . . [12]

—Ha, I have found the way,—I have it—I won't take *Ten Pound for my Thought;* mark—ye me, Mr. Reader, I'll *suppose* I was born alive— for you know a man may *suppose* what he will;—I may *suppose* myself a Conjurer, or you a Rhinoceros. . . . [13]

The academic reader of twentieth-century sensibility may feel that this textual equivalent of a club sandwich, composed of alternating excerpts from Bentley's critical writings and Dunton's autobiography, constitutes improperly loaded evidence. But rapid juxtaposition is the most effective means of showing how, despite the radical disparity of their subject matter, Bentley and Dunton were subverting by the same means and for the same reason the essential decorums of prose as Swift, and such of his contemporaries as were champions of polite learning, saw them. The tone of the two writers, their voices, are essentially the same. The reader may also suspect that extreme and unrepresentative passages have been deliberately chosen to give unfair emphasis and make a point, if only because he supposes that no one, not even Typographic Man, could go on in this way for scores of pages. This last notion is partly true; Dunton's exuberance falls off somewhat in the second and third volumes as he approaches man's estate, and Bentley's exasperation falters, sometimes for pages at a time, especially as he piles up evidence. But the reader may be assured that all of Bentley's polemics abound in such passages (he was censured for the same sort of thing even in his Latin *Epistola ad Millium* of 1691, often considered the *fons et origo* of modern classical scholarship), [14] and Dunton's *Voyage*, at least, is full of tonal surprises throughout.

But what are the salient, subversive, and new characteristics of late seventeenth-century *skaz*? First, there is clearly no decorum of subject, no attempt to regulate the stylistic level in accordance with the generally accepted dignity of the topic, a matter of such importance that Erich Auerbach in *Mimesis* could build a history of Western literature around its decline. The same breezy, offhand manner, with uniformly low diction, will serve for all; and, conformably, no polite or ingratiating concessions to the social rank, education, or possible predilections of the audience are made (a point not lost on Bentley's early critics, at least). [15] The writer ("Here's your justness of thought"; "I could cry I'm so pull'd and tormented") clearly pictures himself as located literally inches away from the reader, rather than upon a rostrum, and the same miniaturization of the communicative scene is evident in his uniform preoccupation with trivia and particularities. The stream of discourse is jerky, if so mild a word will do; if the text were a musical score, legato superscripts and slur lines would be totally absent. And thus it is *talk*, or "table-talk," not composition. Above all, the emphasis is on the writer and on his situation and mood at the moment of writing (including his difficulties in saying what he means), that is, as the writer's thought is seen to veer and evolve, on the *production* of discourse rather than on the finished product. Moreover, it seems to go without saying that the audience will be equally absorbed in all this clutter, will sympathetically care about what is going on—or so the writer assumes. [16]

Most of these characteristics, furthermore, were waspishly noted in passing by the Christ Church wits in their attacks upon Bentley; but we may be absolved of arrogance if at a distance of nearly three centuries we say that they did not know what to make of them. [17] They were desirous above all of defending the Hon. Charles Boyle and obliterating Dr. Richard Bentley as individuals, and we can hardly expect them to have been on the lookout for the ominous heat-lightning of an impending revolution in discourse. They concentrated on depicting Bentley as a lumpish and unpolished pedant in every possible aspect both of character and scholarship, and in trying to pick holes in his logic and his Greek. Not so Swift.

When Swift complained of the torrent of trash which the press groaned under, when he scorned "singularity," when he wrote of the extreme delicacy and evanescence of Modern wit, which is witty only when fasting, or of a summer's morning, or at Hyde-Park-Corner, when he impersonated the blundering, digressive, manic utterance of the Hack, unsparing of the fastidious reader, he was attacking the very phenomena that I have described and illustrated; and a very instructive reading of the whole text of *A Tale of a Tub* can be based upon that fact. But space does not permit even a fragment of such a reading, though I hope in future to offer one. I shall merely remark at present that one scholar has already made a good case for Dunton's *Voyage round the World* as an important source for the *Tale*, while another has argued that the voice of the Hack is chiefly the voice of Bentley.[18]

But before I go on to consider the anti-rhetorical background of these paradoxical brothers-under-the-skin, and proceed to justify my contention that they were in fact brothers-in-*skazerei* and that Swift saw this, it is only fair to answer two objections that may very reasonably be made: first, that what I call *skaz* or Eyethink-prose is nothing more than conventional *sermo humilis,* low style, or rhetorical impersonation, like the hectoring passages in the Martin Marprelate tracts, Milton's pamphlets, or Marvell's *Rehearsal Transpros'd* (which, incidentally, Swift admired very much);[19] and second, that by 1700 the great transformation in seventeenth-century prose style chronicled by Morris Croll and R. F. Jones had produced an easy familiar style in which virtually everyone, including Swift, Bentley, and Dunton, would naturally and habitually write for most purposes. Fortunately, no less an authority than Ronald Paulson, comparing passages of what he calls Restoration satire by Marvell and Bentley, concludes as I do that Marvell's low style is purely adroit rhetorical strategy, while Bentley's exemplifies clumsy but genuine and sincere indignation;[20] as for the widespread familiar style of the reigns of William, Anne, and the first Georges, Paul Arakelian has recently demonstrated with abundance of statistical analysis that the celebrated Croll-Jones transformation did not in fact occur quite as those historians of prose style said it had.[21] Sentences did not get shorter, nor syntax notably less complex. What did happen was that the standard working vocabulary was radically contracted, approaching the austerity of Racine and forcing a Racinian dexterity in the selection and placement of the limited verbal resources (Swift's "proper words in proper places"), while figurative

language shrank essentially to the apologetically-introduced and explained simile and the well-chosen epithet. In short, what David
Lodge has pictured in literary history as the pendulum swing from
metaphoric to metonymic style had taken place.[22] Yet rhetorical can-
ons remained unmoved.

But the style of Bentley and Dunton, at least in the two works I have
mentioned and certainly in others, is very different from the "easy"
style of Addison or Swift. Sentences, and members of the few longer
sentences, are apt to be very short. Connectives are few and simple,
parataxis predominates, and subject matter, point of view, and tone
are prone to veer wildly from phrase to phrase. Moreover, both pieces,
measured against the norms of the oration, seem to have no structure
at all.[23] Dunton's, announcing itself as a rambling autobiography, resembles nothing so much as *Tristram Shandy* (and indeed the resemblance is so close, and appears in so many and such varied aspects,
that a close comparison of the two will convince the reader that the
Voyage is either a most important though unacknowledged source for
Tristram or a case of anticipation truly phenomenal).[24] Bentley begins
his *Dissertation* quite without introduction,[25] and although he does
not let go of a point until he has finished worrying it, the *Dissertation*
reminds one forcibly of a scholar's card file that has been emptied on
the floor and hastily transcribed without resorting.

We have evidence, furthermore, of the circumstances of both works'
composition which, had he known rather than merely suspected it,
would have been grist for Swift's satirical mill. Bentley claims that he
dashed the *Dissertation* off in the odd moments of six weeks, sending
the sheets to the printer unrevised as each was finished, though this
was not his champion performance; he claimed to have drawn up his
proposals for a new edition of the Greek Testament "in haste in one
evening by candle-light, and printed the next day from the first and
sole draught (which haste likewise hindered [me] from revising the
sheet)".[26] And Dunton, we must remember, was his own printer, so
that his effusions did not have to undergo the strictures of a stuffy
corrector of the press, but came virgin to the reader's eye.[27]

A more remote cause of the two men's paradoxical brotherhood in
Eyethink needs also to be mentioned. Both in a curious way had in
fact bypassed a classical education. Dunton, the son and grandson of
Anglican clergymen, spent only a few months at school, because, as
he says, flogging masters teach one to hate Latin; and after a few more
months of attempts at private tutoring his father gave up in despair
and apprenticed him to a bookseller.[28] Bentley of course was no auto-

didact, but rather the bright and shining star of St. John's, Cambridge; yet some facts about his early education may be significant. We are told that he first learned his Latin at his mother's knee; and at Wakefield Grammar School he was punished for not bellowing out the lesson in chorus with the other boys, in the manner traditional since classical Greece (and still preserved in Hebrew *cheders*): "The dunces could not discover that I was pondering it in my mind, and fixing it more firmly in my memory than if I had been bawling it out amongst the rest."[29] This is precisely the difference in learning method to which Eric Havelock devotes an entire volume, *Preface to Plato*, and which, he maintains, is the very foundation of the analytic thought processes which we take for granted as prerequisite to all knowledge and learning.[30] We have to be careful about generalizing on little evidence, but it is surely significant that Bentley first got his learned language informally, from a woman, not a schoolmaster, at home, so that it was in a real sense a "mother" tongue,[31] and at an age when most or all children, as is now generally recognized, have a prodigious natural linguistic ability which is apt to atrophy with adolescence.

But in these two works, at least, the two writers are practitioners of what J. Paul Hunter, in a remarkable study of Dunton's obtrusive ego, has called "collective solipsism,"[32] or what Rabelais called a chimera bombinating in a void. And I think that we need to take notice of one more very important cause of the curious indifference to the susceptibilities of an orator's audience combined with the pertly familiar buttonholing of the reader that we find in this otherwise ill-assorted pair. Both are curiously and unusually conditioned to thinking of words as tangible *things* existing on paper and apprehended by the eye—the most essential characteristic of typographic man. Dunton's page— and Swift was quick to ridicule this fact in the *Tale*[33]—is studded with dashes, italics, Gothic type, marginal index hands, visual cues to the reader and writer as well—e. e. cummings and Lewis Carroll went somewhat further, to be sure, but in Dunton's own era even Sterne scarcely did. And it is surely significant that as a printer Dunton was uniquely conditioned to the visual and very personal transmission of what he had to say: he was his own printer and could be sure that every effect that he wanted and that typography could provide would be exploited to the full, and without interference. Dunton as typographic man is no longer dependent on the sound of his voice, or on the sadly shrunken, intonation-free, nuanceless reproduction of the voice which is all that uniform typography can offer. The book as embalmed oration was what Swift was accustomed to; Dunton gave the naked voice, not dressed in the garment of standard rhetoric, to be sure, but tricked and frounced with the meretricious adornments of visual embellishment and visual mimesis.

The same is true, though to a lesser extent, with Bentley, both as reader and as writer. As reader he was accused of being chiefly conversant with lexicons, glosses, variants, fragments, inscriptions, calendars, lists, tables[34]—all of them minute units of discourse, dissected and disconnected, to be meticulously studied and compared by the eye, in isolation; but on the other hand, not evanescent as oral discourse is, but fixed forever on the page, always ready to be referred to, studied, compared, counted, yet always in disjointed isolation from the larger context. This new, paradoxical combination of precision and disconnectedness could not have been more antithetical to polite learning, with its much-admired but unanalyzed glittering generalities.[35] So too the pages of Bentley's editions were much criticized for their ugly and ungraceful confusion of text and fragments of apparatus.[36] The pages of the *Dissertation on Phalaris* almost rival Dunton's, with their English, Latin, and Greek tumbling over one another, fragments, words, phrases, superscripts, footnotes, capitals, italics. And much of the irregularity is Bentley's own, for he is clearly following no rules, but using capitals and italics for idiosyncratic emphasis (in a manner not uncommon in the 1690s, it is true, but far more capriciously than the average author of that period).

Dunton's tone in the *Voyage*, if he can be said to have a single tone, must be described as chaotic, representing nothing more than whatever whim happens to be uppermost in his mind; or it is no less chaotic if we choose to say that a mad facetiousness predominates, frequently interrupted by passages of a bathetic sentimentality. Bentley's, though somewhat more uniform, is equally irregular and unexpected from line to line; it might be characterized as hiccuping. It is written not as oratory but as though he were talking in a seminar or to a friend looking over his shoulder as he settled *hoti*'s business—a tape recording of an expert scientist leading us through his collection of specimens. Since the facts will speak for themselves, and since they are his own, laboriously sought for and found by him, Bentley can indulge himself in naive displays of vanity, scorn, complacency, and assertiveness. Slang, proverbs, and unrefined modes of speech befit this primitive version of scientific prose; this is an idiom of process, not product, composed as fast as he can write, with no polishing envisaged or required.

The lengthy and heated controversy over the question of how many personae are to be found in *A Tale of a Tub*, or whether indeed the concept of persona is legitimate, has petered out inconclusively, and when for convenience in discussion we use the term "the Hack" to designate the imagined speaker of certain passages in the *Tale*, we are well aware that we do a disservice to Swift's kaleidoscopic genius. Certainly if the Hack is a single person he has had a checkered career. He is an alumnus of Bedlam, he has prostituted his pen to any politician who wanted a quick pamphlet or any bookseller on the make, he is a virtuoso of Gresham College, he is an exponent of Hermetic mumbo jumbo, and he is sufficiently versed in classical learning to cite Ctesias, Photius, and other obscure authorities (unless we choose to assign these last passages to Swift as speaker). But if we consider all the "Hack" passages in disregard of their subject matter, we are justified in perceiving the kind of uniformity that Wittgenstein called a "family resemblance" in their manner, tone, and attitude. If the hands are the hands of Esau and many another, the voice is always the voice of Jacob, and is constituted by the heterogeneous yet causally related characteristics of *skaz*, Eyethink, and typographic man. If the abuses of learning could be detected by Swift in many areas, he saw the minds that were guilty of them as deformed in the same way, and the infallible symptom of that deformity was the utterance of such as Bentley, charging toward the top, or Dunton, rooting about near the bottom, of Parnassus.

The foregoing may strike the reader as a sketchy and disjointed account of a subject that is new enough and paradoxical enough to require a good deal more in the way of qualification, examples for proof, and the filling in of general statements. But it should suffice to establish my principal point at present—that as he composed *A Tale of a Tub*, Jonathan Swift saw a Janus-faced horror rapidly approaching; that he would have called the two faces Pertness and Pedantry; that although Dunton had more pertness and Bentley more pedantry, both possessed the two qualities intertwined. We should now call Dunton's pertness self-expression and Bentley's pedantry scientific prose, but in any event I believe that in them Swift foresaw the disastrous end of an era, and that we by hindsight can see in them the advent of Eyethink and of Typographic Man.

NOTES

The original version of this essay was presented at the annual meeting of the Northeast American Society for Eighteenth-Century Studies at Providence, Rhode Island, in November 1984, and was written during my tenure of an NEH-Huntington fellowship at the Huntington Library, San Marino, California. I wish to express my appreciation for this support of my research.

1 See A. C. Elias, Jr., *Swift at Moor Park: Problems in Biography and Criticism* (Philadelphia: Univ. of Pennsylvania Press, 1982); R. C. Jebb, *Bentley* (London: Macmillan, 1882), 78–83. A concise account of the pamphlet war over the Phalaris question will be found in Reginald J. White, *Dr. Bentley: A Study in Academic Scarlet* (London: Eyre and Spottiswoode, 1965), 92–108. William King's anonymously issued *Dialogues of the Dead: Relating to the Present Controversy Concerning the Letters of Phalaris* (1699), provides a witty and vastly amusing contemporary view of the issues on both sides, with clever parodies of Bentley's style.

2 Perhaps the best introduction to Ong's work, which has appeared in numerous books and articles, is his *Orality and Literacy: The Technologizing of the Word* (New York: Methuen, 1983); for the application of speech-act theory to typographically conditioned discourse, see my article, "Speech Acts, Orality, and the Epistolary Novel," *The Eighteenth Century* 21 (1980): 187–97.

3 It is true that breezy, artfully-artless, colloquial discourse is found in some of the works of Thomas Nashe, for example, in some novels, in satires like the Martin Marprelate pamphlets, and in ballads and chapbooks. But the last two categories received little attention from the learned or polite world, and it is arguable (see below) that all such discourse in the works of university-educated authors is merely rhetorical impersonation for the immediate purpose.

4 One might be tempted to compare this mode of expression with that of Montaigne, who also claimed to present his unmediated self to the reader; but we should recall the considerable degree of organization in Montaigne's seemingly rambling essays, their abundance of classical allusion and reference, and the elaborate and complex revisions (surely rivalling those of Joyce or Proust) that can be seen in his own hand in the Bordeaux copy of the *Essais*.

5 For an illuminating and detailed discussion of *skaz* in fiction (that is, the verbal mimesis by a literary artist of oral narrative in an ideolect), see Ann Banfield, *Unspeakable Sentences* (Boston: Routledge and Kegan Paul, 1982), 171–78, 252–53.

6 Quoted in Perry Miller, *The New England Mind* (New York: Macmillan, 1939), 303–4; and in Barbara Herrnstein Smith, *On the Margins of Discourse* (Chicago: Univ. of Chicago Press, 1978), 127.

7 As in Charles Boyle et al., *Dr. Bentley's Dissertation upon the Epistles of Phalaris Examin'd* (1698), 285–87.

8 It is true, of course, that the famous "naked, natural way of speaking" advocated by Thomas Sprat in the *History of the Royal Society* (pt. 2, sec. 20) was supposed to promote precision in the description of natural processes for scientific purposes by putting the reader in closer contact with *things*: "to

return back to the primitive purity, and shortness, when men deliver'd so many *things,* almost in an equal number of *words"* (a condition which, according to orality theory, could never have existed in preliterate discourse). But the subject of Dunton's naked prose is not natural phenomena, as Sprat took for granted, but himself; and though Bentley analyzes objective data, they are as it were his personal belongings (see below), and he sees no reason in the *Dissertation* to purify his prose by disguising that fact.

9 John Dunton, *A Voyage Round the World* (1691), 1:83–84.

10 Richard Bentley, *Works,* ed. Alexander Dyce (London, 1836–38), 3:304.

11 Dunton, *Voyage* 1:31.

12 Bentley, *Works* 2:233.

13 Dunton, *Voyage* 1:31.

14 Boyle, *Dissertation Examin'd,* 191–92; and see John E. Sandys, *A History of Classical Scholarship* (reprint, New York: Hafner Publishing Co., 1964), 2:402.

15 See, for example, "T. R.," *An Essay Concerning Critical and Curious Learning* (1698), 48–57, passim.

16 The representation of the writer's *persona* inquiring or discovering as it writes is of course far from new; but in earlier writings a whole gamut of degrees of artifice in its presentation could be found, and was recognized; see John M. Steadman, *The Hill and the Labyrinth* (Berkeley and Los Angeles: Univ. of California Press, 1984), 131–33, and the references there cited. On the complexities of reader involvement and of reading as process, so blithely ignored in these works of Bentley and Dunton, see Stanley Fish, *Surprised by Sin: The Reader in "Paradise Lost"* (New York: Macmillan, 1967), and *Self-Consuming Artifacts: The Experience of Seventeenth-Century Literature* (Berkeley and Los Angeles: Univ. of California Press, 1972).

17 See Boyle, *Dissertation Examin'd,* 97, 185–91; in a lengthy discussion of Bentley's style (probably in fact not by Boyle, but by William King) the writer can come no closer to characterizing it than to call it "Doric Dialect" or "country" rather than "court" language. (On the attribution of the passage to King, see C. J. Horne, "The Phalaris Controversy: King versus Bentley," *Review of English Studies* 22 [1946]: 289–303).

18 See J. M. Stedmond, "Another Possible Analogue for Swift's *Tale of a Tub,*" *Modern Language Notes* 72 (1957): 13–18; Jay Arnold Levine, "The Design of *A Tale of a Tub,* (With a Digression on a Mad Modern Critic)," *ELH* 33 (1966): 198–227.

19 "An Apology," *A Tale of a Tub,* ed. A. C. Guthkelch and D. Nichol Smith, 2d ed. (Oxford: Clarendon Press, 1958), 10; and see p. lix. The editors find that Swift echoes Marvell's satire in five or more passages of the *Tale.*

20 Ronald Paulson, *Theme and Structure in Swift's* Tale of a Tub (reprint, Hamden, Conn.: Archon Books, 1972), 45–47.

21 Paul G. Arakelian, "The Myth of a Restoration Style Shift," *The Eighteenth Century* 20 (1979): 227–45.

22 For an exposition of this theory in detail see Lodge, *The Modes of Modern Writing* (London: Edward Arnold, 1977).

23 This last fact militates against seeing the discourse of Bentley and Dunton as little more than a version of the "Senecan amble" or the "hopping style" of Justus Lipsius. For an analysis of the extent to which these generalizations on style correspond with the actual movement of Restoration prose see Robert Adolph, *The Rise of Modern Prose* (Cambridge, Mass.: MIT Press, 1968).

24 Stedmond, in "Another Possible Analogue," has a discussion of this point. Wilbur L. Cross, *The Life and Times of Laurence Sterne*, 3d ed. (reprint, New York: Russell and Russell, 1967), 144–45, speaks of a letter (untraced to date) in which Sterne speaks of being indebted to Dunton for many ideas and devices. I am currently preparing a detailed study of the numerous close similarities that connect the two works.

25 The enlarged *Dissertation* of 1699 has a preface and an introduction, but neither they nor the dissertation itself have anything that could be described as introductory matter in the usual sense; the latter begins, "The Time of *Phalaris's* Tyranny cannot be precisely determined. . . ." See *Dissertations . . . by Richard Bentley, D.D.*, ed. Wilhelm Wagner (London: George Bell and Sons, 1883), 3ff., 71ff., 92.

26 Bentley, *Dissertations*, 65; *Works* 3:509.

27 For a general account of Dunton's life and circumstances, see Stephen R. Parks, *John Dunton and the English Book Trade* (New York: Garland, 1976).

28 Dunton, *Voyage*, I:59–60.

29 See White, *Dr. Bentley*, 28–29.

30 Eric Havelock, *Preface to Plato* (Cambridge, Mass.: Belknap Press, 1963). The reader is also referred to Havelock's *The Literate Revolution in Greece and its Cultural Consequences* (Princeton: Princeton Univ. Press, 1982).

31 See Ong, *Orality and Literacy*, 111–15.

32 J. Paul Hunter, "The Insistent I," *Novel* 13 (1979): 27.

33 ". . . whatever word or Sentence is Printed in a different Character, shall be judged to contain something extraordinary either of *Wit* or *Sublime*." Swift, "Preface," *Tale*, 47.

34 See Jebb, *Bentley*, 7ff., for assorted criticisms on this characteristic.

35 It should be noted, however, that this style is confined to Bentley's polemics and critical works. His sermons, for example, though certainly not rich or poetic, are composed in a smooth style that much resembles Addison's, and are totally free from joky colloquialisms.

36 For details, see James McLaverty, "The Mode of Existence of Literary Works of Art: The Case of the *Dunciad Variorum*." *Studies in Bibliography* 37 (1984): 82–105.

The Man of Law in
Eighteenth-Century Biography:
The Life of Francis North

HAMILTON E. COCHRANE

In his essay "Fictional Representations of the Law in the Eighteenth Century," David Punter studies how novelists of the period "represent the law, legal characters, and legal processes" in order "to uncover a set of attitudes" about the law, crime, and the English legal system.[1] It is important to remember, however, that imaginative representations of legal characters may be found in factual as well as fictional narratives, in biography as well as the novel. One such representation is Roger North's *Life of Francis North* (1742), the biography of his elder brother, a lawyer, judge, and finally, Lord Chancellor.[2] Roger North is not only one of the earliest and most important theorists of biography, he is also one of its most accomplished practitioners, skilled in characterization, the art of presenting a convincing and rounded portrait of a personality through the judicious selection and arrangement of detail. North's version of Francis North's life is of interest not only as history—it documents the life of a Restoration lawyer with enough minute details to satisfy even Samuel Johnson—but also as literature; it is an artful narrative and character sketch in which one may discover a set of attitudes toward a legal character and the law. The biography celebrates a certain kind of hero—the rational and legalistic man. At the same time, North's portrait is complete and complex enough to suggest, implicitly at least, the limitations of this brand of heroism.

139

I

Just as Johnson realized that the "gradations" of an author's life are from book to book and organized his literary biographies accordingly,[3] Roger North emphasizes the gradations of a seventeenth-century lawyer's life—from case to case and from preferment to preferment. Early in the *Life* Roger explains his organizational method: "It will be hard to lead a thread in good order of time, through his lordship's whole life . . . I shall therefore, for distinction sake, break the course of his lordship's life into four stages."[4] These four stages are Francis North's youth and study of the law, his practice after being admitted to the bar, his career as a judge, and his term as Lord Keeper of the Great Seal.

Francis North realized early in life that "his family was not in posture to sustain any of the brothers" and that it therefore "concerned him in the last degree to make the best of his profession" (1:18). He showed no special interest in the law; he was simply "designed" for the profession by his father. He did not find the study of the law pleasant. "I have heard him say more than once," Roger writes, "that, if he had been sure of a hundred pounds a year to live on, he had never been a lawyer" (1:18). Yet he applied himself diligently, knowing that if he were to succeed in the world, it would have to be by his own labors. Roger tells little about his brother's early schooling, but one anecdote is revealing: "Before he went to Cambridge, the master employed him to make an alphabetical index of all the verbs neuter; and he did it so completely, that the doctor had it printed with Lilly's grammar, for the proper use of his own school. This, however easy to be done, (being only transcribing out of the dictionary) was commendable; because boys ordinarily have not a steady application, and, being required, seldom perform, industriously and neatly, such a task as that" (1:12). This performance, demonstrating diligence rather than brilliance, anticipates the way in which Francis studied the law after being admitted to the Middle Temple. He commonplaced all the right books, observed proceedings at the King's Bench and Common Pleas, notebook and pen in hand, and spent evenings with friends discussing what he had learned. Studying the law may have been no more agreeable than alphabetizing and transcribing neuter verbs, but Francis worked "industriously and neatly," hopeful that his labor would be rewarded.

The theme of self-improvement links the first and second division of the *Life*. Even after being called to the bar in 1661, Francis continued his education in the law. He learned what he could from all the judges and counselors he encountered, whether good or indifferent, as, Roger writes, "bees gather honey from all sorts of flowers" (1:72). Dominating this phase of Francis's life are cases in which the young lawyer's expertise and knowledge are displayed. "It is obvious to imagine that a person preferred and in capital practice of the law, must needs be noted for many excellent performances" (1:105), Roger writes, and he includes cases which show Francis as hard-working, clever, and—generally—successful: his first notable performance, an argument in the House of Lords (1:64–67); his timely discovery of an erasure in a will (1:112–27); and his recovery of an estate for his college, St. John's at Cambridge (1:139–41). These cases are offered as representative, evidence of his increasing legal activity and skill. Perhaps not as interesting to students of literature as accounts of a young author's first successes, these cases must be included in a legal life to indicate the subject's development and progress in his profession.

Francis North's mastery was rewarded, first of all, with money. His income upon entering the bar was an annual allowance from his father of sixty pounds; by the time he was made Attorney-General, he was earning seven thousand pounds a year. In addition to money, Francis gained preferments: first an appointment as King's Counsel (1668), then Solicitor-General (1671), and later as Attorney-General (1673). Once his success in the law had "dismissed all fears of the lean wolf" (1:155), Francis decided that it was time to marry. Roger's account of Francis's wooing of several prospects shows him negotiating, presenting his case as persuasively as possible, and eventually winning a wife worth fourteen thousand pounds. For Francis, a favorable match was one of the rewards of hard work in his profession, like the more commodious chambers and coach acquired at this time. His search for a wife demonstrates that his private affairs were as skillfully managed as his professional interests, and that his standing in his profession determined matters as private as the timing of his marriage and the choice of a partner.

Describing the judicial phase of Francis's career, beginning with his appointment in 1675 as Chief Justice of the Common Pleas, Roger emphasizes his brother's concern for upholding and preserving the law. In this section, Francis is depicted on the bench, interrogating witnesses, examining evidence, and handing down decisions. As he narrates these courtroom scenes, Roger insists that Francis managed all cases "with absolute regard to the strictest forms of law, and justice of trials" (1:264). When the laws seemed faulty or inadequate, Francis set out to improve them. He helped to establish a statute of frauds and perjuries (1:224), and made several improvements which hastened the hearing of Chancery cases. He improved the method of conducting trials, controlling repetitive and disorderly counsels. Always his goal was to reduce all questions to "pure management of evidence and arguments of law" (1:230).

According to Roger, Francis, first as a successful lawyer and then as a respected judge, was "in the height of all the felicity his nature was capable of" (1:165). He enjoyed the company of an amiable wife, the esteem of the royal family, and a seat at St. Dunstan's. He had a large house in Chancery Lane from which he could pass easily to his chambers. His typical day included morning church services, a day of business and study, a plain but plentiful dinner and a glass or two of wine with his family and a few choice friends, and an evening devoted to "ingenuities"—music, philosophy, painting, and mechanics. He rose and retired early. It was the regular, tranquil life of a man who was able to balance the demands of public and private life. Like similar scenes of felicity depicted in Johnson's *Lives of the Poets*, however, this was not to last long.

The fourth stage of Francis North's career began with his appointment as Lord Keeper of the Great Seal in the court of Charles II, a place that Francis believed was full of "falseness and treachery."[5] His discovery that the court was not governed by "pure management of evidence, and arguments of law" puzzled him, and eventually led him to a kind of despair. Roger depicts Francis in the court as the sole defender of the law, his unhappy final days an unsuccessful but heroic attempt to preserve the legal authority of church and state. His position on the issues of the day is defined by Roger simply and in legal terms: "His lordship was ever a professor of loyalty; that is, for the legal interest and prerogative of the crown, and the protestant religion by law established" (1:304). As Roger presents it, then, Francis as Lord Keeper remained devoted to the law. The laws he upheld were more fundamental, the disputes more heated, and the outcome of greater consequence, but the same principle was involved: a respect for the law.

Judging from Roger's description in his "General Preface" of what a useful life ought to include—"early application" and "eventual prosperities"[6]—and the narrative so far, a story of hard work and virtue rewarded, one expects this final phase of Francis's life to be the happy and satisfying culmination of his career. But the materials of real life did not conform to Roger's neat formula; in the *Life of Francis North*, there is no poetic justice. Francis's appointment is presented not as a final reward but as the end of his happiness: "And therefore I come now to his lordship's last and highest step of preferment in his profession, which was the custody of the great seal of England. And for comformity of language, I call this a preferment; but, in truth (and as his lordship understood) it was the decadence of all the joy and comfort of his life; and, instead of a felicity, as commonly reputed, it was a disease, like a consumption, which rendered him heartless and dispirited, till death came, which only could complete the cure" (1:410–11). Francis knew what awaited him if he accepted the Seal, but he submitted grimly, "as a person condemned" (1:412), out of obedience to Charles II and devotion to the law.

What awaited Francis, according to Roger, was a court filled with men who cared nothing for the law. The Catholics surrounding the Duke of York, the "faction" trying to exclude him—neither group was concerned with anything but furthering its own interest. Francis is presented as a lonely figure, "mortified" when Sir Leoline Jenkins, another loyal servant of the law, quit the court: "I have often heard him say upon the occasion, that he was absolutely alone in the court; and that no one person was left in it, with whom he could safely confer in the affairs to the public" (2:62). He alone, Roger maintains, was motivated by a desire to uphold the law, to convince the King "to rule wholly by law, and to do nothing which, by any reasonable construction, might argue the contrary" (2:84).

In the court Francis North was a counselor whose counsel was not heeded. He advised actions that would preserve but not abuse the legal authority of the crown; Charles II listened respectfully to his Lord Keeper's advice, but he followed little of it. After the death of Charles II, Francis's health began to fail. He continued to serve James II, however, by predicting the dire consequences of James's foolish actions. Francis foresaw a "confusion to our happy constitution in church and state" (2:153), and, though deathly ill, told James so in a dramatic speech. Francis knew that this performance would have no effect. "So strong were his prejudices," Roger writes of James, "and so feeble his genius, that he took none to have any right understanding that were not in his measures" (2:153). Francis spoke to fulfill his duty, and his words, as quoted by Roger, are indeed prophetic; they conclude with a reminder that "although Monmouth was suppressed, there was a P. of O. [Prince of Orange] abroad" (2:156). According to Roger, Francis's sickness and death in 1685 were caused by "his laying things to heart" (2:156). He was heartbroken to see what his life had been devoted to being foolishly destroyed. For Francis—and for

Roger, his biographer—the succession of the Stuart line represented reasonable order, tradition, and the law, values of greater than just political importance. Francis's efforts to preserve them, though unsuccessful, remained, in his brother's eyes at least, heroic.

II

The essence of Francis North's character—in James Battersby's phrase, his characteristic way of being in the world[7]—is inseparable from his public roles of lawyer, judge, and minister. Andre Maurois suggests that this merging of personality and function is fairly common among great men: "A man who exercises some lofty function . . . reaches the point of literally 'playing' a part; that is to say, his personality loses something of that obscure complexity common to all men and acquires a unity which is not wholly artificial. A great man . . . finds himself modelled by the function he has to perform; unconsciously he aims at making his life a work of art, at becoming what the world would have him be; and so he acquires, not against his will, but in spite of himself and whatever may be his intrinsic worth, that statuesque quality which makes a fine model for the artist."[8] Francis North's essentially legal habit of mind—his faith in reason, his distrust of emotion, his respect for precedent and tradition—is what Roger finds exemplary in Francis's character. It was also his tragic flaw, making him an ineffective and therefore frustrated minister, inflexible and unable to understand those less rational than himself. Here the gulf which separates Roger North from Izaac Walton is obvious; Francis, so admired by Roger, would not have appealed to Walton. It is not just that his employment was secular, while Walton's heroes were churchmen. The lives of George Herbert and Francis North embody opposing beliefs about what the task of life is: Herbert's aim was to fulfill the will of God, which is revealed to the faithful; Francis North had to rely on his own reasoning to determine his course of action. He was guided by man-made, not divine law; he expected to be rewarded or punished in this, not the next, life.

Although Roger does not explain Francis's character simply by identifying a ruling passion, he does emphasize a single trait which accounts for his success and sets him above his contemporaries: the ability to examine logically and carefully any problem or question, whether public or private. Francis, therefore, was very much at home either arguing a case as a lawyer or hearing one as a judge. As Lord

Keeper, Francis demonstrated a strong faith in sound reasoning. His advice to the King, no matter what the crisis, was to publish a pamphlet which clarified the issues and elaborated the reasoning behind the sovereign's decision. Faced with the "popular insanity" inspired by Oates's plot, Francis "was of opinion that a pamphlet might be contrived and wrote with such historical deductions and temper, that might in some measure, if not wholly, qualify the distemper of the public" (1:323–24). Francis wrote such a pamphlet and had it distributed, but the distemper of the public was not in the least "qualified." Whether the King was troubled by the need to dissolve parliament, by the Rye plot, or by disputed elections, Francis advised the same: win public support with plain and forceful reasoning. Nearly all of these tracts were ineffectual, yet Francis's confidence in reason remained unshaken. That the public was unmoved by "pure management of evidence and arguments of law" was something that neither Francis nor Roger, who never questions his brother's tactics, seemed capable of grasping.

The few glimpses readers have of Francis North's inner life reveal that he employed this same carefully reasoned approach to his own problems. From his brother's private papers, Roger reproduces memoranda labelled "speculums." Their purpose was, Roger explains: "That when he fell under any deliberation of great concern to him, and the point was nice, and stood almost in *oequilibrio,* he took his pen, and wrote down the reasons either way, as they fell in his mind, in any words, or manner of expression, and had that paper, for the most part, lying in his way; which gave him frequent opportunities to weigh the cogency of them" (2:255). In these speculums, Francis weighed the advantages and disadvantages of seeking a second wife, of accepting the Great Seal, and, later, of resigning it. Like Robinson Crusoe on his island, he drew up a list of the evils and blessings of his condition. These notes function as do the prayers and meditations in Boswell's *Life of Johnson:* they allow readers to see the subject's most private thoughts, not meant for the world, and to see them directly, not as summarized by the biographer. Here the resemblance ends. Francis's private thoughts are not prayers, but logical arguments; they reveal a private character consistent with the public figure.[9]

Francis's essentially rational character and Roger's admiration for it are both apparent in the way the "common people" are portrayed in the *Life.* Francis's attempts to enlighten them failed, Roger explains, "for the common people are not taken or drawn by the reason of things, but by shows, pretensions, and noise" (1:305). If enough people will affirm nonsense, they will believe it (1:363). Francis dreaded the trials of witches because they brought him face to face with the mob's hysteria and superstition; he feared the same as Lord Keeper. When Roger steps forward to address his readers directly, to comment on the events narrated and to moralize, his subject often is the unreasonableness of the English people, particularly concerning their government. The battle between reason and hysteria is a central tension in the *Life of Francis North,* and Francis's refusal to stoop to "shows, pretensions, and noise" and his strict adherence to reason are, in Roger's eyes, heroic.

It is easy to see why Ketton-Cremer wrote that Francis North lacked "warmth."[10] Even his acts of generosity toward family and friends were performed in a highly formal and strictly legal fashion. Roger records with gratitude that when he was saddened to think what would become of him were he to lose Francis, his best friend as well as his brother, Francis promptly sold him an annuity "at an easy rate" (2:224). To illustrate Francis's affection for his brother John North, a Cambridge scholar, Roger describes how Francis served as his executor, faithfully carrying out his final wishes. Francis loaned money at low interest to his merchant brother, Dudley; he procured favorable marriage settlements for his sisters, and wrote his father's will. While there is nothing unusual about a lawyer who does favors for his family, it is striking that so many of Francis North's dealings with members of his family—even with Roger, his shadow—are legal. Although he may appear cold—to readers if not to his biographer—in such transactions, fulfilling obligations to the letter of the law was apparently how Francis North showed affection.

Another of Francis's traits, his self-control, is also associated with his professional life. A judge cannot make a sound decision in the heat of passion; emotion only impairs reason. Roger includes one anecdote that suggests this lack of passion was habitual: "I remember, at his table, a stupid servant spilt a glass of red wine upon his point band and clothes. He only wiped his face and clothes with the napkin, and, 'Here,' said he, 'take this away;' and no more" (1:398). This "seeming apathy," Roger explains, was the result of his "reason" and "just estimate of things" (1:398). Roger maintains that Francis's ability to control his passions—in the courtroom as well as in the dining room—was not natural but acquired: "And, for all this, I know he was, at the bottom, as much inclined to passion as any one of his race ever was" (1:395).

And so it seems that Francis North worked very hard to make his life, if not a work of art in the sense suggested by Maurois, at least as consistent as possible with the ideals of his profession. Roger, however, in celebrating his brother's life and character fails to notice that adherence to this ideal may not be desirable. Francis's ineffectiveness in the court and his unhappy death may not point at the corruption of the age so much as at the limitations of this legal approach to life. That such an interpretation is even possible is a reminder that biography often offers a kind of complexity—the complexity of real life—not always found in the novel. As Steven Weiland maintains in his essay "The Humanities, the Professions, and the Uses of Biography," biographical analysis—study of lives of members of a particular profession—is, along with historical and operational analysis, one of the most important "styles of humanistic interest" in the professions. [11] As humanists continue to make inquiries into the legal profession and attitudes toward it, let us hope they do not neglect sources as rich as the *Life of Francis North*.

NOTES

1 David Punter, "Fictional Representations of the Law in the Eighteenth Century," *Eighteenth-Century Studies* 16 (1982): 50.

2 Roger North also wrote lives of his brothers Dudley, a merchant, and John, a scholar and clergyman. Known collectively as the *Lives of the Norths*, these biographies were composed and revised by Roger over a period of about thirty years. After Roger's death in 1734, the manuscripts were edited by Montagu North, Roger's son, and published in 1742–44. The *Life of Francis* is the longest of the *Lives* and the first written. The *Lives* are treated briefly in the older critical histories of biography, such as Harold Nicolson's *The Development of English Biography* (New York: Harcourt Brace, 1925), 74–76, and Donald Stauffer's *The Art of Biography in Eighteenth-Century England* (Princeton: Princeton Univ. Press, 1941), 354–69. More recently Peter Millard and James L. Clifford have examined previously unknown manuscript versions of the *Lives* along with a critical preface and have concluded that North, both in theory and practice, was a sophisticated and surprisingly modern biographer. Millard and Clifford make it clear that the *Lives* badly need modern editing; see Millard, "The Chronology of Roger North's Main Works," *Review of English Studies* 24 (1973): 283–84, and Clifford, "Roger North and the Art of Biography," in *Restoration and Eighteenth-Century Literature: Essays in Honor of Alan Dugald McKillop*, ed. Carroll Camden (Chicago: Chicago Univ. Press, 1963), 275–85. Millard has just published *General Preface & Life of Dr. John North* (Toronto: Univ. of Toronto Press, 1984).

3 Robert Folkenflik, *Samuel Johnson, Biographer* (Ithaca: Cornell Univ. Press, 1978), 107.

4 *The Lives of the Right Hon. Francis North, Baron Guilford, the Hon. Sir Dudley*

North, and the Hon. and Rev. Dr. John North (London, 1826), 1:8. Subsequent references will be included parenthetically in the text.

5 For a discussion of Roger North's ideas on politics, law, and the cultural elite, see T. A. Birrell, "Roger North and Political Morality in the Later Stuart Period," *Scrutiny* 17, no. 4 (1950–51): 282–98.

6 *General Preface and Life of Dr. John North*, 64.

7 James L. Battersby, "Patterns of Significant Action in the Life of Addison," *Genre* 2 (1969): 31.

8 Andre Maurois, *Aspects of Biography*, trans. S. C. Roberts (Cambridge: Cambridge Univ. Press, 1929), 48–49. Montagu North's preface to the *Life of Francis* also describes a public man as one who plays a role on the stage of life.

9 One entry is exceptional and very reminiscent of Johnson: "Let me not disquiet myself afresh with lamentable and melancholy apprehensions of what may happen; or renew those excessive and continued groans, attended with fear on every side, which break my rest, and even deprive me of my senses" (2:262).

10 R. W. Ketton-Cremer, "Roger North," *Essays and Studies*, n.s., 12 (1959): 78.

11 Steven Weiland, "The Humanities, the Professions, and the Uses of Biography," in *The Biographer's Gift: Life Histories and Humanism*, ed. James F. Veninga (College Station: Texas A&M Univ. Press, 1983), 43–57.

Transitions in Humphry Clinker

FREDERICK M. KEENER

Addressing *The Expedition of Humphry Clinker*—particularly the scene in which Humphry, having pulled the supposedly drowning Matthew Bramble to shore, assists at his figurative rebirth—Northrop Frye comments, "no one will suspect Smollett of deliberate mythopoeia but only of following convention, at least as far as his plot is concerned." Bridling at the remark, Paul-Gabriel Boucé argues for recognition of a thematic and "moral architectural structure which underpins the entire novel," and elsewhere refers—introducing a metaphor still more appropriate than the one from architecture, I think—to the "protean technique" of this novel's repetitions.[1] I shall examine some of these repetitions, or parallels, seeking to raise in relief a quality that makes this novel quite exceptional in its time: the text's metaphoric, associative quality, a point commentators have often addressed but have certainly not exhausted or even, I think, adequately specified.[2] This quality makes *Humphry Clinker* an extraordinarily poetic novel.

I

Smollett's character Matthew Bramble is the seedbed in which all the other important characters in the book sprout; or, to improve the metaphor, he is the stock upon which either they are growing when the book begins or they burgeon thereafter. In the book as it proceeds, his character engenders those of a good many others, progressively

149

and, in Roman Jakobson's syntactic sense, metaphorically.[3] The plant metaphor, with its implications of "organic" form, is itself in the novel and is developed there.

The name *Bramble*, that of a prickly bush with fruit—the source of bramble jelly—is an emblem of Matt's mixed, self-contrastive character, his oxymoronic amiable humorousness or misanthropic philanthropy. In Bramble's travels he will sail between the botanical Scylla and Charybdis represented by fruitless characters with names like Burdock (a weed with burrs) and Pimpernel (a kind of primrose, thornless). But it is not image clusters of so conventional a metaphorical sort that are my subject.

Bramble's family, as the book opens, is revealed to be made up of several versions, or aspects, of himself. His nephew, Jery, is a younger version, combining Bramble's satirical, Jeremian eye with a Spectatorial lightheartedness Matt may once have had but has no more. Matt's young niece, Lydia, of romantic name, is quite the opposite— all heartfelt sensitivity yearning for, in both senses of the word, engagement; impressionable; entirely unsatirical—the representative of Bramble's more or less covert generosity, but like him also in being blocked, frustrated. Lydia is already in love with a mysterious stranger, possibly of low degree.

But there are characters more significant than these, chiefly Matt's sister Tabitha, as choleric as he but stingy as he is generous. And metaphorically more important than Tabitha is her dog, Chowder, her darling and, as Ronald Paulson says, her "alter ego."[4] Yapping, nipping, underfoot, the troublesome Chowder bears a name suggesting not merely *mongrel* but also the *farrago* of the Juvenalian satirist, and is of a species recalling the sect of Cynics. (The text promotes such associations: Jery at first thinks Bramble "a complete Cynic" [April 18]). Since Tabitha suggests *cat*, as in Tabby ("that wild-cat my sister Tabby" [April 17]), one wonders whether she and Chowder are made for each other. But Tabby has something—something possibly redemptive to a degree—which Chowder shares but which Matt seems to have spent in his youth: note Chowder's attentions to a "female turnspit, of his own species" (Jery, April 24).

As the novel opens, Tabby redoubles Matt, representing, mostly, the harsh side of him, with only a hint of something that could improve her. And Chowder, the distilled essence of that negative aspect of Matt, isolates his and her bitterness: the seemingly unadulterated essence of spleen. Like Matt, Chowder is subject to constipation and possibly dropsy (Matt, April 2, 20; Tabitha, April 2; Win, April 26) and is retentive—recalling Tabitha's avarice. Seemingly Chowder must go, if Matt and Tabitha are to get or become better. Chowder must be vented, purged. What may as well be called the first movement of the novel has to do especially with this process.

The novel leads up to the banishment of Chowder in a fairly conventional eighteenth-century moral-illustrative manner: a Fielding-like, contrastive manner. Matt privately complains of Tabitha's tyranny: "Oh! I shall never presume to despise or censure any poor man, for suffering himself to be henpecked; conscious how I myself am obliged to truckle to a domestic daemon . . ." (May 19). Matt knows, moreover, that the fault is, psychologically, his more than hers, as the "suffering himself" here indicates. Earlier (May 8) he has laid a foundation for our understanding that, when he writes of "suffering myself to be over-ruled by the opinion of people, whose judgment I despise." But the seeds of resistance are being planted. The three letters preceding the showdown, in that moral-illustrative manner, all bear on the way one may cope with dominators and manipulators: Serle weakly shrinks from confronting Paunceford (Jery, May 10); Win Jenkins stands up to dishonest servants (May 15); the militant Parson Eastgate calls Prankley's bluff (Jery, May 17). Earlier in the climactic letter Bramble complains of a political candidate's "effrontery" (May 19).

Jery's very next letter after Matt's complaint depicts a crisis in the Matt-Tabitha struggle—a loss for Matt. There he is in his coach, "that animal sitting opposite to my uncle, like any other passenger. The 'squire, ashamed of his situation, blushed to the eyes." Jery and Matt's "servant John Thomas" are accompanying the coach on horseback when the vehicle overturns (not the only proto-Rowlandsonian touch in the novel); in the confusion Chowder bites Bramble's leg and John Thomas's finger. Bramble, alas, holds his tongue, but John Thomas, aroused, kicks and curses the dog, then insists that it be killed—asserting he himself will do the deed if necessary; then responds in kind to Tabitha's angry outburst; then is fired by the compliant Bramble. Chowder lives; Matt has failed, losing his John Thomas in the exchange with the formidable woman and her dentated Cerberus.

No commentator, to the best of my knowledge, has caught the Lawrentian note in this scene—perhaps, the reader may breathe, because it is not there. But it is, I think. Eric Partridge dates the slang expression "John Thomas" from circa 1840 yet finds an implicit precedent in a play of 1619; not the strongest evidence that Smollett would have intended this sense. However, the name "Thomas" and the expression "man Thomas," with the same meaning, are recorded in Grose's dictionary of 1785, and Bramble's John Thomas is also his servant, his "man."[5] The circumstances of the man's being fired would suggest a sexual dimension even if his name were different.

I return to Smollett's text, to the same letter of Jery's (May 24). *Immediately*, Humphry Clinker enters for the first time and is hired to replace the dismissed servant. That the substitute John Thomas will turn out to be Matt's son, his own wild-oats flower, clinches one or two parallels; that Humphry's natural nakedness must be covered clinches another. But the peculiarly processive quality of the novel's parallelism at this point has only begun to be suggested.

Matt tells Clinker, his "tail" now properly covered, to make peace with Tabitha, which he begins to do in a particularly fawning way—as in the famous Shakespearean association of a dog begging, one might think. Clinker profusely implores "your ladyship's worship" to forgive him, pledging "that my tail shall never rise up in judgment against me, to offend your ladyship again——Do, pray, good, sweet, beautiful lady, take compassion . . . I will serve you on my bended knees. . . ."

Apparently forgiven, Humphry serves at dinner, but his awkwardness and nervousness produce

> repeated blunders . . . At length, he spilt part of a custard upon [Tabitha's] right shoulder; and, starting back, trod upon Chowder, who set up a dismal howl——Poor Humphry was so disconcerted at this double mistake, that he dropt the china dish, which broke into a thousand pieces; then, falling down upon his knees, remained in that posture gaping, with a most ludicrous aspect of distress——Mrs. Bramble flew to the dog, and, snatching him in her arms, presented him to her brother, saying, "This is all a concerted scheme against this unfortunate animal, whose only crime is its regard for me—Here it is, kill it at once, and then you'll be satisfied."

This the irony-proof understanding of Clinker takes as a command and he prepares to act, whereupon Tabitha boxes his ear. "What! (said she to her brother) am I to be affronted by every mangy hound that you pick up in the highway? I insist upon your sending this rascallion about his business immediately—"

The scene parallels the John Thomas confrontation—too closely for Bramble to tolerate a complete reprise—and in addition Humphry represents vulnerable poverty and simple innocence. Virility is reasserted: either Chowder goes or Tabitha does. Matt quotes from Shakespeare's *Henry VIII*, lines addressed to Wolsey as he falls from favor: "to dinner with what appetite you may." A climactic series of parallel episodes comes to its conclusion. It is as if we have walked through an arcade and now through a greater, arched doorway.

But there is another element in the process that an architectural metaphor does not capture. There is a overplus of parallelism in the series, especially in the way Humphry manifests doglike qualities: on all fours, fawning, gaping—a "mangy hound." Even before he confronts Chowder, before being set in significant continuity with the actual dog, Humphry enters as a member of that species. The very names of the beast and servant resemble each other. Clinker, as the scenes unroll, does not simply succeed John Thomas and Chowder; in a pointed manner, he proceeds from them. Moreover, since John Thomas and Chowder are exfoliations of Bramble (the dog via Tabitha as well), Humphry is an exfoliation of exfoliations.

A good many of the intratextual parallels I mention have been noted, in one or another perspective, by students of *Humphry Clinker* and abound in an intricate book by Eric Rothstein, *Systems of Order and Inquiry in Later Eighteenth-Century Fiction.* Appropriately regarding British fiction of the period as distinctively epistemological, Rothstein argues that the central works develop by presenting series of analogous events which test and modify the analogical thinking of the main characters, and of readers. Rothstein reads very perceptively. Yet given his purposes, one element of *Humphry Clinker* escapes direct attention—the element I am pursuing. For example, speaking of Bramble, Humphry, and Chowder, Rothstein says, "Humphry replaces Chowder, to whom Tabby and Win compare him. . . ."[6] The special processive quality of the novel which I am seeking to define is that whereby the word "replace" does not quite do justice to the transition between Humphry's entrance and Chowder's exit. A metaphor entailing metamorphosis would be more appropriate, and not alien to metaphors in Smollett's text, but by itself it would be insufficiently analytical. Humphry, as I have sought to show, proves successively so Bramble-like, so John Thomas–like, and so Chowder-like, and the pertinent confrontations become so fully comparable at numerous points, that the analogies approach being identities, more than analogies usually do.

Parallels here ride a mounting wave of syntactic, metaphorical momentum. Introducing Humphry with what might be called lyric sequacity, on the heels of John Thomas and Chowder in particular, the novel reveals not a gap but an energetic arc. Humphry, subsuming Chowder, shows himself to be a better version, who can prompt not simply Bramble's triumph but a subsequent reconciliation between brother and sister, whereupon "Chowder capered, and Clinker skipped about" (Jery, May 24). Metaphorical contiguity here provides a happier final complement to the scene of Bramble and the dog surly together in the coach, and even suggests the comic redemption of Chowder—who, after his brushes with death, is not destroyed but perhaps fortunately translated to the home of Lady Griskin—who gets him, in a sense, as a consolation prize when Bramble raises his "bristles" at her approaches; and who is not missed by Tabitha, whose heart has temporarily turned toward Humphry (Jery, June 2). Without undue sentimentality, I may note that Chowder's ultimate cheerfulness suggests that, like other characters in the book, including Lismahago, Chowder appears more selfish than he is. And Lady Griskin may be his reward, since a griskin is a morsel of bacon or beef—and might go in and improve a chowder.

Surely the novel discloses a heady confluence of associative forces moving beneath a semblance of architectural form. For a parallel to this quality in earlier English literature, we would have to look to the poets. Bramble's progress, and that of the book, are indeed not unreminiscent of Lear's, and *Lear's*—in form as well as, obviously, in tone and substance. As *Lear* proceeds, Cordelia (a version or an aspect of the King) emanates into the Fool, the Fool into Mad Tom, Mad Tom into Lear again; then Cordelia returns. The action proceeds, the characters emanate, with the fictive equivalent of the "Poetical *Fire*" Pope praised so in Homer,[7] roaring along, swallowing up neat contrasts with wondrous energy of mind.

II

Generally, this novel's emanative processiveness is in the direction of extremity. The emanations become more egregious, as in the original series Bramble-Tabitha-Chowder. Matt's travels bring him into contact with a succession of eccentric characters cut from much the same cloth—especially characters who exhibit various degrees of opinionated assertiveness, even pugnacity. At the start there are Tabitha and, to some extent, Jery. Soon Matt is conversing with a physician in Bath who extols the healthfulness of filth, and then with the Irish knight Sir Ulic Mackilligut, "about the age of three-score, stooped mortally," and "tall, raw-boned, hard-favoured, with a woolen nightcap on his head"—coatless, girding "himself with a long iron sword" (Jery, April 24). There are numerous others to come, especially pretentious or crude or mischievous hosts. There is the angry Irish fortune-hunter Master Macloughlin (Jery, July 18). Even Humphry belongs in part to this sort, witness his positiveness about Methodism and his readiness to fight when called upon.

But the Irishman Mackilligut sharply prefigures the Scots advocate Mr. Micklewhimmen, who is succeeded by that extraordinary Scotsman Lieutenant Lismahago, who represents the summit for the ascent to extremity. Jery cannot help marveling at this "tall, meagre figure, answering, with his horse, the description of Don Quixote mounted on Rozinante," as Lismahago falls from his mount, then leaps up, flourishing a pistol at those who have laughed at him (July 10). "He would have measured above six feet in height, had he stood upright; but he stooped very much; . . . his face was, at least, half a yard in length, brown and shrivelled, with projecting cheek-bones. . . . His horse was exactly in the stile of its rider; a resurrection of dry bones, which . . . he valued exceedingly, as the only present he had ever received in his life."

Like Bramble too, these types of his testiness are, indeed, literally outlandish: extremists from the extremities of Britain. They resemble him in origin, temperament, and age; but with their grotesque angularity, peculiar dress, and frenetically wielded compensatory weapons, they are distilled and attenuated like the biting mongrel already sufficiently prominent in these pages. And Lismahago is certainly the climactic figure in the progression, very fully developed in this respect, especially because Smollett has taken care to plant an array of harsh opinions on various topics, spoken by Bramble early in the book, so that Lismahago, when he turns up, can himself reiterate, exaggerate, or top them. Bramble, in London, had excoriated luxury, the freedom of the press, and so on. Lismahago does so later in still more positive and extreme terms (Matt, May 29, June 2, July 15).

Bramble finds himself most at peace—indeed, within the novel, unprecedentedly disarmed—when in Scotland. Significantly, Lismahago does not accompany him there. Bramble, as it were, travels awhile without his spleen. Then the party returns to England, and to his vexation, Lismahago reappears. But there is more to the structure of this novel as a whole than I am tracing, even regarding Bramble himself—for example, his physiological progress from constipation, through the dangerously clogged hallways of a burning inn, the fire started by a clogged chimney, to the *locus amoenus* represented by Loch Lomond, with its flowing outlet to the sea: the river called the Leven Water which prompts Bramble to break into an ode! The poem is a brief amalgam of Gray's Eton College ode, Pope's "Windsor-

Forest," "L'Allegro," and perhaps Goldsmith's *Deserted Village*. The scene lightly recalls *Paradise Lost*, Book 4, and anticipates "Kubla Khan" : "Above that house is a romantic glen or clift of a mountain, covered with hanging woods having at bottom a stream of fine water . . ." (Matt, September 6). "Oh might I flow like thee" could be Bramble's motto. Now he can—deep, clear, gentle, strong without rage.

Actually, the famous passage in Denham's "Cooper's Hill" to which I am alluding is remembered by Smollett earlier, through Pope's parody:

> Flow Welsted flow! like thine inspirer, Beer,
> Tho' stale, not ripe; tho' thin, yet never clear;
> So sweetly mawkish, and so smoothly dull;
> Heady, not strong; o'erflowing, tho' not full.
> (*Dunciad* B, 3.169–72)

Says Lydia, of a spa near Bristol: ". . . There we drink the water so clear, so pure, so mild, so charmingly maukish" (April 21).

One notable epicycle slows Bramble's progress, however: the most disruptive act he commits, his challenging one of the inhospitable hosts, Lord Oxmington, to a duel after suffering a peremptory after-dinner dismissal. We may be surprised, given Bramble's recent composure in Scotland. But the event is less surprising when we reflect that he has only recently been rejoined by Lismahago. Taking offense, Bramble starts up as Lismahago repeatedly had, and Sir Ulic Mack-illigut before him—Bramble "laying his hand upon his sword, and eyeing him with a most ferocious aspect." Bramble and Jery stalk off, significantly, "through a double range of lacqueys." That is significant because it too initiates a pattern recalling numerous events earlier in the book.

Against Jery's common-sense protest, Bramble sends Lismahago, naturally, to demand satisfaction. Bramble's spleen sorties out. But Lismahago is humiliated by one of Oxmington's lacqueys, a "French valet de chambre," and returns disposed to fight with Bramble. Tabitha, of all people—but now likely to marry Lismahago—makes peace between them. Threatened by Bramble's party, Oxmington yields up the valet, who "asked pardon of the lieutenant upon his knees, when Lismahago, to the astonishment of all present, gave him a violent kick on the face, which laid him on his back" (Jery, September 28). The valet is another version of the fawning dog, as a character mentioned earlier in the book (but not yet mentioned in the present essay) was said to be ("He fawned, and flattered, and cringed" [Jery, July 18]).

He is Dutton, the petit maitre who served briefly as Jery's footman, who nearly stole Win Jenkins from Humphry, and who caused the rage of Master Macloughlin. Dutton in fact has been described, by Matt, as "the very contrast of Humphry" (June 14). But Humphry had fawned in trying to placate Tabitha. As Rothstein suggests,[8] the book depends on resemblances, parallels, much more than on contrasts.

In parallel with the Chowder-Clinker episode, too, Bramble here insists that Oxmington dismiss his dog of a servant, and this demand also recalls the Chowder-John Thomas episode, as does Lismahago's kick, like John Thomas's at the dog. John Thomas, though, had kicked Chowder in the ribs (Jery, May 24); it was Mackilligut who had put his toe to Chowder's jaws (Jery, May 6), that is, to the dog's "face."

Yet gentle Clinker too can provoke a challenge to duel: he did so against Dutton, though with enough presence of mind to resist encouragement to go through with it, "to hazard a thrust of cold iron." The encouragement was delivered by, of course, Lismahago (Jery, July 18). Here was Humphry's main opportunity to ride the Bramble-to-Lismahago progression. Now, later in the book, Lismahago has the opportunity to behave more like Clinker; that is, more like a representation of Bramble's gentler side, Clinker's usual role. Lismahago does so in not letting his pride interfere with his pursuit of Tabitha, which could be regarded as fortune hunting. But the plot lets him do so in other ways, especially when a double of Oxmington, Bullford—ox and bull—another prankster host, rouses Lismahago from his bed with a false cry of fire, and Lismahago ridiculously exposes his "posteriors," as Humphry had upon entering the book (and others do later). In this novel, to be lovable you have to suffer exposure. Lismahago will put up with such redemption only so far. He has his revenge on Bullford by, in effect, sicking a resurrected Chowder on him—baiting Bullford by crying "mad dog!"—falsely—thereby driving the gouty prankster, prankishly, into a pond (Jery, October 3). It looks as though Bullford gets the benefit of some extra, unpurged rancor here, for Oxmington's offensive valet had drawn Lismahago's "person though the horse-pond" (Jery, September 28). Immersion is a large motif in this novel, as Frye and others have noticed; I need not go into it, pausing with the cumulative observation that Lismahago when kicking the valet and later imagining the mad dog is turning the spirit of Chowder against itself.

There are other significant parallels I have not mentioned, in these mere few of the book's many episodes. Truly, as Boucé says, it is a protean novel—paralleling themes, distinguishing them, recombining them as it rolls forward. Doubtless, too, the few strands I have explored could be interpreted differently. But it is not the interpretation I am pressing for, so much as it is the unusualness of this novel, as a novel, in its time: its being so prodigiously, openly, syntactically metaphorical in its construction. And there is more to be said in this respect about Lismahago, who enters the book almost as metaphorically as Humphry does—indeed, does so twice.

III

Not unlike Humphry, Lismahago first turns up abruptly, and, like Humphry, turns up without being heard of before. Like Humphry too, Lismahago fills a void as soon as it opens—as Humphry succeeded John Thomas. Smollett loses not a moment in the transition: the highwayman Martin will "sell his horse" and go to the East Indies, assisted by Bramble in the quest for a new, honorable life. Jery writes of Martin, "He had not been gone half an hour, when we were joined by another character, which promised something extraordinary—a tall, meagre figure, answering, with his horse, to the description of Don Quixote . . . [as before]" (July 10).

This transition is still swifter than John Thomas's into Humphry, via Chowder. The horses are passed over lightly: one disposed of, another coming on the scene. They are certainly figurative horses, however—the fine, disguisable steed indispensable to a highwayman (Jery, June 11) and the transparent extension of Lismahago's world-worn self, a self which has survived scalping—resurrected like the horse's bones (according to Smollett's better locution). There is even a sense in which this transition, like the other, involves Humphry, who is notably associated with horses, having been bred a farrier; who, when appointed as Matt's "life-guards-man," had been provided with a first-rate mount; and who, mounted, had boldly joined forces with Martin to rout highwaymen (Jery, June 23). And Martin has an important, comparably symmetrical relation to Humphry: it was Martin, we recall, who entered the novel to help get him out of jail, and who, Clinker-like—that is, with Humphry's willingness to sacrifice everything for another—seemingly professed himself willing to surrender, to exchange himself, for Clinker (Jery, June 11).

Still, the novel's leap from Martin to Lismahago, despite these earlier filiations, remains provocatively abrupt; has, even, a forced quality. Martin, a Macheath—a paragon of highwaymen, a womanizer, a shrewd and debonair fellow capable of conversing amicably with representatives of the law who have knowledge of his activities but lack the evidence to convict him—poses some structural problems, as if he were occasioned by some reflex excess of the author's associative energies. Martin threatens to become one hero too many for the novel. Tabitha, naturally, is attracted to him, but he is not attracted to her. On the other hand, he is potentially too attractive to Lydia despite her constancy to the mysterious Wilson, who keeps turning up in disguise—though perhaps not fully or often enough, as far as the reader is concerned—to communicate with her. The highwayman's penchant for disguise, and his marginality between gallantry and disreputability, range Martin closely with Wilson. Smollett has to get rid of Martin and supply a match for Tabitha; like Chowder, Martin must be relocated elsewhere; whence Lismahago, who displaces him.

The story, however, has a general tendency to burst its bounds. Despite its inventory of dates and places, in Scotland especially it gets ahead of itself, though it has already moved rather rapidly from London to Yorkshire. On one page Bramble ends a letter at Edinburgh; Jery begins the next viewing the Hebrides. Nearly a month separates these letters (August 8 to September 3), an interval demanding considerable retrospection in the letters that follow—and entailing a certain amount of rapturous circling. The story has comparably gotten ahead of itself in introducing Lismahago so abruptly; and it catches up by introducing him the second time.

Lismahago reenters the novel later than expected, in England rather than on the Scottish border. His reappearance is preceded by Tabitha's wish to see him, after she has failed in her pursuit of more eligible Scotsmen. Jery reports the reappearance or reapparition after the party has come upon the lieutenant's poor horse, dead, drowned (no hydraulic rebirth or second resurrection for him)—his master presumably drowned also. "More meagre and grim than before," Lismahago informs the company that his plans to settle in Scotland have been frustrated, and that he will return to the American Indians. Bramble—"really a Don Quixote in generosity," says Jery, underscoring the parallel between his uncle and Lismahago—explains that the lieutenant's reason for emigrating is his inability to support himself on the inadequate pension given subalterns (September 12). Quixotically generous Bramble will encourage a match between his sister and the veteran. But there is more to all this.

In the next letter, by Bramble, it comes out that Lismahago had been frustrated in his Scottish plans—had indeed been scandalized—when, returning home, he discovered that his nephew, now head of the family, had turned the seat of the Lismahagos into a weaving factory ("the sound of treddles in the great hall"). And his nephew had taken him for the avenging ghost of Lismahago's father; again it is as if the lieutenant had been resurrected. Lismahago, it will be recalled, though born a gentleman, has been so poor that, despite having had the worst of thirty years' military service, he was never able to rise beyond his present rank, being unable to purchase a higher (Jery, July 10). What is more, it appears that he has been too proud to let himself know he would like a promotion, much less pursue it.

It is not garrulity that makes Smollett go into all this. Once again, when Lismahago reenters the novel, he does so metaphorically, for the letter by Jery introduces, beforehand, a new character with a role not unlike that of Martin the highwayman's earlier—making straight the way of Lismahago. A Scotsman, Captain William Brown, is described reappearing in his village after many years, relieving his distressed family—including his jailed brother, who has taken on the debt of his father (who had acted as security for their landlord, been ruined, and now labors outside the prison paving the street). The scene is as if from an opera, and has overtones of Martin's intention of redeeming imprisoned Humphry.

Bramble expresses delight at this quintessentially sentimental display, and above all at the character of the beneficent soldier who, beyond relieving his family, lavishes gifts on its members. Now we learn the particulars of Captain Brown: he had been "bred a weaver," had enlisted for no good reason, but had with the help of his commander worked his way up to a captaincy and a fortune. Now "he promised to purchase a commission for his youngest brother; to take the other as his own partner in a manufacture which he intended to set up, to give employment and bread to the industrious," and so forth. He is a modest, laconic man. Tabitha begins to feel an interest in him until she discovers him too low in "his ideas," notably his idea of tendering "his hand to a person of low estate, who had been his sweet-heart while he worked as a journeyman-weaver" (Jery, September 12). Smollett weaves in these reiterated references to weaving. Double, double; warp and woof.

No one in the book says so, but it will be clear that we have been given all this information about the admirable captain so that we can sense the metamorphic temperature drop when Lismahago reenters—immediately—as we had sensed it drop when he replaced Martin. All Lismahago's disabilities Brown has addressed in his own career and overcome, except Lismahago's defect of temperament; and Lismahago, not Brown, had been born a gentleman. Brown, like Martin, may now be excused as too good for Tabitha. Brown had to be introduced, however, to help put Lismahago in perspective. The final antitheses between the two characters seem almost to cancel the likeness.

But the likenesses between the two characters—the waves of metaphoric association bearing both of them along—are more important, for the men are both needy, capable Scots at first unimproved by Scotland's legislative Union with England in 1707. In Bramble's opinion, expressed earlier, some of the Scots have hampered themselves by clinging to aristocratic habits and not embracing commerce (September 6). Lismahago is the pattern of regressiveness in this respect, Brown forward-looking; yet both shared the same need for assistance. Brown fortunately received it from his English commander, Lismahago did not. Lismahago's miserable, now completely dead horse had represented the only favor anyone had ever done him, was the only gift he had ever received. The generously treated Brown proves generous; Lismahago has proven suspicious, contentious. Their need warrants some reasoning.

The whole framework of the conjunction of the two characters is large, the associations within this book complicated, for Bramble, in the course of his travels, has become—to put the matter briefly—more inductive and flexible in his appraisal of varying social conditions; has become less quick to judge the rest of the world against the ancient manorial standards of Brambleton-hall.[9] Brown, in a world larger than that of the private estate, had become unblocked: had been given, by an outsider, a suitable channel for his energies. Lismahago had not. Both men are characterized by exceptional energy. This context might usefully occasion reconsideration of Martin—but that will not be necessary, except to say that Bramble will assist Lismahago as he did Martin and Humphry.

Given the preponderant likeness between the, in less radical ways, very different Brown and Lismahago, I trust my assertion of metaphoric similitude's linking them will not seem tendentious. Brown alights from an undescribed but probably serviceable horse to relieve and redeem his family. Lismahago's horse was not good enough in the first place, or the lieutenant was unable, unassisted himself, to give it proper care. The barely mentioned horses carry significance, as Chowder had when prefiguring and promoting Bramble's link with Clinker.[10] Lismahago enters and reenters forwarded by—among other figures and forces—Bramble, Humphry, Martin, Brown, and, generally, this novel's distinctive poetic momentum.

NOTES

1 Northrop Frye, *Anatomy of Criticism* (Princeton: Princeton Univ. Press, 1957), 179; Paul-Gabriel Boucé, *The Novels of Tobias Smollett*, trans. Antonia White in collaboration with the author (London and New York: Longman, 1976), 241, 195. My parenthetical references by the dates (and when not obvious the authors) of letters cite the Signet edition of *The Expedition of Humphry Clinker*, foreword by Monroe Engel (New York: New American Library, 1960).

2 Studies beside Boucé's that attend closely to the poetic associations in Smollett's novel include William Park's "Fathers and Sons—*Humphry Clinker*," *Literature and Psychology* 16 (1966): 166–74, which pursues the novel's "dream logic" to parallels anticipating a good many of those mentioned in my text (and some not, e.g., Park's acute linking of Miss Blackerby, Bishop Blackberry, and "the fruit of the Bramble" [p. 173]), and, in attention to the excremental theme, foreshadows some of Robert Adams Day's strong perceptions as recorded in "Sex, Scatology, and Smollett," in *Sexuality in Eighteenth-Century Britain*, ed. Paul-Gabriel Boucé (Manchester: Manchester Univ. Press; Totowa N.J.: Barnes & Noble, 1982), 225–43. Eric Rothstein has also contributed mightily to the recognition of significant parallelism in the novel, as noted below and also in his recent "Scotophilia and *Humphry Clinker*: The Politics of Beggary, Bugs, and Buttocks," *University of Toronto Quarterly* 52 (1982): 63–78; but nearly everyone who has written about the novel in the past twenty-five years has contributed something, beginning with Sheridan Baker, whose 1961 article "*Humphry Clinker* as Comic Romance" suggests an "evolution" of Humphry via "displacement" involving Martin and Lismahago (reprinted in *Essays on the Eighteenth-Century Novel*, ed. Robert Donald Spector [Bloomington: Indiana Univ. Press, 1965], 154–64).

Commentators have not, however, cited the application to the novel of Frye's seminal article "Towards Defining the Age of Sensibility" (1956), reprinted in *Eighteenth-Century English Literature: Modern Essays in Criticism*, ed. James L. Clifford (New York: Oxford Univ. Press, 1959), 311–18). Frye does not cite the application either, giving pride of place to Sterne, but many of the hallmarks of sensibility enumerated—emphasis on literature as process rather than product, on psychological aspects, on the identification of author and narrators with what they write about, on poetic, incremental repetition, and representation of "free or uncontrolled association . . . very like a dream" (most concentrated, conspicuous, and fundamental-seeming in the "Win Jenkins Wake" aspect), even on more particular matters such as "curiously intense awareness of the animal world" (p. 314) and a taste for what may be called the Ossianic feeling—all certainly have affinity with *Humphry Clinker* (e.g., regarding the last see Jery's letter of Sept. 3), but *not*, in general, with Smollett's other novels. Without seeking to settle the proportion with Sterne's fiction, I may record my impression that ideas run in grooves more circumscribed there than those of *Humphry Clinker.*

3 Roman Jakobson, "Two Aspects of Language and Two Types of Aphasic Disturbances," in Roman Jakobson and Morris Halle, *Fundamentals of Language* (The Hague: Mouton, 1956), esp. 81–82.

4 Ronald Paulson, *Popular and Polite Art in the Age of Hogarth and Fielding* (Notre Dame, Ind.: Univ. of Notre Dame Press, 1979), 53; cf. Paulson, *Satire and the Novel in Eighteenth-Century England* (New Haven, Conn.: Yale Univ. Press, 1967), 195, regarding, Bramble, Juvenal, and Pavlov's dog; also, with reference to my general argument, see Paulson's observation (180n) that the repetitions of incidents in Smollett's *Roderick Random* "appear to have no function."

5 Eric Partridge, *A Dictionary of Slang and Unconventional English,* 7th ed. (New York: Macmillan, 1970), 443, 508, 877. Francis Grose, *A Classical Dictionary of the Vulgar Tongue* (1785; reprint, Menston, England: Scolar, 1968), s.v. "Thomas."

6 Eric Rothstein, *Systems of Order and Inquiry in Later Eighteenth-Century Fiction* (Berkeley and Los Angeles: Univ. of California Press, 1975), 137.

7 "Preface," *The Iliad,* vol. 7 of *The Twickenham Edition of the Poems of Alexander Pope,* ed. Maynard Mack et al. (London: Methuen; New Haven, Conn.: Yale Univ. Press, 1967), 4. Quoting a remark of Howard Swazey Buck's about Smollett's novels ("it was the poet that was in him that is the leaven of the lump"), Robert Donald Spector emphasizes Smollett's affection for poetry and Pope (*Tobias George Smollett* [New York: Twayne, 1968], 25–26). Buck also invokes the image of "fire" (*Smollett as Poet* [New Haven, Conn.: Yale Univ. Press, 1927], 81).

8 Rothstein, *Order and Inquiry,* 134.

9 Here I merely touch on a different but complementary subject: the "centifugal" themes of assessment of self and world, themes *Humphry Clinker* also develops to an extent unusual in eighteenth-century fiction.

10 Or (C)linker; see Boucé's cumulative remarks on the name, *Novels of Tobias Smollett,* 249–50, which include etymological information to the same effect.

Garrick's Incidental Lyrics: Supplementing, Not Supplanting Shakespeare

LINDA R. PAYNE

The name of David Garrick is today inextricably linked with that of Shakespeare, primarily because among the twenty-six Shakespeare plays which Garrick produced during his thirty-year management of the Theatre Royal, Drury Lane (1747–1776), at least twelve were his own adaptations. His editing is now generally respected for its recovery of Shakespeare from the Restoration travesties which used Shakespearean characters and plots with little appreciation for their original context.

Yet one aspect of Garrick's adaptations that has received little attention is their context—the way in which they made use of the eighteenth-century audience's taste for the "whole show" by including additional songs not provided by Shakespeare, at least forty of which had lyrics written by Garrick himself. These songs deserve more study for the light they can shed on the Garrick success story. As pioneer Garrick scholar George Winchester Stone, Jr., has said, "without bucking the current of eighteenth-century taste, Garrick provided his contempories with a rather complete Shakespearian banquet, a richer and purer one than their predecessors had enjoyed, and gradually helped to change that taste."

Although his theatrical reputation is what endures, in his own time Garrick was also known for his song lyrics, not only in the theater, but

165

in the street, pub, and coffee house as well. For the theater alone, he composed lyrics to more than 106 songs for plays (his own or others), including ten primarily musical Garrick adaptations or original plays. Many of the lyrics were topical; they were often light, bantering, or satirical, and included love songs, drinking songs, pastorals, dirges, and epithalamia. He collaborated with the important English composers of his day, among them William Boyce, Thomas and Michael Arne, and John Christopher Smith, Jr. We might guess that Garrick put so much creative energy into the musical side of production not only because he wished to please his spectacle-hungry audience, but also because he considered music an intrinsic part of the dramatic effect he sought to achieve. This view is confirmed by a letter he wrote to his close friend, the music historian Dr. Charles Burney, referring to music as "that nice feeling of ye passions (without which everything in ye dramatic way will cease to entertain)." [2]

Given his own general practise as well as the demand of public taste for music and dance, it is not surprising that Garrick provided additional music for those Shakespeare plays that he adapted. He based his contributions to the periodic examination with all-sung English opera on *A Midsummer Night's Dream* (*The Fairies*, 1755) and *The Tempest* (1756). In his landmark history, Burney could recollect "no English operas in which the dialogue was carried on in recitative, that were crowned with full success, except the Fairies, set by Mr. Smith in 1756, and Artaxerxes, by Dr. Arne in 1763." [3]

Although Garrick followed the eighteenth-century tradition of interpolating new incidental songs into plays written by other playwrights, his additions were generally less wanton than the almost ludicrously unrelated bits of spectacle interrupting the course of many period plays. Biographers Stone and Kahrl say of his songs that "the intellectual content of many is slight, but one must bear in mind that the song quality depends on a context of music, play, and theatrical setting." [4] A closer look at Garrick's incidental songs for the Shakespeare adaptations will illustrate his approaches to supplementing the play text, as well as the relationship between the success of the song and the success of Garrick's characterization and fidelity to Shakespeare.

The second edition (1758) of Garrick's adaptation of *Antony and Cleopatra* included a page of verse, headed with the note, "The Song at p. 39, being thought too short, an addition was made to it while the play was in rehearsal, and it is as follows." [5] The song that follows has two stanzas of six lines each, an expansion of Shakespeare's one-stanza, six-line "Come, thou monarch of the vine." This provides the only example of Garrick's words mixed with Shakespeare's within the same song. Shakespeare's lines are these:

> Come, thou monarch of the vine,
> Plumpy Bacchus with pine eyne!
> In thy vats our cares be drowned,
> With thy grapes our hairs be crowned.
> Cup us, 'till the world go round,
> Cup us, 'till the world go round!
> (2.7.120–25)

Garrick did not merely append additional lines to the poem, but instead arranged his new and expanded version to exploit Shakespeare's rhyme and motif in the best way possible:

> Come, thou monarch of the vine,
> plumpy *Bacchus,* with pink eyne;
> thine it is to cheer the soul,
> made, by thy enlarging bowl,
> free from wisdom's fond control,
> free from wisdom's fond control.
>
> Monarch, come; and with thee bring
> tipsy dance, and revelling.
> In thy vats our cares be drowned;
> with thy grapes our hairs be crowned;
> cup us 'till the world go round.
> cup us 'till the world go round.
> (4:4)

Garrick's couplets in trochaic tetrameter follow Shakespeare's quite faithfully both in rhythm and diction. The main stylistic difference is found in the syntax: Shakespeare's couplets are all closed, while Garrick includes an open couplet in each verse to lead into the repeated refrain line. By preserving the rhythm, Garrick not only retained the flavor of the original, but also made it possible to use any extant musical setting by merely repeating the stanza. In 1750, Thomas Chilcot had written such a setting, which Garrick would have known about and had access to.[7]

Despite their brevity, Garrick's six new lines demonstrate his goal of highlighting the work of Shakespeare rather than competing with it. This song is sung by Enobarbus during the scene aboard the ship, when Antony is reunited with Caesar and Lepidus. The scene is designed to underscore Antony's decay, and Garrick's lines 4–6 more blatantly state the case, foreshadowing Caesar's "Strong Enobarbe / Is weaker than the wine" (2.3.53–54). The same lines heighten the justification for Caesar's disgust.

Similarly, for his 1756 adaptation of *The Winter's Tale*, Garrick wrote a song which was not only published with the play but printed with its music in *The London Magazine* (February 1756) and *Universal Magazine* (March 1756). In Garrick's alteration of the play, which had not been successfully produced in the century, the characterization of Perdita became perhaps the most essential element in the success of the three-act *Florizel and Perdita* as a "Dramatic Pastoral."

In order to shorten the play and maintain the unities (which the sixteen-year span of *The Winter's Tale* violates perhaps more outrageously than any other of Shakespeare's plays), Garrick cut much of the second half of the drama, knit the rest together with narrative exposition, and set it all in Bohemia. The sheepshearing event, therefore, becomes the key to the main action. (The Hermione plot is somewhat tacked onto the end, so as not to lose the dramatic potential of the episode of the statue's quickening.) The shortened format and lighter tone made the play suitable fare not only for a mainpiece but for an afterpiece as well, and even rival John Rich used it that way at Covent Garden.

As he often did, Garrick provided in the prologue to the play a rationale or apology for his strategies of adaptation. The entire prologue is an extended analogy featuring the dramatist as innkeeper (at the sign of "Shakespeare's Head"), with images of food and drink and many puns employed. Garrick claims to have altered the play in order to preserve it:

> Lest then this precious liquor run to waste,
> 'Tis now confined and bottled for your taste.
> 'Tis my chief wish, my joy, my only plan,
> To lose no drop of that immortal man!
> (3:225)

This alteration received much criticism from the later bardolaters in the vein of Frank Hedgecock's quip in 1912, "A little more of Shakespeare's champagne and a little less of Garrick's gooseberry juice would have made a better mixture."[8] However, Garrick's biographer and rival playwright Arthur Murphy provides us with the prevailing contemporary view, pronouncing Shakespeare's "business" to be so "complicated and heterogeneous," that the "strictest attention cannot find a clue to guide us through the maze." He judged that "Garrick saw that the public would be little obliged to him for a revival of the entire play, and therefore with great judgment, extracted from the chaos before him a clear and regular fable."[9]

The sheepshearing had already been the focus of a brief musical afterpiece at Covent Garden, and Garrick wanted to make the lasting impression. To introduce the song, he added a line for the old shepherd: "Come, come, daughter, leave for a while these private dalliances and love-whisperings, clear up your pipes, and call, as custom is, our neighbors to your shearing" (2.1.145). Perdita dutifully obeys. The following lyrics were then inserted into Garrick's published version of the play:

> Come, come, my good shepherds, our flock we must shear;
> In your holy-day suits, with your lasses appear.
> The happiest of folk are the guiltless and free,
> And who are so guiltless, so happy as we?
>
> We harbor no passions by luxury taught;
> We practice no arts with hypocrisy fraught;
> What we think in our hearts you may read in our eyes;
> For, knowing no falsehood, we need no disguise.
>
> By mode and caprice are the city dames led,
> But we as the children of nature are bred;
> By her hand alone we are painted and dressed;
> For the roses will bloom when there's peace in the breast.
>
> That giant, Ambition, we never can dread;
> Our roofs are too low for so lofty a head;
> Content and sweet cheerfulness open our door,
> They smile with the simple and feed with the poor.
>
> When love has possessed us, that love we reveal;
> Like the flocks that we feed are the passions we feel;
> So, harmless and simple, we sport and we play,
> And leave to fine folks to deceive and betray.
>   (2.1.149–68)

Perdita's song reveals all the typical illogic of the pastoral form. The city is associated with "passions by luxury taught," with hypocrisy, "mode and caprice," and ambition. Country folk, on the other hand, are "guiltless and free" (the published song sheets read "guileless and free"), happy, content and sweet, and the companions of cheerfulness. Yet the central lovers turn out, of course, to be nobility disguised (Florizel) and undiscovered (Perdita). They leave the Edenic existence they have praised to live at court, where Perdita is to "put on / This novel garment of gentility, / And yield a patched behavior" (3.4.253–55). Polixenes's line immediately following the song points up the paradox well: "This is the prettiest low-born lass that ever / Ran on the green-sord; nothing she does or seems / But smacks of something greater than herself, / Too noble for this place" (2.1.169–72).

Garrick employs closed couplets in this song, grouping them this time in four-line stanzas. He writes in iambic tetrameter, which matches the meter of Shakespeare's "Lawn as white as driven snow," "Jog on, jog on," and "Get you hence," although Shakespeare had used a more interesting 4/3/4/3 stanza for "Will you buy any tape" and "But shall I go mourn for that, My dear." Shakespeare also varies his rhyme scheme between aabb couplets and an abab pattern. Garrick's syntax is sometimes a bit contorted, with unnaturally inverted word order.

The music for this piece (see figure 1) was preserved in Joseph Ritson's *A Select Collection of English Songs with Their Original Airs* (1783) as merely a melody line written by Michael Arne, the young son of the prominent musician and composer Dr. Thomas Arne. Michael Arne played the keyboard instruments in Garrick's band, and often collaborated with him. New settings for the Shakespearean lyrics of the play had been composed within the decade. William Boyce had set at least the trio "Get you hence" and had written instrumental music for the animating of the statue specifically for the Garrick adaptation. Boyce often composed for Drury Lane, so Michael Arne would have worked with him there and thus have been familiar with his style. "Shall I go Mourn" had been set in 1745 by John Frederick Lampe—Arne's uncle. So Arne would have been well equipped to write music compatible with whatever settings Garrick might have chosen to use. (Unfortunately, such decisions were rarely recorded.) His setting for "Come, come, my good shepherds," is bright, tuneful, and easy to sing, with a low *tessitura* suitable for Mrs. Cibber's alto voice. The 6/8 time signature usually denotes a gay tempo, and this piece is no exception.

The only real word painting that Arne attempts with so simple a text and context is to emphasize the characteristic qualities of the shepherd folk, alternately stressing "guileless," "happy," and "free" by setting them as the highest notes in their phrases. In fact, the song's highest note, D above middle C, never occurs except under the word "guileless" or the word "happy." Garrick adds interest to his lyrics by setting up the last two lines in question and answer format, and Arne punctuates his lines with fermatas to retain the separation effectively. The final repetition of the rhetorical "And who are so guileless, so happy as we?" is brought to a more satisfying close by altering the rhythm from the other similar lines, making the final four notes even eighth and quarter notes rather than the dotted rhythms of the final measures in the three previous lines.

The song from the original play which Garrick's new lyrics most closely resemble stylistically is the trio "Get you hence," sung by Nicholas, Mopsa, and Dorcas. The resemblance is significant since the singers of the trio are shepherds like Perdita. Shakespeare's other lyrics are sung by the witty and articulate Autolicus, and they differ in tone and diction from those of the shepherd trio. Garrick is, then, tailoring his song to fit the character, just as he would do with spoken dialogue.

The sweetness and sentimental mood of the sheepshearing song, so suitable for the guileless Perdita, was of course familiar to the midcentury audience accustomed to "sentimental comedy." The strength of that sentiment no doubt enabled the song to stand alone as a "hit" apart from the comedy. It is obvious that the song is longer by far than any of Shakespeare's, and its twenty lines make it considerably longer than the lengthened version of "Come, thou monarch." The length also suggests that it was intended both to support dramatic characterization or motivation and to entertain independently. Dr. Johnson's cynicism about this song only highlights Garrick's sentiment and humanity. When Mrs. Thrale praised Garrick as a master of light, lively verse, she singled out the line, "I'd [sic] smile with the simple, and feed with the poor"; to which Johnson replied, "Nay, my dear Lady, this will never do. Poor David! Smile with the simple! What folly is that! And who would feed with the poor that can help it? No, no; let me smile with the wise and feed with the rich."[10]

Yet many of those contemporary critics who disliked the adaptation spoke well of the song, as did actor and Garrick biographer Thomas Davies: "The sheep-shearing was preserved, with a very pleasing song on the subject, which Mrs. Cibber, in the part of Perdita, sung with that sweet simplicity which became the character."[11] What would have mattered most to Garrick, however, was that, according to Arthur Murphy, the line "The roses will bloom when there's peace in the breast" was "heard for a long time in every street in the metropolis."[12]

The funeral dirge Garrick wrote for Juliet for his 1750 production of *Romeo and Juliet* may not have been sung in the streets, but it was continually sung in the theater into the next century. A 1751 report describes the added scene:

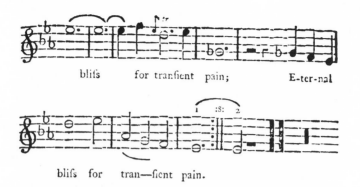

blifs   for tranfient   pain;   E-ter-nal

blifs   for   tran—fient   pain.

Song **XII.** What frenzy muft his foul poffefs. Hoole.

Song **XIII.** To tinkling brooks, to twilight fhades. Warton.

No airs known.

Song **XIV.** Come, come, my good fhepherds, our flocks
[we muft fhear. Garrick.

Set by mr. Michael Arne.

Come, come, my good   fhepherds, our flocks we muft fhear,

In your ho-li-day fuits with your   lafs-es appear; The

happieft   of folk   are the   guile-lefs   and fre, And

who

Figure 1: "The Sheep Shearing Song" from *Florizel and Perdita* (1756). From David Garrick's adaptation of Shakespeare's *A*

172

who are so guileless so hap—py as we?

Who are so guileless, so hap—py as we. The

hap—piest of folk are the guile-less and free,

guile—less and free, guileless and free, And

who are so guileless so hap—py as we?

Song XV. How sacred and how innocent. Mrs. Philips.

Song XVI. Through groves sequester'd, dark and still.
[Hawkesworth.

No airs known.

Song XVII.

Winter's Tale, in Joseph Ritson, *Select Collection of English Songs,* vol. 3, Pt. 3, Song 14 (London: 1783). By permission of the University of Delaware Library.

In the play an entire funeral is represented, with bells tolling, and a choir singing. . . . The scene represents the interior of a church. To my feeling this appears rather profane, but putting this aside, nothing of the kind could be represented more beautifully or naturally. The funeral dirges and the choirs made the whole ceremony too solemn for theatrical representation, especially on the English stage, which has no superior in the world, and on which everything is produced with the highest degree of truth. This effect can be attained more easily here than upon any other stage, owing to the quantity of actors, including dancers and singers, of whom fifty are sometimes to be seen in one night . . . and the quantity of different decorations, machinery, and dresses, which are provided regardless of cost and thorough completeness.[13]

Garrick's processional scene was still being performed by Kemble's company in Paris, and probably inspired a corresponding movement in Berlioz's *Romeo and Juliet*.[14] It had apparently been dropped by 1878 when Fanny Kemble expressed pleasure at its demise. Yet she noted that even during her career the procession had been performed (c. 1830), although her description of the music seems to indicate that the dirge may have been supplanted by traditional funeral music more in keeping with that period.

The circumstances under which the dirge was written are well known, but they provide a colorful footnote to eighteenth-century stage history. In 1748 Garrick had revived Shakespeare's *Romeo and Juliet* nearly intact after his audience had for years seen only Otway's *Caius Marius*. He coached his other leading man, Spranger Barry, and his favorite leading lady, Mrs. Susannah Cibber, in the lead roles; it was immensely popular. After salary disputes, Barry and Mrs. Cibber defected to Covent Garden for the 1750 season, where John Rich hoped to crush Garrick by opening the season with the two great stage lovers in their greatest roles. Undaunted, Garrick undertook the role of Romeo himself and trained Georgie Bellamy as Juliet. On July 27 Garrick wrote to co-manager James Lacy, "Let them do their worst, we must have the best company. . . . I shall be soon ready in *Romeo*, which we will bring out early; I have altered something, in the beginning and have made him only in love with Juliet."[15]

Both theaters opened with the play on September 28, and the subsequent twelve performances at both became known as the "Battle of the Romeos." Rich had a surprise weapon in his arsenal, however, as he announced in *The Gentleman's Magazine*: "Sept. 28. Romeo and Juliet with an additional scene of the Funeral Procession of Juliet, in which was introduced a solemn dirge (The words from Shakespeare) set to music by Mr. Arne."[16] The writer of the lyrics, certainly *not* Shakespeare, has never been definitely identified, but is generally thought to be Theophilus Cibber, son of Colley and ex-husband of Susannah.

Just three nights later Drury Lane added its own "additional scene representing the funeral procession to the monument of the Capulets: vocal parts, Beard, Reinhold, Master Mattocks, Wilder, Mrs. Clive, Miss Norris, Mrs. Matthews, etc. The music of the funeral procession composed by Dr. Boyce." [17] Garrick apparently commissioned William Boyce to set his lyrics as quickly as possible. This aspect of the battle has received far less attention than the clash of actors, yet it illustrates in dramatic fashion Dr. Burney's famous appraisal of the careers of these two most eminent mid-century English composers, Boyce and Arne, as "frequently concurrents at the theaters and in each other's way, particularly at Drury-lane." [18]

During the first week or so, the "battle" got much attention, for there was a great flurry of comparison shopping by the wits and critics, with much debate in the press. The *Daily Advertiser* of 11 October, however, summed up the growing impatience of the general public:

> Well-what tonight, says angry Ned,
>   As up from bed he rouses,
> Romeo again! and shakes his head,
>   Ah! Pox on both your houses!

Even had Drury Lane not outlasted Covent Garden by a thirteenth performance, it is likely that more people would have heard Garrick's dirge than Rich's because once everyone had sampled the two actors, a common practice developed of watching the first two acts at Covent Garden to view Barry's more romantic figure, then dashing over to Drury Lane where the unparalleled tragedian prevailed in the final acts.

In this case Garrick's song did not have to share the stage with Shakespeare's songs. The processional dirge is pompous and majestic, with the weighty lyrics contributing to the overall effect of the occasion. The new lyrics were appended to the end of the second printing by Tonson and Draper:

> CHORUS
>
> Rise, rise!
>   Heart-breaking sighs
> The woe-fraught bosom swell;
>   For sighs alone,
>   And dismal moan,
> Should echo *Juliet's* knell.

AIR

She's gone—the sweetest flow'r of May,
   That blooming blest our sight;
Those eyes which shone like breaking day,
   Are set in endless night!

She's gone, she's gone, nor leaves behind
   So fair a form, so pure a mind;
How could'st thou, Death, at once destroy,
   The *Lover's* hope, the *Parent's* joy?

Thou spotless soul, look down below,
   Our unfeign'd sorrow see;
O give us strength to bear our woe,
   To bear the loss of Thee!
          (6.1.1–21)

The strongly accented dimeter of three lines in the chorus, with which the procession begins and ends, lends the proper rhythmic quality to "*Juliet's* knell." The rhyme of the words "swell" and "knell" also accentuate the bell's tolling. The first and third verses have an even hymn stanza, 4/3/4/3/, matched by an abab rhyme scheme. Garrick achieves variety, and also adds to the solemnity of the second, gravest verse, by rhyming it aabb in a weightier tetrameter quatrain.

Even in this formulaic setting, we again see character detailed through Garrick's lyrics. Juliet is "the sweetest flow'r of May," of fair form, pure mind, and spotless soul. In describing her eyes "which shone like breaking day" and are "set in endless night," Garrick picks up Shakespeare's dawn imagery. That first stanza, containing both the flower and dawn images, is also more lyrical than the others because of its alliteration as the flower "blooming blest our sight." The final verse is given added grandeur by its long vowel sounds.

The competition pitting the Boyce and Arne dirges against each other further highlights what Bertrand H. Bronson refers to as "the Shakespeare revival, of which Arne's and Boyce's settings and incidental pieces are only the most successful musical manifestation among many attractive things."[19] Dr. Thomas Arne had worked with Garrick on many occasions, and is considered by some to have been a more inventive composer than Boyce, although erratic and highly irresponsible. It seems, however, that Garrick would have had no reason to have been disappointed in Boyce's work. Roger Fiske notes that Arne's notorious moral laxness carried over into "slapdash composing." He goes on to compare the two composers' work: "At best his [Arne's] inspiration was loftier, his scoring more imaginative than Boyce's, but too often he wrote below his capabilities. Boyce on the other hand was conscientious and consistent, and made the most of his talents. His quick music is often more virile than Arne's, his counterpoint stronger and less conventional. Perhaps he lacked a little of Arne's ease and individuality when it came to sublimating the English ballad, but he had his own vein of lyricism, and at its best it was infinitely pleasing." [20]

Since the setting (see figure 2) was for a dirge, Boyce was somewhat limited in his range for enlivening Garrick's lyrics. He does find material that suggests itself naturally in a few places, however. The "echo" of Juliet's knell can be heard, as the notes for the second repetition of the word "echo" are the third consecutive repetition of a two-note phrase. In his setting of the first and most lyrical verse, he emphasizes the imagery by harmonizing the words "Flow'r" and "bloom," the only words beyond the opening chords to be harmonized. In the same verse, the words "endless, endless" are given the longest run, the second "endless" being set with more notes to each syllable than any other word in the dirge, as if flowing on endlessly. Garrick's metrical variation of the second verse invites Boyce to vary his melody line, mostly through inversion and ornamentation. (That the harmonic patterns remain very similar is evident in the nearly identical bass lines for the two verses.)

According to Charles Haywood, who first traced a copy of the Boyce setting, long thought to be lost, to the collection of an obscure colonial American composer, the dirge music embodies Boyce's unpretentious personal style. [21] Arne's dirge had featured muffled trumpets and drums, ending with a three-part chorus, "Ah, hapless maid," accompanied by flute and strings. While Boyce's scoring was comparable to Arne's, Garrick's finer lyrics enabled him to produce a dirge which Fiske describes as having "far more substance and genuine feeling." [22]

Still, we might wonder why someone interested in promoting "pure Shakespeare" would have made an opera out of *A Midsummer Night's Dream* or *The Tempest*, or why he would have felt compelled to write a funeral dirge for Juliet or a sheepshearing song for Perdita. Part, but not all of the answer lies in Garrick's intimate connection with the audience for whom he wrote and his uncanny ability to sense their pleasure. Yet, putting generations of theater fashion and of artistic and scholarly concern aside, Garrick was first an actor; therefore, for him the heart of drama was the human heart—and surely part of his love affair with Shakespeare was inspired by a sense of human as well as artistic kinship.

178

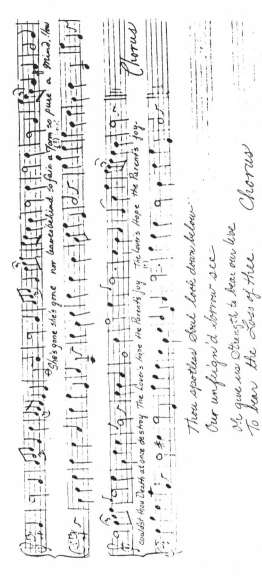

Figure 2: "A solemn Dirge in Romeo and Juliet," in *Francis Hopkinson his Book* (ML96.H83). Microcopy enhanced by Kenneth E. Gadomski and corrected by musicologist David Cohen. By permission of the Library of Congress, Music Division.

179

His devout study of characterization enabled him as an adaptor to retain the full intensity of Shakespeare's characters even in the shorter acting versions of the eighteenth century. A chief purpose of his songs, beyond adding the color and fun his audience craved, was to heighten characterization; through the interplay of music and lyric he could accomplish this economically and forcefully. Song can reveal human emotion and touch human emotion, the essential chord Garrick strove to strike.

Prior to Fiske's work and the Stone-Kahrl biography, Garrick's musical contributions were generally too little noticed and too little valued. While there is little evidence about Garrick's interest in music away from the theater, he was certainly vitally concerned with the role of music in producing dramatic effects. In some respects, his music for the Shakespeare adaptations may give the best indication of what he felt that role should be, because we know the seriousness of his purpose in those adaptations went beyond mere entertainment. He approached the writing of lyrics as a playwright, striving for characterization and dramatic effect, more than as a poet fulfilling convention. These songs, all written within the period 1750–1763, both add to our picture of Garrick's developing writing skills and provide a new perspective from which to appreciate his treatment of "the God of his Idolatry."

NOTES

1 George Winchester Stone, Jr., "Garrick's Handling of Shakespeare's Plays, and His Influence on the Changed Attitude toward Shakespearean Criticism during the Eighteenth Century," Diss. Harvard, 1938.

2 The Letters of David Garrick, ed. David M. Little and George M. Kahrl (Cambridge, Mass.: Harvard Univ. Press, 1963), 1:404.

3 Charles Burney, A General History of Music from the Earliest Ages to the Present Period (1789; rev. ed., 1935; reprint, New York: Dover, 1974), 2:681.

4 George Winchester Stone, Jr., and George M. Kahrl, David Garrick: A Critical Biography (Carbondale: Southern Illinois Univ. Press, 1979), 223.

5 Garrick's Adaptations of Shakespeare, in The Plays of David Garrick, ed. Harry William Pedicord and Frederick Louis Bergmann (Carbondale: Southern Illinois Univ. Press, 1981), 4:4.

6 Quotations from Pedicord and Bergmann's edition of The Plays will be cited parenthetically in the text.

7 Peter J. Seng, The Vocal Songs in the Plays of Shakespeare (Cambridge, Mass.: Harvard Univ. Press, 1967), 213.

8 Frank A. Hedgcock, *A Cosmopolitan Actor: David Garrick and His French Friends* (London: Stanley Paul & Co., 1912), 76. In his book Hedgcock makes too much of the influence of Garrick's French connections on his taste, and overstates Garrick's affinity for the formal unities. He represents Garrick's adaptation of Shakespeare as making the plays less English, more continental.

9 Arthur Murphy, *The Life of David Garrick, Esq.* (Dublin: Brett Smith, 1801), 1:284ff.

10 James Boswell, *Boswell's Life of Johnson*, ed. George Birkbeck Hill and L. F. Powell (Oxford: Clarendon Press, 1934), 2:79.

11 Thomas Davies, *Memoirs of the Life of David Garrick* (London, 1808; reprint, New York: Benjamin Blom, 1969), 1:314.

12 Murphy, *Life of Garrick* 2:286.

13 Frederick Kielmansegge, *Diary of a Journey to England 1761–1762*, trans. Countess Kielmansegge (London, 1902), 221–22. Quoted in *The Plays of David Garrick* 3:411.

14 Roger Fiske, *English Theatre Music in the Eighteenth Century* (London: Oxford Univ. Press, 1973), 217.

15 *Letters of David Garrick* 1:152.

16 *Gentleman's Magazine*, 20 Sept. 1750.

17 *General Advertiser*, 1 Oct. 1750.

18 Burney, *History of Music* 2:1010.

19 Bertrand H. Bronson, "Some Aspects of Music and Literature in the Eighteenth Century," in *Music and Literature in England in the Seventeenth and Eighteenth Centuries* (Los Angeles: William Andrews Clark Library/UCLA, 1953), 23.

20 Fiske, *English Theatre Music*, 359.

21 Charles Haywood, "William Boyce's 'Solemn Dirge' in Garrick's *Romeo and Juliet* Production of 1750," *Shakespeare Quarterly* 11 (1960): 173–87.

22 Fiske, *English Theatre Music*, 217.

The Antagonisms and Affinities of Johnson and Gibbon

MARTINE WATSON BROWNLEY

On both personal and intellectual grounds, the relationship between Samuel Johnson and Edward Gibbon has usually been portrayed in terms of contrasts and antagonisms. From the outside, in respect to appearance and manners, the younger Colman's recollections of an evening spent with the two men when he was a boy of thirteen remain the most striking summation:

> On the day I first sat down with Johnson, in his rusty brown, and his black worsteads, Gibbon was placed opposite to me in a suit of flower'd velvet, with a bag and sword. Each had his measured phraseology, and Johnson's famous parallel, between Dryden and Pope, might be loosely parodied, in reference to himself and Gibbon.— Johnson's style was grand, and Gibbon's elegant; the stateliness of the former was sometimes pedantick, and the polish of the latter was occasionally finical. Johnson march'd to kettle-drums and trumpets; Gibbon moved to flutes and haut-boys; Johnson hew'd passages through the Alps, while Gibbon levell'd walks through parks and gardens. Maul'd as I had been by Johnson [who had been rude to Colman when introduced], Gibbon pour'd balm upon my bruises, by condescending, once or twice, in the course of the evening, to talk with me;—the great historian was light and playful, suiting his matter to the capacity of the boy. . . .[1]

From Boswell on, commentators have tended to see the exterior contrasts between the two men as emblematic of deeper intellectual an-

183

tagonisms, particularly relying on some of Johnson's more reductive remarks about history and others' assessments of these ("There is but a shallow stream of thought in history," for example, and "General history had little of his regard"[2]). Recently, however, John A. Vance has corrected certain oversimplified dichotomies in this area by showing in detail the many similarities in the attitudes of the two toward Gibbon's chosen field.[3] One way of approaching the minds and characters of these two complex men is to take a closer look at some of the contrasts and comparisons that can be drawn between them. Underlying similarities beneath the personal differences and other deeper contrasts beyond certain affinities in their intellectual stances can illumine some of the strengths and weaknesses of both Gibbon and Johnson as men and as thinkers.

Johnson's and Gibbon's habits differed as radically as their appearances. Gibbon, rigidly punctual, rose early every morning; Johnson, chronically lax about adhering to a schedule, found it difficult to get up at all. The affected French mannerisms favored by Gibbon contrasted with Johnson's doggedly English brusqueness. Their approaches toward social conversation succinctly highlight the differences in their attitudes and behavior. Johnson's abilities in fiery and brutally direct intellectual exchanges, and his love of them, are too well known to require comment. In contrast, Gibbon is often thought of as disliking conversation, largely because of Boswell's depictions of him in the *Life*. But Gibbon actually enjoyed talking with others, as long as it was on his own terms; he insisted that he sought conversation "always . . . with a view to amusement rather than information."[4] His contemporaries' complaints—"He appears rather inditing to an amanuensis than holding conversation"; "There was no interchange of ideas, for no one had a chance of replying"[5]—reveal how he dominated groups in which he was the most important person. In conversation, as in life generally, Johnson, aggressively asserting his powers, overwhelmed by force at close range; Gibbon, cautious and retiring, maintained his position by engaging only at a discrete distance. These contrasting modes were strategies evolved to fulfill the same purposes: to protect the self and to control the responses of other people. Similarly, many of the disparities in behavior between the two can be seen as individual adjustments which each made to personal experiences and circumstances which were in important ways markedly similar.

Uneasy family relationships, youthful physical disabilities, and social awkwardness and ineptness were among the factors that in both cases led the two men to compensate in their different ways. Neither one had a happy childhood. Hester Piozzi wrote that "many of the severe reflections on domestic life in Rasselas, took their source from its author's keen recollections of the time passed in his early years."[6] In his *Memoirs* Gibbon entered a protest "against trite and lavish praise of the happiness of our boyish years, which is echoed with so much affection in the World," asserting firmly "that happiness I have never known."[7] Both fathers showed certain instabilities, Johnson's with the melancholy which his son inherited, and Gibbon's with the capriciousness and inconstancy which led William Law to depict him as Flatus in the *Serious Call*. Tensions marked the relationships of both with their mothers. Johnson told Thrale that though he loved his mother, he did not respect her.[8] Gibbon, who considered himself "neglected" by his mother, wrote that he "seldom enjoyed the smiles of maternal tenderness."[9] As children both suffered severe health problems. Johnson remembered his aunt's comment that "she would not have picked such a poor creature up in the street,"[10] while Gibbon recalled "a time when I swallowed more Physic than food."[11] Adulthood failed to markedly improve the physical appearance of either man. Sir John Hawkins's comparison of Johnson to Polyphemus[12] reflects more than physical size, and Gibbon, whose Lausanne nickname of "the Potato" sums up his shape, was once described as looking like a balloon with feet.

Part of the residue of these early experiences was continuing social awkwardness and deeper loneliness in the lives of both men. Although Gibbon and Johnson liked and sought company, neither was entirely comfortable in dealing with other people. Gibbon noted that he had "not been endowed by art or Nature with those happy gifts of confidence and address which unlock every door, and every bosom"—significantly, connecting his problems in part to his "sickly childhood."[13] Johnson admitted that he had never even tried to please until he was over thirty years old, "considering the matter as hopeless."[14] Both men showed a felt sense of isolation throughout their lives. Whether written in London or Lausanne, at Oxford or in the militia, Gibbon's letters and journals reveal that he saw himself as to some extent an outsider in every circle he frequented, never entirely fitting in. Johnson, describing himself as a "straggler," wrote in a letter that he could leave London and travel to Cairo "without being missed here or observed there."[15]

None of these parallels, of course, is meant to suggest that Johnson and Gibbon were actually unrecognized potential soulmates. Religious views alone stood as an insurmountable barrier between them, although even here their opposite stances evolved from mutual deep interests in theological and religious questions. In politics and sexual matters, too, there were crucial differences. Finally, some of their differences were due simply to irreconcilably opposite tastes. The patterns of behavior which Gibbon and Johnson evolved partly in response to similar experiences were in each case precisely those that would most offend the other man. And because each reacted only to the outer defenses of the other, they never became close enough to understand some of the ways in which their pasts, and hence their presents, were alike. But the young man who combined his own attitudes with those of the philosophes to open his first published work with the characteristically general "l'Histoire des empires est celle de la misère des hommes," and the old man who characteristically humanized the same observation to write in a letter only months before his death that "this is my history, like all other histories, a narrative of misery," had more in common than they or their contemporaries were able to see.[16]

Johnson's and Gibbon's different behavioral patterns can be seen partly as reactions to and attempts to control the effects of their similar past experiences in order to function in the present. In intellectual terms, both were also interested in controlling the larger general past—the past of man as it can be known through history—for the use of the present. In his effective demolition of the myth of Johnson as a monolithic detractor of history, John Vance has shown the many similarities between Johnson's views and Gibbon's: their agreement about positive and negative aspects of antiquarians; the informed but not encompassing skepticism shared by both; their dislike of excessive romanticizing of the past; the desire of both for historical foci larger than merely the political; their hesitancies about the "great man" theory of history; and finally, the similar evaluations both made on the role of chance in past events.[17] Their views also coincided in other ways. Johnson and Gibbon agreed on the essential role of chronology in history, while both distrusted excessive systemization imposed on historical evidence.[18] Both followed their age in criticizing the earlier convention of inserting imaginary speeches into histories.[19] Neither wanted the writing of history to be mere compilation, although each saw that such compilations had their uses.[20] Both Gibbon and Johnson were in general intellectual terms in many ways as much direct heirs of seventeenth-century thought as they were representatives of the perspectives of their own era, and their views of history were formed accordingly.

Although the similarities in Johnson's and Gibbon's beliefs about aspects of history do a good deal to clear away perceptions that Johnson's approaches were simplistic and uninformed, the differences in their views are equally important. Some of the divergencies were due, naturally enough, to the fact that Gibbon was a practicing historian and Johnson was not. Godfrey Davies has pointed out that Johnson did not understand how much information was actually available to historians and also failed to appreciate methodological changes in the field.[21] Although both agreed on the importance of eyewitnesses' testimony and recognized some of its shortcomings, Gibbon showed a greater awareness of its limitations than Johnson.[22] On individual historians, Gibbon's and Johnson's evaluations often differed significantly. Both appreciated Voltaire's literary abilities, but despite Johnson's recognition that these very abilities compromised Voltaire's accuracy, he seems to have thought more highly of the Frenchman's work than Gibbon did.[23] Gibbon admired Robertson and Hume; Johnson did not.[24] Their recorded opinions on Knolles, in which they seem to be describing two different historians, sum up the differences in their approaches. In *Rambler 122* Johnson lauds Knolles's content and describes him as having "displayed all the excellencies that narration can admit," with "nothing turgid in his dignity, nor superfluous in his copiousness."[25] Gibbon retorted in a note to the *Decline and Fall* obviously designed to show who could better assess historians. Citing Johnson's praise, he proceeded to demolish Knolles's history as "a partial and verbose compilation from Latin writers, thirteen hundred folio pages of speeches and battles."[26] The reference to the orations is particularly pointed, since they had provided Johnson's only objection to the work. Singling out battles also carries a sting, for Johnson, who considered the "history of manners, of common life" the most valuable branch of history, had written of the uselessness of accounts focusing on "the defeat of generals" and "the stratagems of war."[27] Most characteristically of all, however, Gibbon's strong rebuttal appeared in a volume published after Johnson's death.

Other differences in Johnson's and Gibbon's views on history cannot be accounted for simply by the practitioner's greater knowledge of his craft. On the question of the ultimate purpose of history, for example, they diverge. Johnson's beliefs always reflect earlier traditions that history should offer moral instruction. His strongest praise and his most damning indictments of history all focus on its role in shaping the individual's life and actions. On the positive side, he described history as "that study by which the manners are most easily formed, from which the most efficacious instruction is received."[28] He also ranked "an acquaintance with the history of mankind" second only to the "religious and moral knowledge of right and wrong," "whether we provide for action or conversation, whether we wish to be useful or pleasing."[29] Such statements show Johnson's high regard for what history could do. Unfortunately, because history as written seldom if ever fulfilled such expectations, his resulting dissatisfaction accounts in part for his many negative remarks on it. Thus he wrote in *Rambler 60* that the "general and rapid narratives of history . . . afford few lessons applicable to private life."[30] He complained in *Idler 84* that history offered "useless truth," with examples more for "shew than use": they "rather diversify conversation than regulate life."[31] Positive about history in the abstract, Johnson was substantially less favorable to particular histories because they offered so little information that had direct personal and particularly moral utility.

In the *Decline and Fall* Gibbon expresses the conventional dictum that history "undertakes to record the transactions of the past, for the instruction of future, ages."[32] But his writings make it clear that in this statement, insofar as he is not simply mouthing a platitude—and with Gibbon it is sometimes hard to tell—the instruction to which he refers has little direct utility for an individual's or a group's actions. He had no use for what he described as the "didactic method of writing history."[33] He shared Johnson's pessimism about history as a behavioral corrective. His skepticism surfaced in a query among his notes, "Historians friends to Virtue?," to which his reply was "yes—with exceptions."[34] In a journal written when he was not yet twenty years old, he noted similarities between the contemporary citizens of Berne and the Romans during the early Social War and then commented: "Les Bernois ont lû l'histoire, pourquoi n'ont ils point remarqué que les mêmes causes produisent les mêmes effets? La reponse est facile mais delicate, c'est que la Cupidité particuliere éteint les lumieres de la raison."[35] In the *Decline and Fall* he also remarked that "the experience of past faults, which may sometimes correct the mature age of an individual, is seldom profitable to the successive generations of mankind."[36] Instead, he saw the purpose of history as satisfying what he believed was a tendency innate in human beings: "Nature has implanted in our breasts a lively impulse to extend the narrow span of our existence." It is in this sense that he considered history "a liberal and useful study."[37]

Gibbon's most powerful statement about history's use and instructive potential focused on its broadening of the intellectual scope of the individual:

> A being of the nature of man, endowed with the same faculties, but with a longer measure of existence, would cast down a smile of pity and contempt on the crimes and follies of human ambition, so

eager, in a narrow span, to grasp at a precarious and short-lived enjoyment. It is thus that the experience of history exalts and enlarges the horizon of our intellectual view. In a composition of some days, in a perusal of some hours, six hundred years have rolled away, and the duration of a life or reign is contracted to a fleeting moment; the grave is ever beside the throne; the success of a criminal is almost instantly followed by the loss of his prize; and our immortal reason survives and disdains the sixty phantoms of kings, who have passed before our eyes and faintly dwell in our remembrance.[38]

The very generality and rapidity which Johnson disliked in histories was for Gibbon a strength. In a similar vein he explained after drawing a comparison between primitive and civilized Scotland that "such reflections tend to enlarge the circle of our ideas."[39] For Gibbon, history found its primary purpose in this kind of intellectual expansion for the individual reader. To satisfy this predominantly intellectual priority, he evolved his concept of the "philosophical historian," the historical writer who combines the scholarship of the antiquarian with the reflections and insights of the philosopher.[40]

Dedicated to factual truth in history, Gibbon also demanded more from it. In his early *Mémoire sur la monarchie des Mèdes*, he commented that "aux yeux d'un philosophe, les faits composent la partie la moins intéressante de l'histoire."[41] On these kinds of grounds he censured Knolles, doubting whether his history "can either instruct or amuse an enlightened age, which requires from the historian some tincture of philosophy and criticism."[42] Johnson, eager for history to have direct moral utility, agreed in principle that it had to be more than simply a chronological collection of facts. At the same time, he became uneasy whenever history went beyond strictly verifiable factual evidence. Explaining the sources of this uneasiness requires consideration of the ways Johnson and Gibbon felt history should be written and ultimately involves the extent to which each was willing to accept historical writing as literature.

Again, on the surface, Gibbon and Johnson agreed on the proper form and style for history. Like every commentary on historical writing since classical times, remarks scattered throughout their works indicate that both believed that history demanded a middle style between the overly poetical and the overly prosaic. Both also required that history be written in narrative form. But Johnson's remarks on style show a marked tendency to underestimate the difficulties involved in creating an effective historical style and narrative. "Great abilities," he said in conversation, "are not requisite for an Historian; for in historical composition, all the greatest powers of the human mind are quiescent." He added that "some penetration, accuracy, and colouring will fit a man for the task, if he can give the application which is necessary."[43] In *Rambler 122* he emphasized reasons why the historian's writing should ostensibly be much easier than the poet's or the philosopher's and described the appropriate stylistic level as "that mediocrity of style."[44] Gibbon, of course, knew from experience the many narrative problems faced by the historian and the difficulties involved in attaining the stylistic mean. He portrayed them eloquently and dramatically in his *Memoirs:*

> At the outset all was dark and doubtful: even the title of the work, the true aera of the decline and fall of the Empire, the limits of the Introduction, the division of the chapters, and the order of the narrative; and I was often tempted to cast away the labour of seven years. . . . [M]any experiments were made before I could hit the middle tone between a dull Chronicle and a Rhetorical declamation; three times did I compose the first chapter, and twice the second and third, before I was tolerably satisfied with their effect.[45]

Johnsonian overstatement is usually a reaction against some kind of excess, and such is the case with his frequent reductiveness about the stylistic efforts historical writing required. His criticisms of contemporary historians show the stimulus to which he was responding. Again and again he castigated them for overly poetic deviations from the stylistic mean traditionally considered suitable for history. He complained about Dalrymple's "foppery" and Thomas Blackwell's "luxuriant style" and "gaudy or hyperbolical" epithets.[46] But William Robertson, whom Johnson liked personally best of all the historians he knew, received the most frequent attacks, for his "*verbiage*," "ornaments," "pretty words," and "tinsel."[47] In contrast, Lord Hailes's prosaic *Annals of Scotland* earned Johnson's praise partly because it lacked "laboured splendour of language," while Goldsmith's Roman history pleased him for its concision and its "plain narrative."[48] Just as in family portraits Johnson favored resemblance to the subject over fine art,[49] in historical writing he sought truth rather than stylistic excellence. His concern was that the literary art of contemporary historians— what he described to Boswell as "that painted form which is the taste of this age"[50]—was undermining the truth which he considered essential for history. He reiterated the metaphor of painting in two remarks on Robertson which emphasize his rigid and literal conception of historical truth. In contrasting Hailes's "mere dry particulars" to Robertson's work, he commented: "Robertson paints; but the misfortune is, you are sure he does not know the people whom he paints; so you cannot suppose a likeness."[51] At another time he remarked that

"Robertson paints minds as Sir Joshua paints faces in a history-piece; he imagines an heroick countenance." The conversational context of Johnson's second comment shows the root of his concern. Claiming that Robertson's work "is not history, it is imagination," he asserted that "you must look upon Robertson's work as romance, and try it by that standard. History it is not."[52]

To Johnson, excessively ornamental historical style signaled the presence of the ubiquitous human imagination and its inevitable distortions. Indeed, almost all of his negative remarks about historical writing include references to control of the imagination. When he claims that no great abilities are necessary for a historian, he adds, "imagination is not required in any high degree."[53] In the same sentence which includes his remark on the "mediocrity" of historical style, he notes that the historian must "confine his mind" to an "even tenour of imagination."[54] He criticizes Blackwell because he "seems to have heated his imagination, . . . and to believe that he can affect others."[55] Johnson recognized that "the Spirit of history . . . is contrary to minute exactness,"[56] but he ultimately distrusted anything which might in the least compromise such literal accuracy. He remarked in conversation: "That certain Kings reigned, and certain battles were fought, we can depend upon as true; but all the colouring, all the philosophy, of history is conjecture."[57] He never adequately resolved the conflict between his belief in the need for effective historical style and interpretation and his perception that almost any literary form imposed on historical evidence necessarily distorts the literal truth in certain ways. As much as any other single factor, this conflict explains the apparent contradictions between Johnson's high opinion of history as a pursuit and his almost constant dissatisfaction with its execution.

Johnson's uneasiness with highly mannered historical writing accounts in part for his dislike of Tacitus, who he believed had rather "made notes for an historical work, than . . . written a history."[58] Gibbon, in contrast, asserted that "je ne connois que Tacite qui ait rempli mon idée de cet historien-philosophe."[59] This divergence of opinion shows the orientations of the two: Gibbon remained serenely unconcerned about the very stylistic devices which reflected the presence of the historian's imagination that Johnson feared. To Gibbon, "the style of an author should be the image of his mind,"[60] and the mind of the philosophical historian as he envisioned it was formed by the fullest possible imaginative participation in his subject. As he explained in the *Essai sur l'étude de la littérature*, "cet esprit" necessary for a philosophical approach was developed and exercised by "l'étude de la littérature, cette habitude de devenir, tour à tour, Grec, Romain, disciple de Zénon ou d'Epicure."[61] Insofar as such imaginative participation might make history subjective, moving it away from the kind of truth represented by bare factual evidence, he was undisturbed.

Gibbon himself was of course an extremely conscientious historian, indefatigably collecting and evaluating his materials. He also recognized and disliked linguistic distortions in historical writing, criticizing Ammianus Marcellinus because "it is not easy to distinguish his facts from his metaphors."[62] But that he couches his censure in this instance simply in terms of Ammianus's "bad taste" suggests his acceptance of the role of the subjectivity of the historian in writing. His comment on writers during the reign of Theodosius shows the kind of relativism which he brought to all his evaluations of sources and to historical writing in general: "The complaints of contemporary writers, who deplore the increase of luxury and deprivation of manners, are commonly expressive of their peculiar temper and situation."[63] Gibbon knew that the historian is no more exempt than any other writer from the constraints of his personal vision and of his times. He believed that histories had to be based solidly on the evidence available, but he also recognized that great histories required in addition a uniquely personal perspective, interpretation, and presentation of that evidence. David Jordan and Leo Braudy have both traced in detail how Gibbon evolved this stance, how he gradually came to see, in Jordan's words, the "tentative and personal nature of historical truth," "the historian as the creator of the past," and "a work of history as a self-contained object of artistic unity."[64] Gibbon was able to accept historical writing as literature, with all the limitations that such a judgment implies, in a way that Johnson never could.

Personally, the relationship between Johnson and Gibbon involves violent ostensible disparities with certain underlying similarities between the two men; intellectually, the ostensible differences cover important similarities in viewpoint, which in turn yield to vital differences in their approaches to the purpose, content, and style of historical writing. Just as in behavior and appearance, on basic questions of history Johnson and Gibbon were both concerned with exerting control. In both cases, the kind of control and the amount of control they personally sought and that they expected the historian to seek differed. Their divergent responses to the threats that the imagination and literary art pose to truth in historical writing leave them one final similarity: both show an awareness of and a concern for the relationship between history and literature which far surpasses the attitudes of most of their contemporaries. Johnson's perceptions were rudimentary compared to the more sophisticated insights which Gibbon gained empirically, but nevertheless both dealt directly with problems in the role of literary elements in history which would surface again with urgency only in the mid-twentieth century, in the works of historians like Fernand Braudel and philosophers of history like Hayden White. If in their lifetimes there could be scant significant communication between the big man in his black worsteads and the little man in his flowered velvet, their joint concerns about the nature of historical writing as it becomes literature can finally meet and even briefly merge within the context created by the ongoing twentieth-century debate about the elusive relationship between "fact" and fiction.

NOTES

1 Quoted in D. M. Low, *Edward Gibbon: 1737–1794* (London: Chatto and Windus, 1937), 228. Low has written on Johnson's and Gibbon's relationship in "Edward Gibbon and the Johnsonian Circle," *New Rambler* (June 1960): 2–14. See also W. H. J., "Gibbon and Johnson," *Notes and Queries* 173 (1937): 97.

2 James Boswell, *Boswell's Life of Johnson*, ed. G. B. Hill, rev. L. F. Powell (Oxford: Clarendon Press, 1934–64), 2:195; hereafter cited as *Life*. Arthur Murphy, "An Essay on the Life and Genius of Samuel Johnson, LL.D.," in *Johnsonian Miscellanies*, ed. George Birkbeck Hill (1897; reprint, New York: Barnes and Noble, 1966), 1:451.

3 John A. Vance, *Samuel Johnson and the Sense of History* (Athens: Univ. of Georgia Press, 1984).

4 *The Letters of Edward Gibbon*, ed. J. E. Norton (London: Cassell, 1956), 3:185.

5 Gavin de Beer, *Gibbon and His World* (London: Thames and Hudson, 1968), 110; G. M. Young, *Gibbon* (New York: D. Appleton, 1933), 122.

6 Hester Lynch Piozzi, *Anecdotes of the Late Samuel Johnson, LL.D.*, in *Johnsonian Miscellanies* 1:150–51.

7 Edward Gibbon, *Memoirs of My Life*, ed. Georges A. Bonnard (New York: Funk and Wagnalls, 1966), 43.

8 Piozzi, *Anecdotes*, 163.

9 Gibbon, *Letters* 3:45, and *Memoirs*, 34.

10 Samuel Johnson, *Diaries, Prayers, and Annals*, ed. E. L. McAdam, Jr., Donald and Mary Hyde, vol. I of *The Yale Edition of the Works of Samuel Johnson* (New Haven: Yale Univ. Press, 1958–), 5.

11 Gibbon, *Memoirs*, 29.

12 *The Life of Samuel Johnson, LL.D., by Sir John Hawkins, Knt.*, ed. Bertram H. Davis (New York: Macmillan, 1961), 147.

13 Gibbon, *Memoirs*, 94.

14 Piozzi, *Anecdotes*, 318.

15 *The Letters of Samuel Johnson, with Mrs. Thrale's Genuine Letters to Him*, ed. R. W. Chapman (Oxford: Clarendon Press, 1952), 3:306.

16 Gibbon, *Essai sur l'étude de la littérature*, in *The Miscellaneous Works of Edward Gibbon, Esq.*, ed. John, Lord Sheffield (London: John Murray, 1814), 4:15; Johnson, *Letters* 3:207.

17 Vance, *Johnson and the Sense of History*, 82–83, 145, 148, 156–57, 175.

18 Patricia B. Craddock, "Part I: Introduction," *The English Essays of Edward Gibbon* (Oxford: Clarendon Press, 1972), 1; Allen T. Hazen, *Samuel Johnson's Prefaces and Dedications* (New Haven: Yale Univ. Press, 1937), 88, 182; Johnson, "An Account of the Harleian Library," in *The Works of Samuel Johnson, LL.D.* (Oxford: Talboys and Wheeler, 1825), 5:186; Gibbon, *Essai*, 45; E. L. McAdam, Jr., *Dr. Johnson and the English Law* (Syracuse: Syracuse Univ. Press, 1951), 91–92, 99.

19 Johnson, *Rambler 122*, in *The Rambler*, ed. W. J. Bate and Albrecht Strauss, *The Yale Edition* 4:290; Gibbon, "Marginalia in Herodotus," in *English Essays*, 373.

20 Johnson, review of *Memoirs of the Court of Augustus*, in *Works* 6:9–10; Johnson, *Idler 85*, in *The Idler and the Adventurer*, ed. W. J. Bate, John M. Bullitt, and L. F. Powell, vol. 2 of *The Yale Edition*, 264–66; Gibbon, *Essai*, 22; Gibbon, *A Vindication of Some Passages in the Fifteenth and Sixteenth Chapters of the History of the Decline and Fall of the Roman Empire*, in *English Essays*, 278–79.

21 Godfrey Davies, "Dr. Johnson on History," *Huntington Library Quarterly* 1 (1948): 19–20; see also 6–7.

22 *Life* 2:79, 3:404; Hazen, *Johnson's Prefaces and Dedications*, 55; Gibbon, "Index Expurgatorius," in *English Essays*, 121.

23 *Life* 2:125, 3:404; *Anecdotes by William Seward, F.R.S.*, in *Johnsonian Miscellanies* 2:306; Vance, *Johnson and the Sense of History*, 193 n. 21, 195 n. 53. James D. Garrison surveys Gibbon's attitudes toward Voltaire in "Lively and Laborious: Characterization in Gibbon's Metahistory," *Modern Philology* 76 (1978), 173–78.

24 Gibbon, *Memoirs*, 99, 121; *Anecdotes by the Rev. Dr. Thomas Campbell*, in *Johnsonian Miscellanies* 2:48.

25 Johnson, *Rambler 122*, in *The Rambler* 4:290.

26 Gibbon, *The Decline and Fall of the Roman Empire*, ed. J. B. Bury (1914; reprint, New York: AMS Press, 1974), 7:26 n. 66. For other references to Johnson in the *Decline and Fall*, see George Birkbeck Hill's appendix to his edition of Gibbon's *Memoirs: The Memoirs of the Life of Edward Gibbon* (New York: Putnam's, 1900), 312–13.

27 *Life* 3:333, 5:79; Johnson, *Idler 84*, 262.

28 Johnson, "An Account of the Harleian Library," 184.

29 Johnson, *Lives of the English Poets*, ed. George Birkbeck Hill (Oxford: Clarendon Press, 1905), 1:99.

30 Johnson, *Rambler 60*, in *The Rambler* 3:319.

31 Johnson, *Idler 84*, 262.

32 Gibbon, *Decline and Fall* 2:87.

33 Gibbon, *A Vindication*, 304.

34 Gibbon, "Hints," in *English Essays*, 88.

35 Gibbon, *Miscellanea Gibboniana*, ed. Gavin R. de Beer, Georges A. Bonnard, Louis Junod (Lausanne: F. Rouge, 1952), 53.

36 Gibbon, *Decline and Fall* 4:318–19.

37 Gibbon, "An Address &c," in *English Essays*, 534.

38 Gibbon, *Decline and Fall* 5:258–59.

39 Ibid. 3:47.

40 For Gibbon on the "philosophical historian," see Frank E. Manuel, "Edward Gibbon: Historien-Philosophe," *Daedalus* 105 (1976): 231–45, and David Jordan, *Gibbon and His Roman Empire* (Urbana: Univ. of Illinois Press, 1971), 40–69.

41 Gibbon, *Mémoire sur la monarchie des Mèdes*, in *Miscellaneous Works* 3:126.

42 Gibbon, *Decline and Fall* 7:26 n. 66.

43 *Life* 1:424–25.

44 Johnson, *Rambler 122*, in *The Rambler* 4:289.

45 Gibbon, *Memoirs*, 155–56.

46 *Life* 2:237; Johnson, review of *Memoirs of the Court of Augustus*, 11, 15.

47 *Life* 2:236–37; *Anecdotes by the Rev. Dr. Thomas Campbell*, and *Apophthegms, Sentiments: Opinions, & Occasional Reflections*, in *Johnsonian Miscellanies* 2:48, 10.

48 Johnson, *Letters* 2:83; *Life* 2:237.

49 *Life* 5:219.

50 Ibid. 3:58.

51 Ibid. 3:404.

52 Ibid. 2:237.

53 Ibid. 1:424.

54 Johnson, *Rambler 122*, in *The Rambler* 4:289.

55 Johnson, review of *Memoirs of the Court of Augustus*, 13.

56 Johnson, *Letters* 1:20.

57 *Life* 2:365–66.

58 Ibid. 2:189.

59 Gibbon, *Essai*, 66.

60 Gibbon, *Memoirs*, 155.

61 Gibbon, *Essai*, 59; see also Jordan, *Gibbon and His Roman Empire*, 88–89.

62 Gibbon, *Decline and Fall* 3:72 n. 1.

63 Ibid. 3:196.

64 Jordan, *Gibbon and His Roman Empire*, 103, 99. See also Leo Braudy, *Narrative Form in History and Fiction* (Princeton: Princeton Univ. Press, 1970), 214–15.

A Measure of Power:
The Personal Charity of
Elizabeth Montagu

EDITH SEDGWICK LARSON

Elizabeth Robinson Montagu (1720–1800) is too often perceived in terms of stale images conjured up by Samuel Johnson's sobriquet for her, "Queen of the Blue-Stockings." [1] Disparaging connotations of pretentious self-interest sometimes associated with the bluestockings have made it easy to dismiss her and her friends as women largely superfluous in terms of wielding any real humanitarian power. Curiosity, prolonged acquaintance, and a fresh perspective are all needed to separate Elizabeth Montagu from the hackneyed two-dimensional stereotype evoked by old labels. Happily, her manuscript letters at the Huntington Library can provide such a new perspective and reveal a practical, assertive, humanistic, but financially oriented woman who skillfully wielded considerable power when female dependence was the norm. When reading these letters, I have looked for the letter or phrase which seemed marked by the spontaneity of honesty rather than that which seemed composed with an eye on reputation. I have looked for the unguarded expression and the unconscious pattern.

The pattern I will discuss here reveals that Elizabeth Montagu's power was demonstrated principally through her financial charity. In this paper I will explore some of the ways she dispensed charity and comment on some of the individuals who sought shelter under the umbrella of her influence. In particular, I will focus on individual

197

instances not mentioned in published editions of her letters:[2] on relatives, including those distantly related; on needy women; and on servants, in whom she took a matriarchal interest. Besides the significance of the breadth of the social spectrum encompassed by Elizabeth Montagu's charity, from servants to literary figures like Sarah Fielding, from relatives and friends to strangers like the workers in her husband's coal mines, two important points stand out. First, she saw herself as responsible for approaching the other members of her family, the majority of whom were men, and persuading them to contribute to needy relatives, and second, it was on issues of financial responsibility that she challenged and tested the power of the male heads of her family: her father, her eldest brother, and her husband.

Elizabeth Montagu's self-confidence and assertiveness were encouraged when she was a girl by her grandmother's second husband, Dr. Conyers Middleton, a professor of classical languages at Cambridge.[3] She and her sister Sarah were brought up as members of the landed gentry in the Kentish countryside. Elizabeth Robinson was born at York, October 2, 1720. She was the fourth child and first daughter of Matthew Robinson and his wife, Elizabeth Drake Robinson. Sarah Robinson, the only other girl among the nine children who lived to grow up, was born September 21, 1723. When they were very young, their mother inherited an impressive ancestral estate, Mount Morris, from her brother. Although Elizabeth's father had attended Trinity College, Cambridge, he had no profession. His large family and lack of fortune forced him to take advantage of his wife's inheritance and settle in the country.

One learns from the correspondence in the manuscripts of the Montagu Collection at the Huntington Library in San Marino, California, that living in the country cast a pall over Mr. Robinson's spirits. Furthermore, one learns that Elizabeth's father was always impatient and ill-tempered when confronted with financial transactions. It was Mrs. Robinson who oversaw the management of the estate and the family's records, and who at her death in 1745 left financial matters organized so that her husband had only to follow the pattern she had established. In being a good business manager she set a valuable precedent for her daughters, both of whom were to spend a substantial amount of time worrying about, making, and dispensing money as adults.

Initially, I approached the Montagu Collection, which numbers almost 7,000 pieces, searching for financial information regarding Elizabeth's younger sister, Sarah, who was a translator, novelist, and biographer. Beginning with the year 1762, when Sarah Robinson Scott's most popular novel *Millenium Hall* was published, I combed the letters looking for facts and figures, curious to know how much money Sarah earned. I wondered about her financial goals and what she thought necessary for her upper-middle-class standard of living. And I wanted to know exactly what she and her contemporaries saw as essential to living with a degree of comfort.

During this search I discovered that Elizabeth, who as an adult was in a stronger financial position than Sarah, mentioned money and business as often and almost as obsessively as Sarah did. I came to realize that Elizabeth showed remarkable consistency over many years in her attitude toward money. It was always important to her and dictated her marriage choice as well as her most compelling interests once she was locked into that marriage. I noticed that she was concerned not only with her own financial situation but with that of many others, and that she gradually achieved considerable power over other's lives because she cared intensely about what she saw as the just apportionment of whatever charity she had to bestow, the well-being of all her relatives—even those she disliked—and the general shape of people's lives. In short, she was a controlling person who always realized and guarded whatever financial power she had and she consistently used this power to give and sometimes to withhold favors, positions, influence, and money.

Her financial support crossed boundaries of class and relationship in surprising ways. For example, in 1748 she was supporting the baby of one of her sister's ex-servants by sending Sarah money to pay for the baby's wet nurse, and in 1771 she, with her husband's support, had taken full responsibility for the care of an insane brother, John Robinson. The first charity cost her a guinea every three months and lasted a relatively short time. The second cost £100 a year and lasted until she and her brother both died in 1800. The list of her projects is long and its diversity reveals her involvement in a way of life whose dimensions reach far beyond the drawing rooms and salons where one is encouraged to envision the bluestockings.

She was consistently concerned about the financial well-being of her sister, Sarah. It was she, rather than one of her brothers or Sarah herself, who struggled with her father over the money due Sarah after her separation from George Scott. The Scotts had been married, without Elizabeth's approval, early in 1751, when Sarah was twenty-eight. George Scott was a newly appointed sub-preceptor to the twelve-year-old Prince George who was to become George III. Elizabeth's match to Edward Montagu had been primarily prompted by Edward's solidity in terms of family background and property—he was the grandson of the Earl of Sandwich, an established M.P. from Huntington who owned several estates, and twenty-nine years older than Elizabeth. But Sarah's marriage was based on personal preference and proceeded in spite of strong family opposition. The marriage took place in 1751, and lasted only until the beginning of 1752, approximately a year. The circumstances of the marriage's failure are tantalizingly unclear.

It is clear, however, that Sarah left her husband without making adequate legal arrangements for her separate maintenance. Her situation was made more difficult because she was unable to rely on the good offices of her father, whom she seemed to mistrust almost as much as she did her estranged husband.

In May 1752, Elizabeth's friend, Mrs. Donnellan, wrote to condole with her about Sarah's situation and commented: "all I say is that you entirely justify Mrs. Scott, and I am sure you must know the truth. I hear, too, he has given her back half her fortune, and has settled a 150 pounds a year on her; this, I think, is a justification to her."[4] Although George Scott did, for a while anyway, make quarterly payments to Sarah, they were not always prompt. Her fortune, half of which was £500, was in her father's hands, and she was not prepared to fight for it.

Her goal was to buy a house in Bath, and this she could not afford. Knowing this, and unasked by Sarah, Elizabeth approached their father who was not known for his tractability. She reports the results to Sarah as follows:

> I address'd to him after dinner when he was in good humor, but he said he understood from Morris [their attorney brother] that Mr Scott might claim your fortune of him & he wd not change the property into the form of a house. I assured him I believed he could not be a loser by a purchase of that kind at the Bath & that indeed it was a strange & hard case you should be thus unprovided for, he grew into passion I used all methods of every species of Rhetoric the persuasive the menacing ye flattering ye censuring ect & told him Mr Scott had some handle for a reflection on your family not very honorable to it viz that you had been duped by your Family in regard to your circumstances this I thought a good stimulating argument to a man of pride & passion. . . . My father said the match was not of his making, I told him I did not absolutely think so, for what a Father permits he encourages, & that he had more to do in it than anybody. Mr Montagu says I held him well by the nose, in short he grew cool at last.[5]

On this occasion Elizabeth was manipulative as well as insistent. After presenting Sarah's case, she says, "I kiss'd him & spoke many pathetic sentences about you which after he had spent his fire & fury seemd a little to melt him & so we parted. I should tell you we askd him to dine with us as it was better to introduce this discourse without seeming to make an express visit for it." [6] In this instance Elizabeth's intervention was rewarded with some success. While Sarah was not given enough to buy a house in Bath, her father provided an allowance which Elizabeth attributed to her own insistence.

On another occasion of striking similarity ten years later, in the spring of 1762, Elizabeth approached her father on Sarah's behalf and seems to have forfeited his good will because of her directness. She learned that Lady Bab Montagu and Sarah (Lady Bab was no relation to Edward and Elizabeth), who lived together, were forced by lack of money to give up their summer residence in Batheaston, a spot near Bath, in order to be able to afford to rent a more comfortable and well-situated winter house in Bath. [7] Elizabeth knew what their summer retreat meant to them and went to her father to inquire about an increase in Sarah's allowance. She sent Sarah the following account:

> Two days before I left Town I went to my Father, and after other conversation proposed to him to add twenty pound a year to ye allowance and said Mr Montagu should do the same, that you might not part with a place so necessary to your health and comfort. My Father flew into a passion, & said it was a monstrous proposal & unreasonable, & he could not afford to comply with it. I told him you had had but a thousand pound of him, & you could not have been maintaind for the interest of that sum if you had staid in his house, that he had got back part of that thousand pound, & every one must think you was hardly used, that you was much pitied, & he was not at all free from censure. . . . he said he cared not a farthing for me or what I desired, & he did not desire Mr M to trouble his head with his family & then got up & took me by the hand & put me out of the room. I told him I did not expect to be insulted in that manner, however I was not sorry to find myself on the other side the door where I shall remain till he please to visit me & there ends the chapter of paternal love. [8]

The failure of this confrontational approach helps one understand and sympathize with the necessity of some kind of manipulativeness in dealing with Mr. Robinson. It is significant that on the two occasions outlined, and on others I have not mentioned, Elizabeth went unasked to petition for Sarah. The comfortable position she occupied as Edward's wife and the fact that she need ask her father for nothing for herself freed her to act on Sarah's behalf.

It is also worth noting that Elizabeth seemed to feel it would be improper for her to ask Mr. Montagu to add to Sarah's income if her father would not, or to add more than her father would add. This same principle operated in the case of a more distant relation, one Mrs. Fry, an out-of-the-way cousin, whose desperate case (she was literally starving) was brought to Elizabeth's attention by Mrs Boscawen, and for whom Elizabeth canvassed her family. She wrote to her brother in 1765 about her contribution for Mrs. Fry: "I have fix'd my sum at the same as my Fathers because it wd be improper & disrespectful to him to give more, & my compassion for ye poor Woman will not allow me to give less, even tho I could not conveniently spare it. My private purse is never very heavy, but my heart is still lighter, but wd not be so if ye reproach of a neglected Relation lay at ye bottom of it."[9]

Sarah was a special relation and Elizabeth never neglected her. During the decade between Lady Bab's death in 1765 and Edward Montagu's death in 1775, she loaned Sarah her comfortable London house for several weeks, gave her presents, such as several yards of white satin, and sent her and Sarah Fielding, who was Scott's close friend in Bath, numerous partridges, fresh fowls, bottles of wine, pots of beef, and offers of emergency assistance. All this she did consistently, but she never, as far as I know, gave her a significant amount of money. As far as I can tell, she never gave anyone any significant amount of money while Mr. Montagu was alive. After his death, she gave Sarah an annuity of £200 a year. She was then, at last, at fifty-four, a very wealthy widow, while Sarah was still economizing and moving from one rented lodging to another. Elizabeth explained to her brother Morris what some might interpret as the meanness of the £200 annuity:

> I know she [Sarah] has a great deal of delicacy, and any considerable sum might have distressed her, it is always pleasant to receive little marks of a friends love, but when they are increased to obligations they are heavy, I wd put a gold ring on ye finger of a friend but not a fetter, which they wd be to a mind so generous as Mrs. Scott . . . from some study of human nature, in which I read my own imperfections and those of others, I shall never confer any favour which can create a new set of duties to be expected by me or paid by another, for from such arise uneasy jealousies on all sides.[10]

Although Sarah's continued need for economy may seem unjust in light of the close relationship between the sisters and the relative splendor of Elizabeth's new wealth (she had over £7,000 a year),[11] the annuity was significant. It enabled Sarah to live in London, which she had been unable to afford, and it apparently enabled her to stop writing for a living. She published nothing after 1775 although she lived another twenty years and had published a well-received biography,

The Life of Theodore Agrippa d'Aubigné, in 1772. In fact, Elizabeth's support and her determination to gain others' support for Sarah may have been the factor that allowed Sarah to maintain her upper-middle-class status and which kept her from dying as another eighteenth-century woman writer, Charlotte Lennox, did, alone and destitute.

I have said that Elizabeth seemed never to give away significant sums while Edward was alive. The letters suggest that she simply did not have such sums—say amounts over £20—at her disposal. An incident which illustrates this occurred in 1763 when she and Mr. Montagu were staying in Northumberland on coal mining business. An opportunity arose to help the nurse who had cared for the Montagu's only child who had died years earlier when he was eighteen months old. The woman, Mrs. Kennet, applied to Mrs. Montagu for £50, probably to use as a portion for her daughter. Mrs. Montagu was eager to comply, but the surprising thing is that she borrowed the £50 from her close friend Lord Bath, an immensely wealthy person with a reputation for avarice. More significantly, when she returned to London, she wrote Mrs. Kennet, advising her to keep the matter a secret from Mr. Montagu. On December 28, 1763, she wrote:

> It is with great pleasure I send you the enclosed bond, and you shall not pay interest upon it, & I hope at some time to be able to surrender up the bond itself. The fifty pound is lodged with my Brother Morris Robinson in Chancery Lane from whence you may have it whenever you please to send for it. In any transaction with Mr Montagu you need not mention the fifty pound I lend you, for it is my own money. I heartily wish to hear your daughter is happy in her marriage.[12]

Thus, after twenty-one years of marriage to a man of considerable means who obviously valued her business judgment, and who had valued their dead son too, Elizabeth apparently was not able to borrow £50 from her husband to give to their son's nurse. Furthermore, she seems to have felt there would be unpleasant repercussions if her husband were to find out that she had loaned the woman £50. Elizabeth Montagu was the soul of propriety; she must have seen Mr. Montagu as someone to be placated with great care if she preferred to ask Lord Bath for the loan, and since, it appears, she felt constrained to ask for secrecy from her ex-servant. Her personal means cannot have been extensive, and Mr. Montagu's means were not at her disposal except for selected items which he endorsed.

Although she did not have free access to Mr. Montagu's purse, she seemed to have complete access to his financial decision making, which was often torturously slow and involved. She gained power over him in this sphere because of her constant participation in his coal mining enterprises. By virtue of her shrewd judgment and patience with her husband's hesitancy, he came to value and rely on the business sense which she demonstrated over many years. She went over all the agreements with other mine owners and all the agents' accounts with him. When they were apart, they corresponded constantly regarding negotiations for opening new mines, increasing their property, and hiring new agents. Elizabeth's interest in business was genuine. Two-and-a-half weeks after Mr. Montagu's death at eighty-four, in 1775, she wrote to Elizabeth Carter, "I find business diverts my mind much better than reading at present."[13]

If one word were to be selected to describe Elizabeth's approach to her husband, it might well be "careful." Given her circumstances, this is not surprising. She had grown up in a family where every £100 was significant. When she married at twenty-two, she did not bring her husband her £1000 fortune, but her father's bond for £1000. (Mr. Montagu eventually received the money.) The landscape of her life was dotted with women of good birth whose futures were bleak because they had no money or not enough money: Mrs. Fry, her distant relation, brought up genteelly, but starving with an invalid husband; the Granville sisters, orphaned daughters of Lord Landsdown, living on the uncertain bounty of a half-brother, Lord Weymouth; and her own sister, Sarah Scott, who married for love and spent the rest of her life worrying about expenses.

Sarah's anxiety was made bearable by Elizabeth's support, and Sarah was not the only relative who received financial support from Mrs. Montagu. Her younger brother, John, had had a mental breakdown in 1751 when he was a young man. Apparently he spent many years under the personal care of an individual named Mrs. Hately, whose death in 1771 caused a crisis in the family. Sarah alerted Elizabeth, who immediately went to London to see their father about John's future. In this case she used Edward's increasing wealth and her own skill at hiding her true feelings to best advantage. She assumed full responsibility for her insane brother, who was to live another twenty-nine years. After seeing her father, she reported to Edward:

> What you say is very just, that no one could have acted with the same authority that I have done, but I owe that authority to your kindness, & may Heaven reward you with a long & happy life [he was already eighty] for having renderd me by your kind regard & attachment an object of respect. All has pass'd with great civility between the old Gentleman [her father] & me, but tho I have kept

my temper outwardly I have been inwardly wounded deeply, for tho I knew there was a want of tenderness in his Nature I never imagined there was on Earth a Person so very pityless.[14]

Elizabeth's responsiveness to suffering and her ability to deal effectively with her father must have been clear to Sarah, who wrote to her about John rather than to their eldest brother, Matthew, or their attorney brother, Morris.

This responsiveness was not limited to near relations. When her cousin Lydia Botham's daughters were left penniless orphans by the death of their clergyman father, Elizabeth wrote to her eldest brother, Matthew, who had inherited the Mount Morris estate at Horton, Kent, which had been their mother's during her lifetime. Her theory was, that since as eldest male child in the Robinson family he had received more than the other eight children, he should be willing to donate more of his resources to less fortunate family members, even those with whom he had no immediate acquaintance. Elizabeth suggested that he contribute £10 a year to an annuity for the girls, an annuity to which she and the other relatives would also contribute.

Her eldest brother, who was a sixty-year-old bachelor, did not agree. He responded in an extremely long letter explaining in detail his own responsibilities and his opinions in regard to orphaned clergymen's daughters. Although he agreed to contribute ten guineas, he could not agree to Elizabeth's long-range plan because "such annuities dont suit my affairs." Further, he could not endorse Elizabeth's concept of family obligation. He explained that he felt a crucial difference between relations with whom one had been born and bred and those, like these cousins, with whom he was not acquainted and did not know by sight. Although he could not acquiesce in the annuity, he had some advice for the young women. He commented gallantly to his sister:

> I am used to receive your Ideas with so much respect, that I hardly allow myself to question them. But let me beg of you yourself on this occasion to consider, whether there does not enter the Spirit of Magnificence as well as that of charity into the proposition of finding £100 a year for two young women whose parents have left them without a Shilling. I much doubt whether their mother had in her single State near half that. I don't know that it will be any real kindness to them to teach them to value or set themselves up too high. God knows, such a dependent subsistence may from many & many a cause & accident fail them. I am sure were they my own daughters, & I could foresee such an event, I should most earnestly recommend to them to endeavor rather to assist themselves & to earn,

if possible, in some degree their own bread, than to be totally dependent on the very precarious provision of the generosity & charity of others.[15]

Elizabeth and Sarah agreed with him in so far as they wished to see needy women placed above total dependence on others. Moreover, this wish was not confined to those related to them. They interested themselves in the adversity of women of all ranks, from their own, to servants, to those somewhere in between who might qualify for governess' positions. For example, in 1762, Elizabeth, working with Lady Westmoreland, managed to secure the position of wet nurse to the royal family for one Mrs. Ned Scott, a woman of the same class as herself, whose sister had been Sarah's close friend and who had fourteen children and slender financial resources. This was valuable employment which entailed many benefits such as positions in the royal household for some of Mrs. Scott's children, and a £300-a-year pension for the nurse after the prince was taken from her care. Elizabeth worked hard to convince the royal family that Mrs. Scott was exactly right for the job. She said she was moved "to serve a family of unportioned children" not only because it was her duty, but also, because she herself "was once to a certain degree in the same circumstances." [16]

While Elizabeth could identify with Mrs. Scott's large family of portionless children because she came from a similar one, she also helped many who were of a much lower class. For instance, on October 6, 1772, she wrote imploringly to her close friend, Elizabeth Carter:

> I beg of you to inquire among all yr friends, Neighbours, & correspondents whether they wd accept, as a servant, a modest, sober, ingenious young person who works admirably, can get up fine linen, pickle, preserve, & make jellies, who wd be glad to be housekeeper in a small family . . . I am the more desirous to get her a service, because she has, thus far, withstood ye temptation of her papist relations to put her above servitude if she will quit the Protestant church. She will undergo ye martyrdom of service but ye severer martyrdom of starving may be too much for her.[17]

Because Mrs. Montagu's recommendations were not easily obtained, they were taken seriously. Ten days later, she wrote back to Mrs. Carter, "A thousand thanks for yr goodness about my young Woman." [18]

Finally, Elizabeth Montagu was a concerned and compassionate estate owner who was energetically active in pursuing business interests and in trying to alleviate ignorance and misery among the farm workers and coal mining families on her estates. In the 1760s Mr. Montagu inherited a number of coal mining properties which had been in-adequately supervised because of his relative's incompetence and long sickness. The Montagus invested all the capital they could command in the renovation and development of these mines and they journeyed to Newcastle-upon-Tyne, Northumberland, where in the fall and winter of 1763, Mrs. Montagu worked untiringly on complicated busi-ness problems. As the November cold deepened, Mrs. Montagu wrote to one of her favorite correspondents, Lord Lyttelton, "I have not stirr'd out of my room for some days, & the fireside, which if in Lon-don would be encircled with beaux esprits & blue stocking philoso-phers is now filled by stewards & people who are in the business of the mine."[19]

The mines prospered and as Mr. Montagu aged, his wife's interest in business detail exceeded his own. After his death on May 20, 1775, she spent a short time recuperating and then set off in June to visit the Yorkshire estates and Northumberland collieries which were now hers. The following undated letter to Sarah Scott written in 1772 shows her real concern for others' suffering. She writes in detail, confident of her sister's interest:

> My principal attention has been to providing food for my poor Neighbours, who are in ye most litteral sense starving. We make 8 quarts of rice milk daily for ye suppers of hungry babes, when we do not bake. Baking days said milk & rice is consolidated into pud-ding. Of Broth we make Oceans, yet such is ye general misery that there remains still every day many croaking bowels. I carried a Rice pudding in my chaise tonight to a family of poor Children on Greenham Common. The Father is a Labourer, he earns 6ˢ & 6ᵖ pr week, the Mother is sickly, they have 11 children living, 7 are at ser-vice. The poor man was laid up with ye rheumatism in part of ye winter which put him back in ye World, so that ye 4 little ones at home have only a bit of blanket each to cover them. I saw one of them in this naked condition on saturday I sent to buy cloth for a smock & linsey woolsey for a jacket which I also carried home. The poor Woman was quite astonished & said it was ye first kindness she had ever received except half a crown Mr Griffith got ye Parish to give her when she was very ill in her lying in of her eleventh child. . . . If the rich people do not check their wanton extravagance to enable them to assist the poor I know not what must become of ye labouring people.[20]

This is not the commentary of a woman interested primarily in dominating a crowded drawing room. These are the observations of a woman of energetic versatility, who was as interested in her account books and neighbours' welfare as she was in the *Essay on Shakespeare* which she published in 1769. Elizabeth Montagu accepted many of the conventions of her time regarding proper womanly behavior, but she did not accept them passively. She astutely used the leverage her marriage and her belief in the power of moral benevolence gave her to challenge her father and brothers. She organized support for people of varying conditions and circumstances, and she shrewdly worked to increase her network of friends and business connections so as to maximize whatever independence her conventional marriage allowed and to provide a firm basis for twenty-five years of totally independent widowhood.

Elizabeth Montagu's mother bore twelve children and organized the family's estate. Elizabeth effectively rallied support for dozens of individuals, and helped run considerable coal mining enterprises. Her sister, Sarah Scott, dealt successfully with publishers and booksellers. As one thinks of these accomplishments, one remembers James Mellow's comment that "the famous are only the tip of the iceberg; the generating life of the age lies below the surface."[21] And one is led to question the generalization of female acquiescence in dependence in the eighteenth century. It may have been what society expected, but there may well have been a more significant number of women wielding a measure of power than we have been led to believe. Certainly, Elizabeth Montagu did so, not only in the drawing room, but more important, in the larger world of work and need which appealed to her curiosity, compassion, and sense of justice.

NOTES

1 Almost always these images are pejorative. As Barbara Schnorrenberg remarks after citing two books dealing with bluestockings published in the early twentieth century, "The very name Blue Stockings became synonymous with a learned and hence unfeminine woman." Barbara B. Schnorrenberg with Jean E. Hunter, "The Eighteenth-Century Englishwoman," in *The Women of England: From Anglo-Saxon Times to the Present*, ed. Barbara Kanner (Hamden, Conn.: Archon Books, 1979), 188. This negative attitude to the bluestockings still persists. Lawrence Stone, for example, comments on "the arrogant intellectual claims of the coterie of bluestockings in their literary salons." Lawrence Stone, *The Family, Sex and Marriage in England: 1500– 1800* (New York: Harper & Row, 1977), 356.
2 Early editions of selected letters were edited by her nephew and heir, Mat-

thew Montagu, 1810–1813, her great-great niece, Emily J. Climenson, 1906, and Reginald Blunt, 1925. Also see Dr. John Doran's *A Lady of the Last Century (Mrs. Elizabeth Montagu): Illustrated in Her Unpublished Letters: Collected and Arranged with a Biographical Sketch, and a Chapter on Blue Stockings* (1873: reprint, New York: AMS Press, 1973).

3 Matthew Montagu, ed., *The Letters of Elizabeth Montagu with Some of the Letters of Her Correspondents* (Boston: William M'Illenny, 1810), 4–5.

4 Mrs. Donnellan to Elizabeth Montagu, May 1752, *Elizabeth Montagu, The Queen of the Blue-Stockings: Her Correspondence from 1720 to 1761*, ed. Emily J. Climenson (London: John Murray, 1906), 2:7.

5 Elizabeth Montagu to Sarah Scott, December 1752, MO 5728, Montagu Collection, Huntington Library. Unless otherwise specified, all quotations from the Montagu Collection are here quoted for the first time, as far as I know, and will be designated when possible by their manuscript number. (I have retained the original spelling and punctuation of the unpublished quotations.)

6 Ibid.

7 Sarah Scott to Elizabeth Montagu, 5 June 1762, MO 5294.

8 Elizabeth Montagu to Sarah Scott, spring 1762, MO 5791.

9 Elizabeth Montagu to Morris Robinson, 7 July 1765, MO 4791.

10 Elizabeth Montagu to Morris Robinson, 5 July 1775, MO 4802.

11 So far I have found no evidence in the Montagu Collection regarding a jointure for Elizabeth Montagu. Dr. John Doran quotes Horace Walpole as writing to William Mason after Mr. Montagu's death: "The husband of Mrs. Montagu, of Shakespearshire, [she had published an *Essay on Shakespeare* in 1769] is dead, and has left her an estate of 7000L a year in her own power. . . ." *A Lady of the Last Century*, 193.

12 Elizabeth Montagu to Mrs. Kennet, 28 December 1763, MO 3004.

13 Elizabeth Montagu to Mrs. Carter, June 1775, MO 3362.

14 Elizabeth Montagu to Edward Montagu, 16 September 1771, MO 2775.

15 Matthew Robinson-Morris, 2nd Baron Rokeby to Elizabeth Montagu, 19 December 1773, MO 4852.

16 Elizabeth Montagu to William Pulteney, Earl of Bath, spring 1762, MO 4521.

17 Elizabeth Montagu to Elizabeth Carter, 6 October 1772, MO 3307.

18 Elizabeth Montagu to Elizabeth Carter, 16 October 1772, MO 3308.

19 Elizabeth Montagu to Lord George Lyttelton, November 1763, MO 1428.

20 Elizabeth Montagu to Sarah Scott, 28 July 1772, MO 5930. The importance of even inadequate assistance from propery owners like Mrs. Montagu can be measured against Dorothy Marshall's comments on the subsistence level of existence of the rural poor in eighteenth-century England. "While they had their health and strength and times were not hard they could manage. But they had no reserves and no means of acquiring any. This was partly because wages and earnings were too low, but also because there was no incentive to save, and nowhere except a stocking for savings. Everywhere there was a certain recognized standard of life to which the worker was

supposed to be entitled: what was earned over this went to the beer house. As a result illness, ill luck, or old age pushed most workers over the line that divided the labouring poor from the pauper. The Poor Relief administered by the parish became their only refuge." Dorothy Marshall, *Eighteenth Century England* (New York: David McKay Company Inc, 1962), 35.

21 James R. Mellow, "Determined On Distinction: The Letters of Margaret Fuller," *The New York Times Book Review*, 19 June 1983, 23.

Mrs. Foster's Coquette and the Decline of the Brotherly Watch

FRANK SHUFFELTON

If one makes an informal survey of the novels written by Americans and published in New England before 1800, one is struck by the overwhelming preponderance of sentimental fictions about beleaguered females, hapless orphans, and seduced and abandoned heroines.[1] The earliest of these novels, William Hill Brown's *The Power of Sympathy*, published in Boston in 1789 purports in its subtitle to be "Founded in Truth," but we might well wonder just what truths lie behind weepy epics such as this, seemingly compounded in equal proportions of sentimental effusions about thwarted love and intrusive moralizing about the dangers of seduction. Critics have tended to dismiss the moral injunctions of a writer like Brown as a means to evade vestigial Puritan condemnation of frivolous tales,[2] but in doing so they run the risk of misrepresenting the way in which some of these novels intended to speak to their time by imaginatively projecting their readers' moral situation.

This confusion about the apparently disparate purposes of fiction and moral education is occasionally encouraged by the novelists themselves. Brown, for instance, has a feminine paragon send "a little work entitled 'A Lady of Quality's Advice to her Children'" to a young friend, commenting, "I do not recommend it to you as a novel, but as a work that speaks the language of the heart and that inculcates the duty we owe to ourselves, to society and the Deity."[3] We should, however, emphasize in this sentence not the seeming rejection of the fictional art in which Brown himself is engaged but the connection he

211

makes between heart and duty, and we should further perceive that his notion of the heart may have rather more to do with Jonathan Edwards than with Lawrence Sterne or perhaps even Clarissa Harlowe. Although the literary devices of these American novels depend heavily upon the tradition of the eighteenth-century sentimental novel, it is somewhat of a mistake to read them only in terms of that tradition, for such reading inevitably leads to a focus on what is merely derivative and typical. The best of these novels deserve to be read on their own terms, for they are special cases, written for particular American audiences and, at their most perceptive, addressing particular American concerns.

For example, Hannah W. Foster's 1797 epistolary novel, *The Coquette*, carried on its title page the claim familiar to many of the novels of this period, "Founded on Fact." *The Coquette*, however, notoriously was founded on fact, for its heroine, Eliza Wharton, was clearly modeled on the almost decade-old case of Elizabeth Whitman, a young woman of Hartford, Connecticut, who sought to conceal her seduction and pregnancy by hiding herself from her family and friends. Miss Whitman fled to Danvers, Massachusetts, took a room at the Bell Tavern under the name of Mrs. Walker, and after giving birth to a still-born child in July 1788, died of puerperal fever on the 25th of that month. After the landlord of the Bell placed an account of his mysterious lodger in the Salem *Mercury* for 29 July 1788, Miss Whitman's identity was revealed, and the Boston papers published accounts of her sad story, one of them embellished with a poem by her entitled "Disappointment." The *Independent Chronicle* of 11 September 1788 said Miss Whitman's story was "a good moral lecture to young ladies," for "having coquetted till past her prime, [she] fell into criminal indulgences, proved pregnant and then eloped—pretending (where she lodged and died) to be married, and carried on the deception till her death." The *Massachusetts Centinel* of 20 September, which printed her poem, claimed, "She was a great reader of romances, and having formed her notions of happiness from that corrupt source, became vain and coquettish, and rejected some very advantageous offers of marriage in hope of realizing something more splendid."[4]

In the following year William Hill Brown echoed this latter characterization by including a lengthy digression on Miss Whitman in his *Power of Sympathy*. He suggested that her fate illustrated the proposition that "A Young Lady who has imbibed her ideas of the world from desultory reading, and placed confidence in the virtue of others, will bring back disappointment when she expected gratitude."[5] If Brown first realized the novelistic possibilities inherent in the story of Elizabeth Whitman, he nonetheless failed to do more than repeat the newspaper pieties of the previous year. The ascription of her downfall to romance reading and an almost simpleminded innocence are glib moral clichés which leave unanswered the deeper questions of her motivation and of the roles played by her family, her friends, and her seducer, characters most notably left out of previous accounts. When Mrs. Foster came to portray the characters around Elizabeth Whitman, however, she was guided less by the historical precedent than by her desire to deal with what seemed to be pressing moral and social questions of her age. The story of the seduced coquette had an inevitability to it which did not pertain to the other personages involved in her life.

When Mrs. Foster called her heroine Eliza Wharton, she fooled no one, for all of her readers were aware that Eliza was in fact Elizabeth Whitman, but when readers tried to interpret the rest of the novel in a similar way as a *roman à clef,* they were somewhat frustrated. There was enough conformity to the popular accounts of the Whitman case for readers of *The Coquette* to identify Mr. Boyer, Eliza's suitor, with the Reverend Joseph Buckminster, who had supposedly courted Miss Whitman, but the identity of the seducer, Major Peter Sanford, remained unclear. The popular belief that he was really Pierrepont Edwards was belied as much by the absence of any corroborating evidence as by the failure of their initials to correspond.[6] The female characters around Eliza Wharton conform even less to known historical figures. Too much ink has been wasted in trying to discover the man of Elizabeth Whitman's heart, as one writer put it, but Herbert Ross Brown was more perceptive in pointing to Major Sanford's Richardsonian origins as Eliza Wharton's seducer. He viewed Sanford as a Connecticut Lovelace, his friend Deighton as a Yankee Jack Belford, and Eliza's friend Lucy Freeman as an American Anna Howe.[7] He was certainly right in pointing to the fictional status of these characters as opposed to their being thinly disguised allegories of historical figures, but the parallels to *Clarissa* only go so far. Eliza Wharton has more friends and confidantes than Lucy Freeman alone; she retains her freedom of motion throughout the novel, and there is no domineering family trying to force her into marriage with a repulsive clod. In her other attempt at something like a novel, *The Boarding School*, published in Boston the year after the appearance of *The Coquette*, Mrs. Foster was aware of the exemplary power of Clarissa's fate. "The indiscretion of Clarissa, in putting herself under the protection of a libertine, is a warning to every fair," she wrote, but by imaginatively portraying Eliza Wharton's relations with her friends, suitor, and seducer, she generated a fictive field in which she could address larger concerns than that of merely presenting "a beacon to warn the American fair."[8]

A central problem for Mrs. Foster and her generation was that Eliza Wharton's "criminal indulgences" were for all practical purposes no longer criminal in the strict legal sense of the term. Whereas in early Puritan New England crime was understood first of all as sin and law as the support of religion and morality, in the last decades of the eighteenth century crime began to be distinguished from immorality, and criminal law was increasingly seen as an instrument to safeguard the peace and order of a propertied society rather than as an instrument to enforce individual morality.[9] In studying this change in attitude toward the law, William E. Nelson noticed some rather remarkable statistics from Middlesex County, Massachusetts, a locality he claimed was typical of the state as a whole and perhaps even of the entire United States. Between 1760 and 1774 two hundred and ten of the three hundred and seventy prosecutions in the county's Superior and General Sessions Courts were for fornication, plus one prosecution for adultery and two for cohabitation. In 1786, however, the Massachusetts General Court passed a new law permitting a woman accused of fornication to plead guilty before a justice of the peace, pay a fine, and avoid indictment in the Court of General Sessions. According to Nelson, "The last indictment was returned in 1790, and, after 1791, women stopped confessing their guilt, apparently aware that even though they did not confess, they would not be indicted."[10] In the same period the law's attitude toward adultery was changing; divorces were regularly granted on the grounds of adultery, but after 1793 only one prosecution for adultery was commenced.[11] Whatever the consequences of Eliza Wharton's sin, it was thus unlikely that she or any other errant American fair would be treated as a criminal with the full machinery of the criminal law brought to bear on her.

In the earliest years of the New England experiment legal prosecution was not the first but the last step relied upon to enforce moral behavior, especially for church members who were subject to the brotherly watch of the congregation. Thomas Hooker wrote that by virtue of the church covenant to which all members agreed upon their admission, "I stand charged in a most peculiar manner, to prevent all taint of sin in any Member of the Society, that either it may never be committed; or if committed, it may speedily be removed, and the spirituall good of the whole preserved."[12] New England church discipline came to be an established procedure through which the vigilance of the brotherly watch could be exercised as moral admonition or restraint. As Cotton Mather described it in 1726,

Where a *Scandalous Transgression* is known only to *One* or *Two,* the Proceedings of the Persons that know it, are the same, that they are in the case of a *Personal Injury:* The Steps directed in the XVIII Ch. of Mathew. He that knows the Offence, first of all *himself* goes to the Offender, and seriously endeavours to bring him to *Repentance.* If the Offender be *Obstinate,* he then (having *Proof* to convict him) takes one or two *Brethren* with him, and renews his Endeavours that the Man may come to Repentance. If this be ineffectual, *They* carry the Complaint unto the *Pastor,* who pursues the Designs of *Humiliation* on the Soul of the Offender.[13]

If this process of escalating moral persuasion met with continued obstinacy, the society of saints might excommunicate an errant member and the civil authorities could be invoked, but the aim of the disciplinary process was always repentance and reconciliation with the community rather than punishment. Also, unless the sinner was recalcitrant, the process began in privacy and remained so; so the authority behind the brotherly watch was not public opinion but the covenanted relationship with God and the church.[14]

The effects of the brotherly watch and church discipline as forces promoting moral order and homogeneity were by no means restricted to church members. Many congregations voted to include all baptized members in the watch, and for all practical purposes the whole community fell under its scrutiny.[15] Mather asserted, for example, that ministers were called "*Watchmen,* because They should Watch the Actions of all Men, and with an Aim of Religious Curiosity spy out, how every one liveth with his Household in his House."[16] The effects of the brotherly watch surely cast a permanent expression on the face of New England social life, but after the Great Awakening church discipline became increasingly ineffective as a means to compel moral order.[17] The reasons for this decay were variously social, economic, and political, but changing notions of the value of private judgment in the face of the communal judgment expressed by the forces of the brotherly watch also played an important role.

The bitter arguments of the Awakening over grace resulted in calls from both the Old and New Light sides for toleration of religious differences, one side seeking relief from the recriminations of the evangelicals, the other wishing to gain acceptance of their separating churches. An Old Light stalwart like John Caldwell could in 1742 appeal against New Light censoriousness by asking, "are we to suppose that a Man who can think at all, will be perswaded to lay aside his Reason and Judgment, because others are bold and assuming?"[18] Seven years later Jonathan Mayhew, discussing the right and duty of private judgment, put the question in words with much broader implications: "If one man is to think and judge for all the rest of the species, why was reason given to all?"[19] If all men were to reason in matters of doctrine, would not private moral judgments be equally reasonable? When in the same collection of sermons Mayhew went on to consider the duties of Christians toward one another, benevolence became more important than moral concern. Charity was a more appropriate response to one's neighbors than was moral vigilance; a suitable care was to "do them good either by communicating positive happiness of any kind to them, or by removing the causes of their misery." A man who wishes to find the truth, said Mayhew, "suspends his judgment intirely concerning the truth or falsehood of all doctrines; and the fitness or unfitness of all actions. . . . He that desires to come to the knowledge of the truth, puts himself in a state of *indifferency* with regard to the point to be judged of; that so his mind being as it were in *aequilibrio*, his judgment may be determined solely by reason and argument." Corresponding to this process of rational detachment or indifference in matters of judgment was the pattern of moral responsibility Mayhew advised enlightened Christians to take toward their neighbors. Although charity "pities and laments" the vices of mankind, it does not attempt to interfere directly in the life of the sinner; instead, charity "puts the most favourable construction upon the conduct of others; and is not apt to impute to them ill designs and intentions."[20] After the civil law ceased to prosecute offenses such as fornication, the brotherly watch was almost the only social force remaining to encourage moral conformity, but it had itself been undermined by the logic of benevolist individualism such as Mayhew's.

When Mrs. Foster turned her hand to fiction in the 1790s, she and her readers confronted a world in which the dictates of fashion, "the false maxims of the world" (p. 29) as Eliza Wharton's friend Mrs. Richman puts it, had displaced the power of the covenant bond to regulate behavior.[21] This is the world to which Eliza is consigned to find her place, a world in which charity and moral tolerance have invited libertines into the drawing room. In the beginning of the novel, however, Eliza eagerly anticipates her entrance into this morally ambiguous world; the first sentences of her opening letter describe the "unusual sensation" which possesses her breast. "It is *pleasure*, pleasure, my dear Lucy on leaving my paternal roof!" (p. 5). She has only recently emerged from under the pall of gloom and melancholy occasioned by the death of her fiancée, Mr. Haly. Although "a man of real and substantial merit" (p. 5), he was not, however, the choice of her heart but of her parents'. She agreed to sacrifice her fancy in this affair, she writes, because she recognized his "declining health" (p. 6) would forestall a marriage, and now, released by his death, she desires the freedom of a society with "no other connection than that of friendship" (p. 7).[22]

Freed from the restraints of parental authority, she has gone to visit the Richmans, friends in New Haven, but she is less well prepared for the moral challenges of their social world than she thinks she is. She confesses that even her own mother does not realize that in her engagement with Mr. Haly "my heart was untouched"—a resonant phrase in post-Awakening New England—"and when that is unaffected, other sentiments and passions make but a transient impression" (p. 8). Her sentimental secrets set her against the moral conventions of her society, and when a New Haven acquaintance offers condolences on her recent loss, she writes that "my heart rose against the woman. . . . To have our enjoyments arrested by the empty compliments of unthinking persons for no other reason than a compliance with fashion is to be treated in a manner which the laws of humanity forbid" (p. 11). If at the beginning of her career in the world the secrets of Eliza's heart isolate her from her friends emotionally, the guilty secret of seduction and pregnancy she bears at the end of the novel will separate her from them totally and irrevocably.

We might in addition speculate that there are darker secrets yet that divide Eliza from herself, secrets unconfessed even to herself. Mr. Haly's death supposedly liberates her from her "paternal roof," but we later discover that her father had died at some unspecified time before this, and that, like Haly, he had also been a clergyman. In a very real sense the death of Haly, the unloved minister, is a displaced version of the death of her father, that parental authority she later describes as having imposed shackles on her mind (p. 140). In New Haven she also meets the Reverend Mr. Boyer, another clergyman who wishes to marry her, and while she finds Boyer personally agreeable, she objects to his "situation in life" which entails "cares and restraints" to which "I will not submit" (p. 57). In the same letter to her mother where she admits to these feelings, she refers to her parents' marriage as a "scene of trial" (p. 57), a phrase that provokes an indignant response in her mother's answering letter. Mrs. Wharton implicitly acknowledges the similarity between Boyer and Eliza's father and further points out that since Mr. Wharton's death the whole responsibility for the "expanding virtues" (p. 58) of her children has devolved upon her. "How anxiously I must watch," she writes and urges that Boyer is suitable to take over the role of "friend and protector" (pp. 58–59). But it is precisely this moral vigilance exercised by her

father and then by a succession of ministerial presences that Eliza refuses to submit to. Set free by her father's death, she wants no more
priggish clerical watchmen like Boyer or his friend Selby who seemingly visits New Haven expressly to observe her behavior and report
to Boyer.

Eliza's mother, however, does not exert the same authority over her
as had her father; Mrs. Wharton recommends Mr. Boyer as a suitable
match, but she does not compel Eliza's obedience to her wish as
Mr. Wharton had with Mr. Haly. Eliza's friends are similarly poised in
aequilibrio, to recall Mayhew's term, putting forward the merits of
Mr. Boyer while not insistently trying to determine her choice. When
Eliza encounters Major Peter Sanford, a well-known rake who will be
her eventual seducer, her friends assume a considerably less helpful
position of moral indifference; they enumerate Sanford's vices, but
they refuse to lay an outright prohibition on her seeing him, and they
continue to admit him to their homes. Eliza first mentions him when
she receives an invitation to a ball; showing the invitation to Mrs.
Richman, she says, "I have not much acquaintance with this gentleman, madam; but I suppose his character sufficiently respectable to
warrant an affirmative answer." Mrs. Richman's reply is the first in a
long series of equivocations characters deliver concerning Major Sanford: "He is a gay man, my dear, to say no more; and such are the
companions we wish when we join a party avowedly formed for pleasure" (p. 19). After the ball Mrs. Richman speaks more candidly and
describes him as "a professed libertine" (p. 28), but when Eliza asks
if she should "refuse him admission, if he call, in compliance with the
customary forms," Mrs. Richman equivocates once more. "By no
means. I am sensible that even the false maxims of the world must be
complied with in a degree" (p. 29). By opposing her private judgment
of Sanford to the judgment of the world and then asking Eliza to respect them both, Mrs. Richman fails as a moral guide and merely encourages the contradictions between marriage and pleasure which
Eliza already feels so strongly. When Mrs. Richman subsequently
takes a stronger position on Sanford's immorality and the dangers of
associating with him, her argument has already been undercut by her
own social tolerance of him.

Other friends of Eliza similarly equivocate between moral abhor-
rence and social acceptance, even those who are most candid in their
opinions of Sanford from the very beginning. Lucy Freeman, Eliza's
confidante and closest friend in the first half of the book, feels that "it
is the task of friendship, sometimes, to tell disagreeable truths" and
warns, "he is a rake, my dear friend; and can a lady of your delicacy

and refinement think of forming a connection with a man of that character?" But in a burst of benevolence worthy of Jonathan Mayhew himself she puts the most favorable construction on Eliza's behavior, adding, "I am confident you do not. You mean only to exhibit a few more girlish airs before you turn matron" (p. 38). Lucy Freeman continues to play upon Sanford's immorality, but her letters, too, contrast her judgment with that of society and fail to demonstrate an appropriate moral self-assurance. Reporting that Sanford intends to buy a property in Hartford, she notes that "many of our gentry are pleased with the prospect of such a neighbor." She goes on to denounce his vicious character but follows that by drawing back from her own conclusion: "But I shall not set up for a censor" (p. 44). Something like the old brotherly watch is clearly in operation here, for in the same letter Lucy Freeman adds, "My swain interests himself very much in your affairs. You will possibly think him impertinent, but I give his curiosity a softer name" (p. 44). Yet this watch is for all practical purposes impertinent, irrelevant to the divided nature of Eliza's heart and the perilous moral situation she is in, for it has no authority, no covenant bond, and no way to take action further than a continual nagging. The impertinent curiosity of a friend is not a type of the genuine concern of one saint for another but an epitome of public opinion.

The continued and intensified appeals of her friends to break off the relationship with Sanford do have an effect, however, and Eliza resolves to part with him. Sanford then completes his move to Hartford and promptly calls on Eliza's mother, "for the sake of [her] late husband," he says, "whose memory he revered" (p. 92). When Mrs. Wharton learns that Lucy Freeman does not personally approve of Sanford's character, she replies rather weakly, "His manners are engaging, and I am sorry to hear that his morals are corrupt" (p. 92). Given this compounded judgment of Sanford from her own mother, it is no surprise that Eliza is once more thrown into his path, but it is more deeply ironic that she first encounters him in Hartford by drawing him as a dancing partner at the ball celebrating Lucy Freeman's marriage. Nor are we surprised to learn that "as all neighboring gentry were invited, Mr. Freeman would by no means omit Major Sanford, which his daughter earnestly solicited" (p. 102). Lucy Freeman's failure to exclude Sanford from her own wedding does not augur well for Eliza's ability to keep him at a distance.

The letter in which Eliza describes Lucy Freeman's wedding and the ball marks a crisis in her life. She begins the letter by congratulating Mrs. Richman on the birth of her first child, an event that marks her effective withdrawal from Eliza's life; the letter announcing the birth had come from her husband, not her, and she plays no direct role in the second half of the novel. Eliza confronts her feelings of isolation and abandonment directly when she reveals her fear that Lucy Freeman's wedding conveys to her "the idea of a separation perhaps of an alienation of affection, by means of her entire devotion to another" (p. 101). Lucy's and Mrs. Richman's admonitions to Eliza had already been rendered less effective by being presented as merely private judgments, and their respective retreats into the private world of marriage and motherhood leave her to resolve the ambiguities of her heart and of the social world on her own.[23]

Thrown into an "involuntary gloom" (p. 101) by her reflections upon her alienation, Eliza looks with anticipation to the evening's ball and dances with Sanford while Boyer watches from the side because "his profession prevented him from taking an active part" (p. 102). In succeeding letters Boyer increases his pressure on her to give up her "taste for dissipation" (p. 106) and set a date for their marriage while at the same time Sanford renews his insinuating flirtations. Giving Sanford a promise not to marry Mr. Boyer without first telling him, Eliza grants him a clandestine interview in the garden where she hears him promise to make his intentions known "as soon as [she] should discountenance the expectations of Mr. Boyer and discontinue the reception of his address" (p. 133). Boyer interrupts their meeting, angrily refuses to hear her explanation of her apparent "criminality," and leaves Eliza, "forever," he says, "unworthy of his regard and love" (pp. 134–35). Eliza's distress and isolation are made complete when Sanford, who until now has mainly desired to break up her relationship with Boyer, journeys to the south in search of a wealthy wife.

Her isolation rendered complete, Eliza is forced to realize that she is no longer the central object of sentimental and moral concern on the part of her friends but that her "affairs are made a town talk" (p. 145). She repents her careless treatment of Mr. Boyer and writes a letter abjectly asking him to take her back. In an almost sublimely pompous reply Boyer refuses and in his best ministerial tone professes to rejoice that she has "emerged from the shadow of fanciful vanity" and advises her "to improve the noble talents which Heaven has liberally betowed upon [her] in rendering [herself] amiable to [her] friends" (p. 153). The aim of the brotherly watch was to bring about the sinner's repentance and reconciliation with the community, but for Eliza there is no reconciliation. Just as her friends had been full of admonitions but lacked the old New England confidence in backing them up, so Boyer is willing to accept her humiliation while insisting upon separation and distance. "For your own peace of mind," he writes, "I entreat you to forget that any idea of connection between us ever existed" (p. 154). Boyer's rejection completes the destructive reversal of the moral and social relations that Eliza has with the world. Those who have reason to be aware of and concerned for her private life, the condition of her heart, hold her at a distance, while the impersonal public world that has no such knowledge treats her with familiarity, makes her the "town talk."

Desolate and despairing, Eliza makes one last anguished appeal to her friend Lucy, the one person who most consistently opposed Sanford: "To have some friend in whom I repose confidence, and with whom I could freely converse, and advise, on this occasion, would be an unspeakable comfort!" (p. 156). Lucy, unable to leave her husband, sends Julia Granby to comfort and watch over Eliza, but Julia falls into the same pattern of equivocation we have seen earlier and fails to display that confidence Eliza requires. Sanford returns with his new wife, much to Eliza's chagrin, and sends a note asking for a meeting. Eliza shows it to her mother and to Julia, asking, "What shall I do? I wish not to see him" (p. 175). "Act agreeably to the dictates of your own judgment," says her mother, and Julia advises, "I see no harm in conversing with him. . . . Perhaps it may remove some disagreeable thoughts which now oppress and give you pain" (p. 176). Betrayed once more by her friends' misplaced charity, Eliza's seduction and guilty flight are now inevitable. Consigned to the secrets of her own heart, she falls, as Cathy N. Davidson recently observed, "not because of any ardent passion but out of loneliness and despair."[24] The final chapter of *The Coquette* presents a facsimile of Eliza Wharton's grave stone, the one unequivocal public gesture her friends make for her. "This Humble Stone . . . Inscribed by Her Weeping Friends" at last recognizes that "She Sustained the Last Painful Scene, Far from Every Friend . . . And the Tears of Strangers Watered Her Grave" (p. 260).

All this is not to say that Mrs. Foster's primary conscious concern in this novel was to portray the consequences of the failure of the traditional brotherly watch, but that she inhabited a world undergoing radical social and political changes, a world where the decriminalizing of sin was a symptom both of the loosening of moral bonds which had held traditional New England society together and of the confusion of the appropriate roles of public and private life. The story of Eliza Whitman which she borrows from newspaper accounts is a simple cautionary tale of the price of seduction, but the far more sophisticated fiction Mrs. Foster creates around Eliza Wharton explores the complex questions of personal independence and public life in a postrevolutionary society. Furthermore it explores them in terms of the language and ideas available to her, the ideals of moral order and discipline evolved by the New England churches which after a century and a half were seeming less and less viable.

In her only other attempt at fiction, *The Boarding School, or Lessons of a Preceptress to Her Pupils*, published in 1798, Mrs. Foster attempted to offer a positive response to the problem of the weakened moral fabric of society. This book can hardly be called a novel in any real sense of the word; it has a set of characters who stand in some significant relation to each other, but it has no plot, no real development, and is more like those collections of improving letters popular at the time than it is like a novel. In 1789 William Hill Brown's paragon recommended her young friend read "A Lady of Quality's Advice to her Children"; a decade later she could recommend *The Boarding School*. Mrs. Williams, a clergyman's widow, keeps her school at Harmony Grove for seven young ladies in order "to embellish virtue and soften the cares of human life" for them.[25] She, in other words, will endeavor to do for them all that Mrs. Wharton failed to do for Eliza. Mrs. Williams' "perfect regularity in the government of her pupils" corresponds to "the order of the natural world, and . . . the consistency and harmony of every part."[26] The moral order of the school thus mimics the moral order of the creation almost in analogy to the fashion in which the church intended to echo the larger covenant of God with redeemed mankind.

In the first part of *The Boarding School* Mrs. Williams delivers a series of moral talks to her students who are soon to leave her. In the second half of the book their letters to Mrs. Williams and to each other reinforce those earlier lessons even as they establish an epistolary network of emotional and moral support. As the girls find themselves entering into the public world of society, they are able to express their concerns, their feelings to each other and to Mrs. Williams, receiving in return advice and support. When Harriot Henly marries, she writes to her old teacher, "O madam, how greatly shall I need a monitor like you!" and is favored with the advice to procure a copy of *The American Spectator, or Matrimonial Preceptor*, "lately published by Mr. David West, of Boston."[27] If we may justly doubt that improving books and encouraging letters are really an adequate response to loneliness, despair, and the wiles of the malevolent Major Sanford, we can nevertheless recognize Mrs. Foster's intention to replace the brotherly watch with a sorority of affection and care. This was a doomed hope even as she wrote it, however, for it ultimately depended on the same body of benevolist ideas which had laid the ground for Eliza Wharton's downfall. *The Coquette* is a superior example of early American fiction because it deals with a complex moral and emotional situation both seriously and intelligently. *The Boarding School*, by implicitly suggesting that Mrs. Williams' school can transform New England society into an extended Harmony Grove, descends to moral wish fulfillment. The truth of postrevolutionary men and women is isolation and loneliness in society, and the wishing of *The Boarding School* will not make the truth of *The Coquette* go away.

NOTES

1 In the bibliography to Henri Petters's *The Early American Novel* (Columbus: Ohio State Univ. Press, 1971), 466–75, Jeremy Belknap's *The Foresters* and Royall Tyler's *The Algerine Captive* are almost the only exceptions to this generalization. See also the observations of David Brion Davis, *Homicide in American Fiction, 1798–1860* (Ithaca, N.Y.: Cornell Univ. Press, 1957), 156.

2 E.g., Herbert Ross Brown, *The Sentimental Novel in America, 1798–1860* (Durham, N.C.: Duke Univ. Press, 1940), 9.

3 William Hill Brown, *The Power of Sympathy*, ed. William S. Kable (Columbus: Ohio State Univ. Press, 1969), 88.

4 Quoted in Charles Knowles Bolton, *The Elizabeth Whitman Mystery* (Peabody, Mass.: Peabody Historical Society, 1912), 59–61. Bolton surmised Mrs. Foster might have been responsible for these items in the Boston press, but there seems to be little ground for this belief.

5 Brown, *Power of Sympathy*, 32.

6 Bolton presents the argument against Pierrepont Edwards on pp. 111–16. Caroline Healey Dall, *The Romance of the Association* (Cambridge: John Wilson, 1875), presents some letters of Elizabeth Whitman along with a great deal of silly speculation on this issue.

7 Herbert Ross Brown, "Introduction" to Hannah Webster Foster, *The Coquette; or, The History of Eliza Wharton* (New York: Columbia Univ. Press, 1939), xv.

8 Quoted by Brown, "Introduction," xiv; Hannah Webster Foster, *The Coquette; or, The History of Eliza Wharton* (Boston: E. Larkin, 1797), 244. Citations from *The Coquette* will be identified parenthetically in the text with page numbers from this edition.

9 For early attitudes toward law see George Lee Haskins, *Law and Authority in Early Massachusetts* (New York: Macmillan, 1960). On changes in attitude see William E. Nelson, "Emerging Notions of Modern Criminal Law in the Revolutionary Era: An Historical Perspective," *New York University Law Review* 42 (1967): 451.

10 Nelson, "Notions of Modern Criminal Law," 452, 455–56.

11 Ibid., 456–57.

12 Thomas Hooker, *A Survey of the Summe of Church Discipline* (London: John

Bellamy, 1648), pt. 3, p. 3. On the brotherly watch in New England see Michael Zuckerman, *Peaceable Kingdoms; New England Towns in the Eighteenth Century* (New York: Knopf, 1970), 61–63, and David H. Flaherty, *Privacy in Colonial New England* (Charlottesville: Univ. Press of Virginia, 1972), 151–63.

13 Cotton Mather, *Ratio Discipline Fratrum Nov-Anglorum* (Boston: S. Gerrish, 1726), 148.

14 Flaherty, *Privacy,* 156.

15 Richard L. Bushman, *From Puritan to Yankee; Character and the Social Order in Connecticut, 1690–1765* (Cambridge, Mass.: Harvard Univ. Press, 1967), 159.

16 Mather, *Ratio,* 106.

17 Emil Oberholzer, Jr., *Delinquent Saints: Disciplinary Action in the Early Congregational Churches of Massachusetts* (New York: Columbia Univ. Press, 1956), 239–40. Among other symptoms of the growing ineffectiveness of church discipline Oberholzer notes on pp. 136–37 the discontinuing of the requirement for public confessions of fornication. For parallel discussion of the diminishing authority of the social order see Kenneth A. Lockridge, *A New England Town, The First Hundred Years* (New York: Norton, 1970), 170–74.

18 In Richard L. Bushman, ed., *The Great Awakening: Documents on the Revival of Religion, 1740–1745* (New York: Atheneum, 1970), 135, 159.

19 Jonathan Mayhew, *Seven Sermons* . . . (Boston: Rogers and Fowle, 1749), 50.

20 Ibid., 42, 118.

21 The debates of the 1770s and 1780s over the notion of an external covenant and the practice of owning the covenant were symptomatic of the weakening of the covenant idea. See Joseph Haroutounian, *Piety vs. Moralism, the Passing of the New England Theology* (New York: Holt, 1932), 98–130, who says it "revealed the fact that Calvinism was losing its grip on the masses of the people" (p. 115).

22 Walter P. Wenska, "*The Coquette* and the American Dream of Freedom," *Early American Literature* 12 (Winter 1977/78): 243–55, argues with some force that Eliza's illusory dream of freedom is the central theme of the book and aligns her with frustrated heroines such as Hester Prynne, Isabel Archer, and Edna Pontellier. In doing so, however, he perhaps exaggerates Mrs. Foster's belief that the contradiction between personal freedom and marital union is a genuine issue.

23 Cathy N. Davidson in "Flirting with Destiny: Ambivalence and Form in the Early American Sentimental Novel," *Studies in American Fiction* 10 (1982), 33, interprets Eliza's fall as a consequence of being abandoned by both Boyer and Sanford, but it seems clear that she is effectively abandoned by her female friends as well.

24 Ibid.

25 Hannah Webster Foster, *The Boarding School; or Lessons of a Preceptress to Her Pupils.* . . (Boston: J. P. Peaslee, 1829), 5. (First published in 1798.)

26 Ibid., 8.

27 Ibid., 145, 147.

Variations on the Dialogue in the French Enlightenment

ROLAND MORTIER

Until recently, the dialogue, a victim of the classification system of literary theory, has aroused neither interest nor curiosity among critics. This is all the more surprising since it is in this neglected genre that many of the most important debates of Western thought have taken place. The critical works are almost all quite old: Rudolf Hirzel's *Der Dialog* dates from 1895; it is more historical than theoretical and is primarily concerned with Greek and Latin dialogues, merely giving a rather incomplete list for the rest of literature. On English literature, Elizabeth Merril's *The Dialogue in English Literature* was published in 1911, and, in a comparative vein, John S. Egilrud's *Le Dialogue des Morts dans la littérature française, allemande et anglaise (1644–1789)* dates from 1934. No real literary theory of the dialogue is available; we sketched an outline of such a theory in an article entitled "Pour une poétique du dialogue: essai de théorie d'un genre" published in the *Mélanges Wellek* (Berne: Lange, 1984).

Just recently, several works have appeared that have helped in understanding the problem, either by introducing nuances, or by adding to the theory, or by questioning the very validity of it. I would like to mention here the excellent work of Marie-Louise Blessing and M. K. Benouis on the philosophical dialogue in France, the searching reflections of Eva Kushner on the sixteenth-century French dialogue, the remarkable book by Bernard Beugnot, *L'Entretien au XVIIe siècle* (Montreal, 1971), and the brilliant synthesis of Maurice Roelens in his chap-

225

ter entitled "Le dialogue d'idées au XVIIIe siècle" in *L'Histoire littéraire de la France* ([Paris: Ed. Sociales, 1976], 6:259–89).

Following Eva Kushner, let me insist on the remarkable efflorescence of the genre in the sixteenth-century: Pontus du Tyard, *Le Solitaire premier*; Loys Le Caron, *Claire ou la Beauté*; Etienne Pasquier, *Le Monophile*; Bonaventure des Périers, *Cymbalum Mundi*; Jean Bodin, *Heptaplomeres*, to cite only the best known.

The dialogue form in the Renaissance is concerned with a debate about nature, love, reason, in which the interlocutors are frequently well-known people, particularly writers such as Scève, Ronsard, or Baïf. It pretends to be the formal transcription of real conversations, and its goal, in the majority of cases, remains the exposition of a thesis, which implies a didactic rather than a problematic intention, a situation that is common to other genres of the same period. The most frequent models, apart from the Italian dialogue, are Cicero or Plato, less frequently Lucian.

The end of the sixteenth century marks the decline of the genre: the last major Renaissance dialogue is Bodin's *Heptaplomeres* written in 1588, but not published until 1857. Between 1588 and 1630, not a single important work was written in this neglected form. The seventeenth-century writers who would bring it back to life seem to have been ignorant of their precursors, and they show a certain uneasiness which is expressed in the justifications they think they have to give their readers.

This crisis of consciousness is also the moment of a new realization. We have a precious witness to this in the "Lettre de l'Autheur" which serves as an introduction to *Les Dialogues faits à l'imitation des Anciens* of Lamothe le Vayer, using the pseudonym Oratius Tubero. Lamothe appeals to the classical model to develop his sceptical and relativistic philosophy, and he explains openly: "Aussi ne me suis-je proposé autre but que ma propre satisfaction, lors que j'ay fait eslection *de ce genre d'escrire par Dialogues si mesprisé, voire des-laissé aujourd'hui*." He says he is writing for another century, not knowing whether it will ever arrive, for he has nothing but disdain for the vulgar, the group in which he places "le cavalier, l'homme de robe, et le paysan également." He wants his dialogues to remain "dans l'obscurité d'un cabinet ami." What good would it do to distribute them? They are only "marchandises de contrebande, et qui ne doivent être exposées au public."

If we take him at his word, all he did was write down real conversations, probably with his friends Diodati, Gassendi, and Naudé of the Académie Putéane, all the while hoping to "garder *le secret de nos particulières conférences*"—an obviously contradictory attitude. Lamothe le Vayer believes he is innovating by reviving the philosophic dialogue and by being inspired by "l'antique pleine liberté de parler comme de penser."

It is important to remember that, after 1630, the dialogue appears as the literary form best suited to independent ideas, suspect to both official religion and the dominant philosophy, basically critical, if not really subversive. Lamothe discretely suggests that if he uses the name Oratius Tubero "in puris naturalibus" (that is, naked) under the mantle of a vague Latin, it is in order to avoid having to deal with the Christian message in this debate over the major problems of the period. But his choice is also an esthetic one, since he sees in it a way of keeping, without constraint or hindrance, what he calls his "naïve et soudaine façon de m'expliquer."

If Lamothe really wanted discretion and secrecy, he certainly seems to have got it, at least in part. His *Dialogues* circulated in the eighteenth century primarily in the widely distributed edition of 1716. The feeling that the dialogue is an unusual genre in France is noticeable in a passage of Paul Pellisson's "Discours" that precedes the complete edition of the *Oeuvres* of Jean-François Sarasin, with a "privilège" dated February 1655. Sarasin had left a *Dialogue sur la question s'il faut qu'un jeune homme soit amoureux*, and Pellisson has obvious trouble in defending it: "Ce genre d'escrire a esté iusques icy peu employé par les François, soit qu'on ait cru difficile d'en atteindre la perfection, soit qu'une nation prompte et impatiente comme la nostre, n'ait pû entierement gouster des ouvrages où l'on perd tousiours beaucoup de temps avant que d'arriver au sujet et de trouver ce qu'on cherche, d'où vient, peut-estre, que les Dialogues n'ont iamais esté en si grand honneur qu'entre les Grecs et entre les Italiens, gens tout ensemble de grand esprit et de grand loisir" (pp. 10–11). And he concludes later with rather dubious praise of Sarasin's dialogue: "Je veux qu'il ait pû mieux faire, mais ne luy conterons nous pour rien d'avoir bien fait, et *en un genre d'escrire, où presque pas un de nos François n'a rien fait encore*, qu'il n'ait point mérité tous nos éloges, luy refuserons nous donc ceux-là mesme qu'il mérite?"(p. 16) Pellisson's somewhat involved reservations are indicative of the absolutely minor literary status he assigns to the dialogue. They are also indicative of a very conservative literary taste, since after 1660 the dialogue will have considerable vogue and will move into areas hitherto inaccessible to it.

With his unpublished works Descartes left a dialogue amongst Poliandre, Epistemon, and Eudoxe entitled *La Recherche de la vérité par la lumière naturelle*, which his biographer Baillet tells us enabled him, rather like Plato or Cicero, to "débiter plus agréablement sa philosophie," and which also corresponds to the openly acknowledged ordering of the conversation, in which the interlocutors follow a specific order from beginning to end.

This is the method used by the most Christian of Descartes' disciples, Father Malebranche, in his *Conversations chrétiennes* (1676), his *Entretiens sur la métaphysique et la religion* (1688) between Théotime and Théodore, and above all in a remarkable work which brings us almost up to the Enlightenment, *L'Entretien d'un philosophe chrétien et d'un philosophe chinois* (1707), in which he criticizes both Spinoza and Arnauld, as well as Jesuit practices in China.

Paralleling the exposition of a philosophy or the apology for religion, this type of didactive and directive dialogue is also found in *Les Entretiens sur les sciences* (1684) of Father Bernard Lamy, whose methodological and ideological aims are constantly emphasized by the interlocutors. The best method of studying is based on a knowledge of mathematics and "on en prend l'habitude en lisant l'Evangile assiduement."

The seventeenth century saw many critical debates about literature in the dialogue form. Sarasin's dialogue noted above and Chapelain's *La Lecture des vieux romans* (1647) contain discussions about the courtly romances of the Middle Ages and the moral values that they uphold. Father Dominique Bouhours mixes the most diverse subjects in a peculiar and confused work full of fascinating ideas, *Les Entretiens d'Ariste et d'Eugène* (1671), in which he treats both the preeminent dignity of the French language and the wittiness, that "je ne scay quoy," that captures in a period of classicism the attraction of the indefinable and the sentimental. Bouhours also explains his esthetic preferences in a more coherent fashion in dialogues between Eudoxe, the classicist, and Philanthe, the baroque enthusiast for the Italians and the Spanish, in a work entitled *La Manière de bien penser dans les ouvrages de l'esprit* (1687). In the preface to this book, he says he deliberately chose this form because it is "propre à éclairer les questions les plus obscures," but also, and this is more innovative, because "les gens qui y parlent peuvent aisément dire le pour et le contre sur toutes sortes de sujets." Actually, Bouhours does not balance things out quite so evenly, and we see Philanthe, after having championed charm and brilliance, eventually move towards the completely classical rhetoric of his interlocutor.

It is important to note the importance of spatial localization in these two fascinating dialogues with different titles: Ariste and Eugène converse in the solitary and outdoor setting of the environs of Dunkirk, while Eudoxe and Philanthe have their encounter in a study full of books and they converse with book in hand. In the same way, Desmarets de Saint-Sorlin adopts the dialogue form when he wants to undertake *La Défense du poème heroïque* (1674).

This is the same form of literary debate used by Fénelon in his *Dialogues sur l'eloquence* (1681–1686). The speaking roles are ordered even as to their sequence and no interior progression is noticeable. But it is interesting to note that Fénelon chooses the anonymous A, B, and C as interlocutors just as Voltaire and Diderot will do subsequently. It is also instructive to note that Fénelon, who later becomes the Archbishop of Cambrai (1695), uses dialogue to present his *Instruction pastorale sur le système de Jansénius*. He explains this usage in an introduction in which he says that his taste for "ce genre d'écrit si insinuant" which leads men quietly "à la vérité en leur faisant trouver au fond d'eux-mêmes, par des simples interrogations, ce qu'on ne peut leur enseigner par des leçons directes sans révolter leur amour-propre." This is an explicit acknowledgment of his debt to the Socratic dialogue.

It is obvious that Fenélon's best-known dialogues really belong to the eighteenth century, even if they were written earlier and even if they do not really preview the thought of the Enlightenment. But it is impossible to speak of *Les Dialogues des Morts* (1712) without noting this genre's antecedents, direct descendants of Lucian of Samosata. As early as 1664, Boileau had used this tradition to satirize baroque novels in his *Dialogues des héros de romans,* not published until 1713 in order to avoid hurting Mme de Scudéry during her lifetime. In his case, it is clear that there is nothing more than the purely literary use of the genre.

This is not the case with Fontenelle's *Dialogues des Morts,* published in 1683, but whose sense and meaning are already close to those of the philosophes. Despite a certain brilliance and mannerism for which Voltaire and others would criticize him, Fontenelle is the first to assign to the dialogue a really critical function, in which the "discussants" are merely a mask imposed on modern ideas. He makes fun of man's contradictions and makes clear in his own way the best-known values. Fontenelle brings us into the period of the *open* dialogue, in which the didactic need has been eclipsed by that of investigation. What happens is that our intellectual comfort is upset, our knowledge is disturbed, our certainties are invaded by doubt, and our pride is threatened by our new and valuable knowledge. An ambivalent series of ideas is here transformed into an appropriate form, insofar as it avoids determinative conclusions and categorical formulae. As a work pointing towards an internal crisis in a period of crisis, Fontenelle's *Dialogues des Morts* asks more questions than it answers. It is already in the mental framework of Diderot. Fontenelle is hesitating between confidence in human reason and anthropological pessimism based on history. Just like Montaigne, Fontenelle records our weaknesses and our love of the false (that is, the marvelous) but from that he deduces neither fideism nor renunciation. The only way we can progress towards a more rational and knowledgeable life is by being alert to the traps which surround us. If these dialogues have bothered critics and brought about contradictory interpretations, it is partially because they have been treated as didactic treatises and partially because critics have been looking for the opposite of what the author wanted to suggest. This is really parodoxical thinking, expressed in paradoxical terms, but which also suffers from a kind of deficiency that is inherent in treating complex themes in such an expeditious way. However, it is clear that this complex lesson, both of prudence and of daring, announces the ideas of the Enlightenment, even including its scorn for the majority's opinion and thus for the argument of consensus. In his conversation with Raphaël, Straton says: "Pour trouver la vérité, il faut tourner le dos à la multitude, et les opinions communes sont la règle des opinions saines, pourvu qu'on les prenne à contre-sens." Diderot will say much the same about his *Pensées philosophiques:* "je les tiens pour détestables si elles plaisent à tout le monde." The most important lesson, the one that Voltaire will repeat in his short stories, is the one that Lucretius gives to Barbe Plomberge: "ce que la nature n'aurait pas obtenu de notre raison, elle l'obtient de notre folie." However, the eighteenth-century philosophes will not follow him in his theory of the mobilizing power of the illusionary; they will not say, as does Raimond Lulle: "On perdrait courage si on n'était pas soutenu par des idées fausses . . . si par malheur la vérité se montrait telle qu'elle est, tout serait perdu; mais il paraît bien qu'elle sait de quelle importance il est qu'elle se tienne toujours assez bien cachée." Despite the fact that he is following libertine ideas at this point, Fontenelle is still the renovator of the dialogue as a debate over ideas. In the same vein, Fontenelle will invent the scientific and philosophical dialogue in his *Entretiens sur la pluralité des mondes* (1686) that Michel Delon has properly described as consummating "la ruine des préjugés cosmologiques" while involving "le fondement et la finalité d'une philosophie en recherche."[1]

Diderot is the one who will synthesize all these intellectual and formal initiatives in his *Rêve de d'Alembert,* but he will add to them an audacious visionary approach. However, it is extremely significant that the origins of the Diderotian dialogue, from the dialogue of the dead first contemplated and then rejected, to both the philosophical dialogue and the scientific conversation, are to be found in the period that prepared the Enlightenment, that era that can be called either a "Crise de conscience" or "Frühaufklarung."

This opening up of minor genres could only take place during that esthetic revolution which lies behind the Quarrel of the Ancients and the Moderns. So it is not just by chance that the Quarrel is most coherently and clearly expressed in a remarkable dialogue, Charles Perrault's *Parallèle des Anciens et des Modernes* (1688–1692). This fascinating debate asks some of the major questions about eighteenth-century esthetics, opens the way to innovation while rejecting the absolute and irreversible superiority of the Ancients, and praises modernity, basing its argument on the beauty of the gardens at Versailles, where the conversations amongst the President, the Abbé and the Chevalier are supposed to take place. A work of tolerance and intellectual honesty, the *Parallèle* inaugurates the type of debate in which the point of view of "the other," in this case the President, is treated with respect, sympathy, and consideration, even when it is judged to be out-of-date and of no future interest.

When Diderot writes, in the article "Encyclopédie" of the *Encyclopédie*, "Nous avons eu, s'il est permis de s'exprimer ainsi, des contemporains sous le siècle de Louis XIV," he is referring to Perrault, not to Bayle, and his tribute is important. He also mentions Fontenelle amongst those who have contributed to the progress of "la raison et l'esprit philosophique ou de doute." Wasn't it the illustrious Secretary of the Académie des Sciences who during his youth took the risk of treating science and astronomy in dialogue form, so easily accessible to his readers? Wasn't he the one who braved the criticism of worldliness and frivolousness by giving lessons to a Marquise? By proving that the dialogue could be used in scientific vulgarization, Fontenelle was acting like a pioneer. If there is any doubt on this score, it is only necessary to point to Lessing's remarks to Mendelssohn, reported by the latter in a posthumous tribute, about the innovative and exemplary character of the French writer's dialogues.

Thus all the necessary conditions seem to be united just before the eighteenth century (if you go by dates) or at the dawn of the "Enlightenment" (if you go by the history of ideas or of taste) to make the dialogue one of the most useful vehicles for the new ideas.

The religious and moral debate over the nature of pleasure which was undertaken at this period takes the dialogue form by preference.[2] The same holds true for the debate on feminism which will continue throughout the century.[3]

During the same period, one of the most active practitioners of the genre, Rémond de Saint-Mard, author of *Les Dialogues des Dieux*, wrote a whole discourse on the nature of the dialogue.[4] He is actually writing the apology for a literary genre he believed to be both the oldest and the most natural of all. All human knowledge must have begun in this way, and only the taste for the marvelous caused it to be dropped. Saint-Mard acclaims Plato as the restorer of this literary genre, but he has certain reservations about Plato's literary talent. He acknowledges that he is "gracieux" in his reasoning and poetic in his language, but he finds him rather diffuse and long-winded: "Il s'égare en longs raisonnements . . . souvent alambiqués; sa marche, qui est toujours par demandes et par réponses, est ennuyeuse à mourir" (p. 9).

Cicero's faults are of a quite different order: "Ce sont les plus grands des Romains qui y parlent, mais c'est toujours Cicéron qu'on entend, ce qui est fort mal. Quand quatre personnes sont censées s'entretenir, il est ridicule que nous n'en entendions parler qu'une . . . chacun ayant son caractère à lui, doit avoir aussi un langage qui lui est propre" (p. 16, note). On the other hand, he appreciates the prudence and discretion of Cicero's tone: "il propose toujours la vérité en tremblant, et avec la modestie d'un homme qui examine. Je ne sais pourquoi l'air décisif est aujourd'hui si fort à la mode. On ne songe pas qu'il marque de l'ignorance aussi bien que de la vanité. Quand on a considéré un objet, on se donne l'audace d'en juger: on l'a, dit-on, tourné en tous les sens, on en a bien vu toutes les faces. Qui le sait?" (pp. 18–19).

Lucian is his idol and model: "c'est mon héros, car c'est lui que j'imite, et après lui je fais parler les Dieux. Je n'ai pas cru néanmoins devoir le suivre dans sa manière de les faire raisonner" (p. 23), since the topic of criticizing paganism is outmoded. He likes the fact that Lucian wrote for a wide audience, even including women: "on dirait que les sciences perdraient de leur dignité en devenant faciles, et que l'air mystérieux dont elles sont couvertes soit nécessaire à leur beauté." He makes excuses for Lucian's easy manner: "ce n'est que depuis quelque temps qu'on est devenu chaste dans la manière de s'exprimer. Je ne sais si nos moeurs ont profité de ce changement. Je ne le crois pas" (p. 28).

Rémond de Saint-Mard goes on to give the outlines of a real "poétique du dialogue": it should "présenter des idées simples d'une manière peu commune" or "renfermer une idée singulière et intéressante" (p. 47). The skill of the author allows him "de faire en sorte que les acteurs n'y soient jamais d'accord, qu'ils plaident presque toujours contradictoirement, sauf à eux de convenir à la fin du dialogue et d'établir pour fruit de leur dispute une proposition singulière, mais vraie du moins par le côté qu'on donne à considérer." The best dialogue is a short one, because "l'étendue lui ôte de sa vivacité" (p. 48), but it must not lead directly to the truth: "n'y a-t-il pas de l'injustice à un auteur d'exiger qu'on attrape tout d'un coup une vérité à laquelle il n'est arrivé qu'après bien de la fatigue?" This implies that a literary work is molded by the meandering route taken by intellectual inquiry and that its form should reflect this fact.

Its style should not be too familiar, not an easy thing to achieve when the aim is that of naturalness. Saint-Mard thinks that this kind of style is harder to achieve than that of poetry or treatises. However, making the effort is well worth while: "ces sortes d'entretiens sont d'une ressource admirable dans les matières qui, pour être bien éclaircies, demandent à être discutées, et méritent d'être approfondies" (p. 61n.).

Diderot's dialogue will fully realize this project, even better than Saint-Mard's dialogues. The latter certainly eschew received ideas and traditional morality, but are full of preciosity and mannerisms of the Regency style. But it is important to recognize the interest and originality of this theoretical discourse that points to the maturity of the genre and to a growing interest in it. Saint-Mard doesn't hesitate to acknowledge his predecessors: Fontenelle, whose only fault is his tendency towards frivolity; Fénelon, whose dialogues first seemed to him to be too simple because he was looking for "du vif, du piquant" rather than "du vrai." "Moi et les autres," he acknowledges, "nous jugeons trop vite" (pp. 61–62).

Saint-Mard's twenty *Dialogues des Dieux* and ten *Nouveaux Dialogues* (1711) deserve better than the complete neglect accorded them. These short moral debates are frequently lively and controversial. The author revels in paradox because "les paradoxes piquent et réveillent l'esprit humain" (1.343); he puts forward almost scandalous views because "le dialogue est un genre d'écrire où l'on doit espérer que ce qu'on dit ne sera pas toujours pris au pied de la lettre" (1.348). Dr. Bordeu will do the same thing in his second conversation with Mlle de Lespinasse. And it isn't only his conception of truth and its investigation that brings Saint-Mard close to the Diderot of the *Pensées philosophiques* when he has someone say to Minerva in the third of *Les Nouveaux Dialogues* on the subject of philosophers: "Ce sont des gens modestes, des gens raisonnables, qui peuvent bien quelquefois s'amuser à chercher la vérité; mais je les désavouerais s'ils croyaient l'avoir trouvée." The parallel should not be pushed too far, but it is obvious that the ground has been laid for the full development and spectacular liberation of the dialogue form. Critical thought, political reflections, social analysis will soon take over this medium so well adapted to their objectives.

The way had already been cleared as early as 1703 by the famous *Dialogues curieux entre l'auteur et un sauvage de bon sens, qui a voyagé*, in which La Hontan puts in the mouth of the Huron chief Adario a severe criticism of European laws, customs, medical knowledge, and religion. The intervention of the defrocked Gueudeville in 1705 would reinforce these attacks to such a point that this would become one of the most revolutionary works of the period, going so far as to incite the French army to revolt against its officers.

Contemporary critics quickly noted that Adario was always the victor in these debates and that this so-called noble savage (who will become one of the models of this myth) writes and speaks "comme s'il n'avait ni patrie, ni religion." Maurice Roelens, who has published a critical edition with many comments, emphasizes that it is really a false dialogue.[5] It is clear that the remarks of La Hontan do not reproduce a real conversation; he chose the dialogue because he found it to be the most efficacious weapon against the colonial spirit, diffusing his ideas on hell, property rights, sexual morality, torture, and sorcerers. Although these themes will become dull and banal during the course of the century, they resurface in a more ample and oratorical form in the *Histoire des Deux Indes*, where they will also be better documented.

Montesquieu's political reflections do not follow the same paths. They avoid invective and philippics in an effort to be serene and distanced. When Montesquieu pays attention to the problem of absolute personal power, dictatorship, it is significant that he approaches it through the dialogue form. This will indeed be his only incursion into a literary genre so foreign to his habitual literary stance. Robert Shackleton, the well-known Montesquieu specialist, has tied the genesis of the *Dialogue de Sylla et d'Eucrate* to the elaboration of the *Considérations sur les causes de la grandeur des Romains et de leur décadence* (1734). He cautiously dates the dialogue from 1724.[6] Sylla's dilemma is placed by Montesquieu more in terms of political philosophy than in terms of history. Sylla refuses to become a dictator, even though it is within his grasp, because he needs some resistance to act as an obstacle to his desire for power. Eucrate reminds him of his past and tries to find therein both logic and justification, but Sylla retorts that he had only wanted power in order to put an end to the anarchistic liberty called for by the people. His renunciation is neither patriotic nor humanistic, since he is a man of a certain class who despises humanity. This is obviously a false dialogue, and, by definition in this particular case, the dialogue between Sylla and Eucrate is a warning against the temptation of becoming superhuman and also against the effects of absolutism. If terror is the method of governing and violence is introduced, political relations become perverted by the installation of the logic of violence which can only debase and destroy civic spirit.

Was Mably thinking of Montesquieu when he wrote *Les Entretiens de Phocion* (1763)? There is nothing to prove it, but the main theme is, once again, the foundation of the authoritarian state, now completely revolutionized by Rousseau's political ideas. In a fictional Greece, Phocion expounds to Nicoclès and Cléophane, complacent listeners, a rationally militant and repressive system of thought that founds the strong State on its identity with absolute Reason. Such a set of ideas is hard to fit into the dialogue form he is constantly sidestepping. The only opponent, the young Aristias, is reduced to silence by Phocion: "Aristias changera, je vous le prédis. C'est un bon augure que ce silence modeste qu'il a gardé, pendant que je l'avertissais de ses erreurs" (p. 33). Soon submitting, Aristias becomes an obedient disciple: "Je n'ose marcher sans votre secours" and "Je dévore vos discours." Every question becomes openly rhetorical. The objections are ur.Jermined even before they are formulated: "Je n'attends pas votre réponse, poursuivit Phocion, je la sais" (pp. 42, 51). A discourse that preaches voluntary submission, internalization of the law, one that rejects the passions as leading to disorder, shatters the structure of the dialogue since it suffocates its possibilities in a sort of caricature of the Platonic conversation.

However it is significant that this major political thinker, who has been neglected by critics, should have chosen in such a blatant way the dialogue form in order to express himself. It is surprising that a title like *Des Droits et des devoirs du citoyen* (written in 1758) disguises an epistolary novel that recounts the conversations of the writer and Lord Stanhope in the lovely gardens of the chateau of Marly (which also serve as the basis of a critique of absolutism and a denunciation of the misery of the peasants).[7] It is even more surprising to realize that *Les Principes de Morale* by the very same Mably takes on the appearance of a philosophical conversation amongst four interlocutors. But the desire for rational unification is there just as it was in *Les Entretiens de Phocion*. Mably can only conceive of rational politics, and he can only tolerate the passions "quand elles obéissent à la raison." Such a rigid thought structure does not easily accommodate itself to the suppleness and mobility of a real dialogue. The real development of the dialogue lies elsewhere: in the direction of contradiction and irony, not of authoritarian dogmatism.

Voltaire used the dialogue form only after 1751, quite late in his career. This is also the period when his thought was moving towards the criticism of traditions and clichés using a more direct and militant form, more open to the general public. This polemical vein will grow in the articles of the *Dictionnaire philosophique,* in the caustic insinuations of the "facéties" and the "petits pâtés," in his letters and petitions, but also in the dialogue in which he puts himself forward as a kind of modern Lucian.[8] The dialogue form appears in several articles of the *Dictionnaire philosophique,* such as "Fraude," "Catéchisme," "Liberté de penser," "Nécessaire," which proves just how appropriate Voltaire found it for the general public he wanted to reach. There are numerous individual dialogues, published between 1751 and 1771, varying in subject, length, tone, and style. The dialogue of the dead (*Lucrèce et Posidonius*) takes its place beside the exotic dialogue à la La Hontan (*Un Sauvage et un bachelier*), the esthetic debate (*Les Anciens et les Modernes, ou la Toilette de Mme de Pompadour*), the antichristian diatribe (*Le Mandarin et le Jésuite* and above all *L'Empereur de la Chine et Frère Rigolet*). Some of them are hardly dialogues at all (*Conversation de M. l'Intendant des Menus en exercice avec M. l'abbé Grizel*). Others become so diffuse they seem to take in the whole of Voltaire's philosophy, for example *L'A.B.C* or *Les Dialogues d'Evhémère.*

What they all have in common is their single-minded and preconceived character. Voltaire's dialogue is a work of propaganda in which one of the interlocutors is always overcome. The other is nothing but the mouthpiece of the author, and his irony reduces his adversary to practically nothing, if it does not absolutely eliminate him through ridicule. In *L'A.B.C.,* the triumph of A is complete, B and C serving only as background.

Voltaire's wit, irony, and sarcastic verve don't keep his dialogues from a certain air of monotony. They are all totally without surprises and never really put the master's philosophy to the test. The whole thing is settled in advance. The foolish gullibility of Voltaire's adversaries is only too evident. "Quoi! ne jamais tromper!" exclaims the Jesuit, and Brother Rigolet broaches his discussion with the Emperor Yong-Tching by saying to him: "ma religion est la seule véritable, comme me l'a dit mon préfet le frère Bouvet, qui le tenait de sa nourrice." This is more the tone of parodical pamphleteering than of dialogue, in which the relationship between strength and intelligence should be much closer. Voltaire criticized Fontenelle's dialogues because "c'est toujours lui qu'on voit, et jamais ses héros." It is possible to say the same about his own and come to about the same conclusion: "Fontenelle me paraît le plus agréable joueur de passe-passe que j'aie jamais vu. C'est toujours quelque chose, et cela amuse."

Other authors certainly made more serious use of dialogue, but they lacked the consummate ease, vivacity, and rhythm of the artist. All that is left of them is what history records: whether it is *Le Tel-liamed, ou Entretiens d'un philosophe indien avec un missionnaire français sur la diminution de la mer*, a forceful exposition of Neptunian cosmology,[9] or a curious dialogue by Méhégan in which Alcippe and Oronte discuss the scorn of riches or the status of men of letters in a rustic setting half way between the sea and the mountains.[10] The abbé Galiani's unusual *Dialogues sur les Bles* (1769), one of the real masterpieces of economic thought of the eighteenth century, deserves a special place, distanced as it is from both Turgot's free trade and Terray's protectionism, but it is difficult to tell how much belongs to Galiani and how much to his editor and corrector Diderot.

With Diderot we are truly in the presence of a master of the genre. More than any of his contemporaries, he was open to the complexities of reality and the mobility of thought. He offers no closed system, rather a questioning series of ideas aimed at upsetting rather than at giving solutions. In his *Lettre sur les Sourds et Muets* (1751), he had already declared that he was "plus occupé à former des nuages qu'à les dissiper." He allows his thought to stray to the most improbable hypotheses since "mes pensées, ce sont mes catins" (*Le Neveu de Rameau*), and he is adamant in recommending the experimental method. Diderot refused to write a systematic treatise on morality, such as Helvétius had done, because he found certain questions, quite simple on the surface, to be beyond his powers: "Je n'ai pu trouver la vérité, et je l'ai cherchée avec plus de qualités que vous n'en exigez . . . je n'ai pas même osé prendre la plume pour en écrire la première ligne (*Oeuvres philosophiques* [1956], pp. 594–95).

Since the most important and real problems of life remain open, Diderot will tackle them through the form of the dialogue. The embryonic form of this is found in the *Pensées philosophiques* (1746); it is buried in *La Promenade du sceptique* and reappears in some articles of the *Encyclopédie*. Diderot's reflections on the theater are expressed in the extraordinary dialogues between the author and his character, in the three *Entretiens avec Dorval* (1757). But the true virtuosity of this artist of the dialogue will appear around 1760 in a really amazing display of virtuosity. The *Rêve de d'Alembert* (1769) was supposed to be a conversation amongst the dead; Diderot gave this up, both for the realism of the debate and for its scientific credibility. The first part still belongs to the Platonic type in which Diderot is the master who listens with surprise as d'Alembert is reduced to asking questions. The actual *Rêve* liberates the character from both organized discourse and still hesitant biological constraints, while letting Dr. Bordeu take over from the Academician allowing him to express paradoxes that make Julie de Lespinasse blush.

If the *Paradoxe sur le comédien* and the *Supplément au voyage de Bougainville* remain attached to the classical relationship of Master-Disciple (the Master appearing as B in the *Supplément* and as "le Premier" in the *Paradoxe*), the relationship with "the Other" is freed of didacticism and superiority in the incomparable *Neveu de Rameau*, the remarkable *Entretien d'un père avec ses enfants*, with its extremely ambiguous conclusion, the charming *Entretien d'un philosophe avec la maréchale de ****. Diderot is playing with time, place, setting, characters, but above all ideas. Certainly for him, the interlocutors are neither completely wrong nor completely right. Rameau is the fool who sometimes happens to tell the truth. Diderot's old father is just as respectable as his son, and the Maréchale is right in hanging on to her religion. What is important is to listen to the others, to respect them, to seek truth with sincerity and modesty.[11] Aware of mobility, more questioning than directive, Diderot's ideas are hard to fit into traditional forms, and they are quite at home in the form of dialogue I have called "heuristic" that can be found in a novel like *Jacques le Fataliste*.

An open work, a genial creation without posterity, the Diderotian dialogue merits a much more profound analysis than I can offer here. It represents the summit of a genre that he investigated and exploited to its utmost. Not quite completely however, since Jean-Jacques Rousseau would invent, after the Diderotian dialogue between *Lui* and *Moi*, the dialogue between two parts of the self, Rousseau and Jean-Jacques, subjected to the hostile stare of a third, the Frenchman, who holds Jean-Jacques responsible for all sorts of wickedness. It is obvious that Rousseau did not intend to condemn himself, but rather to excuse his literary double by dissociating him from the monstrous character that had been constructed by proving that "c'est à force d'être naturelle que [la conduite] de Jean-Jacques est peu commune" (Pléiade ed., 850). It is not necessary to take a stand on the whole idea of the conspiracy; all that matters here is that it led Rousseau to invent a new form of dialogue which allowed him to get out of the trap placed there by "the others," those whom he called "les méchants." This both ironic and passionate apology gave to the dialogue form a certain pathetic value in which can be seen the anguish of the modern individual subject to an inquisition both obsessive and incomprehensible. This modern individual, less fortunate than Jean-Jacques, can no longer distance himself from everything and "se résigner à être à jamais défiguré parmi eux" (p. 986).

Less original in literary terms but just as sure as his aims, Sade, towards the end of the eighteenth century (1782), will use the dialogue to expound clearly the principles of his philosophy. The *Dialogue entre un prêtre et un moribond* is anything but an open work. Sade leaves nothing open to his priest, completely dumbfounded by the quiet remarks of this categorical and fluent dying man. In one way, the relationship between the characters is reminiscent of the Voltairian model, even if the apology for voluptuousness and crime or even the affirmation of an out-and-out materialism are completely opposed to the Voltairian ethic which it is possible to discern in his criticism of miracles and prophecies. This resumé of Sade's thought reflects the didactic aspect of a thought process little disposed to doubt or uncertainty.

It is possible to say the same, in another register, of the remarkable, but at times terrifying, *Soirées de Saint-Petersbourg* of Joseph de Maistre.[12] It is symptomatic that it is necessary to wait for the beginning of the nineteenth century to see the resurgence of the dialogue, a form very little in vogue during the Revolution which much preferred the treatise, the pamphlet, or journalism. But it is even more unusual to note that it is the philosophic conversation, the most characteristic literary product of the Enlightenment, that Maistre will choose to question and try to eliminate the eighteenth century. Through the debates of the Russian Senator, the Count, and the little French Chevalier, it is the whole thought process of the Enlightenment that is attacked by a passionate and implacable enemy. Maistre turns his back on the Enlightenment in the same way that he rejects the modern world in the name of a Providence that justifies both war and the hangman. He admires Voltaire, but "ses inimitables talents ne lui inspirent plus qu'une espèce de rage sainte qui n'a pas de nom" (*Entretien* 4). With the conviction of a prophet, he mouths nothing but anathema and curses. However, this displaced person is also a genial writer, this enemy of the Revolution is also absolutely attached to France and to her language, of which the Count says that it is "toujours entendue de plus loin, car le style est un accent" (*Entretien* 6). In this reactionary genius, the eighteenth-century French dialogue finds both its highest and its lowest point. It ends on the very high note that its assertiveness reflects. In Maistre, the Enlightenment found its most formidable adversary, but also its most profound analyst. This fanatic saw in the eighteenth century a decisive moment in history; by denouncing it as a period of absolute evil, he invites us to think about the values of liberty, tolerance, the right to disagree, the usefulness of heretics. In this apocalyptic dialogue, the century of Enlightenment finally found an adversary worthy of it.

NOTES

English translation by Jean A. Perkins

1 Michel Delon, "La Marquise et le Philosophe," *Revue des sciences humaines* 182 (April–June 1981): 65–78.

2 See Baudot de Juilly, *Dialogue entre Mrs. Patru et d'Ablancourt sur les plaisirs* (1701); Rémond de Saint-Mard, *Nouveaux Dialogues des Dieux, ou Réflexions sur les plaisirs* (1711); and N. Dupuy, *Dialogues sur les plaisirs, les passions . . .* (1717).

3 J. B. de Crues, *Les Entretiens de Théandre et d'Isménie sur la préeminence du sexe* (1689); *Entretiens d'un abbé et d'un cavalier su la liberté des dames françaises* (1693); De Vertron, *Conversations sur l'excellence du beau sexe* (1699).

4 Published late (1742) and on the basis of a manuscript in the three-volume edition of the *Oeuvres* of this author. We have quoted from the edition of Pierre Mortier, 5 vols. in 2 (Amsterdam, 1749).

5 La Hontan, *Dialogues curieux,* ed. Maurice Roelens (Paris: Ed. Sociales, 1973).

6 Robert Shackleton, *Montesquieu (1639–1755)* (London: Oxford Univ. Press, 1961), 66–67.

7 On this point it is useful to consult Wolfgang Asholt "'L'Effet Mably' et le problème de l'egalité dans le roman dialogué *Des Droits et des devoirs du citoyen,*" in *L'Egalité* 9 (Travaux du Centre de Philosophie du Droit de l'Université libre de Bruxelles, Bruylant, 1984): 51–71.

8 He makes the claim that he is following the Syrian orator in *Lucien, Erasme et Rabelais aux Champs-Elysées* (1765). In a letter to Frederick II (5 June 1751), he praises Lucian in the following terms: "Ce Lucien est naïf, il fait penser ses lecteurs, et on est toujours tenté d'ajouter à ses dialogues. Il ne veut point avoir d'esprit. Le défaut de Fontenelle est qu'il en veut toujours avoir."

9 Although this dialogue was published in 1749, it must date from the first third of the eighteenth century, since its author, de Maillet, died in 1738.

10 *Dialogue* with no other title following *Les Considérations sur les révolutions des arts* (Paris: Brocas, 1755; registered in 1754).

11 Diderot explained himself in several passages of his *Apologie de l'abbé Galiani* (1770): "vous êtes dogmatiques" he says to Morellet, "et l'abbé est enquêtant," and he has Galiani say, "mes interlocuteurs sont dans mes *Dialogues* comme dans la rue: chacun pour soi; je ne réponds point de ce qu'ils disent, ni eux de ce que je dis" (*Oeuvres politiques,* pp. 74, 80–81).

12 Written between 1802 and 1817, published in 1821, the year the author died.

Diderot from Outside the Research Machine;

or

Recontextualizing Diderot

REMY G. SAISSELIN

In his difficult but devastating *Art as Experience,* John Dewey referred to Dr. Johnson as a philistine and even dared to question Kant.
The book is devastating of the genteel tradition which Santayana saw
as being at bay in the twenties; but which is still far from dead. Dr.
Johnson a philistine! What a liberating thought and one which could
only have been uttered before the creation of ASECS and the Johnson
papers production company got underway. But then there seems
to have been some thinking going on in the university community of
the 1930s.

Now this daring irreverence of Dewey's made me doubt my own
teaching and eighteenth-century-literature experience. Was not the
eighteenth century made up of so many sacred cows not to be disturbed as we made our way through the university obstacle course?
Thus when asked to participate in a panel on Diderot I recalled Dewey
and wondered if anyone had ever been irreverent about Diderot since
the creation of *Diderot Studies.* I also wondered if any one, given the
multinational enterprise of Diderot studies and Diderot papers production, could possibly have anything left to say which had not been
said or written before. Is it still possible to think of Diderot and his
work or works with one's own mind or must all the other minds who
have had thoughts on him and his work be incorporated into one's

thinking? Surely it is impossible for one man or one woman to read all that has been written and is still being written and spoken about Diderot. And surely if the Diderot bibliography is so huge it must be because Diderot is worth this vast research enterprise. The very thought of the task of writing still another paper on Diderot, a respectable, and respectful, learned, footnoted, acceptable-for-publication, innocuous, bland, but solid paper on Diderot stunned me, paralyzed me as I vainly tried again to read through the Diderot works I have in my study only to be reminded of all I had not read on or by Diderot. Yes, I tried to read those sacred texts, read so often, quoted so often, commented, analyzed, explicated, edited, reedited, re-reedited, and I could not. Diderot had interested me some twenty years ago when I first started to work in an art museum and had to edit a journal of aesthetics and learned how wrong aestheticians could be when they wrote histories of aesthetics by mostly dismissing French aesthetics. And I thought I freed myself of Diderot once I was safely in a museum and read a paper in Chicago called *Diderot's Aesthetic Muddle*. But one can't get away from him and some four or five years ago I had to re-read him with care for at least one chapter of a study of the Neo-classic. By early this year I saw no reason for another paper on Diderot. Then came a letter from the chair of this section and I was suddenly haunted by Dewey's *petite phrase*. Dr. Johnson a philistine! Think of the shock and the joy of hearing something like that actually said, written, printed. And think of the implications for all those English departments teaching the Age of Johnson! It was inspiring.

And I suddenly started thinking of other potential shocks: *Diderot serait-il philistin ou Diderot bourgeois? Diderot arriviste! Diderot marchand de tableaux!* After all, *pourquoi pas?* He was a petit bourgeois who made it to bourgeois respectability; and from Grub Street he made it to the editorship of the *Encyclopédie;* and among all those hacks who did art criticism he ended up advising Catherine the Great. Now it may be thought by some that the tone here is in bad taste given that we commemorate the bicentenary of his death. But Diderot is not dead, since he is still being written about, researched, reedited, and spoken of. Diderot even made it beyond the grave. He is still, as they say in certain critical circles, a presence. So much so that I had to write another paper on him. And yet I did not want to do that.

I did not want to study this presence; for that meant going through that ever-mounting Diderot bibliography which merely testifies to the form that his presence takes on now. In other words, to study Diderot on the basis of the latest research and the latest interpretations is really studying not so much Diderot as his interpreters. Diderot, I suddenly recalled, was a historical character who had first existed outside seminar rooms, college courses, and learned congresses. Diderot had lived at a historical moment, of several decades duration, which had made it possible for Dewey to call Dr. Johnson a philistine in the first place, as it had made possible other phenomena not usually associated with Diderot such as aestheticism, snobism, and Kitsch. It was a Hegelian moment, rich in contradiction and ambiguities, and Diderot had been part of it. And so rather than looking at Diderot from within the research machine, I stepped outside to muse upon that first Diderot, actor in a historical moment.

For what, after all the finicky and minute research, the growing number of theses, books, communications, papers, and reports is the significance of the Salons and the rise of art criticism? The slow elaboration of the autonomy of the aesthetic judgment? The seemingly endless discussion of taste, beauty, nature, belle nature, the sublime, *manière*, or grand manner? What the significance of that internal dialogue between Lui and Moi? Why degrade Boucher and praise Chardin? And why did Diderot dislike Caylus? And what is the historical significance of Rousseau's *First Discourse,* or the *Essay on Architecture* of the abbé Laugier, and somewhat later, Winckelmann's *History of Ancient Art?*

Our enquiries into these questions are usually so close to the underbrush that we do not bother with the trees or the forest. For we are professional specialists, and as eighteenth-century specialists from 1700 backwards is not our territory and from 1800 forward is also foreign terrain. For like eighteenth-century producers out of Adam Smith, we work on the principle of the division of labor and the faith that an invisible hand will guide our efforts to some ultimate synthesis.

Now to begin answering these only slightly rhetorical questions, one needs not, like Michael Fried, invent an age of absorption and stick it between the consecrated Rococo and the Neoclassic. All you have to do, at least as concerns France and the purpose of situating Diderot, is to look back to Versailles and forward to Louis Philippe.

From the *querelle des bouffons,* c. 1752–54, to Kant's *Critique of Judgment,* 1790, there occurs a species of Hegelian dialectical moment which you can also turn upside down and call Marxist. The time span includes not just Diderot but also Winckelmann, Reynolds, Rousseau, Glück, Whately and Morel in garden design, Ledoux in architecture, David and his students in painting and others who can be associated with the elaboration of neoclassicism. Now what links all these? Quite aside from contemporaneity and their being grouped under neoclassicism, which label is not all that useful to answer the question? From my post-Dewey reading, that historical moment might be called that of the grand rejection of the Baroque and the consequent elaboration of an aesthetics based on a new concept of the natural. Or you can call it the grand discourse takeover of the arts and see that moment as the beginnings of the genteel tradition. This term is usually associated with a peculiarly American phenomenon, but it rests not only on the New England conscience, but also on the Kantian distinction between Aesthetic Art and merely pleasurable art. The phrase is worth noting: merely pleasurable art.

The distinction is highly important and is a product of that dialectical moment. It is a distinction between high and low, and will turn into a class distinction as concerns valuations of the arts. Thus above, High Art or Aesthetic art, explained by aestheticians, expounded by theoretically minded artists and amateurs, discerned in history by nascent art historians, taught in reformed academies, recognized officially, rewarded by way of gold, silver, and bronze medals to its producers and good students. Below: art as mere entertainment, merely pleasurable enjoyments and feelings, and mere commerce, or at best, art by nonacademicians. Above, spiritual communion and historical signs; below mere sensations, the attractions of the uninitiated. The eighteenth century, far more than the Renaissance, invented Art with a capital A. Which is another way of saying that the philosophes in France and Kant in Germany invented the aesthetics of bourgeois art. They had to make art respectable. One is reminded of Oscar Wilde's mot that there are two ways of disliking art: one is to dislike it, the other is like it rationally. The philosophes rationalized and moralized it.

Consider Diderot-Moi: he believes in all the right things—creative genius, moral actions, moral drama, the moral view of the arts, what will be called culture, and when not Diderot-Moi, Diderot believes in grand history painting, or moralizing painting, Greuze, Chardin, but damns Boucher. As Diderot-Moi he disdains the world of Rameau's nephew, the writers of Grub Street, the literary journalists, the army of hacks, from a moral point of view. And the petit bourgeois in Diderot is shocked that the *neveu* can discuss a criminal or a cheat the way a connoisseur might discuss a work of art or a question of taste. Now we professionals of eighteenth-century studies in general and Diderot in particular (and I do not claim to be such), are usually so intent on close analyses of texts or interpretations according to the latest critical theories that we do not often ask ourselves what is going on in Diderot's historical moment. Thus after years of writing about

aesthetic theories in the eighteenth century, I am less and less inclined to take them at face value. To take them for *argent comptant* as
theories about the arts, and leave them at that, is to fall into the liberal-
aesthetic trap set by the eighteenth century. At this point one must
recall that rhetorical question posed earlier: what is the significance of
the rise of aesthetics in the eighteenth century? Aesthetic discourse is
highly ambiguous, not only because of its vocabulary, borrowed from
metaphysics, rhetoric, literary criticism, as well as the new philosophy, and used to discuss all the arts. Aesthetic discourse is ambiguous
because it veils its primary referents, the secondary referents being
the arts it discusses. At least the case for this hypothesis can be made
for the historical moment in question. Aesthetics is disguised ideology, or if you will the beginnings of ideology.

This becomes apparent when one looks closely at the *querelle des
bouffons*. Philippe Beaussant in a brilliant article on this dispute in his
Rameau de A à Z (Fayard, 1983) points out that the discussion may
seem to have been about music, but that it was really about politics:

> Faillait-il être sourd pour ne pas sentir la valeur intrinsèque de la
> musique de Rameau, et pour lui opposer celle, charmante, mais
> sans véritable densité, de *La Serva padrona?* La réponse est fort
> simple. L'attaque contre la musique n'est qu'un second effet. Ce
> que les Encyclopédistes supportent mal, initialement, c'est que
> cette musique dense, forte, complexe, raffinée, soit au service de ce
> qui leur paraît à ce point futile: un univers de pure féerie, de pure
> irréalité. Puisque cette musique-là ne peut dire que cec choses-là,
> elle participe d'elles: *ergo,* elle est mauvaise (pp. 68 69).

This type of judgment, far more common than the pure aesthetic
judgment defined by Kant, might well be typical of the philistine. Be
that as it may, and without pursuing it here, it is enlightening of what
is happening in that decades-long dialectical historical moment: the
rejection of court culture. Now the aesthetic explanation, within the
classical aesthetic, of a change of style or manner is to say that a form
having been perfected, it must necessarily decline and new forms be
invented, or the corrupt reformed—as if there were some internal
mechanism driving the arts. But in fact the period in which Diderot
lived and acted as art critic and philosophe allows us to see not so
much how given perfected forms decline through their own perfection, but are rejected from outside the aesthetic-artistic system. The
Encyclopedists, the critics of French opera, Diderot, Rousseau, Mercier, David are all engaged in rejecting the Baroque world and its art,
an art of the Church to be sure, but also, more to the point in France,

the court. In this sense, Baroque is an art of representation taken in the class sense of that term: the court was ever *en représentation*, as indeed the great nobility too, and art, taken in a broad sense to include costume and manners, language and gesture, served to make appearances correspond to social and political rank in the grand design of society. As concerns art forms, this Baroque court art is also an art of illusion, pleasure, and luxury. Its grand representative genres are opera and the French formal garden and of course the palace is its architectural form. To be sure eighteenth-century specialists do not often bother with the Baroque; we think of the Rococo; but the Rococo is an aspect of the Baroque. It is par excellence an art of illusion and theatricality, as witness the work of Lajoue, gilding that looks like gold but is not, the *fêtes galantes* within the bosquets of French gardens, the mythological ballets and operas, the small and refined *pièces de clavecin* of Couperin and his followers, not to mention a whole literature of novels and plays which never ended up in college anthologies in part because the philosophes, who are the originators of our anthologies, dismissed these works as frivolous, licentious, and futile. Note too that the rejection of the Baroque through the critique of its Rococo descent is also a rejection of the feminine in the arts. No wonder Boucher became the symbolic figure of that hated style.

Now as any amateur of the arts, or of painting, knows, quite aside from personal taste, aside from the subject matter and, for some, one's taste in color, Boucher was a first-rate draftsman, a grand inventor of forms and theatrical settings, who can still please the amateur of drawings and of *grisailles*, not to mention some superb paintings, as paintings. But he was the court painter, associated with the taste of Madame de Pompadour, and Louis XV preferred his work to the work of some reformist artists who would reintroduce the grand manner of history painting into royal residences. For Diderot he was depraved and his art corrupted. Aesthetic judgment or political judgment? Certainly a moral judgment and ultimately a class judgment. What Diderot might have said with more justice is that Boucher represents the decadence of Baroque painting. But in a society in which there were neither Whigs nor Tories to argue political questions in a Parliament, aesthetic questions became implicitly political because the arts were the mirrors in which the ruling class represented itself and projected itself to others.

But one may go further and suppose that, on the whole, the writers, as hacks, as art critics, and as philosophes and Encyclopedists, did not have much sympathy for artists and painting and linked both to the ruling circles of the rich and the powerful. The critique of art

was also a critique of luxury. Certainly Diderot intensely disliked amateurs, connoisseurs, curieux, those new types produced by the world
of the arts, and here he did not differ that much from Rousseau. As
is well known, Diderot damned the Comte de Caylus in a famous
epitaph:

> Ci-gît un antiquaire acariâtre et brusque.
> Oh! qu'il est bien logé dans cette cruche étrusque!

He also accused Caylus of being a species of tyrant to artists. Yet
Diderot himself was just as presumptuous since as a philosophe he
was convinced, that on the level of theory, he was the superior of
painters and that the philosophes generally knew what they, the
painters, ought to paint.

Now why this dislike of Caylus? The Comte appears, when seen
through other eyes than those of Diderot, to be a rather sympathetic
type of the old nobility, the soldiering nobility, the type that over the
centuries made France. Certainly he was no court flatterer. At the age
of seventeen he distinguished himself at Malplaquet and later on in
the campaign in Catalogna. Later he resigned his commission and fell
in love with the arts in Italy, travelled in the Near East, and turned
antiquarian and amateur of the arts as well as writer on antiquities
and the arts. He also wrote tales which, in their subject matter antici-
pate somewhat the works of a Restif de la Bretonne and also remind
one of aspects of Marivaux's *Paysan parvenu*. In short, in his literary
pieces, Caylus is a genre painter with a real sense of the petit people
of Paris and its life and language. It is not high literature, it is not philosophy, and it is not moralizing. In short, in Caylus you have a man
still belonging to the Baroque on its popular level and as concerns the
art, the type of the antiquarian scholar collector. As such he is far
more familiar to art historians than literary historians. But as in the
case of the abbé Batteux, so with the Comte de Caylus, Diderot did a
good hatchet job on him. It may have been personal dislike, class dislike, or mental incompatibility, but certainly there was no reason Diderot should have disapproved of Caylus as concerns the arts. For
Caylus anticipated some of the reforms called for by the critics of the
Rococo; he also wished to reform the Academy and academic practise; he also worked for the reform of history painting and for better
teaching; and he too was an admirer of Antiquity and the Grand Manner. But he was, for the philosophes a mere amateur, and thus, like
the opera of Rameau, involved in futility. This becomes evident from
reading Marmontel who got to know him at Madame Geoffrin's. Here

too, the word is out: the world of arts, of the amateurs, is one of futility and as Marmontel puts it, *le plus mince des talents* and works of art were dismissed as mere *babioles*. But there is more: "Il [Caylus] avait tant dit, tant fait dire par ses prôneurs qu'en architecture il était le restaurateur *du style simple, des formes simples, du beau simple,* que les ignorants le croyaient et, par ses relations avec les *Dilettanti,* il se faisait passer en Italie et dans toute l'Europe pour l'inspirateur des beaux-arts. J'avais donc pour lui cette espèce d'antipathie naturelle que les hommes simples et vrais ont toujours pour les charlatans" (*Facéties du Comte de Caylus,* with a notice by Octave Uzanne [Paris, 1879], p. xxvi). This rivalry between men of letters like Diderot and Marmontel and the amateurs of the arts is an indication of the great change occurring in the arts and in the aesthetics of the eighteenth century. In the hands of amateurs the arts are a futile amusement and their collections mere *babioles.* Under the pen of the philosophes art is serious, it is a concept, and it will be utilitarian, the instrument of moral reform. Caylus still belonged to the Baroque art world, despite his classical taste.

The dislike of the amateurs by the writers is not too difficult to understand once the question is removed from the genteel discussion of taste and aesthetic theory and once you assume that the judgment of taste is not always disinterested. Obviously neither Diderot nor Marmontel were disinterested when they discussed the taste and activities of Caylus, nor when Diderot judged Boucher. The amateurs were generally rich and belonged to the established powers. It was thus easy to associate the arts with the rich and their life of luxury and pleasure. But to attack the arts on the grounds that they were the arts of the rich and the great was no argument. Art had to be reinvented and one began by attacking luxury art in the name of true art and in the name of nature.

With the abbé Du Bos the rejection of luxury art in 1719 already implicitly meant a critique of the ruling taste of the time, the Rococo. But his critique was based on historical insight: Du Bos thought historically and he had perceived that for the Greeks, for example, the arts had been something more than fine furniture. The Greeks were about to be used to "do in" the Baroque. By the time Diderot wrote his *Salons,* what had begun as a historical understanding of the role of art had turned into a general critique of the ruling taste justified in moral as well as aesthetic terms. If Diderot dismissed both Batteux and Father André and discards the idea of *la belle nature* it is because that concept was used as the critical foundation of the then existing systems of the arts. The philosophes would need a new nature to justify a new opera, a new drama, even new gardens.

Essentially what was eventually invented can be described, from our perspective, as bourgeois idealism. It was not called that at first, but it would become that by the time of Louis Philippe. The new aesthetic and its corresponding neoclassic art would be inherited by the French Revolution, which explains why an art elaborated in the old Regime could become that of the Republic, the Empire, the Restauration, and the age of Louis Philippe. Theories outlast generations. It also explains why an art first considered as an opposition art turns into an Establishment art. That this vast rejection of the Baroque was in fact a political-moral rejection explains the invention of a new nature and the ambiguities of aesthetic discourse, why the great Rameau's music was found unmusical, why Rousseau defined French as unsingable, but Italian naturally musical, why Boucher was depraved but Chardin not, even though he was collected by amateurs and nobles too, why French gardens were found boring but English gardens not, and why the style we call neoclassic, product of a historical moment, was defined as true and universal. This vast politico-aesthetic rejection also explains why Winckelmann and others such as David's pupil Paillot de Montabert reject practically all art between Raphael and Anton Raphael Mengs; why Diderot wrote as he did on *la manière* and the attitudes of the dance, and also why Lui is situated within a milieu of sycophants, sybarites, hedonists, and parasites, namely the losers of the Republic of letters condemned not to receive any place in anthologies destined for American students of the Enlightenment.

For Rameau's nephew as well as his uncle belong to the Baroque while Diderot, as Diderot-Moi, is of the Enlightenment, moral, liberal, proper, realistic, and potentially philistine. What was that poor nephew if not a failed or unsuccessful Baroque musician, a picaro living from hand to mouth, and day to day, motivated by pleasure, gold, and the need to fill the stomach? He had no high thoughts of art or of genius; he was, as the nineteenth century would have said, devoid of ideal. But how different was he from others for whom the arts were making a living rather than a vocation or a dedication to the Beautiful? Though a contemporary of Diderot, the *neveu* was closer to Diogenes than the philosophes whom he instinctively distrusted as if he knew that in the world they were shaping there would be no room for such lucid failures as he. In the person of Diderot and the ideology implied by Moi's attitudes, the *neveu* was up against something far less capricious than the mood of a financier or his mistress; he was up against bourgeois respectability, bourgeois morality, bourgeois aesthetics, and in the person of Diderot the art critic, the reality of the art market glossed over by the discourse of high art.

Viewed then from outside the great research machine, Diderot appears as an active and significant though not unique character in the last act of the Baroque moment, as one of its enemies. As such he was among those who would make possible a world of romantic aesthetes on the one hand and philistines on the other. But Lui saved him from being a philistine and reminded him that he too had to live from hand to mouth and write *Les Bijoux indiscrets* to fill his stomach.

"Impressions africaines":[1]
The Chevalier de Boufflers
in Senegal, 1785–1787

ALEXANDER A. SOKALSKI

Author of the short novel, *Aline, Reine de Golconde*, lionized poet of light satirical social verse, amateur portrait painter, seasoned European traveller, military officer forever in wait for a never-to-materialize engagement, absentee abbot of revenue monasteries in the Lorraine, *chevalier de Malte*, lover of the Countess Eléonore de Sabran, Stanislas Jean de Boufflers had led a life which in no way could be said to have prepared him, and perhaps even more so, many of his contemporaries, for Louis XVI's decision in October 1785 to name the *chevalier* to the post of Governor of Senegal.

Never have the reasons for the chevalier de Boufflers' request nor those behind the king's affirmative resolution been satisfactorily explained. It has been asserted that the nomination was in point of fact a disgrace, the consequence of two songs whose protagonists happened to be the powerfully allied abbess of Remiremont and the queen herself. A number of critics and historians maintain that the petitioner was motivated by strictly personal considerations, a desire to secure income other than that based on his abbeys and perhaps even to refurbish his personal finances, at that time deficient by 60,000 francs, combined with a desire to insure his own social position and thereby be deemed more worthy of his lover. It is highly unlikely, however, that the chevalier ever imagined that a more secure income

251

or a better social rank than the one already his by virtue of family connections would accrue from a governorship considered neither particularly lucrative nor high profile. What this post may really have represented for its seeker, as has been suggested by Paul Bonnefon, was
a last-ditch effort to achieve success, any kind of success: ". . . jouer
son dernier coup de dé et saisir sa dernière chance de réussite."[2] Or,
as another commentator, Pierre Vitoux, observes, although the office
may have had little to recommend it to a man of Boufflers' social stat-
ure, the chevalier may well have felt that, "l'aventure peut faire naître
l'occasion de se distinguer."[3] Indeed, the newly appointed governor
does intimate several times that it is an "ambition folle et barbare,"
that it is this "fatale ambition" which directs him and affirms that his
exile, as he calls it, is due entirely to "le crime des hommes qui ont
donné l'empire du monde à l'ambition, au lieu de ne reconnaître que
l'amour et le bonheur."[4] Consequently, his petition would appear to
have been motivated primarily by a sense of personal ambition, fu-
elled by a passion for adventure and travel. That it was granted would
further seem to indicate an absence of other serious candidates.

During his tenure as Governor of Senegal, the chevalier de Boufflers
made two trips to the tropical colony and resided there altogether approximately sixteen months. Named to the post on October 9, 1785,
he received his instructions[5] on November 18, but it was December 8
before he even boarded the corvette *Rossignol*. His departure, in fact,
was delayed another nine days by unfavorable weather. On January
16, 1786, the new governor disembarked at Saint-Louis-du-Sénégal.
After a stay of only six months he was back aboard ship en route for
France. Boufflers' return without leave seemed precipitous, but had
been contemplated since the end of March, stimulated by outrage at
the conditions prevailing in the colony as well as by an earnest wish to
plead the colony's case before the officials at Versailles. After sixty
days at sea the vessel carrying him finally attained the Atlantic port of
La Rochelle late in the night or early in the morning of August 13/14,
1786. By the following December, the peripatetic governor was once
more bound for Senegal, reaching his destination this time on January
19, 1787. This second period of his government was to last a full ten
months. The chevalier would quit the shores of West Africa on November 20/21 and only upon receipt of royal permission. Late that December he gained French shores, left the *Cousine* at the Ile de Ré on
the 23rd and made his own way to La Rochelle on the mainland,
though as it would turn out, in the wake of his schooner. The title of
Governor Boufflers retained until 1789. When he did resign the office
it was of little if any consequence; on January 25 of that year the statute

of the colony had been entirely altered and the title suppressed by royal decree.[6]

Governor de Boufflers' personal account of his four sea voyages and of his two brief sojourns in West Africa is set down principally in journals he kept for the sake of Mme de Sabran and which she may have considered publishing as early as 1798. At least one critic imagines that the less intimate entries were communicated to the countess's Parisian friends upon receipt and that "les salons parisiens eurent ainsi des images authentiques du Sénégal."[7] This is contentious; what is certain is that the general public only learned of the journals' contents when the daily log of the first trip was edited and published by E. de Magnieu and Henri Prat in 1875 as part of their *Correspondence inédite de la comtesse de Sabran*. Their text is unfortunately, to quote Paul Bonnefon, "fort incomplet, et, de plus, publié assez maladroitement" (B., 194). And it is true that Magnieu and Prat are mistaken in their attribution of their portion of the journals to the chevalier's second voyage. They are also guilty of intercalating entries from the second voyage into the text of the first voyage. Bonnefon, in 1905, undertook the publication of those entries dealing with this second period, an edition he based on the autograph manuscript at that moment in the possession of Gaston La Caille, and which is at present part of the manuscript collection of the *Bibliothèque municipale de Versailles*.[8] If criticism is to be levelled at this latter edition, it is chiefly that of accessibility, the text having been serialized in thirteen installments of the *Revue bleue*, between August 12 and November 4. The Magnieu-Prat *Correspondance* includes a number of letters from Boufflers to an unnamed "cher Maître" and to members of his own family, letters dated from 1786 and of not insignificant interest to the history of his experience in Senegal. The same may be said of other correspondence, edited once again by Bonnefon, and appearing in the *Mercure de France* in 1910. These letters span the full two years of the governorship, late 1785 through late 1787.

On a private level, the record of Boufflers' African experience is a part of a "conversation à distance,"[9] or, more accurately, fragments of an amorous discourse. On the public level, it is the log of an administrator and of his administration. Moments of longing, desire, loneliness, uncertainty, and depression vie with details of plans and projects for the colony, for the governor's residence, details of new hygienic regulations, accounts of successes or failures in a constant struggle with what their author calls "un océan d'affaires" (M. & P., 480). But these are also travel journals. There are many passages, simple reflections, narratives and anecdotes, portraits, in which the chevalier tries to come to terms with the "terre d'Afrique," in which he gives voice and form to personal impressions of the land and its inhabitants. It is this voice and this form which particularly interest me here.

Shortly after his arrival in Senegal, the new governor remarks somewhat jocularly in the letter addressed to the unidentified "cher Maître": ". . . je me sens bien à l'abri de l'influence du climat, et si je deviens Africain, ce sera plutôt par le visage que par le coeur" (January 21, 1786; M. & P., 167). Towards the end of his second sojourn, aboard the vessel bearing him back to France, he confides in a more serious vein to his journal the honest expectation that his safe return in a state of good health will be "un témoignage vivant de la bonté du climat que je viens d'habiter" (December 15, 1787; B., 580). These two citations frame Boufflers' most immediate and most permanent encounter with the African continent: its climate.

If early on, in a letter to his sister, Mme de Boisgelin, the new arrival hints at that familiar, commonplace theme of the debilitating effects of the tropical climate on the human constitution—"Je remarque en général, non pas tout à fait par moi-même, que ce climat est contraire à tout, car le physique et le moral s'y altèrent également" (April 22, 1786; M. & P., 186)—his position and his reactions are, on the whole, far more personal and far more independent. With initial contact he realizes that daily living in this torrid zone will require much circumspection: ". . . j'ai senti que le climat exigeait des ménagements auxquels je ne suis point accoutumé: il faut peu manger, peu boire, peu marcher, peu dormir, peu s'occuper, etc. De tout un peu, mais peu de tout" (to M. le maréchal de Beauvau, March 6, 1786; M. & P., 170). Even though "la sagesse n'est pas toujours récompensée" (April 27, 1786; M. & P., 466), he will learn to be continent and to take those simple precautions necessary to insure that his European body survives under these different climatic conditions. He will refrain from excessive movement. To avoid sunstroke, he will finally take to wearing a headcovering which reminds one of later colonial headgear: "Si par hasard quelque sorcière de tes amies te montre jamais ton mari dans du marc de café, tu le verras toujours sous un grand chapeau rond couvert de papier blanc et grondant (même ceux qu'il gronde) d'être devant lui tête découverte. Dernièrement encore j'avais affaire à un petit officier qui venait de faire une sottise et je lui dis: «Monsieur, quoique j'aie à vous laver la tête, je vous prie de mettre votre chapeau»" (September 12, 1787; B., 481–82). He gives such attention to his body and to his health because he is conscious that even the most innocuous event in this climate might constitute an immense danger to well-being: ". . . le moindre mal peut devenir mortel dans ce pays-ci, puisque notre chirurgien vient de soigner et d'émétiser mon valet de chambre pour une piqûre de cousin" (January 29, 1787; B., 258). And if he does declare that the climate is not at all "propre aux promptes guérisons, à cause de la putridité de l'air et de la disposition pro-chaine de tous les corps à la fermentation" (May 21, 1787; B., 358), he is aware at the same time that the slightest illness can be aggravated by contemporary European medical treatment. He personally refrains from seeking too much the advice, let alone the treatment, offered by the resident medical practitioner when he is indisposed by headaches, stomach disorders, and colic, or suffering from a painful whitlow. This whitlow, in fact, he cures by himself, noting: "Le chirurgien convient lui-même que mon remède vaut mieux que les siens; il ne me faut plus que du temps pour tout réparer, car le temps rétablit tout jusqu'à ce qu'il gâte tout" (July 4, 1787; B., 387–88).

In spite of Boufflers' persistent attention, his almost constant admo-nitions, and his many precautions to insure and preserve their health, the climate does exact its toll on his men. Near the conclusion of his second stay many of them, Boufflers notes, are "morts, malades ou convalescents" (September 14, 1787; B., 482). The others are suffering from heat and fatigue. Some are even foolish enough to request opera-tions whose success is uncertain or which have already proven fatal. Death seems to be lurking all around him. It must have been a de-spondent chevalier indeed who penned this observation on December 4, 1787: "Presque aucun des blancs qui m'ont suivi ne reviendra en bonne santé . . ." (B., 578).

In reality, the West African climate is not without effect on the new governor. The heat he sometimes finds stifling, "extrême," "excessive," "accablante." [10] Twenty-five leagues from the tropics, aboard ship, the tropical zone is already manifest through heat: "Nous sommes à vingt-cinq lieues du tropique, et nous commençons déjà à souffrir de la cha-leur" (January 9, 1787; B., 227). On a trip to Podor, the temperature is so high and the heat so intense that nothing is able to resist; every-thing from freshly caught fish to candles and leather boots, "tout se gâte en peu de temps par l'excès de la chaleur" (April 16, 1786; M. & P., 456). To convey to his "comtesse lointaine" some idea of the heat's tyranny, Boufflers resorts at first to the anecdotal: ". . . tu ne te feras jamais d'idée de la chaleur de cet endroit-ci. Il passe à la vérité pour le poêle de l'Afrique; mais il passe encore tout ce qu'on en dit. Le ther-momètre en dit plus que personne; car je l'ai pendu vers une heure et demie à la muraille, en dehors, au soleil, et l'esprit-de-vin a touché l'extrémité du tube, en sorte qu'on a été obligé de dépendre le thermomètre et de le rentrer, de peur qu'il ne cassât, d'autant plus qu'il était si brûlant que mes gants en ont été marqués" (M. & P., 456). Elsewhere literary references are called on for support; from Sierra Leone, after observing that he has forgotten to speak to her of the climate, he exhorts his Countess: ". . . tu peux consulter là-dessus MM. Milton et Thompson;[11] il est marqué dans les poèmes, comme le Sénégal sur les thermomètres, pour indiquer le dernier degré de chaleur: cependant je ne la trouve insupportable que la nuit, parce qu'alors le vent tombe tout à fait et qu'on perd soi-même la respiration" (April 3, 1787; B., 321). This final pirouette finds an echo in a later entry: "Voilà que nous entrons dans ce qu'on appelle la mauvaise saison et jusqu'ici je n'ai presque point souffert de la chaleur et des autres vices du climat. Au reste, je sens dans mon corps et dans mon esprit, la force nécessaire pour tout supporter . . ." (July 27, 1787; B., 418).

According to Boufflers' experience the West African climate has two seasons: the dry and the "bad." During the bad or wet season, tremendous storms and torrential rains are current meteorological occurrences and replace the overpowering heat of the dry season. One storm, he will claim, "a fait briser les câbles d'un vaisseau marchand mouillé dans la rade" (September 19, 1787; B., 482). Others, those called "tornados," he exclaims in an entry written in Sierra Leone, "nous livrent de furieux assauts et nous mettent en danger" (April 7, 1787; B., 322), and this every evening at approximately the same hour. Moreover, what most attracts his attention about them all is the enormity: "Les tempêtes de la barre ont recommencé," he observes on February 22, 1786, and immediately comments: "Les vagues sont plus hautes que des maisons; on les voit de chez moi, c'est-à-dire de près de quatre lieues" (M. & P., 421–22). French showers, he suggests, cannot impart any idea of the density of African downpours: "Nous avons de gros orages, des coups de tonnerre affreux et des pluies comme on n'en connaît point à Paris . . ." (August 20, 1787; B., 449). "Nous avons de temps en temps des averses dont rien ne peut donner l'idée en France. Imagine qu'il tombe presque autant de pieds d'eau en Afrique que de pouces à Paris et cependant il ne pleut ici que pendant trois mois et dans ces trois mois-là à peine quatre ou cinq jours par semaine. Mais chez toi ce sont des gouttes et chez nous ce sont des cruches" (September 13, 1787; B., 482). In the natural course of events the wet season is accompanied by outbreaks of disease. But not only does the chevalier perceive that "les malades n'augmentent point" (August 20, 1787; B., 449), the superb weather and his own state of continued good health, both mental and physical, in this his last autumn season in the tropics are sufficient proof, he pretends, "que tout ce qu'on dit des maladies et des ouragans perpétuels des automnes de ce pays-ci est un tas d'exagérations, que les marchands inventent pour effrayer ceux qui voudraient venir et que les officiers répètent pour avoir des gratifications et des congés" (September 18, 1787; B., 482).

Among the other climatic "vices" of Africa are the insects. They attack "de toute part et les plus imperceptibles sont les plus cruels; ils ressemblent aux ennemis obscurs qui vous déchirent sans que vous puissiez les connaître" (October 22, 1787; B., 515). The most persistent in their persecution are the "maringoins" (large tropical mosquitoes) and Governor de Boufflers' hatred of them is unswerving. Attracted to him as to a light, they congregate thickly around: "Mes plus fâcheux ennemis sont les maringoins, qui s'attroupent autour de moi comme autour d'une lumière et ils forment au-dessus de mon lit et de ma table des nuages à couper au couteau" (August 14, 1787; B., 421). More annoying than their bite is their presence; sleep becomes an impossibility: "J'ai encore passé cette nuit au milieu de mes bourreaux, les maringoins. . . . Ce qu'il y a de plus fâcheux, c'est de les entendre; leurs menaces sont pires que leurs morsures et leur sifflement est encore plus aigu que leur dard. Ils ne se contentent pas de m'enlever ma peau, ils m'enlèvent le sommeil . . ." (October 4, 1787; B., 485). In the morning, after a sleepless night, he cannot even open his eyes, for they have attached themselves to his eyebrows and eyelids.

It seems to me then that for Boufflers the West African climate has a far greater reality and a greater importance psychologically than physically. I believe that he himself intuits that this will be so in an early observation: "Je crains que le climat n'influe sur mon moral encore plus que sur mon physique, et qu'il ne donne au premier en véhémence tout ce qu'il ôte au second en vigueur" (March 8, 1786; M. & P., 429). It is perhaps this that also explains his generally sanguine attitude towards this climate's various "vices." If it is perhaps too extravagant to think immediately of Proust ("un changement de temps suffit a recréer le monde en nous-mêmes."), it is less so to imagine the chevalier de Boufflers on the threshold of the pathetic fallacy.

In 1786 when the new governor landed at Saint-Louis-du-Sénégal within the sandbar of the estuary of the Senegal river, he found a modest, multiracial community of between "quatre à cinq mille âmes, tant blanches que noires" (January 21, 1786; M. & P., 168).[12] Saint-Louis had only recently, in fact, been returned to French possession through the Treaty of Versailles. Nowhere in his journals, however, does the governor describe the settlement. Nevertheless, it is possible to conceive of his dislike of the community and to imagine both its squalor and its lack of civilized amenities from the account he gives to Mme de Sabran of his own "gouvernement" or official residence located there: "Si tes yeux étaient aussi bons qu'ils sont beaux . . . tu me verrais ici dans ma maison hideuse, délabrée, dont aucune porte ne ferme, dont aucun plancher ne se soutient, dont tous les murs se réduisent en poudre, dont toutes les chambres sont meublées de haillons couverts de poussière; ces haillons, ces bois de chaise cassés, ces tables brisées sont, dit-on, les meubles du Roi, et me font beaucoup d'honneur en me servant" (January 21, 1786; M. & P., 401–2). More relevant proof of the existing state of misery and disrepair is provided in the number of fires Boufflers will record at the start of his residency, with as many as 140 huts going up in flames in one night (January 28, 1786; M. & P., 406). Little wonder that he will thereafter continually apply to Saint-Louis the epithet "triste."

The island of Gorée, on the other hand, immediately attracts the governor. Some 250 kilometres further south, this small island provided a stopping point for the slave traders although it contained a smaller, less prosperous community than Saint-Louis. Boufflers describes the island quite dithyrambically: "Je suis arrivé à bon port, ma chère enfant, et je trouve ici un séjour délicieux en comparaison du triste Sénégal. Il y a une montagne, une fontaine, des arbres verts, un air pur; tout m'y plaît, jusqu'aux pierres . . ." (May 5, 1786; M. & P., 470). The next day he waxes even more lyrical in his descriptions: "Si j'avais de sublimes talents pour le paysage, je t'enverrais une petite vue de Gorée. Imagine-toi un des rochers d'où l'on tire des pierres à Spa, placé sur une surface plane, et [qui] figure comme un jambon. Au-dessus du rocher est un petit fort; au bas est une petite ville, de droite et de gauche sont des batteries aux trois quarts démolies. Les jardins sont bien entourés et bien cultivés; les maisons ne sont point mal bâties, toutes en pierres, et la plupart ont des toits en pailles, en attendant qu'on ait des planches et de la chaux pour les mettre à l'italienne" (May 6, 1786; M. & P., 471). It has been said that the governor asked to transfer his official residence to Gorée but some critics report that permission was not granted. During his stays on the island, he did, nonetheless, occupy two dwellings, neither of which is extant today; the first was destroyed by English bombardment in 1797 and the second, known as the Maison Pépin, demolished early this century.[13]

It may be trite to note that the spectator's initial fascination with the natural opulence of the tropics, with nature's display of her seemingly infinite powers, may quickly turn to horror or as quickly be refined into a sense of idyllic beauty. But it must be stated that it is the latter phenomenon which occurs with Boufflers. Once in the interior, away from the colonial settlements, the African wilderness becomes for him breathtaking, brilliant with flowers and birds, fragrant and aromatic from its woods, groves, and valleys, a virtual earthly paradise: "Une fraîcheur délicieuse, des prés verts, des eaux limpides, des fleurs de mille couleurs, des arbres de mille formes, des oiseaux de mille espèces. Après les tristes sables du Sénégal, quel plaisir de retrouver une véritable campagne . . ." (May 9, 1786; M. & P., 473).[14] Idyllic too, edenic even, is the "position unique" of the native village he will visit a week after the previous entry and of which he will draw this charming verbal picture:

> C'est un mélange pour ainsi industrieux de plaines, de collines, de vallons, de bosquets, de buissons, de prés, de champs, de palmiers, de cocotiers, de mille et mille arbres et arbustes de tous les genres, de toutes les tailles, de toutes les teintes, de toutes les formes, dont les uns se détachent sur l'horizon, les autres se confondent entre eux, et se mêlent dans le paysage. Il semble que tous les singes, tous les rats palmistes, toutes les perruches, tous les colibris s'y soient donné rendez-vous. Tout cela a l'air heureux des bienfaits que la nature prodigue à ce charmant endroit. . . . Partout des plantes qui vous étonnent par leur variété, partout des arbres dont l'ombre vous invite, partout des fleurs dont l'odeur vous embaume (May 16, 1786; M. & P., 478).

Some months later, the chevalier will have occasion to pass through this very same village; at that time he will observe that it still holds for him the same charms as on his first visit (February 5, 1787; B., 259).

Boufflers' orders permitted him to visit different commercial establishments in the colony. One of these expeditions took him south to Sierra Leone. Once again he is ecstatic over the natural beauty of the landscape he encounters: "Nous sommes au calme à la vue du plus beau paysage des quatre parties du monde; nous voyons le cap de Serre Lionne qui s'élève plus haut que toutes les montagnes d'Ardennes, couvert de palmiers et d'autres arbres toujours verts. On voit différentes chaînes qui se reculent en s'élevant, et, si je puis jamais parvenir à la cime, je ne désespère pas de trouver au milieu du brasier du monde une température digne des plus beaux climats de l'Europe" (March 30, 1787; B., 293). A trip up the river Gambia ("cette belle rivière, où chaque lieue nous met dans une nouvelle extase") elicits an equally emotive outburst:

> Il semble que la nature se soit plu à rassembler loin du tout, tout ce qu'elle peut montrer de plus charmant, comme les grands seigneurs qui se plaisent à prodiguer les ornements dans les petites

maisons au fond des quartiers les plus ignorés. Jamais personne de nous n'a vu de plus grands arbres, de plus belles verdures, des vallons plus riants, des enfoncement mieux dessinés. On navigue entre des montagnes à perte de vue et des plaines immenses dans une rivière d'argent qui semble être une ligne de démarcation entre les deux sols les plus différents (March 31, 1787; B., 294).

So impressed was Boufflers by the savage beauty of this landscape that he would rhapsodize at length on it again in a letter written at sea and addressed to a Mme De +++ (April 20, 1787). Curiously, this is the only document of his African experience to have been published during his lifetime.[15]

That we are in West Africa is evident only in the naming of certain flora and fauna. As Boufflers and his companions walk along the river they are escorted, in the distance, "par les lions, les tigres, les hyènes, les léopards," and in the foreground "par les crocodiles et les hippopotames dont le fleuve fourmille" (April 11, 1786; M. & P., 452). Mention is made of red and yellow parrots, of monkeys, of parakeets, of a "poule sultane ou porphirion" and of a "spatule" (July 9, 1786; M. & P., 508). Of all of these birds and animals destined as gifts, the "spatule" (spoonbill) alone merits more than a brief verbal description— "a peu près grosse comme une oie." According to Magnieu and Prat and verified by my own reading of the autograph entry, the chevalier actually provides his countess with a tiny sketch (2.4 cm × 1.9 cm) of the feathered vertebrate in his text. This is the height of his exoticism. As for the African flora, he is even more content with generalities ("mille et mille arbres et arbustes"). "Je remets," he tells his Countess, "à d'autres temps à te faire la description de ce pays-ci . . ." and then adds, "Contente-toi de savoir que la nature y est encore plus admirable dans les détails que dans l'ensemble et que je suis aussi fâché de n'être point botaniste en me promenant dans ces jardins-ci, que je le serais d'être sourd quand tu me parleras ou d'être aveugle quand je recevrai de tes lettres; car c'est ici comme chez toi, il n'y a rien qui ne soit piquant, qui ne soit nouveau, qui ne soit charmant" (April 2, 1787; B., 321).

Sparing in his descriptions of African flora and fauna, Boufflers is less so when it is a question of narrating a good story such as the one apropos a plant whose fruit has rather devastating effects upon himself, his Swedish and French companions. "Mon enfant, je l'ai échappée belle," he begins, and having whetted the Countess' appetite, he continues:

> Je viens de me promener au continent avec trois savants suédois, qui voyagent par curiosité et en herborisant avec ces messieurs, j'ai

trouvé un bel arbuste portant des coques pleines de graines qui m'ont tenté. J'en ai goûté et jamais je n'ai rien mangé de plus délicieux. J'ai ensuite monté à cheval; j'ai couru à une lieue et demie et je suis revenu le même train. Je me suis aperçu sur la fin de la course que mon aide de camp et mon nègre ne me suivaient pas, et j'ai vu qu'ils s'arrêtaient de temps en temps avec l'air très affairé: ils étaient occupés en effet à vomir comme s'ils avaient pris de l'émétique. Messieurs les Suédois que j'ai retrouvés en faisaient autant, et dès que nous avons été en pirogue pour revenir dans l'île, j'en ai fait autant. J'ai su depuis que la graine en question est le plus puissant des vomitifs, qu'il n'en faut que deux grains pour émouvoir l'homme le plus fort, et j'en avais mangé plus de vingt, et un Suédois en avait mangé plus de cent. Enfin tout va mieux qu'on ne devait l'espérer . . ." (October 20, 1787; B., 515).

Whatever he may have lacked in botanical savvy, the chevalier de Boufflers certainly makes up for in narrative skills.

Referring to one particular pictoral description from the chevalier's pen, Paul Bonnefon pronounces it, "digne par son luxe de pointes et de *concetti* d'un familier des jardins de Versailles."[16] Romanticism has predisposed us to expect both more local colour and more interest in the exotic, but as Bonnefon appears to infer and as Roger Mercier indicates in *L'Afrique noire dans la littérature française* (p. 164), Boufflers' descriptions are quite classical and would not have been substantially different were it a more familiar European landscape being described. There is, however, no mistaking the sincerity of his feeling for the nature he contemplates nor is there any doubt about his sense of awe as he confronts various African panoramas.

For the most part, Boufflers considers the native black population to be "l'indolence et l'insouciance personnifiées" (May 11, 1786; M. & P., 475). If by the end of his second stay, he will claim a minor victory over their inertia—"j'anime un peu l'inertie africaine" (November 2, 1787; B., 517)—during his tenure he generally qualifies them as ignorant and stupid and claims that communication with them is difficult: "Il serait presque aussi aisé de parler à des briques qu'aux nègres" (February 7, 1786; M. & P., 413). He insists on their lack of self-control and eventually pronounces them clumsy in all they do except in robbing him: "Je me trouve presque entièrement à la discrétion de mes nègres, qui sont maladroits pour tout, excepté pour me voler" (November 15, 1786; B., 547). Apparently their only quality seems to be their skill in swimming: "mes nègres . . . nagent comme des poissons" (March 13, 1786; M. & P., 433); "l'on m'assure qu'un nègre ne peut pas plus se noyer qu'un poisson" (March 19, 1786; M. & P., 438).

That this skill is also knowledge of and familiarity with the dangers lurking in coastal waters does not seem to have impressed the chevalier. In spite of these minor bits of ignorance, he does, in the end show himself to be a generous man of heart, moved by compassion for the blacks and with a considerable amount of benevolence towards them.

Nevertheless, both Boufflers' compassion and benevolence are highly tinged with condescension and a sense of the conscious superiority of the civilized man is evident in the irony with which he describes certain of the blacks he encounters as well as in the description of their customs. Though always gentle, his irony reveals many of his own as well as contemporary prejudices and thought patterns and marks the limits of the average, cultivated eighteenth-century European's acceptance of the African and African civilization. There is the kindly portrait of his black maidservant with her "petit nègre" French: "Ce matin, ma bonne négresse est venue me dire: «Comment portes-tu toi sa matine?» Je lui ai dit: «Assez bien, mais je n'ai point dormi.»—«Tu l'o pas doremi. . . . non . . . c'est que tu penses loin.»" (June 1, 1786; M. & P., 489). Boufflers' sympathy is unmistakable but so is his superior air. Much more patronizing is his description of this African queen, a curiosity not only because of her colour but also because of her physical appearance and her habits:

> Je viens de recevoir chez moi une des grandes reines du pays qui est venue avec une cour nombreuse, mais seulement en hommes. La reine est grosse comme madame de Clermont. Elle a deux dents de sanglier, et le tour des yeux barbouillé d'une vilaine graisse noire. Je lui ai donné de l'eau sucrée, du vin, de l'eau-de-vie, des biscuits; elle a tout avalé, et je me serais donné moi-même qu'elle m'aurait avalé aussi. C'est une second Garganelle, femme de Grandgousier. Elle m'avait demandé un logement chez moi, je n'ai pas pu le lui offrir; mais elle veut revenir demain; cela me gênera beaucoup à cause de toute sa cour, qui pue comme un troupeau de boucs (April 2, 1786; M. & P., 446).

In the portrait of the King of Podor, the author's European prejudices are by far the most apparent. Not only the black monarch's character but also his observances of Muslim rites are openly derided:

> Je ne t'ai point encore fait la peinture d'un roi maure, et sûrement sans cela tu ne pourrais pas t'en faire une idée. Celui avec qui je viens de passer deux jours est un homme fort puissant, mais fort doux et en même temps fort dévot. Il n'aime que les femmes et les prêtres, et passe sa vie le plus qu'il peut à Podor, pour être loin de son camp, loin de ses ennemis, sous la protection de notre canon, à

portée de piquer l'assiette de nos pauvres officiers, et de faire demande sur demande au gouverneur et aux marchands. Il habite une mauvaise chambre du fort avec une femme en titre et trois ou quatre dames d'honneur qui en manquent de temps en temps, livré aux conseils de ses marabouts, qui lui laissent faire toutes ses sottises et toutes ses fredaines pourvu qu'il porte une centaine de leurs petits scapulaires qu'ils appellent grigris, et qu'il leur paye bien cher, et qu'il fasse par jour environ huit à dix prières ridicules sur une peau de mouton qu'on étend à ses pieds. Il se lève debout sur cette peau; il étend les bras; il s'abaisse, met la tête à terre et le derrière en l'air, marmottant des passages de l'Alcoran qu'il n'entend pas plus qu'il n'entendrait le bréviaire de Paris. C'est là ce qu'on appelle faire l'isalem. Le reste du temps il converse (cela s'appelle palabrer) sur les intérêts de sa prétendue couronne . . ." (April 17, 1786; M. & P., 457).

It is perhaps of interest to note that the very day he sketches this portrait, the governor would conclude an historic pact with this same Ahmad Maktar (Achmet Moktar or Hamet Moctar), emir of the Brakna. Later, when there is some trouble with the emir's subjects and his own men, Boufflers' patronizing superiority is in no way diminished by his show of mettle but, in fact, becomes even more marked. On no account will he suffer injury to the dignity of France. His attitude is that of a father admonishing a naughty child:

Toi-même, Achmet Moktar, [he writes] tu n'es pas prudent et dans les menaces ridicules que tu nous fais tu te conduis comme Moktar Boubi. Tu as reçu et tu reçois tous les jours mille bienfaits du Roi, mon maître, et tu injuries la compagnie qu'il protège. M. Bonhomme a sauvé la vie à ta femme et à tes parents et tu lui cherches dispute; il revient de Podor par mon ordre et tu prétends qu'il devait t'attendre, sans penser qu'il ne connaît d'autre autorité que la mienne, enfin tu annonces qu'aucun mulâtre ne commandera de bâtiment dans la rivière, comme si tu pouvais faire la loi aux sujects du Roi de France, ton protecteur. Il paraît aussi que tu as oublié que les mulâtres sont les enfants des blancs et que par là seul ils méritent que les autres peuples les respectent (M. de F., 82).

Most likely it is this same personage who also figures in an entry of November 9, 1787, in which the frustrated governor fulminates in utter exasperation: "Ce maudit roi que j'ai si bien traité l'année dernière ne vient-il pas de rompre tout commerce avec le Sénégal, sans doute par quelque mécontentement particulier de la Compagnie" (B., 546).

There is no indication in any of the passages dealing with aboriginal inhabitants of any effort on the chevalier's part to attempt to bridge the gap between benevolent condescension and real intellectual understanding. Boufflers is no Diderot; for him Africans and African mores are merely strange and curious. Eloquent witness of this is the scene of the black women who do him the honour of "singing" and "dancing" for him. For Jore the "déroulement des tam-tam" is of such realism as to defy description (p. 96), and it must be admitted that the author-poet is a master of technique: "Hier encore," begins his narrative of the encounter, "j'ai été, à quatre lieues d'ici, faire une chasse de petits oiseaux aux filets." Enter the main protagonists and the main event: "Les femmes de l'endroit m'ont fait l'honneur de me chanter et, suivant l'expression du pays, de me danser." And so he continues:

> Je n'ai pas bien compris ce qu'elles chantaient, mais il était difficile de se méprendre à la signification de leur danse. Un homme jouait d'un instrument, toute l'assemblée battait des mains, et une danseuse à tour de rôle sortait, en contrefaisant toutes les crises de Mesmer. . . . Elle s'avançait vers moi en roulant les yeux, tordant les bras, faisant mille petits mouvements, que ma chaste plume n'ose pas vous rendre, et après un instant d'anéantissement total, elle rentrait dans le cercle pour faire place à une autre pantomime, qui essayait de surpasser la première; le bal a fini par une espèce de joûte des trois plus habiles, dont une jouait un rôle de femme, et les deux autres des rôles d'hommes, avec une vérité et de petits détails dont on ne se fait point d'idée en Europe. Après le bal, je les ai toutes récompensées par de petits présents; celle de toutes qui m'avait paru la plus gentille m'a dit qu'elle était bien fâchée de n'avoir pas pu mieux faire, mais qu'elle était encore faible à cause qu'elle relevait de couche. Comme je lui marquais de l'intérêt et de la compassion, elle m'a beaucoup remercié, a été chercher son petit enfant de quinze jours, et m'a demandé la permission de lui donner mon nom (to M. le maréchal de Beauvau, March 6, 1786; M. & P., 175–76).

The raw edge of the observer's curiosity is invariably tempered by a substantial dose of compassion and sympathy.

No one brought to Africa, so asserts the governor's *premier aide-de-camp* and *ingénieur militaire* Xavier de Golbery (or Golberry), "des intentions plus libérales, et des vues plus nobles et plus pures que celles qu'y portait M. de Boufflers."[17] Nobility and pureness of intentions did not prevent the governor from personally becoming involved in the purchase and export of human souls, for example slaves acquired at substantial savings for "la charmante petite Ségur" (February 4, 1786; M. & P., 411), or house servants for members of his own and of the royal family. In a letter to his sister, he recounts that he has found "un petit Maure très-joli" whom he intends for the queen, "et qui pourrait trouver place dans la maison de M. le Dauphin." Directly he adds: "j'attends aussi une petite Mauresse de vingt mois, qu'on dit charmante" (May 27, 1786; M. & P., 190). In his journal, he notes for the benefit of Mme de Sabran: "J'achète en ce moment une petite négresse de deux ou trois ans pour l'envoyer à madame la duchesse d'Orléans. Si le bâtiment qui doit la porter tarde quelque temps à partir, je ne sais pas comment j'aurai la force de m'en séparer. Elle est jolie, non pas comme le jour, mais comme la nuit. Ses yeux sont comme de petites étoiles, et son maintien est si doux, si tranquille, que je me sens touché aux larmes en pensant que cette pauvre enfant m'a été vendue comme un petit agneau. Elle ne parle pas encore, mais elle entend ce qu'on lui dit" (February 8, 1786; M. & P., 413–14). The children mentioned in the letter to Mme de Boisgelin are quite probably the celebrated "belle Hourica" who became a member of the household of Boufflers' aunt the *maréchale* de Beauvau and Jean Amilcar whom Marie Antoinette had baptized at Notre Dame de Versailles and whom she handed over to Müller, one of her houseboys, to be looked after.[18] Both came to tragic ends. Ourika was to die of consumption or some mysterious disease, at sixteen say some, at twenty according to others,[19] while the young lad, driven from his boarding place after the imprisonment of his chief benefactress, succumbed to cold and hunger. Of the black girl destined for the Duchess of Orleans, I have found no further references although Nicole Vaget Grangeat does mention two other infants bought for Mme de Blot and for Mme de Sabran. One of these is perhaps the child of this touching little verbal portrait forwarded from Sierra Leone: "Je ramène avec moi une petite négresse qui a l'air d'être la continuation de la belle Hourica; mais je ne sais par quelle fatalité, malgré toutes mes caresses, elle a l'air de ne pouvoir pas me souffrir" (April 5, 1787; B., 322). It is safe to conclude that the fate ultimately awaiting all these children was not much different from that awaiting the plantation slaves destined for the West Indies.

Nor does Boufflers do himself proud when it is a question of acquiring land. He arrives at an agreement with an African monarch, but when the king has a change of heart the chevalier claims he will pretend not to have understood and will insist on the terms of the accord. He recounts the event in detail:

> Voilà mon ambassade revenue de chez Sa Majesté le roi Damel. Il me cède en toute propriété le terrain que je lui ai demandé et j'ai entre les mains le traité signé de lui; mais il a fait courir après mes

gens pour leur dire que tout était rompu et qu'on lui avait dit que, s'il cédait ce pays-là, il mourrait dans l'année. Je n'en prendrai pas moins possession de mon nouvel empire en feignant d'ignorer le dédit et de m'en tenir à la signature du monarque. Je prends cependant la précaution de lui renvoyer mes ambassades avec une belle lettre et le beau présent qu'il ne connaissait que par un simple récit. J'espère que l'or et l'argent l'éblouiront au point de l'aveugler sur la mort qui le menace et que, pour une selle et une housse brodée et deux ou trois assiettes d'argent, je me trouverai en possession d'une petite province (October 12, 1787; B., 514).

A rare example in Boufflers' journals and letters of one of the worst aspects of the colonial mentality.

Between the conception and the act, between the liberal ideal and its pursuit, there is a whole gray area of possible concessions. Governor de Boufflers was not, as some decidedly apocryphal stories are wont to imply, a great philanthropist. Certainly he did not seek nor accept the governorship of Senegal in order to work against the slave trade; in fact, although appointed by royal authority, the governor was very much the instrument of the Compagnie du Sénégal which had a vested interested in the continuation of this trade and profited from it to an immense degree. Of paramount concern to Boufflers as governor of Senegal was the smooth functioning and the well-being of the colony, the maintenance and protection of the honour of the mother country—concerns not entirely compatible with an abolitionist bias.

The chevalier de Boufflers' final statement on Africa was made not in his journals nor in letters from that continent but in his reception speech before the *Académie Française* on December 29, 1788. In Grimm's *Correspondance littéraire* the beginning of this address is called, somewhat ironically I believe, "une véritable églogue nègre," its author taking to task the speaker's imagination: "On est tenté d'oublier un moment que des hommes qui vendent leurs semblables ne valent pas mieux au moins ceux qui les achètent, et des rives du Sénégal on se croit transporté au milieu des bergers de l'Arcadie ou sur les bords riants du Lignon. . . ."[20] The judgment is maybe too severe. For, as the *Année littéraire* of March 1789 declares in its summary of the new academician's presentation, if he spoke forcefully and elegantly of "le séjour qu'il a fait dans les contrées incultes & presque désertes de l'Afrique, parmi des Sauvages dont il peint les maux & la barbarie . . ." (p. 99), it was to lead up to the following *pointe:* "J'ai vu ce que la Nature avoit fait de l'homme; je vois ce que l'homme a fait de la Nature. . . . Dans les déserts de l'Afrique, l'esprit de chacun ne sert qu'à lui seul; dans nos climats, l'esprit de l'homme appartient à tous, & celui de tous à chacun. . . ." (pp. 115–16). A conceit not at all surprising in the mouth of a man who had written previously in his journals: "Le sentiment ni la philosophie ne sont pas faits pour l'Afrique" (February 14, 1786; M. & P., 417). Roger Mercier believes that the chevalier "ne parvient pas d'emblée à une attitude cohérente et réfléchie envers les Africains," this because he is still too engaged in "les problèmes matériels et les manières de penser de son temps" (p. 165). Also perhaps because Boufflers' real existence lay elsewhere. It is apparent that he was never comfortable in the company of Africans and lower class colonials: "Au lieu de tant de charmantes créatures dont je me verrais entouré chez toi, je ne vois que des nègres, des négresses, des maures, des mûlatres et des coquins plus noirs que tout cela. Je me crois au milieu de l'enfer de Dante . . ." (July 21, 1787; B., 417). In all things, his is consistently the white European's vision: "J'ai essayé de peindre pour me désennuyer, mais tu n'imagines pas combien je me suis trouvé dépaysé à la vue d'une mûlatresse; ce mélange informe de couleurs et de traits si opposés, ces visages qui nous parlent tantôt du père, tantôt de la mère, qui par conséquent disent tantôt blanc, tantôt noir, te donneraient à toi-même de la tablature" (June 18, 1787; B., 386).

The experience of Boufflers in West Africa was hardly of long enough duration for new attitudes or new visions to evolve. His impressions of the land and its people, constantly tinted by a sophisticated European sensibility and civilized superiority may seem to us now simplistic, idyllic, or lacking in depth, and even at times too inflated. I consider that they are, nevertheless, the fruits of a genuine and sincere if limited interest. Given time, they may have grown in depth, in perceptiveness, in realism. In any case, the chevalier de Boufflers must stand as a precursor of Romanticism, his conception of climate influencing mental states and mental states affecting reactions to climatic conditions, his involvement with the body and the body's comfort, his idyllic vision of nature, his curiosity about another culture— albeit on a still fairly superficial level—his generous humanity, all this, without a doubt, indicates a distinct movement in the direction of Romantic sensibility.

NOTES

1 This expression is borrowed from Louis Cario and Charles Régismanset's *L'Exotisme: La Littérature coloniale* (Paris: Mercure de France, 1911), 54.

2 Introduction to "Journal inédit du second séjour du chevalier de Boufflers au Sénégal," *Revue politique et littéraire: Revue bleue* (12 août 1905), 194. Hereafter, reference to this portion of Boufflers' journals is cited parenthetically in the text as B., followed by the appropriate page number.

3 "M. de Boufflers au Sénégal," *Miroir de l'histoire*, no. 67 (Aug. 1955), 222.

4 *Correspondance inédite de la comtesse de Sabran et du chevalier de Boufflers, 1778–1788*, ed. E. de Magnieu and Henri Prat (Paris: Plon, 1875), 366, 370, 371. The portion of the Boufflers journals found in this volume is cited parenthetically in the text as M. & P., with page number.

5 Of these, Christian Schefer writes: "On peut estimer . . . que ces instructions résument tout le système et toute la politique que l'Ancien régime était enfin parvenu à préciser touchant les côtes occidentales d'Afrique." Many passages reproduce prior instructions provided the former governor Repentigny and these in turn reproduced those of Repentigny's predecessor Dumontet. However, there are a number of new points added to the Boufflers document. His instructions are in two parts. The first is a general survey of "les diverses parties qui intéressent le commerce de la France sur les côtes d'Afrique, depuis le cap Blanc jusqu'au cap de Bonne-Espérance" and the second contains details on those places directly under his administration, that is Senegal and the island of Gorée. Treated in some detail are subjects such as the slave trade, gold mines, forts and warehouses, defence, the administration of justice. Royal interest seems generally to have coincided with the commercial interests of the Compagnie du Sénégal. See: *Instructions générales données de 1763 à 1870 aux gouverneurs et ordonnateurs des établissements français en Afrique occidentale* (Paris: Librairie ancienne Honoré Champion, 1921), 1: 127–62. The citations above are to be found on p. 127 n. 1 and on p. 136.

6 Léonce Jore, *Les Etablissements français sur la côte occidentale d'Afrique de 1758 à 1809* (Paris: Société française d'histoire d'Outre-Mer, 1965), 114–18.

7 Roger Mercier, *L'Afrique noire dans la littérature française: les premières images, XVIIe–XVIIIe siècles*, Publications de la section de langues et littératures no. 11 (Dakar, 1962), 163.

8 I am endebted to my French colleague François Moureau for bringing to my attention the existence of this manuscript and its location. The autograph manuscript is complete for the second trip, but there are lacunae in that of the first.

9 Boufflers travelled with a portrait of Madam de Sabran. In his entry of February 27, 1787, we read: "Adieu; je lève les yeux vers ton portrait; il me semble qu'il prie en ce moment avec un redoublement de ferveur" (B., p. 289). On her side, the Countess also kept a journal which she forwarded to her lover. It seems, therefore, quite appropriate to speak of a conversation between the two.

10 On February 21, 1787, Boufflers does complain, however, that "Il fait un froid de chien et nous ne trouvons pas de bois pour nous chauffer. On ne croirait pas que ce fût là une plainte datée d'Afrique" (B., 261). He then adds that up until this moment he has suffered more from cold than from

heat and concludes: "La preuve en est que j'ai tous les jours regretté ton feu et toutes les nuits ton lit bleu."

11 Is Boufflers thinking of the following lines from Thomson's *Summer*?

> Now, while I taste the Sweetness of the Shade,
> While Nature lies around deep-lull'd in Noon,
> Now come, bold *Fancy*, spread a daring Flight,
> And view the Wonders of the *torrid* Zone:
> Climes unrelenting! with whose Rage compar'd,
> Yon Blaze is feeble, and yon Skies are cool.
>
> (ll. 629–34)

The Seasons, ed. James Sambrook (Oxford: Oxford University Press, 1981). Apart from the famous reference to Abyssinia in his *Paradise Lost* (4.280–84), I have been unable to find any others to the African continent in Milton.

12 Others have established this population at between 6,000 and 7,000 souls. See: Marcel Chailley, *Histoire de l'Afrique occidentale française, 1638–1959*, (Paris: Editions Berger-Levrault, 1968), 129; Jore, *Les Etablissements français*, 260; Martin A. Klein, *Islam and Imperialism in Senegal: Sine-Saloum, 1847–1914* (Stanford: Stanford Univ. Press, 1968), 31.

13 Armand Lunel, *Sénégal* (Lausanne: Editions Rencontre, 1966), 99. Earlier in his text Lunel offers this contemporary description of the island of Gorée: "Toute petite! Un îlot basaltique de seulement neuf cent mètres de long sur trois cents de large, dont la silhouette évoque celle d'un fer à repasser. Un site, m'avait-on prévenu, au premier abord assez ingrat et sans attrait. Point de source, par exemple, sauf dans le roc une maigre fontaine qui tarit en saison sèche, si bien que, de nos jours, la population (guère plus de neuf cents habitants, dont beaucoup ne sont là que par force, dans l'attente d'un logement à Dakar) reçoit l'eau douce par bateau-citerne. Oui! mais justement pour avoir la révélation de Gorée dans sa grâce secrète et émouvante, je ne savais pas moins qu'il faut là, plus qu'ailleurs, s'abandonner sans hâte, paresseusement, au plaisir de la découverte . . ." (p. 95).

14 Jore claims this is on "la presqu'île voisine de Cap Vert" (p. 88), but Boufflers clearly indicates that the promenade takes place "à la grande terre."

15 "Lettre écrite des parages d'Afrique à M^e De + + +," *Oeuvres du C. Stanislas Bouflers* [sic], seule édition avouée et corrigée par l'Auteur, où se trouve un grand nombre de pièces inédites (Paris: L. Pelletier, An XI [1803]), 122–28.

16 "Le Chevalier de Boufflers au Sénégal: Lettres et documents inédits," *Mercure de France*, no. 86 (July–Aug. 1910), 82. Other references to this text are cited parenthetically as M. de F., with the page number.

17 *Fragmens d'un voyage en Afrique, fait pendant les années 1785, 1786 et 1787, dans les contrées occidentales de ce continent* . . . (Paris: Treuttel et Würtz, 1802), 1:9.

18 Philippe Huisman et Marguerite Jallut, *Marie Antoinette* (Lausanne: Patrick Stephens Limited with Edita Lausanne, 1970), 143.

19 Twenty, says Nicole Vaget Grangeat, *Le Chevalier de Boufflers et son temps: étude d'en échec* (Paris: Nizet, 1976), 69 n. 14; at sixteen and "emportée par un mal mystérieux" writes Léon Fanoudh-Siefer, *Le Mythe du nègre et de l'Afrique noire dans la littérature française (de 1800 à la 2e Guerre mondiale)*, Publications de la Faculté des lettres et sciences humaines de Paris-Nanterre, ser. B, Essais, 3 (Paris: Klincksieck, 1968), 27.

20 Grimm, *Correspondance littéraire*, ed. Maurice Tourneux (Paris: Garnier frères, 1881), 15:400.

"The Lover Crowned" in Eighteenth-Century French Art

ANNE BETTY WEINSHENKER

French art from the time of Watteau to the Revolution and beyond was particularly rich in the iconography of love. Among the many pictorial themes devoted to that topic was the coronation of the loved one with a floral garland. Subject to literal or symbolic interpretation, this motif allowed considerable variation and was susceptible of a range of nuances in meaning. It was used by a large number of the century's painters, sculptors, and printmakers, including most of the major ones, and appears in other art forms as well.

The theme had a long previous development. Since antiquity the image of wreathing in general had been a frequent subject. Representations of garlands held over or placed upon the heads of individuals to be honored for merit or victory are common on ancient works of art.[1] In these cases the wreath is ordinarily foliate rather than floral.

Coronation with a garland or chaplet of flowers is depicted in many works of art from the later Middle Ages. They are usually secular in subject. With them the theme takes on the two aspects that will so frequently henceforth—and particularly in the eighteenth century—accompany it: the association with love and the pastoral context. Depictions of a woman placing a garland on the head of her beloved appear on ivory mirror cases from the fourteenth century; sometimes the scene is found alone, and sometimes as part of a sequence that also includes a portrayal of the couple weaving the crown (fig. 1).[2] Fifteenth-century engravings, also devoted to the theme of love, portray the weaving of the crown and the floral coronation.[3] The flower

271

Figure 1: Mirror case: lovers meeting, the weaving of the crown, the lover crowned, the departure. Ivory, first half of the fourteenth century. The Louvre, Paris. Courtesy of the Musées Nationaux.

wreath was a standard accessory of courtly gallantry and a frequent object in medieval love literature. It was also presented by suitors to their ladies.[4] Floral coronations, like other medieval representations of lovers, were commonly set amid park-like or pastoral surroundings, marked by the presence of trees and other forms of vegetation and of domestic animals.

Of direct relevance for eighteenth-century French practice is the popularity of the floral coronation in seventeenth-century Holland.[5] Again it is found in a bucolic setting and refers to love. A number of works by Pieter Lastman, the teacher of Rembrandt, include this motif. One of them conveys most explicitly the sexual meaning that the wreath carried in folk tradition: virginity and in particular the female sex organs (fig. 2). A woman's bestowal of the wreath on her suitor signified her consent to giving up her virginity. The accessories in Lastman's painting enlarge upon this theme: while sheep are seen in the distance, two prominently placed goats, symbols of unbridled eroticism,[6] gaze at us as directly as do the young human lovers. The lower right corner of the work displays a still-life grouping consisting of a large ripe melon, partly open to reveal its soft and inviting interior—a clearly erotic reference—along with a shepherd's staff and a set of bagpipes. This musical instrument was also considered symbolic of sexual activity.[7]

A relief made by Clodion in 1765 again places the floral coronation in an overtly erotic situation. It presents a nymph, a satyr, and a satyress involved in a sexual act; the wreathing denotes and completes their unification.[8] Less obviously erotic are the numerous eighteenth-century floral coronations portraying a male figure placing the wreath on the head of his beloved. In some instances this action may merely refer, as Posner has indicated, to an early stage of courtship.[9] Such is the impression created by Boucher's *Hommage champêtre* of 1732[10] or Lancret's *La bergère couronnée* of 1743.[11] On the other hand, Pater's *La bergère couronnée* (fig. 3)[12] sets its personages beneath a herm of Pan, a woodland deity related, like the satyr, to goats and also known for mischievous deeds and constant readiness for sexual activity.[13] Clodion's more explicit reliefs, made several decades later, include similar statues. The Pater coronation is accompanied by a flute player. While this instrument is traditional in representations of shepherds, it also has a long history of erotic associations.[14]

The Boucher, Lancret, and Pater paintings again take place in garden-like or pastoral surroundings; the Lancret includes a flock of sheep. Yet they are a far cry from the earthy image by Lastman. Reviving the medieval courtly mode, they are peopled by dainty, elegantly clad figures who gesture with grace and decorum. The floral coronation, by this time carrying a variety of references to love and placed in its usual shepherd's setting, has been absorbed into the repertory of *fête galante* activities.

While the flower crown was at home in an aristocratic courtly milieu, it was also specifically associated with the lower levels of the social scale, particularly in the subject of the rustic wedding. Because of its connection with the idea of virginity, the wreath was a traditional bridal accessory. In several German, Flemish, and French depictions of weddings—including those in religious themes involving marriage celebrations, such as the marriage of the Virgin or the wedding at

274

Figure 2: Pieter Lastman, *Pastoral Scene*, 1619. Private Collection and the Worcester Art Museum, Worcester, Massachusetts.

Figure 3: Jean-Baptiste Pater, *The Shepherdess Crowned* (La bergère couronnée). Versailles, Palais du Petit-Trianon. Photo courtesy of the Musées Nationaux.

Cana—from the fifteenth century through the seventeenth, the bride and sometimes the groom wear wreaths.[15] The settings of these scenes are frequently rustic and appropriate to shepherds or peasants.[16] In this context the wreath is a mark of the low social and economic status of the participants.

A tradition going back to the Middle Ages connected the lover's garland with poverty: the God of Love in the *Roman de la rose* refers to the "chapel de flor qui petit coste."[17] From the late sixteenth century on the brotherhood of the Sacred Rosary in Rome annually gave dowries to a large number of poor girls who wore crowns of flowers for the occasion.[18] A French treatise of 1672 states that a marriage with the bride wearing a floral wreath is one where there is no dowry.[19] The custom gave rise to an expression, the same text continues: "*Chapeau ou chapel de roses. C'est un petit mariage, car quand on demande ce qu'un père donne à une fille, et qu'on veut repondre qu'il donne peu, on dit qu'il lui donne un chapeau de roses.*"

A variation of the bridal wreath is found in a painting by Watteau of a festive betrothal ceremony in a rural village (fig. 4).[20] The principals are seated at a table before a cloth of honor. A garland of flowers hangs in front of the cloth, over the young woman's head. It relates to her, but she does not wear it because she is not yet a bride.[21] The outdoor setting here recalls the pastoral tradition. The participants' status is not emphasized, yet the rustic milieu locates this event toward the lower levels of the social hierarchy.

Fragonard's painting of *The Lover Crowned* from his series called *The Progress of Love* has been demonstrated by Sauerländer to be essentially a wedding picture.[22] Yet while the extensive vocabulary of symbolism it utilizes points undeniably to that interpretation, one must note that the painting is somewhat at variance with the usual iconography of country wedding scenes. They generally depict the bride or bridal pair as already crowned, while Fragonard's work presents us with the act of coronation. Since that action relates to the well-established tradition of the pastoral lovers, we are justified in seeing this painting as translating that tradition into the eighteenth-century mode of *fête galante*, in much the same manner as the Lancret and Pater versions of the *bergère couronnée*.[23] The Fragonard is enriched by thus blending themes belonging to the upper and lower ends of the social scale, the aristocratic *fête galante* with the rustic wedding, the erotic and playful shepherd idylls with the social institution of marriage.

Madame du Barry, for whom Fragonard painted the series, rejected it in 1773 in favor of a set by Vien. Among the Vien paintings is also a

Figure 4: *Village Betrothal* (L'Accordée de Village). Engraving after painting, c. 1712–15, by Antoine Watteau. The British Museum, London. Photo courtesy of the Trustees of the British Museum.

Figure 5: Joseph-Marie Vien, *Lover Crowning His Mistress*, 1773. The Louvre, Paris. Photo courtesy of the Musées Nationaux.

floral coronation, *The Lover Crowning His Mistress* (fig. 5). Since the next painting in Vien's series depicts the wedding of his lovers, the coronation, as Posner has shown, represents an earlier stage in their relationship.[24] It must nevertheless be pointed out that the girl is reaching for a wreath with which to crown her lover in return, an indication of the imminence of their union. Although neoclassical trappings and forms in this painting have replaced some of the courtly elegance of the *fêtes galantes* from earlier in the century, a pastoral flavor is retained. Vien again turned his attention to the immediately prenuptial stage, although now with cupids supplying wreaths to the principals, in a late drawing entitled *Preparations for the Wedding Night*.[25] The subject tends to draw attention to the sexual implications of wreathing even though the drawing contains no erotic actions.

The floral coronation of the lover in a pastoral setting became an even more popular theme because of the widespread success attained by Giovanni Battista Guarini's play *Il Pastor Fido*. Produced in 1585, this pastoral tragicomedy was published in numerous editions, including several in France and the Netherlands, in the seventeenth and eighteenth centuries.[26] It was set to music a number of times; Rameau made it the subject of a cantata. It became a frequent source of themes for painters, especially the Dutch, and for tapestry designers.[27] In the episode most often selected for portrayal the hero, Mirtillo, is crowned with flowers by the heroine, Amarillis, for whom he nourishes an undeclared love. Disguised as a woman, he had just been judged by her to be the winner in a contest among her companion maidens to determine which one could provide the best and sweetest kiss.[28] This floral coronation, then, mingles the tradition of the crowned lover with that of the crowned victor. The situation becomes even more complex when Mirtillo proceeds to transfer the garland to Amarillis' head, whereupon she places on his the wreath she has been wearing.

Many Dutch painters of the seventeenth century illustrated some part of this scene: an example by Ferdinand Bol (fig. 6) depicts Mirtillo, bearing his bow and arrows and accompanied by his hounds, kneeling to receive the wreath from the garlanded Amarillis. Jacob van Loo, in a considerably more animated conception, painted around midcentury, combined the coronation with the bestowal of the prize-winning kiss (fig. 7). This artist provides a significant link between seventeenth-century Holland and eighteenth-century France. He moved from Amsterdam to Paris in 1661 and became the ancestor of a major dynasty of French eighteenth-century painters.[29]

The most famous artist to treat the *Pastor Fido* episode was Anthony van Dyck, in a painting known to exist in at least four early copies besides the original (fig. 8).[30] Remarkably similar to the pose of Mirtillo in this painting is that of Zephyrus crowning Flora in a work by Watteau (fig. 9). Recently destroyed, this composition symbolized Spring in a series of *Seasons* painted for the Baron de Crozat. As Levey has shown, however, the figure of Flora in Watteau's work is more closely related to drawings of Zephyrus crowning Flora by Charles de Lafosse.[31] Lafosse was housed by the Baron de Crozat when Watteau also came to live with his patron; the older artist probably began work on the *Seasons* and then turned the project over to the younger one.

The theme of Flora's coronation with flowers may also relate to that

Figure 6: Ferdinand Bol, *The Crowning of Mirtillo*. Oil on canvas, 55 3/8 x 76 3/4", c. 1660. The Fine Arts Museums of San Francisco, Museum Purchase.

Figure 7: Jacob van Loo, *Amarillis and Mirtillo,* c. 1650–60. Photo courtesy of the Rijksdienst Beeldende Kunst, Den Haag.

of the marriage wreath. In Ovid's *Fasti* Zephyrus, having ravished Flora, makes her his bride. Ovid writes of the pair together with Bacchus and Ariadne, another mythological couple.[32] Tiepolo, in his frescoes in the Palazzo Labia,[33] makes the floral crown, here given by Flora to her lover-spouse, a pendant to Ariadne's crown of stars created by Bacchus.

In eighteenth-century France the messages of the floral crown grew ever more varied. It might again designate the victor: in a lost painting by Boucher preserved in an engraving a young girl leans toward one suitor, listening to his whispered entreaties. She reaches in the other direction, however, to confer the floral crown on his delighted rival, who points to his twin arrows in the bull's-eye of a target, another object carrying several connotations.[34] In literature the love itself, rather than the beloved, could be described as receiving the crown: Dorante, the hero of Rousseau's *L'Engagement téméraire,* convinced that he has finally won his lady's affections, exclaims, "je pourrois voir, enfin, mon amour couronné!"[35]

Figure 8: Anthony van Dyck, *Amarillis and Mirtillo*, scene from Guarini, c. 1632. Göteborgs Konstmuseum, Göteborg. Photo courtesy of Göteborgs Konstmuseum.

The floral wreath also served in the delineation of some of love's problems. An illustration by Charles-Nicolas Cochin the Younger, published in 1754,[36] depicts two pastoral couples (fig. 10). One is happily united, but the other shepherd tries to embrace his love and to place a garland on her head, only to meet with rejection. In an opera-ballet entitled *La Guirlande* with music by Rameau and libretto by Marmontel, the garland remains eternally fresh when belonging to a faithful lover, but withers and fades to reveal infidelity.[37] In *La Cruche cassée* of 1784 by Simon-Louis Boizot the removal of the wreath symbolizes the end of love as well as loss of virtue.[38] During his long tenure as director of the sculpture atelier for the royal porcelain factory at Sèvres, Boizot furnished many models for reproduction in porcelain. Several of these small-format works are complex and rather ambiguous allegories. Although the broken pitcher in this statuette conveys the notion of lost maidenhood in the same terms as Greuze's paint-ing,[39] Boizot embroiders on his theme by means of a bemused cupid, who removes a garland from the young woman or perhaps offers it to her in vain.[40]

Apart from its place in coronation narratives the floral wreath, like

Figure 9: *Spring,* from Crozat, *Seasons.* Engraving after painting by Antoine Watteau, c. 1713–16. The British Museum, London. Courtesy of the Trustees of the British Museum.

Figure 10: "Two Young Shepherd Couples in a Landscape," by Charles-Nicolas Cochin the Younger, illustration to Tito Lucrezio Caro (Lucretius), *Della natura delle cose*, 1754. Courtesy of The New York Public Library.

the bow and arrows, was one of Cupid's prime attributes; examples are found in works by Boucher[41] and Fragonard.[42] In Boizot's *Prix de Cythère* of 1778 a cupid is congratulated on his success at creating a love-match (symbolized by two doves) and a wreath—of love and victory—is given to him.[43] Connected in this way with the ideas of youth and love, the garland is also an appropriate symbol of spring, the season of blossoms and beginnings. In Bouchardon's relief of *Spring* for the fountain in the rue de Grenelle (1739–45) (fig. 11), two babies or cupids crown one another with flowers, while a third catches doves. It must have been for such associations that the subject of Zephyrus crowning Flora was chosen for Watteau's painting of Spring (fig. 9). More than eighty-five years later, that myth received one of its most beautiful visualizations in the statuette made by Clodion in 1799 (fig. 12). In this terracotta, the ardor of the embrace which accompanies the coronation gives it a heightened romantic intensity. At the same time, the work's forms are much more fully classical than those of the artist's earlier production.[44]

In a terracotta made about three decades earlier, Clodion had represented a satyr crowning a bacchante (fig. 13). The relaxed and playful mood of this statuette contrasts with the exalted fervor of the artist's *Zephyrus and Flora*, but is much like that of a rustic idyll painted by Boucher in 1755 (fig. 14), whose figural grouping it seems to have translated into three dimensions. Instead of shepherds, however, it presents us with Dionysiac beings. This terracotta occupies a transitional position between the rococo *fête galante* formulation of the pastoral tradition and Clodion's more directly antique-inspired works. Like most of his statuettes of classical figures, its relationship to the

Figure 11: Edme Bouchardon, *Spring*. Reduced version of relief from the fountain, completed 1745, in the rue de Grenelle, Paris. The Metropolitan Museum of Art, Harris Brisbane Dick Fund, 1935.

Figure 12: Claude Michel, called Clodion, *Zephyrus and Flora*, 1799. Copyright The Frick Collection, New York.

antique world is not limited to theme and details, but extends to the concept of nature. In these works, nature no longer takes the form of accessories such as trees, meadows, and animals, but instead exists as a living, animating force.[45]

This concept appears more fully developed in his statuettes, which like the *Zephyrus and Flora* (fig. 12), but long before it, combine the floral coronation with a fervent embrace (fig. 15).[46] Clodion's nymphs

Figure 13: Claude Michel, called Clodion, *Satyr Crowning a Bacchante*, 1770. The Louvre, Paris. Photo courtesy of the Musées Nationaux.

Figure 14: François Boucher, *Spring*, 1755. Copyright The Frick Collection, New York.

Figure 15: Claude Michel, called Clodion, *Nymph and Satyr*, 1772.
Private collection, New York. Photo by Betty Schlossman.

289

and satyrs embody neither the artificial naturalness of the rococo courtly pastoral nor the heroic Renaissance-Baroque tradition of the loves of the gods. They are instead anonymous personifications of life dominated by the instincts and senses, of a jubilant vital force, of the bounty and fertility of nature. These woodland spirits neither have nor need any material possessions; the association of the wreath with rustic simplicity and poverty is here affirmed as a positive value. The grapes are transformed into symbols of release from inhibitions and the floral crown into an emblem of genuine passion. We are given glimpses of the Romantic movement soon to come.

NOTES

1 For examples, see the paintings on ancient Greek vases by the Berlin Painter and the Leningrad Painter in John Boardman, *Athenian Red Figure Vases: The Archaic Period* (New York: Thames and Hudson, 1975), figs. 161, 323; also the Roman cameo called the *Gemma Augustea* (Ranuccio Bianchi Bandinelli, *Rome, the Center of Power* [New York: Braziller, 1970], 195, 197). For an ancient example from the nonclassic world, see the Sassanian plate in Ilse Seibert, *Women in the Ancient Near East* (New York: Abner Schram, 1974), pl. 112. I am grateful to Dr. Betty Schlossman for the last example.

  Visual and literary representations of wreathed figures constitute a huge body of material. See, for example, Charles Joret, *La Rose dans l'antiquité et au moyen age* (Paris, 1892; reprint, Geneva: Slatkine, 1970) and J. B. Trapp, "The Owl's Ivy and the Poet's Bays: An Enquiry into Poetic Garlands," *Journal of the Warburg and Courtauld Institutes* 21 (1958): 227–55; also the extensive wreath symbolism in seventeenth-century emblem books, such as Cesare Ripa, *Iconologia* (Padua: Tozzi, 1611; reprint, New York: Garland, 1976), 20, 142, 185, etc.; I. Baudoin, *Iconologie* (Paris: Guillemot, 1644), 3, 17–18, 31, 62, 153, etc.; Otto van Veen, *Amorum emblemata* (Antwerp, 1608; reprint, New York: Garland, 1979), 3. This paper will deal, however, only with portrayals of the floral coronation and only in the context of love. It will not discuss wreathing in other circumstances or wreathed figures in general.

2 Raymond Koechlin, *Les Ivoires Gothiques Français* (Paris: Auguste Picard, 1924), 2, nos. 997–1013 and 3, pls. 176, 177; Margaret Longhurst, *Victoria and Albert Museum: Catalogue of Carvings in Ivory*, pt. 2 (London: Board of Education, 1929), pls. 42, 43. For French fourteenth-century ivory writing tablets portraying similar scenes, see O. M. Dalton, *Catalogue of the Ivory Carvings of the Christian Era of the British Museum* (London: British Museum, 1909), nos. 359, 360, 362. I am indebted to Nancy A. Williams for this information.

3 See *The Planet Venus*, from a series of Florentine engravings attributed to

Baccio Baldini, reproduced in A. P. de Mirimonde, "La Musique dans les allégories de l'amour," *Gazette des beaux-arts*, 6th ser. 68 (1966), fig. 1; also *The Large Garden of Love*, by the German Master of the Garden of Love, illustrated in James Snyder, *Northern Renaissance Art* (New York: Abrams, 1985), fig. 281.

4 For example, the illustration from a fifteenth-century manuscript of the *Roman de la rose*, in Guillaume de Lorris and Jean de Meun, *The Romance of the Rose*, trans. Charles Dahlberg (Princeton, N.J.: Princeton Univ. Press, 1971), fig. 36. Also see fig. 57 of this edition and, for textual references to garlands, pp. 42, 180, 555 and esp. 219–21.

5 See Alison M. Kettering, *The Dutch Arcadia: Pastoral Art and Its Audience in the Golden Age* (Montclair, N.J.: Allanheld & Schram, 1983), 88, 93–94, 97.

6 Ibid., 57, 97.

7 Ibid., 160; de Mirimonde, "Musique dans les allégories," 287.

8 For an illustration, the catalogue of the exhibition, *France in the Eighteenth Century*, Royal Academy of Arts, London (Winter 1968), no. 799, fig. 352. The sexual significance of the wreath in this work is mentioned by Donald Posner, "The True Path of Fragonard's 'Progress of Love,'" *Burlington Magazine* 114 (1972): 530. Another relief by Clodion with a floral coronation accompanying an erotic scene is illustrated in Florent Fels, *L'Art et l'Amour* (Paris: Éditions Arc-en-Ciel, 1953), 2:7.

The wreath carries similar meanings in the eighteenth-century engraving called "Vice," from *La Route du Monde* by L. Truchy after N. Debare; it is illustrated in Georg Hirth, *Kulturgeschichtliches Bilderbuch* (Munich: Knorr & Hirth, 1882–90; reprint, New York: Benjamin Blom, 1972), 6:2128, pl. 3137. In it a crown of flowers hangs over a scene involving a young man, a procuress, and a prostitute. Representations of Zephyrus wreathing Flora also carry sexual connotations. Their wedding followed a rape; see above, p. 281.

9 Posner, "Fragonard's 'Progress of Love,'" 530–33.

10 Alexandre Ananoff, *François Boucher* (Lausanne-Paris: Bibliothèque des arts, 1976), 1:213–14, cat. no. 81.

11 Georges Wildenstein, *Lancret* (Paris: Les Beaux-arts, 1924), pl. 126.

12 Three other paintings by Pater are also of *La bergère couronnée*: Florence Ingersoll-Smouse, *Pater* (Paris: Les Beaux-arts, 1928), nos. 355–57.

13 Lynn F. Kaufmann, *The Noble Savage: Satyrs and Satyr Families in Renaissance Art* (Ann Arbor, Mich.: UMI Research Press, 1984), 2, 4–5, 16.

14 Ibid., 19–27; Kettering, *Dutch Arcadia*, 162. For an example by Watteau, see Donald Posner, *Antoine Watteau* (Ithaca, N.Y.: Cornell Univ. Press, 1984), 26–27.

15 Walter S. Gibson, "Some notes on Pieter Bruegel the Elder's *Peasant Wedding Feast*," *The Art Quarterly* 28, no. 3 (1965): 203. Examples include *The Marriage Feast at Cana* by Juan de Flandes, illustrated in G. C. Bauman, *The Jack and Belle Linsky Collection in the Metropolitan Museum of Art* (New York:

Metropolitan Museum of Art, 1984), no. 20; also the *Marriage of the Virgin* by Barent van Orley, illustrated in Max J. Friedländer, *Die Altniederländische Malerei.* (Berlin: Cassirer, 1930), 8, pl. LXXIV.

16 See the raucous *Peasant Wedding* in a woodcut of ca. 1527 by Erhard Schoen, illustrated in M. Geisberg, *Der deutsche Einblatt-Holzschnitt in der ersten Hälfte des 16. Jahrhunderts.* (Munich: Hugo Schmidt, 1928), 33, pl. 20. The Parisian artist Abraham Bosse made a series of three etchings entitled *Le mariage à la campagne* (ca. 1633). In two of them the bride wears a floral wreath. His related series, *Le mariage à la ville* (1633) does not include bridal wreaths. See Nicole Villa, *Le XVIIe Siècle vu par Abraham Bosse* (Paris: Dacosta, 1967), 25, pls. 98–99 and André Blum, *L'Oeuvre gravé d'Abraham Bosse* (Paris: Morancé, 1924), 19, nos. 116–21, 45, nos. 962–64.

17 Guillaume de Lorris et Jean de Meun, *Le Roman de la rose* (Paris: Champion, 1970), 66, l. 2149. He goes on to advise (ll. 2151–52) that everyone can have one because great means are not needed for them.

18 Michel Benisovich, "A Sculpture by Pierre Julien in the United States," *Art Quarterly* 12 (1949): 370–72.

19 *Les Origines de Quelques Coutumes Anciennes* (Caen, 1672), 53, quoted in John Brand, *Observations on the Popular Antiquities of Great Britain*, ed. Sir Henry Ellis (London: Henry G. Bohn, 1849), 2:124–25.

20 Posner, *Watteau*, 21–26.

21 Brand describes another circumstance in which a wreath is suspended over the recipient rather than being placed on her head: "In some Country Churches 'tis customary, to hang *a Garland of Flowers* over the Seats of *deceased Virgins,* as a Token of Esteem and Love . . ." (*Observations on Popular Antiquities* [Newcastle Upon Tyne, 1777], 39.)

22 Reproduced in *The Frick Collection: An Illustrated Catalogue* (New York: The Frick Collection, 1968), 2:101, 117. See Willibald Sauerländer, "Uber die Ursprüngliche Reihenfolge von Fragonards 'Amours des Bergers,'" *Münchner Jahrbuch der Bildenden Kunst* 19 (1968): 140–42.

23 The *Progress of Love* series is described in Bachaumont's *Mémoires secrets* of July 20, 1772 as portraying "les amours des bergers" (*Frick Collection*, 104). In the *Portrait of a Couple as Shepherds* by the seventeenth-century Dutch artist J. G. Cuyp the husband, in the guise of shepherd, is shown crowning his wife, portrayed as a shepherdess, with a wreath of flowers. The pastoral gear and the wreathing are intended to frame their portrayal as a married couple within a convention for the representation of romantic love. There is no indication, however, that this painting was made for the occasion of their wedding. For an illustration, see David R. Smith, *Masks of Wedlock* (Ann Arbor, Mich.: UMI Research Press, 1982), fig. 70.

24 Posner, "Fragonard's 'Progress of Love,'" 533. See p. 273 above.

25 From a series made 1791–99 entitled *Le Bonheur de la vie ou l'union de l'Hymen et de l'Amour.* See Arlette Sérullaz, *Dessins français de 1750 à 1825: le néo-classicisme,* Exposition du Cabinet des Dessins, Musée du Louvre (Paris, 1972), no. 8 and the illustration in the review of this exhibition in the

Burlington Magazine 114 (1972): 574. Also see Vien's frontispiece to this series of drawings in the exhibition catalogue, no. 7 and pl. 3.

26 There were twenty-five editions in France (in six translations); see Walter F. Staton, Jr., and William E. Simeone, *A Critical Edition of Sir Richard Fanshawe's 1647 Translation of Giovanni Battista Guarini's "Il Pastor Fido"* (Oxford: Clarendon Press, 1964), ix.

27 Kettering, *Dutch Arcadia*, 193–98 lists some—but not all—of the paintings, book illustrations, print cycles, and tapestries based on it.

28 Act 2, sc. 1.

29 On Jacob van Loo (c. 1614/15–1670), see Oliver T. Banks, *Watteau and the North* (New York: Garland, 1977), 196–200; Bob Haak, *The Golden Age* (New York: Abrams, 1984), 488–89; J. M. Nash, *The Age of Rembrandt and Vermeer* (London: Phaidon, 1972), 249.

30 On the history and derivation of this painting, see Carl Nordenfalk, "Ein Wiedergefundenes Gemälde des Van Dyck," *Jahrbuch der preuszischen Kunstsammlungen* 59 (1938): 36–48.

31 Michael Levey, "A Watteau Rediscovered: 'Le Printems' for Crozat," *Burlington Magazine* 106 (1964): 53–59. Levey believes that the Watteau figure of Zephyrus is not derived from the Van Dyck Mirtillo but that each of these figures is independently based on that of the man pouring wine in Titian's *Bacchanal of the Andrians.* It must be noted, however, that both the Van Dyck and the Watteau figures are placing floral crowns on the heads of their loves, while the Titian figure is performing a very different kind of action.

32 Ovid *Fasti* 5.183–346.

33 Painted c. 1757; see Eduard Sack, *Giambattista und Domenico Tiepolo* (Hamburg: H. von Clarmann, 1910), ills. 123–24.

34 Ananoff, *Boucher*, 2:9, no. 313, fig. 902.

35 Act 3, sc. 2. Posner, "Fragonard's 'Progress of Love,'" 530, quotes a sentence from Casanova's *Histoire de ma vie* in which the crowning of love serves as a symbol of consummation.

36 From an Italian translation of Lucretius' *De rerum natura:* Tito Lucrezio Caro, *Della natura delle cose* (Paris, 1754), 160; see Gordon N. Ray, *The Art of the French Illustrated Book* (New York: Pierpont Morgan Library, 1982), 1:27.

37 Jean-Phillippe Rameau, *La Guirlande,* ed. Georges Beck (Paris: Heugel, 1981).

38 See Emile Bourgeois and Georges Lechevallier-Chevignard, *Le biscuit de Sèvres: recueil des modèles de la manufacture de Sèvres au xviii* siècle (Paris: Lafitte), pl. 35, no. 162.

39 Jean-Baptiste Greuze's painting, *La Cruche cassée* (1773) is in the Louvre, Paris. See Anita Brookner, *Greuze* (Greenwich, Conn.: New York Graphic Society, 1972), pl. 49.

40 Boizot's *Le larcin de la rose* also defies exact interpretation, but the wreath held over the head of the young woman as she pays homage to Cupid points toward a happier outcome. See James D. Draper, "New Terracottas by

Boizot and Julien," *Metropolitan Museum Journal* 12 (1978): 141–47 and esp. fig. 2.

41 Ananoff, *Boucher*, 2:104, no. 416: *L'Amour vainqueur*. Also see 89–91, nos. 389 and 390 for the juxtaposition of the floral crown with the flute and tambourine, musical instruments associated with love.

42 Georges Wildenstein, *The Paintings of Fragonard* (New York: Phaidon, 1960), 208, no. 63: *Amour triomphant* and 212, no. 81: *Amours vainqueurs*.

43 Bourgeois and Lechevallier-Chevignard, *Le biscuit de Sèvres*, pl. 27, no. 523.

44 A combination of romantic fervor with classical detail—if not form—had appeared in Boizot's *L'Amant couronné* of 1784; see Emile Bourgeois and Lechevallier-Chevignard, *Le Biscuit de Sèvres: Recueil des modèles de la manufacture de Sèvres au XVIIIe siècle* (Paris: Lafitte), pl. 29, no. 13.

45 Kaufmann, *Noble Savage*, 29, 30 and 43 points out medieval and Renaissance instances of satyrs conceived as personifying the wilderness.

46 Dated 1772; private collection, New York. Similar works are illustrated in H. Thirion, *Les Adam et Clodion* (Paris: Quantin, 1885), ills. facing 192 and 240.

Alexander von Humboldt
in South America:
From the Orinoco to the Amazon

SONJA KARSEN

> *Every great advance in science has issued*
> *from a new audacity of imagination.*
> John Dewey

It was an auspicious period in history into which Alexander von Humboldt was born because it ". . . saw the demise of the monarchs of enlightenment: Frederick of Germany, Catherine of Russia, Maria Theresa of Austria and Charles III of Spain. It was the age of the 'great change,'"[1] Friedrich Wilhelm Karl Heinrich Alexander, Baron von Humboldt was born in Berlin, then the capital of the kingdom of Prussia on September 14, 1769, and died there on May 6, 1859. During his lifetime he explored vast expanses of Latin America, took part in the scientific life of Paris for almost a quarter of a century and also found time to go to the Urals and Siberia. In his later years he served as chamberlain at the royal court in Berlin. The German scientist was bound by no national barriers because he was a European in the best sense of the word. He was preeminently a child of the age of enlightenment and was equally at home in England, Spain, Italy, or Russia all of whose languages he spoke fluently. He studied geology, physics, mathematics, and astronomy at the universities of Frankfurt on the Oder, Göttingen, and the School of Mines in Freiberg in Saxony.[2] While at Göttingen he became the friend of Joh. Georg Adam Forster, one of Captain Cook's companions on his second voyage around the world. It was Forster who was largely responsible for Humboldt's desire to travel and who awakened his interest in exploring the yet little known parts of the globe.

In 1798 the scientist went to Paris, at a time when the revolution of 1789 had spent itself and produced Napoleon Bonaparte who had defeated the Italians and the Austrians and was preparing for the conquest of Egypt. For Humboldt it was an exciting time to be in Paris where all the famous scientists of Europe were gathered, among them Cuvier, Jussieu, Laplace, and Fourcroy. During his stay in the French capital he was invited by Lord Bristol to participate in an expedition to Egypt. However, the English nobleman never reached Egypt, as he was arrested in Milan on order from Napoleon, suspected of being an agent of the British government.

Humboldt then was invited for a second time to become the member of a scientific expedition around the world sponsored by the French government and to be led by Captain Baudin. This trip too was a disappointment since the voyage was postponed indefinitely on orders from Napoleon. Also chosen for the expedition was Aimé Bonpland, a French physician turned botanist. The two scientists became fast friends and decided to undertake an expedition of their own to Egypt. However, the political situation at the time prevented them from ever reaching their destination, and so they changed their plans again and went to Spain instead. There, the idea of exploring the Americas was suggested to them by Baron von Forell, a friend of the Humboldt family and the court of Saxony's ambassador in Madrid. This fortuitous encounter changed the scientist's destiny forever and in March 1799 Humboldt was presented to the Spanish court at Aranjuez. He explained to King Charles IV "the motives which led [him] to undertake a voyage to the New World. . . ; and [he] presented a memoir on the subject to the secretary of state." Don Mariano Luis de Urquijo "supported [his] demand, and overcame every obstacle."[3] Humboldt was issued two passports, one by the secretary of state, the other by the Council of the Indies. In order to allay all fears that the viceroys or captains-general might have regarding the purpose of his trip the passport issued by the *primera secretaría de estado* stated that Humboldt had permission to use his scientific instruments fully while in the Spanish colonies. "Never had so extensive a permission been granted to any traveller, and never had any foreigner been honored with more confidence on the part of the Spanish government" (*Narrative* 1:7). These permits were quite unusual; "the Spanish government kept its colonies completely shut off from contact with the outside world."[4] Jean-Marie de la Condamine in 1735–1745 had been the last foreign scientist to have visited the Spanish colonies.

Humboldt and Bonpland left Madrid in May 1799 for La Coruña, from where they sailed on June 5 for the New World, careful to avoid the English frigates which were cruising off the Spanish coast. After a stop in Teneriffe, they arrived on July 16, in the Captaincy General of Venezuela. They landed in Cumaná exactly forty-one days after their departure from the Iberian peninsula.

After a few months in Cumaná exploring the surroundings and making scientific observations Humboldt and Bonpland continued on to the port city of La Guaira and from there proceeded to Caracas on a perilous mule trail up the mountains.[5] The months of November, December, and January were spent in the Venezuelan capital, climbing the Cerro de Avila and in making preparations for their long-awaited trip to the Orinoco. On February 7, 1800 they left Caracas, traveling southward through Venezuela on their way "to determine just where the connection between the Orinoco and Amazon waterbeds took place" (Hagen, 106). With their instruments and collections the two naturalists made their way over the most remarkable plains in the world, the *llanos* of Venezuela. According to Humboldt they are very green during the rainy season, but during the dry season they look like a desert. "The grass is then reduced to powder; the earth cracks; the alligators and the great serpents remain buried in the dried mud, till awakened from their long lethargy by the first showers of spring" (*Narrative* 2:87).

At Calabozo more than halfway from Caracas to the Orinoco, Humboldt studied the famed electric eels or *tembladores* as they are called in Spanish. These gymnoti are five to six feet in length and are strong enough to kill the largest animals when they discharge their electric organs. "All the inhabitants of the waters dread the society of the gymnoti. Lizards, tortoises, and frogs, seek pools where they are secure from the electric action" (*Narrative* 2:130). Later, Humboldt wrote that he could not remember "having ever received from the discharge of a large Leyden jar, a more dreadful shock than that which [he] experienced by imprudently placing both [his] feet on a gymnotus just taken out of the water. [He] was affected during the rest of the day with a violent pain in the knees, and in almost every joint. . . . We seem to feel, at every stroke, an internal vibration, which lasts two or three seconds, and is followed by a painful numbness. Accordingly, the Tamanac Indians call the gymnotus . . . *arimna*, which means something that deprives of motion" (*Narrative* 2:118–19). When he wrote about the electric eel upon his return from South America, Humboldt astonished the scientific world.

On March 26, 1800 the scientists arrived on the banks of the Apure, a tributary of the Orinoco. They would be traveling on this vast river system for the next seventy-four days accompanied by Nicolás Soto, the brother-in-law of the governor of the province of Varinas. When they finally beheld for the first time the waters of the Orinoco, it was not without emotion. "An immense plain of water stretched before us like a lake, as far as we could see. White-topped waves rose to the height of several feet, from the conflict of the breeze and the current. The air resounded no longer with the piercing cries of herons, flamingos, and spoonbills, crossing in long files from one shore to the other. . . . All nature appeared less animated. . . . in this character of solitude and of greatness, we recognize the course of the Orinoco, one of the most majestic rivers of the New World" (*Narrative* 2:174). Up the Orinoco they went to the junction of the Río Meta which Humboldt considered "a great spectacle." A little over a month after leaving the Capuchine mission at the Río Apure they arrived at the Mission of San Antonio de Yavita. "At this point there is a curious phenomenon that explains the connection between the Orinoco and the Amazon. At San Fernando de Atabapo, a distance of about 300 miles from the confluence of the Apure, the Orinoco makes a right angle eastward. . . . But halfway between its source and where it turns eastward at Atabapo, there is a branch, the Casiquiare" (Hagen, 120), "whose existence has been alternately proved and denied during half a century" (*Narrative* 2:371). The Casiquiare is simply an arm "of the upper Orinoco . . . which gets lost on a low wide plain and wanders over into the territory of the Amazon. There it joins the Río Guainía, rising far to the westward in Colombia to form the Río Negro, the largest affluent of the Amazon from the north" (Hagen, 120).

In Humboldt's own words: "After all [that] we had endured it may be conceived that we felt no little satisfaction in having reached the tributary streams of the Amazon, having passed the isthmus that separates two great systems of rivers, and in being sure of having fulfilled the most important object of our journey, namely to determine astronomically the course of that arm of the Orinoco which falls into the Río Negro (*Narrative* 2:371). On the 10th of May they embarked to go up the Río Negro as far as the mouth of the Casiquaire, to devote themselves to researches on the real course of that river, which unites the Orinoco to the Amazon (*Narrative* 2:402). Humboldt determined the connection of the Río Negro and the Orinoco to take place at 2° 0' 43" north latitude, off only a little more than a minute according to the most modern calculations (Hagen, 122).

Although Humboldt was absorbed by his experiments he keenly felt the insignificance of the human being in the midst of this virgin nature and reflected rather sadly that "this aspect of animated nature, in which man is nothing, has something in it strange and sad. . . . Here, in a fertile country, adorned with eternal verdure, we seek in vain the traces of the power of man; we seem to be transplanted into a world different from that which gave us birth" (*Narrative* 2:371).

Humboldt and Bonpland after a voyage up the Orinoco, their boat bouncing in waters teeming with crocodiles, alligators, and piranhas, had finally pinpointed the link of the Orinoco Río Negro canal, discovered numerous medicinal plants, and laid the groundwork for the botany of South America. In a relatively short time "they had made known more than had been unearthed in centuries" (Hagen, 126).

From Venezuela the two scientists went to Cuba, in the hope of joining there the expedition of Captain Baudin. Upon learning that the ship was on its way to Cape Horn, the naturalists returned to South America in April 1801, by way of Cartagena de las Indias thinking they would meet the expedition in Lima. This would make it possible for them to explore Colombia, Ecuador, and Peru. After the hydrographical exploration of Venezuela's river system, they now turned their attention to the Andes, a volcanic mountain range among the highest in the world. After a forty-five day trip from the coast they reached Santa Fé de Bogotá by way of the Magdalena river, and a road through the mountains hardly wide enough for the mules to pass through. They spent several weeks in the capital of the viceroyalty of New Granada, as guests of Dr. José Celestino Mutis, then known as the greatest authority on South American plants. Mutis was the last and most famous of a series of scientists whom King Charles III had sent to the New World. Then the expedition was on its way again and in January 1802 they arrived in Quito. During their eight months in the Ecuadorian capital they began to prepare for the ascent of Chimborazo.

Near the town of Riobamba, where the lofty mountain soars to 20,561 feet above sea level, Bonpland and Humboldt began their record-breaking climb on June 23, 1802. At 17,979 feet they could no longer see the summit and were suffering from the effects of the high altitude. Suddenly "the fog which made it impossible for [them] to see what lay ahead lifted, and they saw again quite close the dome-shaped summit of Chimborazo. It was a spectacular view and the hope of conquering the volcano animated them with renewed strength." They had reached 19,289 feet, the highest man had ever climbed, and lacked a little more than a thousand feet to the summit when they reached "a chasm which proved impossible to [cross]." They stayed only as long as was necessary to pick up some rock samples as they were certain "that Europeans would be eager to see a fragment of Chimborazo."⁶ Although they did not reach the summit their feat would remain unsurpassed for three decades. "When [Humboldt] sat in 1859 for his last portrait . . . he insisted that he be painted with none of his decorations. Instead he suggested that great Mount Chimborazo be placed in the background; of all that he had accomplished in his ninety years of life, he regarded 'this as the greatest'" (Hagen, 147).

After their descent they had word from Captain Baudin informing them that his trip around the world would begin by going around the Cape of Good Hope rather than Cape Horn as had been expected and announced. With that prospect lost forever, Humboldt and Bonpland decided to leave Quito and began their thousand mile journey to Lima. The impression of the scarcely inhabited deserts of the cordilleras is increased in an unexpected manner because in these regions there still exist wonderful remains of the great road of the Incas. On the sides of these roads there are *tambos* or huts built of stone. Humboldt marvelled at the old roads which appeared even superior to the Roman roads he had seen in Italy, the south of France, and Spain. "The Inca road is the more extraordinary, since, according to my barometrical calculations it is situated at an elevation of 13,258 feet. . . . We saw still grander remains of the ancient Peruvian Inca road on our way between Loxa and the Amazon."⁷ In writing of the roads and structures of the Incas "Humboldt became the first archaeologist of South America" (Hagen, 148). From the mountains they gradually descended into the plains of the upper Amazon where "an unknown world unfolds itself, rich in magnificent vegetation."⁸ It was scenery different from the treeless *páramo* and from the Venezuelan *llanos* and the virgin forest of the Orinoco. They remained seventeen days in the hot valley of the upper Amazon river. Humboldt was bent on improving the map of Charles-Marie de la Condamine who had preceded him here and had started his journey down the Amazon from the village of Jaen. Turning back from the tropical regions Humboldt and Bonpland crossed the Andes near Cajamarca "at a point where the inclination of the magnetic compass passes from the north to the south. They had traversed the magnetic equator."⁹ Only five days were spent in Cajamarca, the ancient capital of the Incas where their descendents dwell "amidst the dreary architectural ruins of departed splendor."¹⁰

They had traveled in the Andes for a year and a half and had yet to see the Pacific. "The longing wish I felt to behold the Pacific from the lofty ridges of the Andes was mingled with recollections of the interest with which, as a boy, I had dwelt on the narrative of the adventurous expedition of Vasco Nuñez de Balboa." When they were finally able to view the ocean, it was from the foothills of the Andes: "the plains of Chala and Molinos, as far as the sea coast near Trujillo, lay extended before our eyes, with a wonderful effect of apparent proximity. We now, for the first time, commanded a view of the Pacific. We saw it distinctly; reflecting along the line of the coast an immense mass of light, and rising in immeasurable expanse until bounded by the clearly-defined horizon." [11] At last Humboldt had seen the Pacific, the sea of Captain Cook's travels, which had been so vividly portrayed in Forster's descriptions. The road gradually led them down from the mountains to Trujillo, "founded by Pizarro . . . [and] close to the ancient walled city of Chanchan, now a ruin . . . but once a great metropolis, the key city of the ancient Chimus" (Hagan, 152). From Trujillo they continued south along the Pacific coast to Lima. As had happened in Caracas, Bogotá, and Quito, here too they were received with great enthusiasm. While in the Peruvian capital, a "successful observation of a transit of Mercury enabled Humboldt to make an accurate determination of the longitude of Callao," [12] the port of Lima.

The scientists left Peru bound for Acapulco on January 3, 1803. The voyage from Callao to Guayaquil gave Humboldt "the opportunity to measure the temperature and course of the famous cold current which bears his name." However, "on his own maps, it [was] always called 'Peruvian current'. He strongly objected to the designation 'Humboldt current.'" [13] During the weeks that the ship was in port at Guayaquil, the travelers witnessed the eruption of Cotopaxi and its rumblings were audible although they were two hundred miles away. "At night, far out to sea, Humboldt could see its top glowing like the end of a lighted cigar" (Hagen, 158). They reached Acapulco in March 1803, to spend the last year of their expedition in Mexico. Their stay there "did not lead to new geographical discoveries but to a thorough geological, geographic and political investigation." [14] After a short second stay in Cuba, Humboldt and Bonpland sailed for Philadelphia, where they arrived in May 1804. While in the United States the German scientist was the guest of President Jefferson at Monticello.

With his return to Bordeaux three months later the momentous journey ended. Humboldt and Bonpland had travelled "1,300 leagues by land, and 650 leagues by water." [15] Humboldt had spent close to four years in South America and had explored with Bonpland the lands known today as the republics of Venezuela, Colombia, Ecuador, and Peru. Shortly after his return to Europe from Latin America he would meet Simón Bolívar, who later said of him: "Baron de Humboldt did more for the Americas than all of the conquistadores" (Hagan, 159).

NOTES

1 Victor Wolfgang von Hagen, *South America Called Them* (New York: Alfred A. Knopf, 1945), 89. Hereafter cited parenthetically in the text as Hagen.

2 See L. Kellner, *Alexander von Humboldt* (London: Oxford Univ. Press, 1963), 15.

3 Alexander von Humboldt, *Personal Narrative of Travels to the Equinoctial Regions of America during the Years (1799–1804)*, Trans. and ed. by Thomasina Ross (London: Henry G. Bohn, 1852), 1:7. Hereafter cited parenthetically in the text as *Narrative*.

4 See Kellner, *Alexander von Humboldt*, 29.

5 At the time it took Humboldt and Bonpland three hours by mule; today the trip from La Guaira to Caracas takes less than an hour by car on a superhighway.

6 Alexander von Humboldt, *Vom Orinoco zum Amazonas* (Wiesbaden: F. A. Brockhaus, 1964), 384–86 (translation mine).

7 Alexander von Humboldt, *Views of Nature*, Trans. E. C. Otté and Henry G. Bohn (London: Henry G. Bohn, 1850), 394.

8 Humboldt, *Views of Nature*, 390.

9 Kellner, *Alexander von Humboldt*, 59.

10 Humboldt, *Views of Nature*, 411.

11 Ibid., 418, 419.

12 Kellner, *Alexander von Humboldt*, 59.

13 Ibid.

14 Kellner, *Alexander von Humboldt*, 59–60.

15 Hagen, 159. Humboldt's "complete works on the Americas would number twenty-nine volumes of immense folios, quartos, and octavos, illustrated with upward of 1,426 maps and plates. [He] would directly inspire other scientists—Darwin, Schomburgk, Linden, Funck-Brentano, Moritz, Wagner and Carl Sachs among them—to embark on a continuation of his investigations" (Ibid., 162). Also see p. 301, "With the exception of his explorations in Venezuela, he never wrote a continuous narrative of his American travels. . . . the greater part of his American odyssey was published in French as: *Voyage aux régions équinoxiales du Nouveau Continent (1799–1804)*" (Paris, 1808–1834). See Alexander von Humboldt, *Vom Orinoco zum Amazonas*, p. 29.

Executive Board, 1985–86

303

Institutional Members

of the American Society

for Eighteenth-Century Studies

Arizona State University
University of Arkansas
National Library of Australia
University of Calgary
University of California, Davis
University of California, Irvine
University of California, Los Angeles/
    William Andrews Clark Memorial
    Library
University of California, San Diego
California State University, Long Beach
Carleton University
Case Western Reserve Univerity
University of Cincinnati
City College, CUNY
Claremont Graduate School
Cleveland State University
Colonial Williamsburg Foundation
University of Colorado at Denver
University of Connecticut
Dalhousie University
Delta State University
Detroit Institute of Arts, Founders
    Society
Emory University
University of Evansville
Folger Institute of Renaissance and
    Eighteenth-Century Studies
Fordham University
Georgia Institute of Technology
Georgia State University
University of Georgia
Gettysburg College
Herzog August Bibliothek, Wolfenbüttel

University of Illinois, Chicago Circle
Institute of Early American History and
    Culture
John Carter Brown Library
The Johns Hopkins University
University of Kansas
University of Kentucky
Kimbell Art Museum, Fort Worth
Lehigh University
Lehman College, CUNY
The Lewis Walpole Library of Yale
    University
Los Angeles County Museum of Art
McMaster University/Association for
    18th-Century Studies
University of Michigan, Ann Arbor
Michigan State University
University of Minnesota
Mount Saint Vincent University
State University of New York,
    Binghamton
State University of New York, Fredonia
University of North Carolina, Chapel
    Hill
Northern Illinois University
Northwestern University
The Ohio State University
University of Pennsylvania
University of Pittsburgh
Purdue University
University of Rochester
Rockford College
Rutgers University
Smith College

305

Smithsonian Institution
University of Southern California
University of Southern Mississippi
Swarthmore College
Sweet Briar College
University of Tennessee
University of Texas at Austin
Texas A&M University
Texas Tech University
Towson State University
Tulane University
University of Tulsa
University of Utrecht, Institute for
  Comparative and General Literature

University of Victoria
University of Virginia
The Voltaire Foundation
Washington University, St. Louis
Westfälische Wilhelms-Universität,
  Münster
The Henry Francis du Pont Winterthur
  Museum
University of Wisconsin, Milwaukee
Yale Center for British Art and British
  Studies
Yale University

Sponsoring Members

of the American Society

for Eighteenth-Century Studies

Stephen J. Ackerman
G. L. Anderson
Mark S. Auburn
Mary-Margaret H. Barr
Jerry C. Beasley
Pamela J. Bennett
Carol Blum
Martha Bowden
George C. Branam
Leo Braudy
T. E. D. Braun
Patricia Brückmann
Max Byrd
Joseph A. Byrnes
Rosemary M. Canfield
W. B. Carnochan
David W. Carrithers
Richard G. Carrott
Ellmore A. Champie
Henry S. Commager
Brian Corman
Howard J. Coughlin
Robert A. Day
John Dowling
E. L. Eisenstein
A. C. Elias, Jr.
Lee Andrew Elioseff
Frank H. Ellis
Robert Enggass
Carol Houlihan Flynn
Frank J. Garosi
Morris Golden
Stephen H. Good
G. Jack Gravlee

Josephine Grieder
Dustin H. Griffin
Walter Grossmann
Leon M. Guilhamet
Phyllis J. Guskin
H. George Hahn
Roger Hahn
Elizabeth Harries
Karsten Harries
Phillip Harth
Donald M. Hassler
Alfred W. Hesse
Stephen Holliday
Robert H. Hopkins
Adrienne D. Hytier
Margaret C. Jacob
Thomas Jemielity
Frank A. Kafker
Shirley Strum Kenny
Svetlana Kluge
Richard Kneedler
Gwin J. Kolb
Carl R. Kropf
Colby H. Kullman
Catherine Lafarge
I. Leonard Leeb
J. A. Levine
Herbert Livingston
Albert M. Lyles
Michael J. Marcuse
H. W. Matalene III
Georges May
Arthur McDonald
Donald C. Mell, Jr.

Paul H. Meyer
Earl Miner
Nicolas H. Nelson
Melvyn New
Robert C. Olson
Hal N. Opperman
Nicholas A. Pappas
B. A. B. Pasta
Harry C. Payne
Jean A. Perkins
Ruth Perry
Leland D. Peterson
Peter W. Petschauer
J. G. A. Pocock
John V. Price
Irwin Primer
Jules D. Prown
Richard E. Quaintance, Jr.
Ralph W. Rader
Clifford Earl Ramsey
Thomas J. Regan
Hugh Reid
Walter E. Rex
John Richetti
Jack Richtman
Ronald C. Rosbottom
Constance Rowe
E. L. Ruhe
Kathleen L. Russo
Peter Sabor

Barbara Brandon Schnorrenberg
Robert E. Schofield
Richard B. Schwartz
Robert Shackleton
English Showalter
Oliver F. Sigworth
John E. Sitter
Henry L. Snyder
Robert Donald Spector
Mary Margaret Stewart
Albrecht B. Strauss
Amie Tannenbaum
Madeleine Therrien
James Thompson
Connie C. Thorson
James L. Thorson
Betty Perry Townsend
Daniel D. Townsend
John A. Vance
David M. Vieth
Tom Vitelli
Morris Wachs
Renée Waldinger
Janet L. Walker
Howard D. Weinbrot
David Wheeler
Raymond Whitley
Roger L. Williams
Samuel H. Woods
John W. Yolton